SHOWDOWN AT OPAL CREEK

SHOWDOWN AT OPAL CREEK

THE BATTLE FOR ✸ AMERICA'S ✸ LAST WILDERNESS

DAVID SEIDEMAN

Carroll & Graf Publishers, Inc.
New York

First Carroll & Graf edition 1993

Carroll & Graf Publishers, Inc.
260 Fifth Avenue
New York, NY 10001

Library of Congress Cataloging-in-Publication Data is available.

ISBN: 0-88184-867-0

Manufactured in the United States of America

To the memory of a dear friend,
Bill Smith,
and to my loving parents

Contents

Acknowledgments

First, I'd like to express my eternal gratitude to three special people no longer here to receive it. By his words and deeds, Bill Smith, a beautiful man, inspired me to act on my idealism through the power of honest writing. At *Time*, his other dear friends and I still feel his reassuring presence. Bill Baumgarten was a thoughtful guide through Opal Creek and dedicated public servant who took every logger's injury or fatality personally. Wilbur Harlan, Mill City's venerable logger and accomplished saw painter, personified his breed's sweat and dignity while never losing sight of the forest from the trees.

Also in Oregon, Bill Florence, Dan Postrel, and Corinne Hamilton at the *Salem Statesman-Journal* gave me hot tips and opened their rich archives to me. The paper's superb coverage of news in Mill City and Opal Creek has been in regional journalism's finest tradition. Mill City's Charley and Marie Stewart proved it was possible to export cross-country the hospitality they show friends and customers in their general store each day. I deeply appreciate their packages of newspapers and videos. Michael Donnelly was always close enough to telephone to keep me abreast of the latest events in the Northwest. Cherie Copeland shared her original historical research with me.

The National Wildlife Federation's Rick Brown and Environmental Defense Fund's Mark Wilcove lent their expertise in reviewing the manuscript. Mark Wexler served as an important sounding board from his editing post at *National Wildlife* magazine.

Numerous colleagues at *Time* offered me moral support on the long days and longer nights we worked together. Among them are Charles Alexander, Barbara Burke, Margaret Carlson, Tresa Chambers, Wendy Cole, Tom Curry, Sally Donnelly, David Ellis, Paul Gray, Ted Gup, Walter Isaacson, Susan Kaufman, Jim Kelly,

Steve Koepp, Michael Kramer, Ursula Nadasdy, Rudi Papiri, Andrea Sachs, Tom Sancton, Jill Smolowe, Marianne Sussman, and Sidney Urquhart. Kevin Kelley and Lamarr Tsufura, the magazine's resident computer wizards, saved me many megabytes of lost text. Special thanks to Betty Satterwhite for selecting me for *Time*'s fellowship at Duke University. Dee Reid, the fellowship's director, assisted me in taking full advantage of the program's opportunities for research and reflection.

On the publishing side, my talented and tireless agent, Jane Dystel, championed this project from its outset and sharpened its focus. Kent Carroll of Carroll & Graf dared to buck commercial trends on a serious subject because he believes it matters. Laura Langlie, his able aide, sheparded the book's various pieces. William Drennan's copy editing gives perfectionism a good name.

It goes virtually without saying for any reader of *Showdown at Opal Creek* that George Atiyeh and Tom Hirons are two unique individuals, sincerely true to their beliefs and poetic in expressing them. On top of that, I'm indebted to their families and to them for their supreme patience and kindness, often under trying circumstances.

Above all, I'm fortunate to have so special a family to lean on, beginning with my supportive mother and father. His healthy spirit and incisive editing improved every page during his two readings of my manuscript. My brother and sister cheered me on, as did my wonderful new in-laws Bob and Sally Hersh. Finally, I'm blessed to have met Jennifer Hersh. She had the courage to marry me at the delicate cusp of *Showdown at Opal Creek*'s completion, while keeping a smile on her face and putting one on mine, too, when we needed it most.

I

Introduction

A damp breeze and bare-limbed trees show faint signs of the Pacific Northwest winter releasing its grip to spring, 1989. George Atiyeh, a conservationist from Mill City, Oregon, bounds up the state Capitol steps in downtown Salem, a man on a mission. He steals a glance at the Golden Pioneer, a twenty-four-foot-high statue straddling the tower and projecting the spirit of Oregon's first settlers.

This moment marks the apex of a long fight to protect Opal Creek from being logged for lumber. Legislation under consideration would grant permanent protection to as fine a place as there is on earth, at sixty-eight hundred acres one of the largest stands of virgin forest in the western Cascade Mountain range. Opal Creek is a rare jewel in the necklace of old-growth forests that once stretched uninterrupted for hundreds of miles from Canada to northern California. Majestic groves of trees dating back hundreds of years and soaring hundreds of feet high host northern spotted owls and a healthy population of black-tailed deer. Liquid turquoise cascades from one waterfall and plunges in a pool to the next in a joyous symphony.

Atiyeh has cherished Opal Creek for most of his 41 years. As a boy he hiked, swam, and fished it. "The majesty of Opal Creek grabbed me and never let go," he declares in today's testimony. "Opal Creek is unique in its beauty. It is special." As a young adult, he confronted the U.S. Forest Service, a federal agency bent on seeing the area logged—at gunpoint—rather than let it harm a single tree. Atiyeh then moved his newlywed to Opal Creek for three years to stand constant guard. Since then, the dashing bush pilot has led the Northwest flank of a flying service dedicated to exposing the ravaging of ancient forests. At every turn, his mastery of the legal system's finer points has foiled the Forest Service's best-laid plans to log Opal Creek.

An adept grass-roots activist, Atiyeh has championed his cause so fiercely that he has landed in the national spotlight. He has been featured on all the network evening news shows, NBC's *Today*, ABC's *Prime Time Live*, and a PBS special; as well as in *The New York Times*, *The Washington Post*, and *Time*. The instant recognition he enjoys—and is unafraid to exploit—as the nephew of a recent governor of the same last name enhances his reputation as an insider in Oregon and Washington D.C. He has testified before Congress more than a dozen times.

Outside the Capitol, Tom Hirons, a logger from Mill City, glows from the success of a rally he has helped orchestrate to protest the bill conserving Opal Creek. Last night, he canvassed friends in town and across the state by phone. Today, a caravan of one hundred log trucks rumbles past the Capitol, horns blaring so loudly they rock state workers out of their seats. Rubber chickens representing the northern spotted owl, a denizen of virgin forests and the environmentalists' surrogate for shutting down logging operations, dangle from sideview mirrors.

Hirons and Atiyeh are each conservationists in their own right. Against staggering odds, Hirons, fifty-one, who has spent half his life logging, strives to conserve a proud way of life rooted in the frontier's soil. As owner of Mad Creek Logging, a modest outfit with ten employees in the best of times, it's all he can do these days to pay his bills, and fight off creditors closing in on his equipment, let alone prepare for retirement and hand over the company's reins to his son. The cold, hard numbers economists project for job losses in the logging industry fail to convey Hirons's real-life trauma. Watching his American Dream slip away, Hirons fears radical shifts in the economy will ruin his career and community. His financial hardships reflect middle-class anxieties in general.

Matching Atiyeh's public performances, Hirons has appeared on *Today*, a Bill Moyers special, and on a TBS documentary. *Time* and *The New York Times* have featured him as well. Congress has heard his gripping testimony on numerous occasions, and he has argued his case all the way to the White House.

From the second he wakes up well before dawn till he collapses on the couch late at night, Hirons, a self-made man, embodies the national credo of hard and honest work. Most urbanites and suburbanites have lost sight of the ranchers, farmers, and other yeomen who wrestle with nature to bring home the bounty of our abundant resources. Hirons's timber ends up in the finest homes across the continent.

Among America's rugged individualists, a logger faces unremitting danger in providing the material Americans need for shelter. On any given job, often in unimaginable weather, a tree may flatten his head or a cable slice him in half. Loggers' freewheeling ways and tenacious independence spring out of the legend of Paul Bunyan, the lumberjack symbolizing the American genius for Getting Things Done.

Atiyeh and Hirons were once, by their own estimates, as inseparable as the closest brothers. For two years, these two best friends lived with their wives in the camp at Opal Creek, where the harsh winters demanded trust and teamwork. Their families vacationed together. When Hirons's father passed away, Atiyeh agreed to become guarantor of his children and executor of his estate. Joint ventures in lumber, before Atiyeh converted to environmentalism, and mining united them professionally. In the highest form of American male bonding next to war, the two men went hunting, fishing, and on and off the wagon in tandem.

On opposite sides of a national issue, their once abiding friendship has erupted into a dispute of Hatfield-McCoy proportions. The competing visions of ancient forest they hold drive them to lock horns from Mill City to Washington. The dialogue between them in media and political forums has degenerated into personal mud-slinging as ugly as a political campaign in Chicago. Since they began exchanging polemics instead of backslaps, Atiyeh and Hirons communicate through interlocutors. "The town is so polarized, we're not communicating at all," Hirons explains. "I can't be on the phone with George for more than two minutes without getting into a shouting match. Atiyeh has approached me at conferences and I've said, 'Look, I think it's better if you and I don't even talk.' "

At these tense moments, they circle one another almost as if on the verge of a dogfight. "The loggers are like drug addicts— they're addicted to cheap timber," Atiyeh declares. "Tom Hirons doesn't recognize it's over. He's in complete denial. We've had a very hard time maintaining our friendship." The conflict's outcome will affect not just their personal lives, but also those of

the millions of Americans who want both the wood Hirons produces and the wilderness Atiyeh strives to conserve.

Their estrangement illustrates the conflict's tragic intensity.
The showdown over Opal Creek is at the forefront of a conflict
engulfing logging country. "What started out as a disagreement
between friends became a conflict. It's rapidly turning into a civil
war," Atiyeh says. The conflicts have split apart siblings, spouses,
and best friends such as Atiyeh and Hirons. By ostensibly pitting
one man's paycheck against another's paradise, the stakes could
not be higher. "Either you're fer us or agin' us!" rings the loggers'
battle cry in timber towns. "Better not stand in the middle of the
road," Hirons is fond of warning, "or you'll be run over by a log
truck." Atiyeh regards the exhortation as so apt he borrows it in
his conservationist pitch. He freely attributes it to Hirons, a bow
to their warmer past.

In a packed Capitol hearing room, Atiyeh is resolved to play
the power game to its hilt, lining up sponsors for Senate Bill 500
like an accomplished parade marshal. The measure would carve
the Opal Creek Ancient Forest State Park out of federal forest
land fifty miles east of Salem. He has stacked the testimony with
witnesses from the environmentalists' side. A slick slide show
accompanied by bouncy music takes a page from Madison
Avenue.

In timber towns up and down the Santiam Canyon, the gentle
slope in western Oregon beneath the Cascades, timber workers
are off with pay and schoolchildren are let out to ensure a good
turnout at the rally outside against Senate Bill 500. Families hoist
handpainted signs proclaiming "PEOPLE, NOT PARKS" and
"OPAL CREEK IS NO GEM," a swipe at Atiyeh's own slogan
on T-shirts, "OPAL CREEK, THE UNCUT GEM." Much of the
demonstrators' rage against their number one nemesis turns personal: "KISS MY AX, GEORGE," "WHAT PART OF THE
WORD 'NO' DON'T YOU UNDERSTAND, GEORGE," and
"TAKE A HIKE, GEORGE."

"This will teach him to mess with us," Hirons fumes. He and
his fellow loggers who make their living off the national forest
Atiyeh seeks to preserve have decided to draw the line in the
sand at SB 500 as a bulwark against conserving other forests in
the Northwest. "What do you do in the small timber-dependent
economies?" he asks. "I've read so much about Appalachia and
the steel mill towns. There's a turmoil, with social upheaval and
more drug abuse when people have to give up a life-style they're
used to. There are a lot of people out there who would like this

life-style to become extinct." Dozens of timber towns like Mill City may run out of a lumber supply, he argues, until the next ripe harvest of second growth comes on line in about fifteen years.

Atiyeh is stunned by the drama unfolding before him. Over the past few years he has grown accustomed to being attacked by the timber industry's hired guns, but not by his own neighbors and friends of twenty years in Mill City. In his testimony, Mayor Charlie Tate describes Opal Creek as nothing more than Atiyeh's "mistress." Though Tate later denies the metaphor was ever intended as a swipe at Atiyeh's recent divorce, citizens of a town too small for anyone to keep a secret snicker nervously. Social decency, a hallmark of Mill City's closely knit community, is the first casualty in the battle for Opal Creek.

Distraught, Atiyeh storms out into the narrow hallway with his companions. Townspeople pour out of the room to confront Atiyeh for the first time since he embarked on his crusade. Randy and Gary Moberg, brothers and the fourth generation of loggers in their family, are struggling to figure out Atiyeh's descent from their hunting partner in the fall to a traitor in the spring. "Why are you turning our backyard into the focal point?" demands Randy. "You're knifing us in the back." Before Atiyeh can complete a sentence, Garry chimes in: "Why, George? Why? You're trying to shut us down." "What do you think you are trying to do to me?" retorts Atiyeh.

On the heels of their sons, Verl and Sue Moberg arrive to get their licks in. Verl is too shocked at what he perceives as Atiyeh's betrayal to recall his deep fondness for him. "Why'd you join that marriage with environmental tourists?" Verl implores. Sue bulls her way through the throng toward Atiyeh. In an instant, they are engaged in a heated argument. Reeling from the sort of terror a rabbit must feel circled by a pack of coyotes, Atiyeh suddenly realizes that he has passed the point of no return.

At this moment, he's confronting more than a few industry hacks; it's his entire town turning on him. The ostracism mists his eyes. Sue Moberg refuses to grant him the moment's raw emotion. "He can turn the tears on like the waterworks," she reminds Verl, "and lie at the drop of a hat faster than you can talk." A young lady from the radical environmental group Earth First! sides with Atiyeh. Sue spins around to tell her, at an ear-splitting level, to find a real job. In the middle of a screaming match, Verl pulls them apart.

Across the hall, Dave Alexander, the local forest ranger, stands erect over every inch of his six-foot-nine frame. As the local timber czar determining Opal Creek's fate, Alexander has found himself caught between the warring factions. He recalls growing up in the South in the late 1950s and early 1960s at the time of the civil rights struggle. The first black did not attend his segregated high school in the hardscrabble country of East Texas until the year Alexander graduated, in 1963. He remembers people being lynched and effigies burned. "I don't want to imply it's quite as confrontational, but there's a possibility of violence," he says. "I can't overemphasize the fact that when you start touching people at their core values, their ability to provide for their families, and their existence in the communities they grew up in, you're starting to move in some pretty dangerous ground."

Thirty years after the civil rights revolution, citizens of small rural communities throughout the Northwest are combating comparable threats to their core values. Why any agitator, particularly from their own midst, would want to deprive families of the only existence they have ever known exceeds their comprehension. "Either Atiyeh is extremely gutsy or dumb," Alexander muses. "He'd better mend some fences or he's history in this canyon." A few weeks later, he braces for violence over a controversial timber sale in the vicinity of Opal Creek.

Up in Mill City, Pastor Aaron Veach preaches calm from the pulpit. "If a staunch environmentalist were to come into this community and open a counteroffice to the timber industry's on the highway [run by Hirons] in favor of the owl," he says, "I wouldn't be surprised if it were fire-bombed."

In the hallway, ten of Atiyeh's newest antagonists continue to mix it up with him. He struggles to convince the Mobergs of the park's benefits to their community, insisting that he has their best interests at heart. His seeming obliviousness to the rising danger around him amazes Alexander and Hirons, who keep a safe distance. "You goddamn tree-hugger," hollers a scruffy, twenty-year-old logger from Southern California, reeking of beer. Parrying the barrage of invectives with a few of his own, Atiyeh prepares for blows. Hirons understands that allowing an altercation in the state Capitol would only damage his cause by reinforcing the image of loggers as drunks. "Christ," he muses, "you're not going to win this out in the hallway." Deeper down, part of him fears for Atiyeh's safety.

Yet Hirons balks at intervening on Atiyeh's behalf because he might rouse the suspicions of his peers in the timber industry. Instead, he scurries through the hallways to hunt down Chuck Bennett, an old acquaintance and Atiyeh's chief lobbyist for Opal

Creek. "George has gotten himself into a big mess. Sue is like a fighting sow and liable to paste him," he gasps. "If you're a friend, get him out of it." Bennett hustles back to the melee. "Hey, the majority leader needs to talk to you," he says, leading Atiyeh away. Unbeknownst to Atiyeh, one of his fiercest public enemies of the past twenty-four hours just emerged as his private savior. As a couple of heavyset loggers grab the young troublemaker and drag him off, Bennett sits Atiyeh down on a couch in the majority leader's office, out of harm's way. "No, I'm not prepared to get into a fistfight in the state Capitol," he tells Bennett.

Atiyeh mulls over a tormenting episode earlier in the day when he ventured out through the rotunda's revolving doors onto the south Capitol steps. On his survey of the familiar faces from Mill City milling about the timber rally, he spotted Hirons. Atiyeh could scarcely believe it, since he thought he would be the first to know about Hirons's involvement in the demonstration. After all, for almost two decades the two friends had been tighter than the grain of a good two-by-four.

As Hirons knows from years of observation, whenever Atiyeh becomes tense his upper lip starts to quiver like an electric toothbrush. At the moment, it flapped more like a flag in the breeze. Atiyeh was too distraught even to look him in the eye, so he turned to Rick Schaefer, a mutual friend and a neutral observer. "What's he up to?" Atiyeh asked him. "Looks like he's defending his livelihood," Schaefer answered.

Atiyeh confronted the man on his mind. "It's nice to see you, Hirons. Well, what the hell are you doing here?" he roared. "I thought we'd agreed you wouldn't be part of this."

Hirons returned the glare. "Never," he shot back. "Jesus, George, how can you expect me to stay out of it?"

The conservationist still holds a deep grudge against his ex-friend. "When Tom and them went after Opal Creek it was like going after my kids or members of my family," Atiyeh says. "Hell, I'm in a wrestling match with a guy. Until he screams 'uncle!' or calls quits, you can't very well walk away because he's going to clobber you upside the head. The only thing I can keep doing is keep tightening the screws."

The Northwest's painful dilemma is the nation's, for the region's forests produce one third of America's plywood and have fed the housing boom since World War II. Odds are that any wood house built since 1946 contains materials from these woods. The trees Hirons mostly logs, Douglas fir, are the most valuable in timber commerce worldwide. Overall, the U.S. Forest Service has proclaimed timber the nation's number one agriculture crop, comprising about one fourth of the value of such products. In most regions of the United States it ranks among the top three manufacturing industries.

For those in Hirons's field, the Damoclean sword hanging over timber towns portends the end of the homesteaders' pioneer spirit. Logging suffuses Northwest culture as thoroughly as cotton did the Deep South. It drives the economy and shapes the school system. Politicians do the industry's bidding as if their careers depend on it, because they do.

Yet the false choice between environmental protection and economic growth George Bush and Dan Quayle struggled to exploit in the 1992 presidential election to scare voters about Bill Clinton and Al Gore appears particularly disingenuous in the Northwest. Over the past two decades, the timber industry has declined less from environmentalism than from automation in the mills; the shift of jobs to the South; and the export of raw, uncut logs that eliminates additional work in the mills. In coming decades, thousands more employed in the wood trade will lose their jobs when the last irreplaceable trees fall anyway, regardless of the spotted owl.

This past spring, Clinton and Gore held a historic forest conference in Portland to find solutions to the dispute. "We owe it to our children and to every generation that follows to preserve this unique treasure with a balanced long-term policy that recognizes," said the vice president, "we don't have to sacrifice jobs to protect a unique natural resource." Ultimately, the trees will pay far more dividends left alone in an upright position. The day ancient forests are gone the booming tourist and real-estate businesses will lose their best drawing card. Seattle and Portland will have to spend more to keep water supplies pure. Drug companies will have to look elsewhere for the cancer-fighting chemical derived from the Pacific yew that grows primarily in such places as Opal Creek.

Opal Creek has emerged as the flagship in the Northwest's war in the woods. It ensnares judges and legislators in three states and in Washington, D.C. The fault for the present crisis clearly lies with the politicians on the Potomac. Myopic expedience has led to cut-and-run practices on private lands and, since the 1940s, the outright mining of many national forests. Contrary to popular perception, the U.S. Forest Service administers 75 percent of the nation's remaining virgin forest for timber rather than parks. For the past two decades, at Congress's behest, the Forest Service and the Bureau of Land Management have accelerated cutting schedules to put most of the remaining virgin stands straight in the chainsaw's path. Until temporary court injunctions three years ago, more than one square mile of ancient forests belonging to all Americans disappeared each week. The region's landscape has not been so radically altered since the withdrawal of the glaciers during the last Ice Age.

Preeminent ancient-forest scientists have observed that the rate of timber cutting in the Pacific Northwest exceeds the rate of cutting in tropical forests. Brazil has nothing on the Northwest. A team of U.S. government scientists found in its latest satellite pictures far more damage to the Northwest's temperate rain forests from logging and road construction than in Brazil's tropical rain forests. The images contrast big blankets of the Amazon to the shredded, moth-eaten rags of the United States' richest forest.

While up to 15 percent of Brazil's Amazon forest has vanished, 95 percent of this nation's original endowment has been lost to agriculture, development, and logging. Most of its fragments may be doomed to go the way of songbirds in spring in the next fifteen years. Politicians who have long kept their campaign chests full from the Northwest's green gold stubbornly refuse to deal with the lives of two endangered species running out of habitat, the spotted owl and American loggers.

The Northwest's old growth constitutes the most spectacular conifer, or cone-bearing, forests anywhere. The trees—Douglas firs, redwoods, hemlocks, cedars, and spruces—are the biggest and oldest in the world. The species often attain five hundred years and sometimes thirty-five hundred. They have been known to reach 330 feet in height and 16 feet in diameter, though today's trees are mostly smaller because the biggest ones were logged first. Indeed, these trees are the largest and oldest living beings on earth. The Northwest forest contains twice as much mass of life from wood as do tropical rain forests, and the world's most productive salmon fisheries.

In the past three decades, the world has plundered half of its forests at the rate of fifty acres per minute. Global deforestation may lead to the extinction of one quarter of the earth's five million animal and plant species over the next several decades. It contributes to global warming. The loss of temperate rain forests in the Northwest and Alaska is quietly joining tropical deforestation in the Amazon and elsewhere at the top of the world's environmental crises. These ecosystems provide food, pure drinking water, and clean air. Their destruction borders on planetary suicide.

The United States is squandering a natural heritage on the

order of Yellowstone and Yosemite. The cathedral-like groves of ancient forests offer a spiritual and recreational haven from modern life's pressures. Opal Creek, a vestige of the virgin woods that once blanketed America, is one of the last living links left to the early Middle Ages, centuries before white settlers arrived.

Today, the amount of pavement in the United States equals the amount of pristine wilderness, about 2 percent of the land base. If current trends continue, parking lots will soon outnumber parks in total area. Opal Creek's significance extends well beyond its geographical boundaries or Mill City's economy to the heart of the nation's soul. It calls on a nation to reject the false choice between "beauty and bread," as John Muir once defined it, by saving ancient forests for everyone's benefit.

II

The Big Trip

At the break of an April dawn in 1970, state trooper Glen Bigness gropes in the dark for warm clothing. This morning he is venturing out of Willamette Valley, cuddled by spring's balminess in the high fifties. His destination is the mountains. But abrupt shifts in weather patterns can drop temperatures like hailstones. From his dresser, he removes long underwear, a pair of rain pants to put over his jeans, a long parka coat for warmth, and a slicker on top of that. In his holster Bigness packs a Colt.

A steady mixture of snow and rain greets him at the Opal Creek gate leading down the three-mile road to Jawbone Flats, the old mining camp at Opal Creek. Shivering slightly, he wipes moisture from his glasses. Three Forest Service employees join him on a stakeout to investigate vandalism to their equipment over the past few days. From their police barricades in Mill City, Bigness's force has maintained a state of high alert for more than a year around the renegade community George Atiyeh and his cousin Tom have maintained at Jawbone Flats.

The previous summer, in the Atiyehs' absence, Bigness's partner Tom Drynan arrested one of their friends living at Jawbone Flats for illegal possession of marijuana. Drynan had suspected something was afoot among the enigmatic characters from the odd assortment of vehicles parked in camp, from a green 1969 VW bus to a silver 1938 Chevrolet paneled truck to an armored car. While two Forest Service officials pretended to be road survey crews to distract Jim Hewitt, the camp's ill and bedridden owner, Drynan uncovered a cultivated marijuana patch along the Little North Fork of the Santiam River, and a watering jar nearby. He returned in the company of a Forest Service worker to set up an observation point across the river, eighty feet from the marijuana patch. Drynan observed the suspect, William Lee Duff, through seven-power binoculars and photographed him. As the officer later recounted in his official report,

> At 5:00 PM, the subject, later identified as Duff, came to the area, looked both up and down the river and then walked to the Marihuana [sic]. He sat down cross legged, facing writer [Drynan], pulled out some cigarette papers and began pulling the yellowed leaves from the plants and rolling them into joints. After rolling several, he put one in his mouth and left.

Duff was jailed on a thousand dollars' bail, but a narcotics search by Drynan, Bigness, and two other officers came up empty. The camp's residents felt violated by the invasion of their privacy and the underhanded tactics employed against Hewitt. Over the next year, as the Forest Service stepped up its activities in Opal Creek, the clash continued.

By 1970, Atiyeh has left school and the military service an angry young man. "It's damn stupid to kill over an economic system when the people don't care how their rice bowls are filled," he hectors anyone within earshot. Friends of his return from Vietnam in body bags. With student unrest sweeping across the nation, he applauds campus activists who have blown up the ROTC building at the University of Oregon. One by one, his cultural icons fall by the wayside. The deaths of Jimi Hendrix, Janis Joplin, and Jim Morrison—all favorites of his—compound a generational paranoia of distrust of traditional institutions. Two weeks after Bigness's trek to Opal Creek, Ohio National Guard troops at Kent State shoot down four students. Atiyeh continues keeping company with Students for a Democratic Society and the Black Panthers. Against his better nature, he gravitates toward the Maoist philosophy that power comes out of the barrel of a gun.

Dropping out of society, Atiyeh and his cousin Tom play out their romantic notions of the wild West. Disaffected urbanites are reclaiming old mining camps left and right at the peak of the 1960s' back-to-land-movement. The Atiyehs take over Jawbone Flats with the consent of Tom Atiyeh's grandfather Jim "Grandpa" Hewitt, who operated a small mining operation at Opal Creek for four decades and now lives in a Portland nursing home. Poor as dirt, they maintain the mining roads by hand and can only afford to do the barest assessment work to keep title to the land. George's hair grows wild, from a military crewcut to below his waist. He lets it go south uncut until his firstborn's arrival. George and his cohorts further effect the appearance of crazy mountain people by wearing Bowie knives. He and Larry McDonald, a friend and another caretaker living in camp with his wife, post an illegal no-trespassing sign and stand guard duty twenty-four hours a day. On and off the job, they like playing with guns—among them an M1 carbine, a Colt .32 automatic pistol, and a Winchester .30-.30 rifle with a sawed-off barrel—to scare off un-invited guests. The entire camp has been jolted from bed by the sound of McDonald blowing away roosters for awakening him too early.

A number of visitors from Salem that year provide police with personal accounts of harassment at Opal Creek. The Atiyehs and Larry McDonald stop two men on motorcycles at gunpoint. Wearing a rifle strapped over his shoulder, George escorts them out on his own cycle. A group of four is met at the camp entrance by three men, including one in military fatigues, tot-ing sidearms and a rifle. Six other "accomplices" in camp ap-pear to be armed as well. Upon being advised that they were trespassing, the guests beat a hasty retreat. One terrified man gasps to police that he would sooner go to Vietnam than risk returning to Opal Creek.

On infrequent forays into town, Atiyeh and McDonald revel in their roles as outcasts. A tavern near Mill City hangs a sign NO GUNS OR KNIVES ALLOWED and a wooden box for checking them. "Hey, girlies, when you gonna cut your hair?" the regulars inquire. "There's a red neck behind there," Atiyeh responds, lifting his pigtail. "Why don't you give me a haircut?" The ensuing brawls account for his two capped front teeth.

Throughout the year, a series of episodes appear to bear out the police leads that, according to their intelligence reports, "hip-pie types" are converting Jawbone Flats into a training base for urban guerrillas. The Vietnam War's domestic fallout intensifies authorities' vigilance of subversive elements fomenting unrest. At Opal Creek, FBI agents are investigating connections between dynamite found at the mines and the destruction of buildings at the University of Oregon. An undercover officer from the Port-land Police Department's Intelligence Division has infiltrated the ranks of People's Army Jamboree (PAJ), a radical fringe group in

the vein of SDS or the Weathermen. The police believe they
have already found evidence, through authorized traces of phone
records, of links between a People's Army foot soldier and at
least one mine resident. The PAJ leaders unwittingly assign an
undercover agent to rent a U-Haul and join the suspect assigned
to retrieve a load of automatic weapons, handguns, and explosives
at the mines and ferry them back to headquarters in Portland.
For reasons unknown, the van never makes it to the mines and
returns empty. "The mine area, it is rumored," the official police
records state with evident equivocation, "is being used as a stopover for militant persons and persons on the run." The troopers
stick by their guns. "Radical individuals," the troopers are convinced, pose an imminent danger.

Atiyeh ridicules his classification as a political suspect. His
agenda is as mainstream as living out the principles of the first
Earth Day celebrated one week earlier in the Eden he has known
since childhood. All he and his friends ask is to be left alone in
splendid isolation, unmolested by the U.S. Forest Service's invading enemies. Timber planners have long eyed the millions of
board feet of Opal Creek's ancient forest. In 1964 they began
bulldozing a logging road from the gate. Four years later, the Opal
Creek Timber Sale was announced. In early 1970, the logging of
nearby Mount Beachie, on thin topsoil, caused Opal Creek and
rivers to run muddy for thirty-four miles for a week after the first
rains. Two decades later, from his plane Atiyeh still provides a
bird's-eye view of the permanently bald spot from logging.

Atiyeh becomes an Earth First! member in spirit, if not in
name, well ahead of his time. A decade before the environmental
terrorist group first springs on the scene, he practices his own
brand of "ecotage," the Earth First! term of destroying logging
equipment and other environmentally unsound machinery. Forest
Service workers are as welcome as military recruiters on a college
campus. "We generally made their lives as miserable as we could,"
he recalls two decades later. Atiyeh and Larry McDonald follow
the surveyors on their daily rounds, pulling their stakes out of the
ground as fast as they can plant them. Strategically placed mining
equipment blocks the passage of government vehicles on the main
road. They periodically engage the foresters in heated conversation in a futile effort to convince them of the error of their ways.
On top of that, Atiyeh and McDonald put snow in the gas tanks
of the surveyors' tote goat, a motorcycle with a sidecar, and, for
good measure, urinate in them.

On arriving in the morning for the surveillance, Bigness is

certain fresh dog and human tracks in the snow confirm his hunches. The only people with access to the area, Atiyeh and company, are almost always accompanied by a dog or two. The oddest is Claude, a black Labrador sporting a nose disfigured from a bear's punch, who howls to Led Zeppelin rock music. Recently Claude knocked a Forest Service employee off his tote goat, bouncing his helmet into Battle Ax Creek, where it floated for weeks. A few weeks later, McDonald and Atiyeh race in the water for the trophy. McDonald wins, and—to the loser's amazement—flings it on the ground and shoots a hole in it from one side to the other. McDonald starts greeting Forest Service workers wearing his bullet-riddled headgear. "That's what happened with the last one of you who messed with us," he jokes. The hapless butts of his jokes take him seriously.

After they park their motorcycles beside a weathered building housing old mining equipment, the Forest Service's Hurston Nicholas parts ways with two coworkers who are lining out a new road through Opal Creek and checking the boundaries of timber for cutting. Burrowed in the bushes a hundred yards away, he and Bigness spend all day observing the vehicles through binoculars to build a case for vandalism of federal property. On this day they come up empty.

By 3:30, Bigness and Nicholas are wet and weary from the snowy rain. A pair of Forest Service employees, Jim Monroe and Frank Homar, join them for a smoke before heading out. At the bridge spanning Battle Ax Creek, a pickup truck parked in the middle at a slight angle prevents them from crossing. The men must dismount from their motorcycles to lift them around the pickup. Riding double in the lead, Homar and Bigness return a greeting they mistakenly deem friendly from a resident emerging from the last cabin in camp. Nicholas and Monroe follow far behind. They pull up in camp when Atiyeh flags them down, wearing a .32 Colt automatic pistol strapped to his hip.

"You're a damn liar! You said you would stop and tell us when and where you'd be working in this area!" Atiyeh yells. "You didn't stop this morning, you fucking liar!" He and Larry McDonald are sure that Frank Homar is armed and the Forest Service intends to burn down the camp.

"You're not hurting me saying that. When we came through yesterday to pick up the damaged tote goats you asked us what we're gonna do," Monroe replies. "We told you we'd be back in the morning and will be in the area for four days. I don't think

we have to stop every time we come through here on a Forest
Service right of way to let you know we're doing our job."

"You're a damn liar and I am telling you to your face, you're
a liar!" Atiyeh shouts again.

Nicholas and Monroe have already passed through camp when
they note the disappearance of their two companions. They put
the brakes on immediately and return to camp on foot. At the
sight of them, McDonald, who has been sitting on his cabin's
front porch enjoying the action, stands up with a walkie-talkie in
hand. He goes inside to communicate with an unidentified party,
then reappears moments later brandishing a .30-caliber M1 carbine. Even under normal circumstances, this twenty-three-year-
old Indian halfbreed cuts a terrifying figure. To this day, Atiyeh,
acknowledging a certain unease in his presence, calls him "part
Indian, full fanatic." McDonald has green, beady eyes—the shade
of an army jeep—and shoulder-length charcoal black hair. A single feather sticks out of the Smoky the Bear hat usually atop his
head. "Hippie from the word go" is Bigness's initial reaction.
McDonald's fingertips are in perpetual motion twirling a handle-
bar mustache. The quirk reminds a friend of Atiyeh at the camp
of someone else he cannot quite place. Years later, he remembers:
Snidely Whiplash, a cartoon villain from his childhood, who ties
the distressed damsel Nell to the train tracks.

"You're gonna stop in the mornings and let us know you're
here because I'm here to protect my family and property," Mc-
Donald snarls through a loud barrage of profanity.

"Don't think you can rape the forest and get away with it,"
Atiyeh chimes in. "And I'm real pissed off about you screwing
Grandpa Hewitt out of his rights just because he's sick and not
here to defend himself."

"Maybe if I shoot at you," screams McDonald, waving his carbine, "I'll get your attention. You're gonna get shot the next time
you come through here."

"How are our people a threat to you and your families riding
tote goats through here and carrying out work details? We don't
have to tell where we're going or what we're doing," replies Nicholas, who so far has remained quiet. "Up to now this has been a
problem between the mining company and the Forest Service.
You start shooting, it's gonna get personal."

McDonald takes a step toward him and sticks his gun's sawed-
off barrel in Nicholas's face. "You gettin' hard on me?" McDonald
shouts at him.

"Don't point that rifle at me," Nicholas pleads.

"I'll point it wherever the hell I want. You gettin' hard on me?" McDonald asks.

"You wanna call it that?" Nicholas says. "Yeah, I'm getting hard."

"Get hard, man!" McDonald screams. In one sweeping motion, he jumps back, operates the bolt, and jacks a live round of ammunition in the weapon's chamber. Fingering the trigger, McDonald points the gun in Nicholas's stomach. "Get hard, man." At the same time, Atiyeh unsnaps the strap across his pistol.

From his vantage point ten feet away, Bigness knows McDonald is not bluffing. He himself fired the M1 in the military service. (A star of the Korean War, it has since become defunct.) As a gun collector, he is also familiar with the model's operation from illustrated magazine articles. The gun's downward angle affords him a clear view of the shell entering the chamber. With one hand on the stock and trigger, McDonald reaches the gun's far end to grab the slide. He cocks that back and lets it snap forward in a single, smooth motion. The magazine clip extending three inches below the gun permit him to fire fifteen shots before reloading.

Bigness takes a step forward and begins unzipping his outer coat for his Colt. "Do you know who I am? I'm the man," he announces. "Bigness, state trooper. The man."

"I know you're the man and you've got a gun," McDonald thunders, turning toward him and aiming the carbine at his feet, "Don't move or else. If you draw a gun, I'll shoot. I've been ready for this for a long time."

"Don't do it," Atiyeh begs Bigness. "Don't do it."

McDonald takes a few steps toward Bigness, who keeps unzipping his parka. "Stop it," McDonald yells, "unless you want to take the Big Trip."

"Larry, don't point that gun," Bigness pleads. "You'll hurt somebody."

All the hours of training at the academy can never prepare an officer for the real world's flash points. The mind races through the options. "Either I must get us out of here peacefully or shoot McDonald before he can shoot somebody else. He's got Hurston and me covered. Atiyeh hasn't drawn his automatic, but he's just as dangerous and unpredictable," Bigness recalls thinking. "Can't make a sudden jerk to retrieve my retriever, which is buried beneath three layers of clothing. I'm not scared, but one move and McDonald unloads. If I neutralize him, it inflames the situation.

Thank God, I'm not equally armed. I'd better let things cool down."

Through the corner of his eye, Bigness spots movement on a cabin's front porch. "Another hippie from the word go," he says. McDonald's wife—the embodiment of a flower child from head to toe—may be the calmest soul at Opal Creek. She's standing outside drinking the whole scene in. At odd intervals, her hands curl a thin log, a crossbar tied to two sections of rope overhead. Back and forth the human pendulum swings. Bigness wonders if he has lost his mind.

He decides the wisest course is retreat. Any attempt to force an arrest would ensure a deadly melee. Bigness can return later with a warrant. Meanwhile, the trooper keeps a steady conversation going to cool down Atiyeh and McDonald. Tempers subside as rapidly as they flared up. The foursome leaves, drained of energy. The encounter certainly left Bigness bowed. From now on, he promises himself always to keep an exposed gun on his belt at the ready. Whatever face he may have lost, Bigness can take solace that his mild response probably saved lives.

"Just don't come back," McDonald rejoices. His victory celebration sets the stage for the next phase of assault. Atiyeh happens on him stuffing dynamite in pipes in the garage. McDonald is plotting to blow up log trucks and booby-trap the half bridges into camp. Heaving a sigh, Atiyeh admonishes him to relax. They are already in one heap of trouble.

Down in the valley, Bigness contacts local, state, and federal authorities over the next four days. A battery of state officers and undersheriffs agree to assist him in devising a "plan of action to effect the permanent removal of McDonald and George Atiyeh from the area." They will terminate the menace once and for all. The twelve-man posse he finally forms runs the lawn enforcement gamut, from Marion County deputies Clipfell and Grossnicklaus to officers Seales and Smith. Bigness briefs them of McDonald's statements that he would resist apprehension. At 6:30 A.M. on Saturday they convene in Mill City to plot the strategy. The posse surrounds the camp in the woods. Aircraft hover ahead at a distance for backup. Bigness enters alone to make the arrest, since a show of firepower could induce a reverse effect. Bigness takes out handcuffs and reads the suspects the charges. "Looks like you're taking a Vietnam village," Atiyeh tells Bigness, admiring the heavy weaponry. Atiyeh and McDonald go quietly.

Atiyeh and McDonald laugh about their adventures on their way down to Mehama jail in the squad car. After all, in their circles, they can wear this new notoriety as a badge of honor. That night in jail, cowboy inmates threaten to give the longhairs lessons in grooming. McDonald is moved to the segregation cell for his own safety. Alone in his thoughts, Atiyeh feels the humiliation of incarceration. Here he sits on a hard bed waiting for friends or family to post two thousand dollars in bond, trapped behind bars and far from Opal Creek in body and spirit.

Vic Atiyeh, acting on behalf of his father-in-law Jim Hewitt, Jawbone Flat's owner, steps in to defuse the crisis. The state senator, who would rise to the governorship eight years later, can ill afford the potential political bombshell. On his orders, George informs McDonald he is fired. McDonald takes it hard, renewing his threat to use his stash pipe of bombs—this time against George. He finally packs up and heads down the road. Atiyeh assures Bigness and his partner Tom Drynan that henceforth he will be a model citizen. On their future encounters in the woods, Bigness is struck by the sincerity of Atiyeh's regret and new maturity.

Atiyeh and McDonald's days in court go well. A grand jury does not indict Atiyeh because he never drew a gun. Although McDonald is not convicted of assault with a dangerous weapon, he is found guilty of the lesser charge of "pointing a firearm at another." The Court later orders McDonald's acquittal and his record expunged on account of a technicality.

This episode marks the turning point in Atiyeh's spiritual odyssey. The showdown leaves him no closer to staving off Opal Creek's destruction. Those with the power to imprison him, Bigness, and to exonerate him, the jury, hold the upper hand. Yet he wins. "I recognized the judicial system works," he recalls. "There are so many ways to address your grievances other than going to violent extremes." Atiyeh shifts his tactics from lawlessness to politics. In that venue, he would beat them at their own game.

Atiyeh grasps the true depths of his devotion to Opal Creek. His belligerence toward Bigness and the foresters was purely a reflex action. Squaring off against an armed officer, he has proved beyond a doubt to the Forest Service and himself that he is willing to put his life on the line for Opal Creek. Twenty years later, his will to fend off persistent threats refuses to bend. "They are going to have to kill me or lock me up before they ever kill that forest. My life is not that significant in relation to it," he says today. "It's like one of my children. I'd be willing to sacrifice myself for that piece of forest." Over the past two decades, the likelihood of Opal Creek losing its soul to loggers has risen in direct proportion to the overcutting of the rest of the forest. While foiling the Forest Service and politicians at each turn, Atiyeh cannot afford to let his guard down.

"Been up with Atiyeh? Been up with Atiyeh?" That is the first question anyone with a stake in the Cascades asks a visiting reporter. Forest Ranger Dave Alexander poses it in the middle of his forestry tour. So do a timber baron in Mill City and a top congressional aide to U.S. senator Mark Hatfield. Atiyeh can deliver stirring speeches, write cogent newspaper columns, and work the capital like Lyndon Johnson. But the weapon in his arsenal his foes most despise is his Cessna 170 Aztec Piper Twin, a small single-engine plane he deploys to expose the wanton abuse of American forests. "It's a major part of his media approach," says Jim Morgan of Young and Morgan Lumber, a former friend who learned to fly under Atiyeh. "If you showed me George's slide show with all the music and took me over some of those lands like he does, I'd ask, 'Where do I sign up?' " A gas station owner in Mill City has overheard customers plotting to ground George for eternity with a few choice holes plugged into him and his plane.

No visit for politicians, scientists, and members of the media is complete without a tour from Atiyeh. "I firmly believe that if we could get everyone in Washington and Oregon into the air to see this logging," Atiyeh says, "it would stop tomorrow." In testimony in Washington, D.C., he extends an open invitation:

> You, the Congress, have heard all kinds of conflicting figures as to how much of Oregon's ancient forests is left and you're probably wondering what the truth really is. Come to Oregon or send your staff. I will fly you over Oregon's timberland and you can see with your own eyes what we have done to Oregon and what little of Oregon's ancient forest is left for future generations.

Starting in the mid-1980s, the indelible images of masticated forests on television and in newspapers and magazines had the same galvanizing effect on public opinion as oil-soaked otters at the time of the *Exxon Valdez* debacle in Alaska. Once Americans began waking up to an environmental issue that they were unaware existed, the clamor in Congress became too loud to ignore.

Atiyeh became an aerial crusader purely by accident. In 1974, at age twenty-five, he had a few hours to kill waiting for an order at an auto parts store in town. At a field nearby, he plunked down five dollars for introductory flying lessons, and has been hooked ever since.

On his early forays into the skies, it gradually dawned on him that something was wrong with the sweeping panoramas at his wingtips. "The thing that changed me the most was learning how to fly an airplane. It didn't compute at first, since we've done most of the cutting since 1970," he recalls. "Once I got up over national forests, I could see just how much has been cut. On a clear day, when you can see for a hundred miles, it all looks the same. You get shown the reality right smack up against the face." For the first time, Atiyeh realized he was unable to allay nagging doubts about his own involvement in the logging business with Hirons. "I could see what happened when my friends and I cut the forest," he adds. "My eyes told me it was going very fast and we couldn't continue doing it. In the past twenty years we've cut too much." The Wilderness Society, which has done the most comprehensive inventories, estimates that more than 40 percent of Western Oregon's old-growth forests that existed on the first Earth Day in 1970—556,000 acres—has been logged over the past two decades.

Seventy years ago, the philosopher and ecologist Aldo Leopold chastised Americans for taking their wilderness for granted by reminding them that only "when the end of the supply is in sight [do] we 'discover' that the thing is valuable." Or as Kewpie Zeke, an Oregon logger, recently put in on television: "You never miss the water till the well runs dry."

Atiyeh's Cessna 170, a four-seater from 1952, has a stylish wood interior. To accommodate the maximum load of passengers and the heavy weight of camera equipment often on board, Atiyeh, an indefatigable tinkerer, has souped it up with a powerful engine. With runways in short supply in the mountains, special landing gear and beefy tires allow for emergency landings.

Donning silver aviator's sunglasses, Atiyeh leaps into his 170's cockpit. A grassy airstrip runs right by his double-wide mobile home, dragged up to these gentle grounds known as King's Prairie, down the road a piece from the town cemetery. He once enjoyed earning extra income operating a flying service from home until environmentalism took up his time and his customers in Mill City's logging community boycotted him. With steady spring rains and stubborn clouds grounding him all week, this afternoon he is raring to exploit the fluttering lens of clear weather's bright light. "According to a pilot's adage, there are old pilots and bold pilots, but not old and bold pilots," he says, almost apologetically. Challenged to identify a hawk in our view, Atiyeh warns: "Be nice or I'll fly upside down."

Of all the means devised by man to duplicate the bird's gift of flight, perhaps none approximates nature's way as much as the bush plane. Powerless, hot-air balloons and gliders are at the mercy of the wind's gyrations. Helicopters numb any human sensation with noise. The commercial airlines' modern jets shelter passengers in little more than a winged hotel, as distanced from the world rushing by as the subway rider speeding through dark tunnels beneath city pavement. In a bush plane, a passenger sits close enough to windows in front, beside, and behind him to feel his breath touch the glass. The elements are always in full force. On a sunny day, the heat warms the skin. In stormy weather, the plane skips to and fro as thumping rain on the fuselage drowns out the engine. A good pilot teases the clouds, darting in and out of the mysterious altitudes to gaze at specks large and small on the ground. Far off, on the transparent horizon, the sky seems to kiss the earth. On this point, Atiyeh's detractors are dead wrong. A bush plane's God's-eye view doesn't lie about the loss of ancient forests.

At first glance from the air, the Northwest's singular splendor appears immortal. Snow-capped mountains pierce the three-thousand-foot layer of swirling white cumulus. The Cessna's tiny shadow floats above endless evergreen and black lakes shimmering beneath our feet. In their hunt for dinner, eagles and hawks graze the old growth's craggy canopy—compared to the cookie cutter symmetry of planted trees—and meadows glisten with a fresh coat of morning rain. Sheets of mist drape over peaks and valleys in the sunset. Against the big sky's backdrop, the pale shape of the moon emerges to introduce a crystal-clear night.

Atiyeh rudely shatters the serenity. Forty-eight square miles of steep valleys have been scraped to the naked earth, leaving a brown barrenness as inviting as a moonscape. "We're heading over Weyerhaeuser land, the tree-growing company. Hard to believe, isn't it? They cut all the way down to the lake," Atiyeh says. "Look at that, it will never grow back. That was a forest once like Opal Creek. The entire watershed is gone. When that's cut, the forests' creeks will dry up. Those deep ridges used to be drinks." Water trickling downhill in dead creeks will evaporate as soon as the snow finishes melting, leaving dry gulleys. Atiyeh notices a pair of cutters dropping timber. "Hey, look, they're getting the last of it," he exclaims. "The whole fucking watershed," Atiyeh considers buzzing them, but thinks better of it.

The nation's first law regulating such private lands did not even exist until 1971, when Oregon sought to protect streams and set standards for replanting. It did not put restrictions on the size of clear-cuts, the felling of all trees on a site, until 1991. At 250 acres, the state exceeds the federal legal limits by almost five times.

At Opal Creek, Atiyeh has a perverse affection for a small man-made break in the virgin forest left over from a short-lived logging venture fifty years ago. Ninety percent smaller than the cuts sanctioned by the Forest Service today, the five-acres have begun reverting to their original state without ever needing to be replanted. "If a clear-cut is small, it's like a burn that heals," he says of the natural transition from old to second growth. "Even though man wounded it, the forest is recovering itself." The well-spaced patch contains a mixed, tall stand of deciduous (leafy) trees and conifers. First, alder, a weedy and tenacious tree, pops up. The nitrogen it releases nourishes the soil for budding Douglas firs, hemlocks, and cedar. In a few centuries, the relatively new forest ought to be as good as ancient.

Continuous clear-cuts on private tracts ravage rivers and fish. Natural tree cover plays an instrumental role in regulating fresh-water supplies. Forested slopes enjoy the maximum capacity for absorbing rainfall, and release it gradually through streams and springs. Deforestation removes the elaborate network of tree roots and logs, known as the "stairstep" effect, that secure the soil in place. In the Northwest, where rainstorms can dump several inches of water a day, the runoff tears down the hillsides in sheets. Many of the wastelands below will never bear old, young, or any growth again. The quick-buck specialists strip-mined and ran.

One corporate raider has behaved so rapaciously that most loggers, including Hirons, rue him for blackening their breed. For decades Pacific Lumber Company, a family-run business in northern California, had practiced the model of sustainable forestry on 193,000 acres of redwoods. Environmentalists applauded its custody of the biggest holding of ancient redwoods, some of which are two thousand years old, outside public land. (Just 4 percent of the redwoods remains scattered in parks.) Pacific Lumber had sold thousands of acres to conservationists for parks in the 1920s. It selectively cut the rest to ensure that it would last through the twenty-first century. In 1985, Charles Hurwitz, president of the Maxxam Group in New York, took over the company with $795 million worth of junk bonds sold through Drexel Burnham Lambert, the Wall Street brokerage house that specialized in leveraged buyouts. To retire the debt and bankroll Maxxam's other take-overs, Hurwitz almost doubled the rate of cutting, to 330 million board feet a year. In its 1989 annual report the company attributed its ninefold jump in earnings to Pacific Lumber's cash cow, the redwood forests.

Environmentalists and the firm's own employees protested the irreparable devastation. "There's a story about the golden rule," Hurwitz responded. "Those who have the gold, rule." Says Hirons: "That ain't logging, that's rape. He gives all us loggers a bad name." The California Department of Forestry has turned down Pacific Lumber's application to log more than half the ancient trees on 564 acres on the grounds that the forest serves as a breeding ground for the marbled murrelet, an endangered seabird.

Thousand-acre clear-cuts and the liquidation of prehistoric redwoods call into question private property's sanctity in society in and outside the public domain for the common good. "A land ethic changes the role of *Homosapiens* from conqueror of the land community to plain member and citizen of it," wrote the ecologist and philosopher Aldo Leopold. "It implies respect for his fellow members and also respect for the community as such. The land ethic simply enlarges the boundaries of the community to include soils, waters, plants, and animals, or collectively the land." Even in private hands, land should be accorded protection for healthy air and water. These natural resources are part and parcel of one community, as the cumulative impact of pell-mell logging demonstrates.

Atiyeh's plane cuts through a groove in a mountain. "Now we're in the Detroit Ranger District. They got it pretty good, didn't they?" Atiyeh says. "Remember, this is *your* national forest." Over the past twenty years, when most of this logging occurred in the Northwest, the Forest Service sought to disperse the impact of the high cut levels set by Washington, D.C. The Service limits clear-cuts in the Douglas fir zone from forty to sixty acres. In 1992, the agency finally came to the conclusion that it had better begin switching from the clear-cut to new forestry that leaves some trees standing to help regenerate plants and wildlife. A directive from the chief calling for a more "ecological approach" could reduce clear-cutting up to 70 percent. At this point, though, he has less than 10 percent of the ancient forests on which to test his methods.

The federal government has already allowed the forest to be chopped to pieces. As far as the eye can see, clear-cuts checkerboard the land like midwestern farm fields, giving lie to the premise of sustainable forestry. "I call it a moth-eaten blanket or mangy dog," Atiyeh says. "Look at this one, you'll love it. They clear-cut here and a windstorm came. It's like pulling a thread of yarn and watching it unravel."

The violent gale accelerated through the man-made caverns, razing every object in its path. Terming the whirlwind wreckage from clear-cuts the "edge effect," they have documented its devastation to the spotted owl's precious habitat. Trees lie jackstrawed on the ground like toothpicks dropped from a table. The forlorn few still standing are all but stripped of branches and limbs cheek by jowl to clear-cuts.

A plane ride exposes "scenic corridors" or "view-sheds," those thin curtain of trees the Forest Service leaves standing along busy roads to shield the harsh truth from passersby. Behind the scenes, foresters refer to the buffer zone as the "fool-'em strip." "It's like Hollywood false fronts on a movie set. We don't see our clear-cuts. From British Columbia to northern California, my argument with Tom Hirons is, 'Where are you gonna go?' " Atiyeh says. "They say there's twenty-five years left. My eyes tell me there's five left. It's obvious to me it's going to come crashing down on their heads. They cut too fast."

Though shreds of forests scattered among the bald spots still stand, Atiyeh has already written them off. "I don't get too upset about these parts of the ancient forest because they are biologically dead," he says. "That is what we should give Tom. It's his methadone program to buy the loggers some time to make the change." Federal scientists caution against surrendering those precious pieces as bargaining chips because they serve as critical passageways for wildlife looking for food or mates in larger stands. The elimination of links between islands of forests could spell doom for countless species dependent on old growth.

Logging roads snake their way through the mountainsides. Next to cutting itself, they are old growth's worst enemy. The Washington State Department of Natural Resources estimates that each square mile of commercial forest needs about 5 miles of logging road. Roads cross and disrupt 200,000 streams. On public lands, the Forest Service has become the largest road-building agency in the world. Its road system, at 365,000 miles (almost a square mile of road for each square mile of land), is eight times longer than the interstate highway system. Over the next fifty years, the agency plans to construct 262,000 miles of new roads and rebuild more than 300,000 miles of roads. The total mileage would reach the moon and back and then circle the globe four times.

The dynamite and bulldozers shoving tons of earth and rock out of place compound the erosion already under way from logging. After downpours, torrents of mud and avalanches of logging debris silt up streambeds. Their pure waters become polluted with fertile topsoil too valuable to waste. Thin, unstable soils on exposed hillsides are especially vulnerable to landslides. An entire mountain, 30 miles southwest of Eugene in the Coast Ranges, is on the verge of collapsing since being logged.

Fifty miles north in Washington State, forty-five minutes by plane, a column of smoke spirals toward the heavens parallel to a majestic mountain peak. "It's a slash-burn near Mount Hood," Atiyeh explains. Until recently, the Forest Service took great pride in the modern methods it employed to dispose of slash— the organic mess of limbs, tops, and unused logs left after land has been logged. The purpose is to clear the area of/for eventual replanting and reduce the "fuel load." Accumulating slash quickly becomes tinder, or food for forest fire. With a mixture of gasoline and diesel, "fuel specialists" torch the duff, the top layer of fine debris.

Such burning deprives the next forest of essential habitat for small animals and retards the release of nutrients that replenish the soil. On newly logged and slash-burn sites, mice, chipmunks, and other small mammals have no hiding places. They then become easy prey for snakes, hawks, and foxes. Occasionally a fire burns out of control, scorching the earth and wiping out the surrounding forest. If only Smoky the Bear knew that logging is the biggest man-made cause of forest fires in the Northwest and slash-burning the biggest contributor to those fires. "Over there, they burned it so hot, they sterilized the soil," Atiyeh says, hovering over an outsized charcoal pit. Out in the brush, Forest Service workers I've met describe this occurrence as "nuking" a site. Slash-burning also contributes up to half of the Northwest's raw air pollution, a blemish on Oregon and Washington's otherwise sparkling air. These two states rank fifth and thirteenth, respectively, among the fifty states in controlling this type of pollution.

On my first trip with Atiyeh, in 1989, an acrid haze from fires raging all over the forests cloaked the valleys. For an instant, in the mind's eye, there seems at least a superficial symmetry between this scene and the Brazilian rain forests going up in smoke. (In the Amazon, of course, they make little pretense of replanting.) At the very least, the scene brings to mind Lincoln Steffens's description of Pittsburgh at the turn of the century as "hell with the lid off." One retail merchant I met in Mill City on an overcast day claimed that the smoke-seeded clouds bring rain. This assumption holds true insofar as rain condenses around particulate matter. The Forest Service plans its burns when the wind blows east, away from urban areas. The Willamette Valley's air currents lift and disperse the smoke over the mountains.

On an official forestry tour, Dave Alexander, the Detroit District Ranger for the U.S. Forest Service to whom Atiyeh and Hirons answer, expounds on "flashing the units," his agency's term for burning a logged site. On a good day, ten sites may be burning at once in the district. "In the right air current we can smoke Bend [population: twenty thousand, in the eastern Cascades] out. Burning slash is one of the emerging issues in the Northwest that is probably going to be as significant as owls and wildlife. One of the things the public doesn't want is polluted, smoky air," Alexander says. "We burn a lot less than we did in the past. Maybe the public is going to have to accept more forest fires. There are no free lunches in this deal. Every time we think there are breakthroughs, you want to ask what the end result is. The public doesn't deal well with trade-offs. You get clean air now, and every once in a while you'll get a forest fire." Of course, less logging would leave less flammable slash in the first place.

The public lumps the Forest Service's practices with the field burning that farmers do in the Willamette Valley to prepare for their next crop. In the summer of 1988, dense smoke enveloped Interstate 5 near Albany, Oregon, after a fire set on a farm field escaped. Blinded motorists slammed on their brakes, triggering a chain reaction over a half-mile stretch of the highway. Seven people died and thirty-seven were injured in the fiery crashes.

Swinging around, Atiyeh and I hug the base of a mountain. "I hope I didn't piss it off," he chortles. "See this line? This is one of the few areas we got in the Middle Santiam Wilderness area and we had to scream bloody murder." A few miles away, the federal government's decision to set aside a tract fueled resentment, too. "They cut through the mountains right up to the boundary because good timberland was locked up," Atiyeh observes. "Nice, huh?" Jagged gouges in the national forests abruptly stop at the edge of the Mount Jefferson wilderness area, the most popular in Oregon. Its namesake's 10,497-foot glazed peak glistens in the sunlight, wreathed by evergreens dark as night.

On closer inspection, the firs look scraggy this high up. Opal Creek's low elevation—2,300 feet, in a drainage cupped by

5,000-foot-high mountains—has heightened the stakes for both loggers and environmentalists. The trees grow bigger further down, in moderate climates, among a wider variety of animal and plant species. Elevation is the single most significant factor in maintaining the Cascades' wildlife simply because there is more life lower down. "There's damn little of the lower-elevation forest set aside," says Jerry Franklin of the University of Washington. "The wilderness areas don't do a good job of protecting biological diversity. And the parks, with the exception of the Olympic National Park, don't really do a good job either." More than one third of the ancient forests are so fragmented as to be uninhabitable for animals dependent on old growth. In the United States the parks exist primarily because of their dramatic scenery instead of their biological importance.

In drawing up maps for wilderness areas under federal protection, the politicians gave loggers the first dibs at the best timber. The Wilderness Society, which has done the most extensive surveys of ancient forests, estimates that a mere one quarter of the remaining ancient forest is below 2,500 feet. One independent scientist estimates that in the Willamette National Forest—where Opal Creek is situated—only one tenth of the cut occurred above 4,000 feet until the 1970s. Since then, the lower stands' depletion has accounted for 65 percent of trees being cut at such high elevations and even higher. In the Northwest, the wilderness loggers complain ferociously about being "locked up," but the areas they're talking about are confined mostly to rocks and ice on mountains, with a ring of old growth thrown in below. Since the 1984 Wilderness Act, less than 10 percent of the areas set aside have commercially valuable timber on them.

As if by divine providence, our plane suddenly collides with an eddy of air spilling out of the peaks above Opal Creek, bumping us up and down. To avoid meeting their Creator, mountain pilots earn their stripes as bush pilots. "When you're in mountains as tight as we are," Atiyeh says, "they act like rocks in the middle of a stream." In the air's lifts and sinks over a ridge, a plane can enjoy a free ride or end up in a stall as deadly as the Sirens' songs luring sailors to their destruction. Stories abound of flatlanders piloting tragic sightseeing trips in unfamiliar canyons. The stranded victims run out of altitude and places to turn around. Then, as they say in the game, it's time to "eat it." Atiyeh knows the currents of Opal Creek's waters as well as he does its winds. With a deft touch, he exercises a combination of aeronautical maneuvers to reach safety.

For a look at Opal Creek, Atiyeh banks over its perimeter at a forty-five-degree angle. Down in the drainage, Flume Creek's silver streak sparkles through the emerald treetops. It provides his mining camp's water and, close by, a monument to a glaring Forest Service mistake. Twenty years ago, timber was cut on the thin, fragile layer of topsoil better left alone. He's waiting for the first tree to grow there since. "George has surely shown you clear-cuts at the upper end of Opal Creek from the 1960s that haven't come back. If you break any basin into thirds, the lower will be the most productive, the middle will be mixed, and the third will be the least due to the environment's harshness," Ranger Alexander says, anticipating my question. "Today, I might not have harvested those units. If we were to cut in Opal Creek, where we have plans, it would be low. We have very productive lands there. We know more about soils, hydrology, and wildlife. There's things we're doing today we wouldn't have done two or three decades ago."

Massive erosion following the first rainfalls meant there would be no growth. "Look at 'em, they're not coming back for a good long time," Atiyeh laments. "It's all rock." High up, the camp's cabins appear as quaint as dollhouses. Atiyeh proudly points out the hike he took as a small child from there up to a magic grove of one-thousand-year-old cedars.

All the way from Stony Ridge, on Opal Creek's other side, clear-cuts pockmark the pretty landscape's face. "That's the price we had to pay to keep the rest from being logged," Atiyeh says. "Little Cedar Creek and Elkhorn Creek were cut last summer; they just tore the hell out of them." Any skeptic of Opal Creek's uniqueness will be struck, in a plane, by its utter isolation from human enterprise. It looks like a state compared to the small communities of forest beside it. Still mourning the loss of a recent Opal Creek park proposal in the state legislature, Atiyeh worries about the fate of the thirty two thousand acres left unprotected. "They have chiseled away at the edges. Unfortunately, I still don't know if we'll be able to save it."

Atiyeh slows the plane down to prepare for landing. Pulling on the flaps checks the speed and adds extra life to the wing. The resulting drag allows him to push the nose over for a steeper angle. The short, bumpy runway and bright sunset in his eyes call for a stall landing. He bleeds off until the plane cruises harmlessly over cattle belonging to the farmer next door. As gently as a falling leaf, we touch down on Atiyeh's airfield, with the sun sliding behind the mountains. On the ground, dusk darkens the valley, which had been shining in daylight moments ago.

Atiyeh's active participation in a group known as Project LightHawk carries his environmentalism's clout well beyond Oregon. For years Atiyeh had directed ancient forest flight missions on his own before Michael Stewartt, a fellow bush pilot, tapped him to join the extraordinary green air force. The Santa Fe-based group deploys planes, pilots, and volunteers to give the conservation movement wings. Besides Atiyeh, the pilots include a lawyer in California; an auto mechanic in Idaho; a pumpkin farmer in North Carolina; a doctor; a fire fighter; a sculptor; and a forest ecologist. Each year they log hundreds of thousands of miles on missions ranging from tracking wolves to rescuing the world's last fourteen of an endangered grouse species. The nonprofit flying service is winning over skeptical national environmental organizations accustomed to releasing technical studies. LightHawk brings home the breathtaking visuals Atiyeh exploits and Hirons dreads.

For more than a year LightHawk toured Alaska's Tongass National Forest in southeastern Alaska. Three times the size of Massachusetts, it comprises the largest remaining temperate rain forest in the United States, with 5 million acres of old growth. LightHawk's tours with congressional and conservation leaders exposed the folly of the federal government's $40 million annual subsidies mandating the cutting of 4.5 billion board feet of Tongass timber each decade. Since the 1950s, two corporations holding fifty-year contracts have been paying as little as $15 for enough timber to build a house. Stewartt coordinated planes and pilots to allow photo and network camera crews to see for themselves the extent to which the forest had been plundered, resulting in stunning images on television and in newspapers. In 1991 Congress finally passed the Tongass Timber Reform Act, shutting down almost a quarter of its old growth to loggers and modifying the contracts to reflect market demand accurately. Even so, critics charge the Forest Service with gutting the law and preparing to sell Tongass timber off faster than ever.

Thanks to a fleet of Atiyehs, LightHawk has played a leading role in putting the old-growth debate on the nation's agenda. Flying environmentalists have turned the patchwork quilt of clear-cuts in the Cascades from the conservationists' pet project into a national cause. Televised on TBS and PBS, the Audubon program "Rage over Trees" featured Atiyeh's aerial footage.

Five months after Atiyeh began piloting for LightHawk in

1989, ABC's *Prime Time Live,* a newsmagazine show, approached Stewartt about doing a program on the flying service. Stewartt turned their attention to the loss of the Northwest's ancient forests, and hooked them up with Atiyeh. LightHawk's newsletter hailed it as "the best coverage of the tragic plight of our public forests broadcast on network television news to date." The television program iced Atiyeh and Hirons's relationship. "Tom was coming by my place till *Prime Time Live,*" Atiyeh says. "When the loggers saw that, they knew it was over."

On a cool and drizzly morning, Atiyeh leads a pilgrimage through Opal Creek. A hiker in the Northwest had better bring a poncho in the spring or stay home waiting for the weather to break. Lately, some loggers have gone to wearing baseball caps emblazoned with the slogan "I LIKE SPOTTED OWLS FRIED." Rain drips today from the brim of Atiyeh's counterpoint: "SAVE AN OWL, EDUCATE A LOGGER."

From its alpine headwaters in Opal Lake 3,500 feet high in the Cascades, the creek by the same name flows northward through a mountain for more than 4 miles past rows of towering Douglas firs clinging to steep and rocky banks, then cascades 1,200 feet through dozens of waterfalls, some 240 feet high. Melted ice trickles among the immense roots' fingers and through the banks as it plunges over green boulders and under mossy logs, before tumbling with a symphonic splash into crystalline aqua pools. Atiyeh and I take a short side trip down a steep path, pine needles crackling underfoot. We stand at the edge of a gorge, staring straight down through the mist at Opal Pool's turquoise sparkle 100 feet below. The iridescent bodies of rainbow trout glide beneath the glassy surface. "That water's so clear," Atiyeh shouts above the crashing falls, "it's like looking, with goggles on, at diamonds and emeralds at the bottom of a pool and seeing fish swimming around." Opal Creek earned its name from an early forest ranger. Upon discovering it, he was at a loss to think of anything so beautiful except for his wife, Opal.

Opal Creek, a 6,800-acre basin connected to other tracts of comparable size equaling about 30,000 acres, belongs to a narrow belt of forest running north to south for 1,000 miles. From California redwoods to the Douglas fir, hemlock, spruce, and cedar farther up, these trees grow bigger and faster in this mist-washed Promised Land than anywhere else on earth. The ancient forests contain five times as much timber per acre than did virgin forests once standing tall in Maine and Michigan. David Douglas, the

Scottish botanist for whom for the Douglas fir is named, hailed it as "one of the most striking and truly graceful objects of nature."

Atiyeh steers us over a flume line, a plastic chute channeling water into the camp at Jawbone Flats. He rebuffs my compliments of the neat trail his crew has kept up for the past five years. "The bears built it, not us," he glowers. The construction of the Opal Creek Trail we're on, or any trail without authorization, is illegal on Forest Service land. "This is not a Forest Service system trail. The trail was built without permission by an unknown party," warns a bureaucrat on a sheet detailing the official directions of Opal Creek; he knows full well the unknown party's identity. "The Forest Service maintains this trail for public use. Expect some very steep sections." The agency's permission to Atiyeh to lay out the trail would amount to an endorsement of recreational potential at the expense of the timber it intends to remove. The agency offered to put proceeds from timber sales into trail maintenance. "Nice, huh?" Atiyeh responds. "Clear a trail for clear-cuts."

Our boot soles leave fresh tracks in the snow, marking the first entry into the forest's heart since autumn's first deep freeze six months ago. We fall in and out of snowbanks reaching our knees, then we head into a clearing where it appears as though a bomb went off. In January violent windstorms toppled as many trees in the Willamette National Forest as the legendary Columbus Day storm of 1962. If the 140 million board of feet timber leveled in this year's storm were milled into lumber, they would provide enough for more than 10,000 three-bedroom houses. This year's storm had winds only half as strong as the 170-mph gusts of 1962. Yet the two tempests exacted a comparable toll owing to years of intensive Forest Service logging and road-building. The resulting tunnels in the forest exposed the remaining trees to the merciless wind, toppling them like toothpicks.

Though Opal Creek's heavy-set forests mitigated the storm's damage, the destruction is still beyond belief. Only the biggest, healthiest hemlocks and Douglas fir survived the onslaught. The rest fell like titanic matchsticks. Lying on their sides, they still stand fifteen feet above the ground. At the end of the trunks, clenched fists of soil and rock, known as rootwads, could fill a two-story house. The upended roots have scooped out deep craters in the earth. Water from rain and snowmelt has since filled them up as clear pools. To break through the obstacle course, Atiyeh and I must climb over the blowdown. We climb the steps of branches to continue. The drop from up here seems less perilous walking up and down logs as wide as a sidewalk and, in many cases, half a city block-long. The natural bridges they form go all the way up to our destination. After the 1962 storm, the fourteen-year-old Atiyeh hopscotched in circles for miles atop the fallen trees.

Most people are probably unaware how dead and down trees, in their afterlife, contribute to the forest's well-being. On their downward crash, they take along neighboring branches, opening up paths of sunlight to penetrate to the forest floor. A thousand-year-old tree takes almost half as long as it took to grow to return to the soil completely. A humble hemlock grows out of a nurse log that, by Atiyeh's estimate, has been slumping farther into the ground under a rug of moss since the American Revolution. Trees and plants die and decay, replenishing invaluable nutrients to the living forest. In its stages of decomposition, nature's own fertilizer yields a soil rich and ripe for spawning new life. A log contains enough moisture to act as a reservoir for dry summers and protection against fires and floods.

"You'd be amazed about the life in there," he says. Trillions of bacteria, billions of ferns, millions of insects, and thousands of salamanders are crawling at our feet. At least 163 species of mammals, birds, reptiles, and amphibians—among them black bears, bobcats, and skunks—may find shelter in or eat from a decaying log because the soft wood allows them to sink their claws, paws, or beak into it. Nature's delicate balance between life and death rests on recycling.

Fungi known as mycorrhizae create webworks of root hairs threading across the forest floor, drawing nourishment from the roots of trees. In turn, the trees, in their sunlight-powered sugar factory, extract their own food from the soil. The fungus provide trees with the phosphorus, nitrogen, and water essential to their growth. The antibiotics in fungus inoculate the roots from root rot and parasites. "The Forest Service is trying to design a forest based on isolated products, that is, wood fiber. Nature has designed everything with an order that must be respected if we are to succeed in achieving a sustainable forest," Atiyeh argued in his appeal of the Opal Creek Timber Sale in 1988. "You do not see Nature's order; you can only perceive a Kaleidoscope of ever-changing relationships which you don't understand because you focus on the product rather than the processes that built and sustained that order."

The truffle, a mycorrhizal fungus, grows underground. (Its European counterpart, the black truffle, commands up to $600 a pound as a delicacy. Oregon has begun harvesting its own lucrative crop.) "Truffles emit strong and distinctive odors—fruity, fishy, cheesy, garlicky—so that the rodents hone in on them with a minimum of digging," writes David Kelly, author of the book *Secrets of the Old Growth Forest.* Squirrels, chipmunks, mice, and other gourmets then disperse the truffle spores in their droppings across the forest or bury them beneath the floor for future meals, thereby continuing the cycle. The spotted owl, in turn, consumes rodents in nature's closed circle of interdependence, programmed over the millennia by natural selection. A drop in its population may indicate an inadequate supply of the mycorrhizae on which the trees depend. The spotted owl has thus earned the Forest Service's designation as an indicator species, a gauge of the whole forest's health and all its inhabitants.

Precious little was even known about nature's intricately balanced life until two decades ago. "We're really just learning what old growth is," says scientist Jerry Franklin. Professional foresters use phrases such as "decadent," "overripe," and "wasteful" to dismiss old growth they believe should be replaced with new stands. In 1952, a Forest Service silviculturist dismissed the great forests as "biological deserts." In 1984, a Reagan administration official claimed "old-growth foresters remind me of an old folks' home, just waiting to die."

"Living beings so old have so much experience we can learn from. A 1,000-year-old tree has experienced a thousand springs and a thousand winters. It's sat there watching the huge evolution of man," Atiyeh says. "That's my Druid side. There are certain levels of consciousness. Imagine mountains that have been here for 20 million years. Their experience can be translated into ours. Native Americans believe the earth is conscious, not only as our mother, but as part of us.

"Why should someone in Chicago or New York care about Opal Creek? You may never see a Rembrandt or the Sistine Chapel, but aren't you glad as a human being they are still there? I would be incensed if I owned something so magnificent and somebody else was destroying it. There's the appreciation of arts, appreciation of beauty," he says. "Probably the only thing that does separate us from other creatures is that we aren't limited by our basic needs, like food and water, but we have this sense of the whole. Art is the perfect example. People are willing to spend their entire lifetime in complete poverty and go through personal torment to give us so much beauty. That's what makes us human."

The light mist caresses our hands. Passing through the windfall, we bend down over a stream to slake our thirst. Tasting sweeter than wine, the water running through these creeks is the purest known on earth. The secret lies with pristine watersheds such as Opal Creek, plus the carbon and organic matter of the forest floor. "It's almost as if nature invented the original Mr. Coffee filter," says Lou Gold, an Oregon-based conservationist. Mountain-fed streams supply drinking water to almost 3 million Oregonians and Washingtonians. The U.S. Forest Service manages 211 watersheds encompassing 4 million acres across Oregon and Washington. The 1897 Organic Act setting up the national forest system codified a built-in conflict by promising both clean water *and* timber. Unfortunately, the Byzantine regulatory system of federal and state agencies has failed to monitor adequately the increasing sedimentation of water from logging.

"After the dogwood blooms, the steelhead will be here," Atiyeh says. "I fish this in the summer. You literally lie on your belly right up to the water. If the fish see you, they know your bait is fake and they're gone." As a boy, he camped out at Opal Lake and hiked all day back down to camp, nourished by freshly caught fish broiled over an open fire. Farther down, he cast his line for salmon weighing up to fifty pounds each, on their swims upstream over rapids and waterfalls. Opal Creek is the rare waterway in the Willamette National Forest, running its entire course unimpeded by logging clutter.

Salmon once abounded in these parts. In his youth while returning home from work, Oscar Nystrom, a retired ninety-year-old logger in the Mill City area, would go to the "meat market." All he had to do back then was cast his line in the local river now occupied by a man-made fish hatchery. Salmon constituted a significant part of Native Americans' diet. Before Lewis and Clark arrived, the rivers were so pregnant with fish the Indians said you could walk across on their backs. The horses of early miners reared and bolted rather than wade through the hundred-pounders nipping at their hooves. Urban pollution, excessive fishing, erosion from ranching, and Asian drift nets that strip-mine the oceans have all but wiped out many of the wild fish runs outside hatcheries. Since the 1930s, a series of dams that produce one third of the United States' hydroelectric power has severely obstructed the migration of these fish. Salmon and trout runs are dying off from southwestern Oregon to Montana. On Oregon's southern coast coho salmon and fall chinook are edging close to extinction. On the state's northern coast, wild chum and coho salmon, steelhead and cutthroat trout are plumeting in numbers as well.

In 1991, the National Marine Fisheries Service formally designated the Snake River sockeye salmon an endangered species. Only four of the fish that year completed the epic nine-hundred-mile trek from the Pacific to spawn in an alpine lake in Idaho's Sawtooth Mountains. Scientists removed the solitary female in that group in a last-ditch effort to create hatchery-raised fish with genetic characteristics of the native species. The National Marine Fisheries Service has also proposed to list two other Snake River salmon populations, the spring/summer and fall chinook runs, as threatened, a preliminary step toward receiving protection from the federal Endangered Species Act.

Logging has played a significant role in hastening the decline. It allows as much as eight times the silt and debris as in a pristine ancient forest to wash into a creek, scouring the gravel beds needed for spawning. Naturally, fallen trees on slopes and in streams prevent erosion. In their absence, sediment may suffocate the eggs and clog the gills of hatchlings. In cloudy waters, salmon can go hungry struggling to find food. They may perish in summer waters, overheated for lack of the cool that shade trees provide. A Washington wildlife biologist who studied the phenomenon described steelhead as "panting." The dearth of large fallen trees across a creek deprive salmon of hiding places from predators and of the insects on which the salmon feed. Their vital link in the ecological chain—as meals for raccoons, bears, eagles, and other species—serves as a measure of a healthy forest.

Indeed, at least three fourths of all wildlife species depend on streamside areas. Yet Oregon allows loggers on private lands effectively to strip all vegetation down to within fifty feet of the streambank. Inside the riparian zones, narrow buffer strips, loggers enjoy considerable latitude. Soil and rocks from logging operations have scoured the river bottoms beyond recognition. The U.S. Fish and Wildlife Service recently noted that most loggers follow laws protecting large streams, but eliminate most, if not all, vegetation beside smaller ones.

The forest's melody serenades us. A rhythmic creaking of dead trees rubbing against the living accompanies a pileated woodpecker's distant drumbeat. (The pileated, a stately bird sporting a brilliant red crest, is North America's largest woodpecker after the ivory-billed woodpecker. That bird, which depends on virgin hardwoods, hasn't been seen in the U.S. for 50 years.) Creeks thunder a steady, wet crescendo. Even the clean air sounds good.

Evergreens fill the nose with a galaxy of Christmas mornings past and to come. Scented breezes through the pine needles whisper tales of prehistoric ages. It feels as though we're treading where no one has before; except maybe the dinosaurs, among their primordial breathren.

The air's crispness feels healthy. Each year one acre of temperate forest yields more than six tons of oxygen to keep us breathing. An excess of carbon dioxide creates a greenhouse effect by locking heat in the earth's atmosphere. Levels of the gas have jumped 25 percent since the previous century due to deforestation and the burning of fossil fuels. About one fifth of the most recent increase stems from deforestation, since the logs are burned or decay. Each acre of old growth leveled releases as much carbon dioxide as two hundred cars driven for a year. The world is in no position to eliminate these natural defenses against global warming.

The spongy trail of decomposing wood is as bouncy as a trampoline. The thick material developed over centuries keeps soils and nutrients in place. A huckleberry's gossamer blossom pokes its head out. Atiyeh picks up a skein of pale green lace from the ground. Lungwort—so named because it looks like the inside of a human lung—belongs to the group of lichens and mosses dangling from the old growth's canopy of twigs and branches. It grows not as a parasite sponging off other plants, but it sucks nutrients from rainfall and other particles in the air. Lungwort, as do all lichens, fixes its own nitrogen for growth. On the forest floor it supplies nitrogen for the soil and food for browsing animals. Lungwort survives only in pure air, and thus becomes one of the first living things in an ancient forest to die of pollution. Two years ago for a Halloween party, Atiyeh dressed himself in limbs, lungwort, and moss as the "old-growth man."

He wishes we would run into the real Sasquatch, or Bigfoot, the humanlike creature believed to inhabit these woods. For generations, the thick-furred, long-armed, broad-shouldered, and short-necked beast has been reported in the mountains of California, Oregon, and Washington. His ten-foot-high, five-hundred-pound hulk supposedly leaves footprints as wide as tire tracks. "I believed in Sasquatch as a kid and till recently, everybody did. I remember the footprints and sightings. The forest was so vast, there had to be something there," he says. "Now it's hard to believe in Sasquatch. Either he never was or he's extinct because he ran out of habitat.

"One of the sad parts for me is that we used to think we could disappear in the mountains. In the 1960s, when we thought the revolution was going to happen, I figured nobody would stumble across me for a few weeks. You can't really find those places for solitude anymore. There's so many people it's scary," Atiyeh says. "I want to see purely wild places where you can be alone. It's not wilderness unless there's something bigger than you are that can eat you. I mean that's truly part of it. Not a goddamn amusement park. It's truly a place where people can get in touch with the core of who they are. These are places where people get back to their roots and find the primitiveness."

Atiyeh speaks from experience about encounters with creatures larger than he. On a night his truck had two flat tires, he came face to face with Opal Creek's grandest creature this side of elk or moose. An adult bear, six feet tall standing on its hind legs, sniffed him out on his walk into camp. A mad dash in the opposite direction ended abruptly when he smacked straight into an old-growth tree. Atiyeh and a friend later returned in a pickup to investigate. As soon as Atiyeh—carrying a rifle just in case—stepped out, the driver locked the doors and began driving away in a fit known in these parts as "bearanoia." The omnivorous mammal had faded back into the woods, while Atiyeh raced down the road after his lift home. "Thank God, at least I was armed," fumed Atiyeh, banging on the window. "Yeah, kinda," muttered the driver. "I forgot to tell you we're all out of bullets."

Throughout the twentieth century, humans have heralded their insulation from nature as a sign of technological progress. "What's Wrong with Plastic Trees?" asked a contributor to *Science* magazine in the 1970s. The World Forestry Center in Portland recently stages a multimedia exhibition on ancient forests. "Don't miss this chance to find out what an old-growth forest really is!" proclaims the advertisement in the *Oregonian*. Presumably many Portlanders stand to be enlightened by the slide shows and photography of an ecosystem they have taken for granted in their own backyard. At the gift shop I purchase a cassette tape. "Pacific Northwest Wilderness," of chiming winds and chattering brooks. Over the past few years, a thriving industry has sprung up offering consumers "atmosphere recordings," from "American Forests and Lakes" to "Garden Birds." The drop in real-life songbirds in the United States, resulting largely from the destruction of the Amazon rain forest, only heightens the appeal of artificial noises.

Worst of all, we may be growing too distant to know the difference between the authentic calls of the wild and man's synthetic noise. On a spring visit to Opal Creek, a husband and wife complain to Tin Cup, one of Atiyeh's employees, about the incessant racket of jackhammers. "One, we don't work on weekends, and two, even if we did," Tin Cup thinks, "we don't use them." Tin Cup later realizes the sound they hear is a pileated woodpecker rattling away on a tree.

Opal Creek, as an idea, challenges the nation to choose between wood as a product and its natural heritage. "America is becoming Europeanized," says Roderick Nash, author of the book *Wilderness and the American Mind* and professor of environmental studies at the University California at Santa Barbara. "We are losing qualities that made this nation special." More than 1 million acres of open land cease to exist each year to pave the way for cities. A congressional report estimates that an additional 19 million acres—about the combined size of Massachusetts, New Hampshire, Rhode Island, and Vermont—will be gone by the year 2000.

Concerned citizens and grass-roots activists are drawing battle lines with federal officials, who over the past 12 years saw nothing inconsistent between the custody of natural resources and rapid exploitation of them. Under the Reagan and Bush administrations, Washington encouraged logging, strip mining, oil exploration, and commercial development in or on the edges of many of its wild holdings. Bill Clinton has pledged to take a more balanced approach.

Anxieties about a paradise lost have already filtered through the country's heartland, where early settlers once likened the sight and sound of the windswept tall grass prairie to the ocean's waves. In a few generations, the prairie's original endowment of 140 million acres across the Midwest were plowed from fence post to fence post, river to river. Today there remains less than 3 percent of the original prairie, and the "Prairie State" of Illinois has only .10 percent of its native prairie left. The government's liberal leasing practice for oil and mineral excavation in the Midwest could doom the last remnants of America's natural splendor.

Over half the wetlands—the wet foundation of survival for wildlife and fish—that existed before the Declaration of Independence have vanished. More than a thousand acres of these vital swamps, bogs, marshes, tidal estuaries, and potholes disappear every day. They are drained for agriculture, municipalities dump garbage in them, or developers bury them under pavement.

The most famous wetland of all, the Everglades, is thirsty and threatened. In the 1960s, the U.S. Army Corps of Engineers straightened and dredged one of its major tributaries for flood control and navigation. Since then, wildlife populations have fallen and pollution from agricultural runoff has soared. We are finally coming to understand how wetlands filter pollutants for much of America's drinking water, replenish aquifers, and absorb floods. One third of the nation's endangered species, including the manatee, live in these bastions of nature. President Clinton is reevaluating regulations from the Bush administration allowing the development of millions of acres of wetlands.

The land rush is on in the Northeast. Real-estate developers' encroachment threatens Vermont's Northeast Kingdom, New Hampshire's north country, the Maine woods, and New York's Adirondack Mountains. For more than a century, most of the pine trees and lakes belonging to a few large paper companies were open to the public for recreation. In the past five years, the corporations have begun to cash in their vast timberlands for pulp and real estate. This development—combined with scattershot subdivision for second homes and resorts in New York and the three northern New England states—has spawned a land trust movement unequaled in the nation, whereby public-minded businessmen buy up private property for preservation.

Every year more than 10 million visitors—exceeding the number going to Yosemite, Yellowstone, the Grand Teton, and Rocky Mountain parks combined—flock to the Great Smoky Mountains National Park straddling the border between North Carolina and Tennessee, making it the nation's most popular park. The park's splendid diversity of wildlife habitats and its convenient location (within a two-day drive of two thirds of Americans) raise the risk of it being loved to death. Retirement and resort communities abut the park's edges. The government's plans to log national forests surrounding the park further endanger the ecosystem's integrity. Black bears, songbirds, and other animals living in the park do not follow dotted lines on a map.

Today, Atiyeh believes visitors can still enjoy an abridged version of the Opal Creek Experience: "They won't have the complete solitude, but they know they can disappear here for an entire day immersed in peace and beauty. Sometimes I camp for days in Opal Creek by myself. It's very cleansing. Your thought process tends to be better when you're out by yourself in the woods. There's a tremendous freedom, like being up in a plane. There's nothing man imposes. You're about alone as being in the middle of the ocean. That kind of freedom is rare in our society."

A heroic grove of Douglas fir thrusts skyward. They had already survived a few centuries by the time Columbus was born. Nine-foot-thick trunks, storing thousands of gallons of water beneath insulating bark, protect the trees against death from fire. Your head spins gazing past the bare lower trunk toward the first branches ten stories up, where the daylight squints through. The high rise keeps going twenty stories past that. On a hike through Opal Creek, the forest scientist Jerry Franklin observed that he had seen bigger trees and older trees, but never so many big old trees in one place.

"That we would trade a place like Opal Creek for green paper is absurd. I can't believe the people's values have gotten so distorted. Happiness comes from living in beautiful surroundings, maybe having enough to eat, and warmth in the winter. Most people in this culture run around trying to fill the hole that's inside them by buying stuff. And that hole never does get filled. Does it?" Atiyeh asks. "The only solution is to buy more. The more they consume, the more they damage the planet and the worse it is for the quality of life for the planet and people. We have to break the consumer ethic that more will bring us happiness. The happiness you'll get is the tranquillity of going into the wilderness and sitting by a clean stream."

By definition, a stand of old growth includes at least eight large Douglas fir or other coniferous trees per acre, all at least two hundred years old, long past the age when tree farms are cut. It contains a variety of species compared to a tree farm's machinelike uniformity. There are large numbers of conifers at least thirty inches in diameter and a multilayered canopy of shade and broken sun above. The large standing dead trees are known as snags. Fallen trees and rotting logs crisscross the ground and streams.

More than 1,500 invertebrate species may dwell in a single stand of old growth and more than 150 species of mammals in a forest. Four dozen vertebrate species, including the northern spotted owl, live and eat nowhere else but in old growth. While grizzly bears, wolves, and other carnivores may be less particular about living second growth than spotted owls, they require several thousand acres to range for food. The most dramatic carnivores—the grizzly, gray wolf, fisher, lynx, and wolverine—are virtually extinct in the Cascades.

Ancient forests tend to be warmer in the winter and cooler in the summer than younger forests. A balanced equilibrium, coupled with a variety of plant life, inoculates them against disease, insects, and fire far better than conditions in tree plantations. In addition, it affords an even-temperatured habitat for deer, elk, and other species. The Roosevelt elk and blacktailed deer seek shelter beneath the canopy's thermal cover in the winter because the forest floor remains dry and the food is not buried under drifts.

Snow accumulations are up to six times deeper in clear-cut forests, a leading cause of floods during the thaws. "I used to think hunting was best in the logged places because the deer could forage there," Atiyeh says. "Now I know the trophy deer are in old growth."

High up in the trees a creature rustles. "The funny thing about it is we spend our whole lives on the forest floor," Atiyeh says, "and we have no idea what goes on above us in the canopy." A Douglas fir's tall crown, spraying out in all directions, can carry more than 60 million needles covering more than 30,000 square feet. The canopy contains 264,000 gallons of water per acre. A fifth of a forest's annual rainfall may come from needle drip. It can add eight inches of precipitation in dry months to maintain stream flow. The tiny red tree vole, like the spotted owl, lives exclusively in these forests. At least thirty of them may live in a single tree. Yet its feet never come down from the Douglas fir in whose upper limit it nests. Red tree voles may reproduce for generations on the same ancestral family tree. The creature eats Douglas fir needles and drinks by licking rain and dew from the needles. Under attack from a predator, it can dive more than 50 feet to escape.

In a cool, wet grove grows a twisted and ragged tree, about 15 feet high, whose green-needle leaves are the darkest of all evergreens. The Pacific yew, a species common to ancient forest, was considered a weed until recently. After finishing their clear-cuts, most loggers torched it in slash piles. In the days they ran a small logging company together, Atiyeh and Hirons collected it as scrap for the bigger logging outfits. Unbeknownst to them, or almost anyone else at the time, its purple, papery bark contains a potent cancer-fighting chemical called Taxol. In clinical trials conducted only since 1984, scientists have proved the drug to be an extremely effective treatment in preventing the replication of cancerous cells, particularly in forms affecting the ovary (which kills 10,000 women a year), breast (45,000), and lung (143,000 people). Researchers marvel at Taxol's extraordinary prowess.

To the dismay of patients and the National Cancer Institute, the yew's fruit appears forbidden. It takes six one-hundred-year-old trees to treat a single cancer patient. Perhaps the world's slowest-growing tree, a yew expands ten inches in diameter every century. Only a tenth of them reach that size, the minimum for producing Taxol. It suffers the added misfortune of growing sparsely, about one per twenty-five acres, in forests that have been mostly logged in the domain of the U.S. Forest Service and Bureau of Land Management. Only enough Taxol exists now to treat a thousand patients a year on an experimental and emergency basis. That may change since Bristol-Myers Squibb, the company that produces Taxol, announced in early 1993 that it has made such rapid progress in synthetic creation of the drug that it can stop logging yews immediately. Caught off guard, the Forest Service was scheduled to allow Bristol-Myers to cut 10 percent of all yews through 1995. Still the news is already too late for thousands of patients who never lived to be treated because ancient forests were little valued for their health benefits.

Our nation is eradicating an irreplaceable bank of species and gene pools whose significance we haven't begun to grasp. Myriad other medical benefits may await future discovery. "To take your life support system and exchange it for green paper is the height of absurdity," Atiyeh says. "Would you take out your left lung and trade it for money?" It makes hardly any economic sense either. Even George Bush, who hyped the false choice between owls and timber workers, admitted that the Taxol derived from yews has generated jobs and millions of dollars for local economies.

Everything is larger than life in this land of giants. A dark white fungus called a "conk" protrudes from a tree. The spiral shape once reminded woodsmen of the conch shell. Conks can reach two feet across and weigh more than twenty pounds—some of the biggest fungus-fruiting bodies in the world. Loggers used to sink their pocket knives into the fleshy wood to draw elaborate scenes in their own version of whalers' scrimshaw. Once the conks dried and hardened, the designs assumed a rich brown luster. Sadly, the finer folk art of etching on conks appears to have disappeared.

Today's hike performs a miracle in relieving Atiyeh's work-induced stress. With every bounce up the mountain far ahead of me, the conservationist dispels any doubts about his fitness after being stuck in his office lately. His slender build slithers almost as smoothly through the rolling slopes of thickets as his fleet-pawed Doberman pinscher, Codi. Atiyeh breathes easily in answering all the questions I huff and puff. "So Hirons says I'm out of shape," he growls to himself. "He's pretty out of shape too, that SOB. I go through this every year. I'll be out in the brush this summer, working."

To the degree physiognomy is destiny, Atiyeh is a publicist's dream. His solid bone structure, supporting a firm jaw and chiseled nose, are usually found in *GQ*'s pages. High cheekbones

highlight his sky-blue flinty eyes, projecting sincerity above reproach. An easy smile and quicker laugh, showcasing a perfect
set of teeth, soften some of his arguments' harder edges delivered
in a radio pitchman's mellifluous voice. His flowing chestnut mane
and a mustache reinforce the image he cultivates in Mill City of
a cocksure cowboy. The cowboy boots fit Atiyeh as well as they
do the Marlboro man. One level-headed female visitor to Opal
Creek gushes to me about "the environmental movement's Robert
Redford." Coed fan clubs turn out for his appearances on college
campuses.

Atiyeh's exalted appreciation of his own assets enrages his foes
among the loggers. His photogenic package ensures a flattering
presentation, whatever the medium. While most subjects are
lucky to receive head shots in newspaper stories and magazines,
his sleek physique ennobles Opal Creek's image. Television cameras dote on him on his rambles through the woods. On *Prime
Time Live,* light snow dusts him at Opal Creek, as if in a Nativity
scene. After the show, the mother of an employee at Opal Creek's
mining camp writes her son for the identity of "the hunk."

We hurdle another patch of windthrow up a twisting trail. The
piney sweetness of needles crunching underfoot tingles the ears
and nose alike. A twenty-two-year-old Forest Service marker grins
at us from its lofty place on a Douglas fir. It marks the logging
road the Forest Service planned to build through Opal Creek.
While the road surface may have been only fifteen feet wide,
the agency's common rights-of-way punch eight-foot-wide holes
through the forest. About ten acres of trees are felled for each
mile of road. Atiyeh has left the markers up as historical memen-
tos and reminders. "We've never been able to get permanent
protection for Opal Creek. Each day the trees have stood is a day
they've lived and won," Atiyeh says.

Atiyeh enjoyed a classic northwestern childhood. Born in 1948,
he identified more with cowboys than with Indians. When lumberjacks still stood tall as folk heroes to the nation's youth, young
George toted around a little yellow log loader, stacking miniature
Lincoln Logs into orderly piles. The stories in picture books of
forest fires and lumberjacks fired his imagination. His father, of
Syrian descent, had run Atiyeh Brothers Oriental Rugs and Carpets. His mother regaled him with tales of being reared in
Chiloquin, a logging town in southern Oregon. Her grandfather,
a foreman at Pacific Lumber (the company now under attack for
ravaging California redwoods), moved to Chiloquin to take over
a sawmill. Her father had other ideas about raising his daughter

among brawling loggers. Worst of all, he feared she would marry
a millworker and never leave Chiloquin. As soon as he could, he
shipped her and her sister off to a Catholic convent in San Francisco. The family soon left the logging business altogether, only
to have George revive it in the company he formed with Tom
Hirons in the 1970s.

Growing up in Beaverton, on the outskirts of Portland, Atiyeh
enjoyed running through farm pastures with his dog after school.
Life in the rural suburb scarcely prepared him for Opal Creek.
Once the eleven-year-old began spending summers there in 1960,
his life changed forever. The riffles beckoned him to ride them
and the deep pools to dive. One day he violated the strict orders
of Uncle Vic, a future governor of Oregon, by hiking beyond
designated limits in Opal Creek's upper reaches. The younger
Atiyeh leaned his fishing pole against a tree and kept climbing
higher and higher. The farther he went, the more his love for
Opal Creek grew. Atiyeh finally reached two gigantic western red
cedars he has called his "friends" ever since. He stood transfixed
for as long as the daylight held out, then realized it was time to
start heading back down to camp. First, he anointed his discovery
"Cedar Flats."

Running down the trail, the boy flew through the air in excitement. At the dinner table that night he rhapsodized about the
beauty unknown to him till a few hours ago. His heavy hearted
grandpa broke the news to him gently. The strange people living
in camp were Forest Service employees surveying a road through
Opal Creek's guts. "I was mad. It was like someone had told me
they were going to shoot my dog," Atiyeh recalls. "I vowed right
then that I was never going to let that happen. It didn't." His
resolve led him on a collision course with the Forest Service,
culminating in the armed showdown in 1970.

At Cedar Flats, Atiyeh introduces me to his two buddies. "Hi,
you guys," Atiyeh exclaims. "You'll be immortal in this book. Of
course, you're immortal anyway. The book is biodegradable. You'll
still be standing here." The pair of thousand-year-old western red
cedars had already reached half a millennium the day Columbus
set sail for the New World. On the East Coast, the explorer had
marveled at giants "stretching to the stars with leaves never shed"
that surely paled in comparison to these. Those at Cedar Flats
have massive trunks, over ten feet in diameter, or wider than the
tallest man is tall. Red cedars, with their swell-butted trunks,
have reached twenty feet in diameter—the broadest of northwestern trees.

In contrast to the stalwart Douglas fir, the cedar projects the emotional uncertainty of Mona Lisa's smile or frown, depending, perhaps, on the beholder's own disposition. The flat sprays of foliage, like ferns, offset the bark's reddish cinnamon brown coloring. Your neck hurts craning to find the crown's head start toward the heavens. Strands of moss are draped over the lower limbs. The honied aroma of wet cedar sweetens the air.

"We need all these special places to wash away civilization's intensity. In a city, going down by a river will do it. Some people don't feel comfortable in a forest. For me, it's like a security blanket. No matter how bad things are, all I have to do is get here. There's a spiritual recharging, like those endorphins you get from exercise. They're far more satisfying than any drugs."

On a visit to Opal Creek, Calvin Hecocta, a Native American of the Paiute tribe, laments the spiritual loss he will suffer returning to the city. His ancestral home in the woods is wherever he goes. A few years ago, in midtown Manhattan, the city's chaos began to overwhelm him. Hecocta stepped into a doorway to "frame a vision" of the forest primeval back in Oregon. The cool thoughts pacified him sufficiently to resume his business.

"We've had to share Opal Creek with the rest of the world. Opal Creek would never have been saved unless everybody saw what they had to lose. The only way is to encourage people to go out and make that contact with nature, even if they live in the depths of the city. If it means just going to a park or farm or just a window box with flowers, you've gotta get back in touch with the land. A lot of the people have gardens in their backyards in cities because it's soothing and satisfying," Atiyeh says, advising everyone to find his or her own Opal Creek. "Rather than thinking every piece of real estate has to be developed, why not let it become a natural place? If people like their surrounding environment, the value of housing and everything else goes up. Central Park is a classic example. New York City is making lots of money from people with views. Why not create more Central Parks?"

The original Central Park owes its existence to Frederick Law Olmsted, the nineteenth century's leading landscape architect, who argued that natural beauty combated "nervous irritation" and "constitutional depression." "The enjoyment of scenery employs the mind without fatigue and yet exercises it; tranquilizes it and yet enlivens it," he wrote, "and thus, through the influence of the mind over the body, gives the effect of refreshing rest and reinvigoration to the whole system." The urban toxics Olmsted despaired of have only grown worse during the past century. Affluent New Yorkers pay some of the highest real-estate prices on earth for the privilege of looking out of their penthouse windows at an oasis. Inside the park itself, people from all backgrounds bike past ponds, jog through meadows, picnic under trees, or just loll about on the Great Lawn—all delighting in their escape from the city's asphyxiating asphalt.

Life takes on a new meaning in an ancient forest's green lushness. Old growth, left alone, reaches a state called climax. The sexual connotation befits the orgasmic consummation of green growth. Trees here absolutely grow mad. New generations spring out of the old. One cordial cedar hosts a young hemlock in the rotten part of its trunk. The upstart, sandwiched at a forty-five-degree angle between two branches, forms a pronounced V shape. Loggers have traditionally referred to pairs of tree legs spread out in the air as "schoolmarms," a secular term Atiyeh prefers to omit from the sermons he delivers today.

Atiyeh raises a hand above his head to give a cedar a warm pat and a good-bye, reaffirming its attractive and durable use for roofing, siding, decking, and fencing. "Can you imagine someone like Tom coming in and knocking these suckers down?" he demands. "He's been up here to the flats, you know."

Once upon a time, forests blanketed much of the earth. Centuries of flooding followed the deforestation of China's uplands in about 3,000 B.C. In Homer's era "deep, endless, shadowy" woods blanketed the landscape until Greek civilization depleted them by 400 B.C. for ships, homes, and heat. Syria was anything but a desert, and Lebanon was home to immense cedar forests. Oak and beech forests filled England and Ireland. By the end of the Roman era, one quarter of the land that currently comprises Germany had been cleared. The "great wood crisis" at the end of the medieval period eventually led to the first planned forest economies. Norway spruce and Scotch pine replaced the indigenous hardwoods chiefly because they grew faster. Since 1950, almost half the world's remaining natural forests have vanished.

At the time of the arrival of European settlers, almost 1 billion acres of virgin forest cloaked North America. What the settlers missed cutting or clearing for crops and settlements, the loggers soon turned into lumber—America's first industry. The timber went into cabins, carriages, bridges, stockades, and towns. The New World's tall, straight conifers were fit for royalty. In the seventeenth century the British Crown, which had annihilated its own trees, paid handsomely for pine ship masts from the colonies.

England reserved for the Royal Navy all pines at least two feet in diameter and within three miles onshore. Any colonist cutting trees bearing the mark of the broad arrow faced penalties rivaling those for swearing, heresy, fornication, and murder. The mills kept right on consuming the timber, broad arrow and all. Thirteen times as much acreage was cleared for farms, though, than to feed sawmills. The American plow followed the American ax. By the Civil War, the lumbermen had skinned the Northeast's great hardwood and white-pine forests.

Another green bonanza always awaited them just over the next ridge. The pines, cypress swamps, and live-oak stands in the South, and pine and hardwood forests in the Great Lakes states soon surrendered to the ax and the saw. Once the virgin forests tumbled, so, too, did the eastern elk, bison, timber wolves, cougars, Carolina parakeets, ivory-billed woodpeckers, and passenger pigeons—all of whom suffered dearly from hunters as well. The 100 million acres of forests cleared in the mid-1800s—as much as had been felled since 1600—helped house the influx of immigrants and lengthen the railroads. Hewing to their motto "cut and get out," the timber barons, or anyone else, never broached the question of replanting.

Once all the eastern virgin forests had become history, investors began gobbling up stands of Michigan's abundant white pine, the wood most commonly used for construction. From 1869 through the rest of the century, Michigan maintained its position as the top lumber state in the Union. The colossal trees—three hundred years old and reaching two hundred feet in height and five feet in diameter—gave their lives for houses, barns, fences on the treeless plains, and ties for the nation's growing rail system. At the beginning of the era, surveyors estimated the amount of standing pine to total 150 billion board feet. They missed by 10 billion. By the turn of the century, 160 billion board feet of pine had been cut—enough to build 10 million six-room houses or to floor all of Michigan's land one inch thick and to cover the state of Rhode Island in the bargain. The bonanza netted $4 billion, $1 billion more than the California Gold Rush did from 1848 to 1898. Michigan had been scraped bare.

The Panic of 1893 scattered the lumbermen before they could drop eighty-five virgin acres in the stand destined to comprise part of the Hartwick Pine State Park in the Lower Peninsula. In 1941 a hurricane-force wind, accelerating up the local highway tourists took to the woods, slashed the last scrap to forty-nine acres, on which private developers still entertain designs. Each year more than 250,000 visitors from as far away as India and China—where they know a thing or two about deforestation—flock to Hartwick Pine to skirt the stumps of the big trees felled in the past century and to imagine the twenty-thousand square-mile forest from Lake Huron to Lake Michigan, and north to Lake Superior. Or as Joni Mitchell sings:

> They paved paradise
> and put up a parking lot.
> They took all trees
> And put 'em in a tree museum.

In 1905 the federal government reported that Washington State, a place where few men had gone, generated a lumber output almost as much as Wisconsin and Minnesota combined. The second migration westward followed unbelievable tales of trees drawfing even those of Maine and Michigan, in a land the first explorers ranked the most fertile in the world for growing timber. Early settlers described the dense forests as "thick as hair on a dog's back . . . reaching to God's elbow." Squirrels could commute from California to Canada 250 feet up without touching the ground.

> Oh! What timber! These trees so enchain the sense of grand and so enchant the sense of the beautiful that I am loath to depart. Forests in which you cannot ride a horse—forests into which you cannot see, and which are almost dark under a bright midday sun—such forests containing firs, cedars, pine, spruce, and hemlock—forests surpassing the woods of all the rest of the globe in their size, quantity and quality of the timber. Here can be found great great trees, monarchs to whom all worshipful men inevitably lift their hats.

Such was the ecstasy not of John Muir, but of a lumberman rejoicing over his supreme fortune.

Behind the awe, however, the new arrivals—loggers and farmers—carried with them their traditional biases against forests in uncut form. From Maine to Michigan, loggers had exalted their manifest destiny as conquering the "Green Desert" or "letting daylight into the swamps." In the Willamette Valley, homesteaders had to penetrate the dark, forbidding woods to weed fifteen-foot-thick, three-hundred-foot-high nuisances before availing them-

selves of the fifty-foot-deep topsoil for crops. It often took them
years to burn away the stumps.

The timber barons continued their inexorable march toward the
mother lode of all "Green Gold" in the nation's far corner. Railroad
companies received vast timber tracts from the federal government
to extend their lines. Under the arrangement, Northern Pacific
helped itself to a 39-million-acre land grant covering prime old-
growth parcels. Frederick Weyerhaeuser, fresh off his success cutting
Wisconsin and Minnesota to the bone, bought 900,000 acres at a
meager six dollars per acre. In doing so, he became the world's
biggest private timberland owner. Today the company of his name
controls 13 million acres in the United States and Canada. Weyerhaeuser, a loud voice against the so-called socialists defending the
spotted owl, swilled at the federal trough long before smaller timber
outfits struck it rich off national forests.

The giant redwoods in northern California fell first, although
they were less prized for lumber than Douglas fir. The lumberjacks
started on the most accessible trees in the lowlands where they
could skid the tall timber straight downslope to the rivers with
oxen and horses. "As she had so often done in the past," wrote
Sam Churchill in *Big Sam*, a timberman's account of his way of
life in the Pacific Northwest, "Nature underestimated the capabilities of this creature, Man, she had spawned." The ax, the don-
key, and the steam locomotive hastened the job. Mills evolved
from two-man rip saws to high-speed band saws capable of producing lumber a hundred times faster than before. The bulldozer and
chainsaw's muscular advent following World War II connected
loggers to forests once thought too steep to touch. "They'll be
logging here a thousand years from now," Sam Churchill's Uncle
Marsh had sworn in 1902. "You mark what I say, Sam. A thousand years." To his nephew's eternal regret, he was off by about
900 years. Loggers had finally backed up against the Pacific.

The forest primeval—thriving since the last Ice Age 11,000
years ago and survivors of wind and fire—had met its ultimate
match. By the mid 20th century, almost all virgin forests had
been cut from private lands in the lower 48 states. Since then
logging on federal lands has eliminated most of the rest. Today
only 2 million acres at most, or 10 percent of the old growth that
once covered western Oregon and Washington, remain. In
Alaska almost half of the densest forests are gone. In British
Columbia 60 percent of the coast stands have vanished. Before
a series of temporary court restrictions in the 1980s, loggers
consumed ancient forests at the rate of 71,000 acres per year

in Oregon and Washington national forests. If northern California, Alaska, and British Columbia are added, almost 200,000 acres of ancient forest were felled each year, or 500 football fields a day.

Ambivalence toward nature runs deep in our national consciousness. From the instant that white visitors first set foot in the New World, a puritanical distrust of wilderness as a mysterious barrier to progress and prosperity competed against a provincial pride in American scenery. Andrew Jackson asked in his 1830 inaugural address, "What good man would prefer a country covered with forests and ranged by a few thousand savages to a Republic studded with cities, towns, and prosperous farms?" The prevailing view regarded the primitive environment as a place best suited for conquest in the name of almighty progress.

In the mideighteenth century a growing number of Americans rose to embrace nature as a distinctly national treasure, well worth preserving. "Friends at home! I charge you to spare and cherish some portion of your primitive forests," Horace Greeley wrote in 1851, "for when these are cut away I apprehend they will not easily be replaced." Henry David Thoreau saw it as next to godliness. "From the forests and wilderness come the tonics and barks which brace mankind," he declared that year. But the second Eden he worshiped continued to surrender to the frontiersmen's ax and plow. At this moment his beloved Walden Pond is under threat from developers.

By 1890, with the Industrial Revolution in full swing, the Census indicated the frontier's official end. The pioneer had run out of continent to subdue. Frederick Jackson Turner mourned the loss of the forest's lofty democratic ideals. The Old World's lifeless landscape reinforced tyrannical influences. By contrast, America's great supply of wilds nurtured "social regeneration—the freedom of the individual to seek his own." The free ride had reached its final stop.

Today's argument for old growth replays earlier debates over American wilderness. More than a century ago, sportsmen and other nature enthusiasts backing measures to create a preserve in New York's Adirondack Mountains shifted from spiritual to utilitarian rationales. The lumber and mining companies were ravaging forest watersheds, the fountainheads of municipal water supplies and bulwarks against floods. "Watershed destruction will seriously injure the internal commerce of the state," argued no dyed-in-the-wool romantic, but the head of New York City's Chamber of Commerce, acting in his and the city's self-interest.

"Old-growth forests are a blueprint of God's handbook on how

forests work," Atiyeh says. "It's like we're throwing out the instructions before figuring out how things work." Intensive management of forests in the United States began after the Second
World War. Land managers replaced the system nature designed
to run in 400- to 1,200-year cycles with one of only 80 to 120
years—plus a lot of fertilizers, herbicides, and pesticides. "How
good are farmers with one crop after they've taken all the nutrient
capital from the earth?" Atiyeh asks. Chris Maser, a forest ecologist, argues that no people have ever maintained plantation-
managed trees beyond three rotations. Europe's Black Forest, a
plantation, is dying at the end of the third rotation due to the
soil's depletion. Almost half of German and Scandinavian forest
plantations are perishing. Poor management and air pollution
have combined to plague them with a mysterious disease, *Wald-
sterben*, or forest death. In China, just two rotations have exhausted the soil.

In the mid-1980s the U.S. Forest Service observed a 25 percent
drop in annual growth rates and a dramatic rise in mortality rates
in the United States' southeastern tree plantations. Part of the
damage stems from acid rain, but Maser faults modern forestry for
removing the natural, diverse ecosystems' checks and balances
preventing infestation and illness. Time will tell about the long-
range impact of current practices in the Pacific Northwest's new
forests. Recent years have seen outbreaks of Douglas fir tussock
moth, western spruce budworm, barkbeetles, laminate root wat,
and red ring rot. Natural forests have proved to be self-sustaining
and self-repairing for millennia. "If we liquidate the old-growth
forests—our living laboratories—and our plantations fail, as plantations are failing over much of the world," Maser argues, "industry will be throwing the bathwater out with the baby."

Managed second-growth tree farms are an ancient forest's distant cousin or, usually, no relation at all. The tedium of single-
species monocultures resembles a cornfield—only this crop takes
about a half century to ripen. The uniform canopy rests on trees
of the same age and height; this blocks out sunlight and robs the
floor of plants that take to it so easily in old growth. The thin
boughs are bare of moss and lichen. Spotted owl and dozens of
other species are deprived of the snags in whose cavities they
seek shelter from predators and harsh weather, because dead trees
interfere with intensive tree farm management. Nor can they eat
the insects colonizing downed logs. Until biologists recently en-
forced regulations to leave some fallen idols behind, there was

none to be found. The lack of snags and fallen trees may account for a third less wildlife species in young-growth forests.

We have reduced the last remnants of primeval North America to rocky soil, scrubby brush, and antiseptic tree plantations. "A lot of our effort, when you're talking about a supertree, is nothing more than breeding a better cow," a veteran forester with Crown Zellerbach once boasted. Foresters talk of "reforestation," an oxymoron if there ever was one. Nature's ineffable wonder and complexity defy imitation. "The problem is that the forest is almost gone," Atiyeh says. "It's analogous to what happened to the Great Plains. When you bust the prairie and turn it into wheatfields and cornfields, it's no longer prairie. It's a field. We've converted the forest into plantations. They're tree farms."

After a quick lunch, the noontime sun penetrating the clouds melts the air. Shafts of green light filter the needled spires into dappled elegance on the forest floor. On the opposite ridge, puffs of fog roll across the mist-shrouded crowns. The sun irradiates the white peaks of Whetstone Mountain. "This is my cathedral," Atiyeh says. "No one has the right to defile it any more than I would have the right to desecrate anyone else's church."

As a nation, we can easily affix dollar signs to wilderness values, either intact or exploited. From the forests' raw abundance, Americans built the richest civilization ever known to mankind. The forests yielded fuel for warmth, shelter for comfort, and books for enlightenment. Urban and rural communities depend on watersheds for safe drinking water. People pay good money to vacation in wilderness. Research in plants and animals is leading to the development of miracle drugs. In old growth and every wild area there exists a biological diversity integral to survival of all species—including, ultimately, humans.

In the end, though, wilderness's priceless virtues transcend practical considerations. "In wildness is the preservation of the world," Henry David Thoreau observed in 1861. Down through the ages, the romantics among us have recommended escape to the trackless wilds to refresh the body and spirit. A hike through wilderness provides the ultimate relaxation. Our continent's contraction deprives Americans of the chance to be alone in nature's sublime solitude for a few hours. The loss of the last frontier's remaining fragments robs us of a basic ingredient of our national character. "In the United States there is more space where nobody is than where anybody is," Gertrude Stein wrote. "That is what makes America what it is."

And some of the finest space America still has to offer mankind is in our ancient forests. They are all things special to all people. Kathy Diamond of Oregon Economic Development views Opal Creek through the popular prism of mass culture as "otherworldly, a fantasy out of place and out of time. It's like stepping into Disneyland. I have this fear that my children will not be able to step into it as adults." Dave, the U.S. Forest Service district ranger responsible for Opal Creek's fate, is willing to grasp old growth's aesthetic significance in the context of national landmarks, "just like Gettysburg, the Lincoln Memorial, and [the] Washington Monument. The Vietnam Memorial gives you a real shaky feeling if you're my age. If I have those feelings when I'm standing in those places, I can understand there is at least as much spiritual value in a stand of old-growth timber that was growing when this country was established."

In the footsteps of Opal Creek's antiquity, we have one of the best hopes for saving the last pieces of America's natural heritage. While wilderness protection will always remain subject to human whim, the decision to turn it into timber is irreversible. Once logged, Opal Creek will be lost forever. Borrowing Atiyeh's analogy, how many Notre Dames are enough? Would we fill the Grand Canyon for a swimming pool; dam Niagara Falls for a reservoir; cork Yellowstone geysers for baseboard heating; and, if they still lived, kill off dinosaurs for dog food? Future ages would condemn our short-term folly as we do today the reckless buffalo and whale hunters. Opal Creek's intimations of immortality tie us to our past and future.

III

The Butt End
of a Nubbin

"Hi, Tom. What was that crap you tried to feed ABC?" booms Atiyeh by phone.

"What do you mean?" Hirons asks.

"You know, the shit that I never was a logger. What a crock that was."

"Hey, look, we are always being portrayed as the bad guys, and you're always the good guy trying to save Opal Creek. We are going to defend ourselves and you're a hard guy to hit. So if it means attacking your credibility, we are going after it."

Marlene Hirons cups her hands over her ears, shielding them from the din of the loudest phone fight yet. Her husband is railing at Atiyeh about an interview hours earlier with Chris Wallace, a correspondent for ABC Television's newsmagazine show *Prime Time Live*. Hirons blames his ex-friend for casting him as the villain to Atiyeh's hero in a black-and-white morality play.

With December's icy winds snapping through him that day, Hirons did a slow burn while waiting for Wallace to introduce himself as his crew set up. His temper flared when Wallace asked him, in one of the first questions, what crossed his mind while cutting down a thousand-year-old tree. Hirons bit his jaw, suppressing a growing urge to pop him: "How the hell to get out of the way, so it doesn't fall on me."

Wallace's provocative questions about Atiyeh's past as a logger and possible motives purposely fanned Hirons's ire. "What motivates George? Ego. You got the biggest one of all of us," he fumed. "You sat out there in that goddamn car and wouldn't even talk to anybody until the cameras were ready to roll." Wallace glared at him until stalking off with crew in tow. The Hirons footage ended up on the cutting room floor back in Manhattan.

In the phone call Atiyeh initiated, he unleashed his own fury. Although Wallace and the ABC producers took a shine to him, they challenged Atiyeh to defend himself from Hirons's salvo. He held his erstwhile pal and once-upon-a-time logging partner accountable for forcing him to send ABC old North Fork business cards and photos of him at the wheel of a logging truck. Atiyeh had heard his contributions to their company mocked. "George's hand fits an ax about the way mine fits a pick," Hirons told Wallace, a dig at his career as a miner. Atiyeh inveighed against that desperate ploy of denigrating him to obscure hollow arguments for continuing to cut old growth.

"Tom, didn't I pay my dues out in the brush?"

"Nope. I did most of the day-to-day operation."

"Bullshit. How about all the operations that I took care of every day? Like the trucks? Working on the equipment? Setting chokers? Running the side [crew] when you weren't around? Doesn't that qualify me in your opinion?"

"No. You're not a logger. A logger is a guy who has spent years on the landing or on the butt end of the nubbin." (A nubbin is a round metal piece for hooking chokers, the cable loops used in yarding logs.)

"I'll remember that next time I see your truck parked all day at the coffee shop instead of up at the job. I'll bet all those green kids you got working out there this year are going to be real surprised to find out they haven't made the rank of logger yet, but you have."

"Fuck 'em."

"I helped you build that company from scratch."

"Yeah, but now you are trying to destroy it. So far as I'm concerned, you've lost your claim to be called a logger."

"Go fuck yourself, Hirons. My family was logging when yours were a bunch of dirt farmers in Salem. When you met me you were a crummy choker setter. I helped you from the very beginning. I never lied to you about you and the industry. You've really gotten sleazy this time. So piss up a rope, Tom."

"You're full of shit. Every time you open your mouth, I take it personally. I got you this time and I plan to keep it up until we shut you up. Maybe you just better accept it."

"Thanks a lot, asshole."

" 'Bye."
" 'Bye."

The fierce pride Hirons takes in his work compounds his hyper sensitivity toward lumber jack poseurs. "Out of everything that has happened, I probably resent George calling himself a logger the most," Hirons says. "It's a question of paying your dues." Few other jobs in the world demand comparable dues. Logging's backbreaking danger and dirtiness rob young men of their youth and older men of a future. They move gargantuan objects in brazen defiance of natural laws. The physical intoxication endows them with the sense of invincibility. Risking life and limb under a wide-open sky in weather's worst extremes, loggers come as close to old-time cowboys as any folk heroes in America's mythology.

There is a modicum of ironic truth in the bumper sticker on pickups across the Northwest, "EVERY DAY IS EARTH DAY FOR A LOGGER." As much as office bound environmentalists are loath to admit it, the average logger probably does enjoy a deeper affinity for nature than most. He spends his entire working life in the great outdoors weaning his livelihood from the land. To observe Earth Day, Hirons shared his thoughts with students of Linn-Benton Community College in Albany, Oregon, where he attended school on the first Earth Day in 1970, and with readers of the newsletter he writes for the local chapter of a logging group:

I've had my nose in the dirt for the last 25 years. You just don't get closer to it than when you come home filthy, with muck all over you, splinters sticking out of your shins, your shins scraped, and your hands full of slivers. I celebrate Earth Day on those days at 4:30 A.M. when it's pouring down rain and I'd be just as well off if I got dressed and took a cold shower because that's the way I'm going to be all day. I celebrate it on those days when I have laid awake until 3:00, too hot to sleep, knowing that 4:30 was coming soon and that the Southwest slope was going to be 90 degrees as soon as the sun hit it.

I've celebrated Earth Day on those days when the weather was just right, the air was cool, but not cold, the sun was shining, but not hot, the ground was good and not steep. The logs were high and the wood moved good.

I've seen Mother Nature's awesome hand at work, lightning strikes, windstorms, bug kill, disease, gully washers, and the hand of man, for we are part of nature, too.

On a cool evening in early May, I stay over at the Hironses to shadow him from dawn to dusk the next few days. They built their pleasant home a mile down the road from Atiyeh's in 1974 in the style of a modest, outsized chalet. The living room's exposed wood, capped by crossbeams made from Opal Creek mining timber, is Hirons's implicit salute to the wood products industry. A bearskin hangs high above, opposite a sliding door leading to a deck. A Middle Eastern rug on the wall doesn't hail from the Atiyeh family.

Unless overcome by exhaustion, Hirons prefers staying up late reading in bed to retiring early. Years of practice have taught him to function on remarkably little sleep. Loggers, like farmers, stretch the mornings. As long as woodsmen in the Northwest can remember, they have called their predawn jumps into the day "working at first light," or "hoot-owling," because the only other living beings still up are nocturnal birds of prey. Lumberjacks favor the cooler weather. During a tough fire season, in late spring and summer, the Forest Service frequently orders early closures or bans logging altogether. South-facing slopes in the direct sun can reach up to fifteen degrees higher than those facing in other directions, affording comfort in the winter but hell the rest of the year. By noon, the thermometer is liable to top one hundred. A flick of a cigarette, with a dry east wind blowing, can turn the woods from a tinderbox into a conflagration. Hirons recalls two recent summers when it had already hit eighty at 7:00 A.M. Hirons leaped back into his rig and went home. "On those hot summer days, I don't even start up in the mornings," Hirons says. "Sometimes the Forest Service tells us it's okay to work. I say it ain't. I don't want to get in that hole today. If a fire started, I couldn't ever get out. It's worse than a prairie fire."

The constant fear of an inferno haunts the lumberjack. Even as we shiver one day in what he refers to as marine weather—cold and wet—Hirons grows nervous kicking the dry, woody debris left in the wake of logging. A few days later, out in the brush, a cable vibrating against a stump emits sparks. "I know there's not much you can do, but it's going to be eighty degrees tomorrow," he cautions the crew. "A week more of this weather, we'll have fire trucks and piss cans [extinguishers] out here." Once a significant fire breaks out, local loggers spring to action faster than a volunteer army to stop their subsistence from going up in smoke. Seven years ago, at Monument Peak, Hirons and his son Wes ran up and down hills all night long snuffing out flames with five-gallon cans, until dropping from exhaustion at 3:00 A.M. Hirons and son thanked God they would see another dawn in a few hours.

At 4:00 A.M. sharp, Hirons awakes me from my deep slumber. Just before emerging from his covers, he gave Marlene a soft kiss. His amorous side shines through mostly after a full night's sleep because, on most evenings, he lies in an exhausted daze on the living-room couch. I am served the coffee I begged him to brew before going to bed. In the slim hope I might steal a few extra winks, I had asked him then whether he planned to shower in the morning, a question I wished I could have retrieved halfway out of my mouth. Hirons, who does not suffer fools gladly under the best of circumstances, shot me the unmistakable look known by his crew to crack rocks. "I shower the night before. It's like that old saying," he says, abruptly convulsing with laughter. "You can always tell a workingman. He don't wash his hands after he pisses. He washes them before."

His physical features encapsulate Hirons's bifurcated personality. The penetrating gaze, concentrated through intense eyes behind aviator glasses, can turn fiery at the outset of one of his legendary lumberjack's tantrums. The tension he wears in his face is of a man wound tighter than the spools of cable in his logging equipment. Yet moments later, on the whim of an amusing thought presented or occurring to him, the laugh lines on both temples can emerge from the creases of his happy eyes. Freezing for an instant, Hirons suddenly erupts into a volcanic outburst of laughter.

Hirons jets out of his driveway in his red and white pickup. Having approached this ungodly hour from the night side for most of my life, my cottonheadedness shows. "Shit, this is one helluva time to get up in the morning," he chirps in a halfhearted effort to keep me from nodding off. "Been doing it forever and it still hurts." In five minutes, Hirons has saturated the car with Camel smoke and country music blaring from the radio:

> Black coffee, blue morning
> Rain keeps pouring
> The toast is burning
> Bad feelings, I'm losing you

Wedged between five-thousand-foot ridges on both sides, we listen to the singer's doleful melody in stereophonic static.

At the Cedar's Restaurant, a Detroit institution catering to logging clientele, Hirons plops onto a stool. A nod to the waitress standing behind the counter signals the usual. She pours black coffee into his mug and into an immense, heavy-duty metal Thermos. Sitting, he slugs down white china mugs of it. So far Hirons has stripped his monosyllabic conversation of pronouns, sputtering like a car engine turning over on a cold morning. I order from the menu, fearing it may be a long while until our next meal. In my several weeks on the active trail with Atiyeh and Hirons, their casual indifference to sustenance amazes me. These two intense, thin men shunt aside food as a nuisance in life's larger scheme. "I eat to live, not the other way around. It's just a biological necessity," Hirons says. Five hours into a fishing trip I took with him and Randy Moberg, another Mill City logger, our early-morning breakfast consisted of hot dogs, Snickers bars, Pepsi, and coffee. But that was at the more civilized hour of 9:00 A.M. This morning Hirons looks disgusted eyeing the fried eggs and hash browns I'm wolfing down. He says he'll grab a bite later.

The primary reason Hirons skips food at this hour is to beat his crew to the job. It allows him to prepare all the equipment and, in cold weather, build a pile of tree limbs and branches lying around into a big pot-roaster fire. He also likes to set a good example. My meal has cost him precious minutes. In the parking lot I jog to catch up. Slate-gray darkness envelopes the mountains in that hazy netherland between night and day.

"Damn, the crummy is already ahead of us," Hirons grouses, peering beyond the headlights' beam and pockets of fog. "I'd rather it behind." A few hundred feet ahead, his son Wes, in the loggers' bus—a pickup with benches and a "ten-pack box," or can, built on top in the rear—blares loud rock music for the enjoyment of the men switching from sneakers to boots. Hirons pushes the speedometer in the midseventies, like a mill tail from hell, as he is fond of saying. Ten years ago, at a faster clip, the flashing lights he noticed in his rearview mirror forced him to pull over. "No bitching, Tom," a state policeman intoned. "Just write the SOB," Hirons pleaded, "and let me get to the saw shop before it closes." The ticket-writer discreetly informed him the coast was clear between there and the saw shop.

Hirons admits financial woes lend an added urgency to his commute this morning. Loggers customarily face two- or three-month layoffs due to high snows in the mountains. Lately, however, environmental restrictions and the industry's volatility have extended the duration of Hirons's inactivity. The scarcer work distances his eight-man crew and him farther and farther from home. His last job, around Christmastime four months ago, in Oakridge, seventy five miles from Mill City, required all of them to live in a seedy motel for weeks on end. Such is the life of a gyppo, or contract, logger. Hirons must go wherever and whenever he finds jobs. His client Jim Morgan, the vice president and co-owner of Young and Morgan, rarely lets their friendship interfere with business decisions.

Young and Morgan, Mill City's largest logging company, recently bought a salvage sale—Forest Services for removing only dead timber, either standing or on the ground—at Pamelia Creek in the Willamette National Forest twenty miles from town. Other commitments obligated me to turn down Hirons's two invitations to investigate it with him. He had coveted the job for a month while waiting for Young and Morgan to decide which gyppo to hire.

In the middle of a late lunch at Giovanni's Pizzaria last week, Hirons suddenly dropped a cheesy slice on his plate to clench a fist. "I need that salvage operation. I need that. I need to go out there. I need the challenge of logging," he exclaimed. "You gotta do something in this life. You gotta do something you like. You gotta do something you're half-ass good at," he rasped through a grimace. "By God, I'm a good logger. I'm proud of it. You know what? And this's no joke. Some of the best loggers in the world are right here in the Santiam Canyon. Damn, I'm proud to be part of it. You know something? I have worked long and hard. I was given an opportunity by the people in this canyon and by God and I have lived up to it. I ain't the best, but God, I'm among the best. It's kinda like playing golf. You know you always play better when you're playing with someone better than you." Hirons got the job.

The died-in-the-wood logger would just as soon leave the politicking to someone else. "I won't deny there is a certain amount of excitement. I've got to meet a real lot of neat people and get to keep expanding the network of like-minded people," he says. "But I want to work myself out of a job doing it and go back in the brush." Hirons points to his heart with his stubby fingers.

He hangs a sharp left past Idanha onto logging roads into back country seldom seen by the public. The winding, paved one-lane Forest Service 2246 branches left to a graveled spur, 750, as the first light begins to tint Mount Jefferson's nearby peaks. Hirons kicks up clouds of dust for a half mile. At Pamelia Creek, he laces up his thick-leather, knee-high calk (sometimes pronounced cork) boots. The rows of long, needle-sharp spikes set in the soles to keep woodsmen from slipping off logs would put a football lineman in cleats to shame.

Hirons and his eight-man crew are outfitted in virtually identical uniforms. Loud suspenders, emblazoned with the logos of logging equipment companies, drape snugly over plain work or hickory shirts. The hickory, a favorite of Northwest lumberjacks for generations, comes in one style only. (When purchasing one for myself at Stewart's Grocery in Mill City, my inquiry about color choices engendered waves of laughter from everyone in the store. Atiyeh reminded me of Henry Ford's line about the Model T: "You can have any color you want, so long as it's black.") The tightly spaced navy stripes and a pair of chest pockets resemble the uniform once favored by railway men. The gray zipper running halfway down the shirt to the belly button reveals a brightly colored T-shirt underneath. Jeans, chopped crudely below the boottops, have frayed, unhemmed edges to mitigate the risk of a low-slung pant leg catching on a limb or bush and hurling a man into a log in motion or pocket of dangerous rigging. For further safety, the loggers top it all off with tin hats bearing multiple dents and flecks of peeling paint.

The dirt perpetually encrusted on lumberjacks appears as natural as an extra layer of clothing. At North Fork Logging, Atiyeh once watched in amazement as Mike Broili, an employee and friend of his and Hirons's, started the day by rolling in muddy puddles on the road. "What the hell are you doing?" Atiyeh asked. Broili looked up at him from the ooze: "Just getting it over with."

The modern logger's appearance tends to be deceiving. In the hundreds of hours I spent with Hirons, I have yet to see his wardrobe vary, except while testifying before Congress in Washington, D.C., from blue jeans, a hickory or T-shirt, and a baseball cap. Yet his sinewy, taut frame clashes with the classic, burly image of many lumberjacks. Scarcely any loggers I've met wear glasses—they fog up too easily in the wet weather. In addition, loggers are notoriously renowned for their poor personal hygiene. (When loggers once talked about "getting their teeth fixed," the expression meant a trip to a saloon, not a dentist.) Hirons's large aviator frames dominate his thin face. He uses them to read. A lot. A history buff long before he majored in the subject in college, Hirons boasts perhaps the biggest library in Mill City. From floor to ceiling, the living room's shelves overflow with European and American histories and biographies of his heroes, from Washington to Churchill. Hirons laughed out loud when a visiting lumberjack once asked him what they were for. Ross Miller, a humanities teacher from Mill City High, needed no prompting from me to express his admiration for Hirons as the best-read man in town. The thinking man's logger, Hirons can cuss the wallpaper off a wall with the best of them in one breath and quote Thomas Jefferson on the rights of man in the next.

For all the sentimental attachment he professes to the golden era's heroic gyppos, contract loggers, Hirons typifies the new breed of woodsman. Starting in the 1960s, the public outcry against the forests' destruction led to comprehensive environmental regulations covering all facets of the loggers' job. Technological know-how has become an economic must to stay competitive and the essential tool for limiting damage to the forests. Hirons is required to be a trained technician, well versed in the matrix of laws demanding scientific and engineering expertise. His Forest Service contract can run about two inches thick. He wields a calculator and an ax with equal finesse.

The modern logger spends almost half his time in rigging complex and heavy machinery. In the big woods' golden age earlier in this century, it took hours for pairs of Paul Bunyan look-alikes to drop trees using heavy crosscut saws, and then to drag them out by mule or ox. In modern skyline logging, the timber flies fast. This morning Hirons directs his yarder around a tight corner, waving his arms like a traffic cop. The treacherous move nearly sends it over the edge of a cliff. Once the bolt of terror flashing across his face melts into a smile, he beats his chest with relief. His two yarders, the 50-foot-high 0-71 Madill now in use for midsize timber and the 110-foot-high 208 Washington sitting idle down in Albany for lack of old growth to log, set him back $335,000. Once upon a time, prior to this mighty machine's invention, sprightly timbermen had to remove tops and limbs for mighty spar trees at enormous cost in time—not to mention their own limbs and lives. Blocks and tackle operating from cables in the air helped yard, or yank, logs down the hill.

Hirons's "tin spar" consists of a five-story-high steel tower mounted on a four-wheel-drive flatbed truck for optimum mobility. Snaking down from the top of the tower to trees and stumps Hirons has spotted with pink ribbons, a dozen guy wires anchor the yarder.

Nothing can stop this mechanical behemoth from rocking up and down from the weight of the downed trees. Hirons climbs aboard a small yellow booth jutting out of the side and from which he can power the whole operation. The tower connects to a steel skyline suspended from its top to a tailhold, or fastening seven hundred feet up the mountainside. A computer-driven carriage—as big as a station wagon—shuttles back and forth on pulleys up and down the skyline. It carries a mainline with chokers, flexible steel necklaces, for yanking one or two logs in a single four-ton snatch. Hirons eases his foot off the haulback brake to let the wasteline run down to the tower and shifts a lever to slacken the skidding line. A good yarder engineer needs perfect hand and eye coordination. Running the cables too taut may snap them, too loose and the logs can become stuck behind a tree. However tightly the lines are spooled in the yarder, one "rat's nest," or knot, on the yarder drum can unleash a backlash like a fishing reel gone amok. The whipsawed cable, at five pounds to the foot, can shred a man.

Downhill yarding, what Hirons is doing today, poses far more hazards than working uphill. It can hurl any unmoored object, and some that are fixed, toward the men below with the velocity of an avalanche. Uprooting a stump may bring down the guy line. Some runaway stumps have been known to slice the roof off a yarder and the operator's head in one fell swoop.

Technically, Hirons wins environmental points for strictly adhering to Forest Service regulations. Twenty years ago, before the advent of skyline logging, the Big Sticks tore gulleys on the slope too deep for nature to heal. Hirons now shortens the mainline, jerking the logs up at a forty-five-degree angle and floating them aboveground on their descent. No sooner has he brought an early load home to the landing than a Forest Service agent happens to drop by to check up on this very phase of the operation. "Good lift," he says of the full suspension, then leaves as quickly as he came. Hirons scarcely pays him mind, so sure of the job he is doing. "I know it looks like we're just slam-banging around," Hirons says, ostensibly preempting criticism he expects me to lodge. "You gotta care about what you're doing around here, or you won't be doing it for very long. The Forest Service doesn't think you're doing a good job, they can blackball you right out of here.

"I don't want to be known as a half-ass logger. I derive a helluva lot of satisfaction from either meeting or exceeding the contract's specifications." As proof, Hirons can point to a plaque on his living-room wall bearing the inscription "Logger of the Year 1989," his occupation's most prestigious award, presented to him by Oregon Associated Loggers, an association of contract loggers. "Tom was one of the better students I've had because he had an interest," says Larry Smith, his forestry professor at Chemeketa Community College in 1969, "and he had already worked in the woods." In a drawer Hirons saves letters from the Forest Service's timber sales officers congratulating him on his fine work. No less a critic than his number one tormentor readily sings Hirons's praises. "Tom is a good logger. There are a lot of guys who don't give a shit. He doesn't log sloppy or take short-cuts," Atiyeh says. "He's very careful about doing things right."

Each of the men on Hirons's crew has a precise role to play. The hook tender steers the carriage's load of logs into a neat pile at the landing, command central on the road where the yarder and other heavy machinery is stationed. The "tin" pants he wears derive their name from the heavy, water-repellent denim they're made of. After accumulating a few days of mud, they also tend to stand up by themselves. The hook tender trims off limbs that the buckers, men who saw trees into neat logs, lift and stamp the ends with a long hammer dipped in yellow paint and bearing the federal stamp. Timber from national forests may be sold abroad in a processed form only.

A sixty-foot-long truck hooks a broken U-turn a half mile down the road and backs up toward the landing. The loader's operator clutches a log with mammoth, hanging claws. He cradles it gently onto the truck's bed. The logs must be well balanced and tight in their bunks, no mean feat considering that the engineer has just a few minutes—when time is money in a highball, fast opera-tion—to ensure that the cargo falls within a hundred pounds of the eighty-thousand legal limit. A side-heavy load can turn a logger's short haul on mountain roads into a long ride to eternity.

Hirons protects his investment as though his life depends on it. A few Easters ago, he permitted an employee to take the holiday off. On Monday, they discovered all the radios, saws, hydraulic cylinders, and tools missing. The bandits who had struck could have easily pocketed eight thousand dollars on the black market in Portland or Seattle from their haul. From that point on, Hirons had a watchman look after the equipment and, as required by the Forest Service, for fires during warm seasons. Howard Hall, an affable fellow with a mean guard dog, draws the energy for his small trailer from a generator and solar panels on the roof. As an antidote to loneliness, he has invited mail-order Filipino brides from a booklet to share his taste for "rustic living." So far he's still waiting.

Hall's predecessor, "Weird" Willard Fleetwood, frightened ban-dits and Hirons's crew alike. The Mill City native and ex-Marine captain free-lanced for Hirons while in town. In his real job as a mercenary, Fleetwood hopped the globe from Oman to Rhodesia (now Zimbabwe) making the world safe for democracy. "I was trained not to take any crap from the enemy." Hirons recalls him saying of his tactics after participating in the invasion of Grenada. "Better yet, mind their crap and shoot the wounded." Fleetwood wore camouflage-fabric fatigues, the pant legs stuffed into tall black boots, and a helmet or beret tipped to the side. The odd belt buckle he sported came from the body of a Cuban killed in Rhodesia. His story proved irresistible to Oregon feature writers. "We're up against the full power of the Soviet Union," he warned readers of the *Salem Statesman-Journal* in 1982. "Whether America choses to admit it or not, World War III is on."

Hirons arrived one morning to find Fleetwood sitting atop the company's trailer cross-legged, an M-16 poised across his lap and grenades strapped around his shoulder. He peered intently into binoculars to scout the area. "What do you want me to do if I see anyone?" Fleetwood asked his stunned boss. "Waste him?" He left Hirons's employ for the CIA in the mid-1980s at the height of the conflict between the contras and the Sandinistas.

All the impressive hardware tends to obscure the soul of a logging operation out in the brush. "I call this being in the jaws of the devil," Hirons says with a laugh. "This is a real herculean task." Chokers, cable necklaces, are slipped over both ends of logs with screwy hooks connected to odd pieces known as bells and the nubbins. The ex-tree flops about like a harpooned whale flailing against its captors. Where the whip of jackstrawed piles of logs comes down in the ensuing chain reaction, nobody knows for certain. A man diving for cover seventy feet away may be clipped. "You're getting haywire in the eye of the haulback. Right?" asks Hirons, splaying lingo around. "You're gonna skim it around baldheaded. Don't forget the ginny line." "Mad" Jack Stevenson, Hirons's rigging slinger—the yarding crew's foreman— has the battle scars to show for it. Four years ago, a log butted into a stump and swung around like a baseball bat. Stevenson's leg was in a cast for four months.

He knows the tricks of the trade to ensure maximum production under the safest conditions. Plotting every step taken in the brush, the rigging slinger thinks two moves ahead of the yarder engineer running the tower on the landing. In this minefield of deadly objects, he chooses the logs for each turn to achieve the right balance. Upon helping his choker setters hook on steel ca-bles, Stevenson guides them to locations out of harm's way. Admirers have said he is so smooth he can water-ski on those chokers. Hirons watches the latest challenge his crew man just mastered float through the air downhill.

"Come on, mama. Get your ass in gear," he shouts, babying a giant into the air. "There's another damn cord to Japan. (In fact, most of Hirons's wood goes to the domestic market, but the joke still elicits a few chuckles.) Ain't no way we get that other one without getting killed. We ain't going to do that today." He will return later to tackle a log Hirons identifies as a "thumper in the pumpkin patch" stuck in the slope, even if it means digging a trench underneath or shooting a hole with a stick of dynamite to thread the choker around. Today's timbermen can afford to waste nothing.

Hirons spots a thick clump of tentacles and soil at the end of a trunk far exceeding the average log's forty-foot length. The "root wad" popped out of the ground in the same storm that created the windfall Atiyeh and I hiked through at Opal Creek. Loggers refer to uncut logs still containing the root wads as "Russian Couplings." Outsized and lopsided, they can run wild at severe risk to loggers below. "I never trust 'em," Hirons says. Buckers would sooner back off from Russian Couplings like this than take their chances. Electing to dispose of the menace himself, Hirons retrieves a chainsaw from the crummy. As soon as a puff of sawdust and a loud pop signal a clean cut, he waves for his crew to resume work.

As rigging slinger, Stevenson serves as the whistle punk, sounding signals to the rest of the crew on a little red radio-tipped transmitter. It sounds a whistle atop the yarder through a simple code: three short toots to go ahead and pull the logs to the landing; one short toot to stop and let the man out of harm's way. To a lumberjack's ears, seven long toots and a short one—the longest sequence in code—chill the body and soul.

The seasoned instincts of Stevenson, fifty-two, and Hirons, the same age, dispel the old saw about logging as a young man's game. By rights, both men ought to have retired from running up and down hills all day twenty years ago. Their woods smarts have taken them as far as their legs. I'm in top shape and twenty-three years Hirons's junior, yet I straggle far behind him as he effortlessly alights from logs higher than our chests, screaming and streaming sweat. Where Hirons leaps from one to the next, exploding through the brush, I crawl on all fours. "It ain't easy. You gotta be able to climb up and down felled and bucked timber. You spend as much time on your hands and knees as you do on your feet," he says.

"Fall on your belly. Hand over hand. End up running around with one leg shorter than the other from walking on steep slopes all your life."

He repeatedly extends his hand to help pull me up. I grimace at the sight of a deep cut on my wrist from a sharp nub. Hirons throws a dismissive wave with a lumberjack's hand and arm bearing a panoply of black-and-blue welts. "When I was a ringing slinger at twenty-six I thought I was hot shit," Hirons says, flashing a smile as though to restore my confidence. "One of my choker setters, Wiley Potter, was sixty-five and running circles around me." Potter knew, as Hirons admonishes me to do now, to judge a log before scaling it. Two years ago, a log rolled over a young choker setter for Young and Morgan, crushing him to death. It hardly assures me to learn this morning most accidents occur in the morning hours and in the first six months of a rookie's season.

The wide latitude Hirons gives his men on the job bolsters their rapport. With maturity, he is less disposed to throwing "rigging fits" than in his temperamental past. Today he takes charge of the operation mainly as a troubleshooter. A cable needs splicing. "Hey, you want an ax?" he asks Stevenson. "Hit it like you live, Jack, hard and fast," whereupon Stevenson slips on a branch. "Just like I live, I fall down the whole damn time," he replies. "If it's not one bill collector, it's two." Hirons cautions a choker setter against picking up a heavy block by himself: "That makes for dead babies."

A few nights ago Hirons called his wife to bring home *Never Give an Inch*, the 1970 movie version of Ken Kesey's *Sometimes a Great Notion*, from her video store in Mill City. Watching the video on the VCR, we sat spellbound by the size of trees being logged. "Now, that's old growth," Hirons gushed. He then treated me to a running critique of Paul Newman's credibility in the lead role as a lumberjack. "Look at that. He's chopping the stumps the wrong way; not sliding his hands," Hirons grumbled. "Hell, no, that's not Paul Newman climbing that tree. It's too fake. You know he was only five feet off the ground and a stuntman did it. Newman's afraid of heights. I read that when he was making the movie down there on the coast. He didn't wear suspenders. I'm sure he did his own motorcycle riding." I initially assumed Hirons's rancor belongs to that of any red-blooded male envious of Newman's charm and good looks. On closer inspection, watching the genuine article in action for a few weeks, I come to realize

Hollywood cannot do justice to the real-life lumberjack in the woods.

Hirons revels in the controlled chaos. "Logging is a big kick. There's nothing else I'd rather do. I love to watch the wood move. No two logs are the same. I love to plan a job from beginning to end and make it happen," he enthuses. "I love the challenge of always reaching over your head. Every night you go home with all that you've accomplished during the day." At the corner of a hill, he orders his choke setters to polish off a two-acre triangle of blow-down.

At its best, the modern logging show presents a kinetic rivalry between man and nature. Lilliputians fight to tame giants. No matter how many times the lumberjacks fall down or puncture their skin from busted-off limbs, the very endorphins that Atiyeh calls forth hiking Opal Creek numb the lumberjacks' pain. One rolling log or guillotine cable can kill a lumberjack in a flash. Still they persevere, emboldened by machines they know will ultimately prevail. The yarder's tower looms over the landing, its cables slanting against the horizon like the rigging of a tall ship conquering the ocean.

The cacophony reverberating throughout the mountains overwhelms the bucolic setting. Preeminent logging historian Stewart Holbrook likens the logging show to a "factory without a roof." Chainsaws roar and wail. The shrill whistle cries out over and over again. An engineer wears earplugs to block out the yarder's rumble. The vibrating skyline pings like a guitar string off key. Logs drop at the landing with resounding thuds. Trucks trundle up and down the road, belching their exhaust. No less a hardened environmentalist than Atiyeh admits to holding this triumph of human ingenuity in awe.

At the turn of the century, in *The Education of Henry Adams,* the author explored his young nation's transition from agriculture to industry and from reason to force. At the Great Exposition in 1900, in the gallery of machines, Adams beheld the forty-foot dynamo as a "symbol of infinity . . . a moral force, much as the early Christian felt the Cross." Overcome by "natural" instinct, Adams prayed to the object. The "occult mechanism's" substitution of the "dynamo for the Virgin" ultimately drove him away from technological entropy back to the church's emotional succor. Atiyeh's embrace of Opal Creek as a metaphor for his cathedral mirrors Adams's own soul-searching.

Hirons, in turn, can scarcely live half his waking hours outdoors and avoid falling under its spell. He stands atop a stump, inhaling the panoramic majesty of the Mount Jefferson wilderness area on the federal boundary's other side across the ridge, removing the 35mm camera from the case strapped around his neck to shoot photos of trees being transformed into timber. The plush, dark green fir demarcates a universe off-limits to lumberjacks on workdays. "My God, it ain't all rock and ice," he says. "Those are two fair-sized basins we're lookin' at." His sentiments conform to the loggers' standard public-relations campaigns against the greedy "lock-up" of choice timber that flies in the face of a quick plane ride over scraps of forest scattered among rocks and ice. Hirons also acknowledges, in effect, Mount Jefferson's intrinsic beauty. He is attuned to the dilemma society faces in choosing between the forest primeval and the wood products he makes possible. "No, there sure aren't any free lunches," Hirons explains. "And we have a blessing we should use wisely."

The rhetoric rings true, however, only as long as Hirons can keep the wood moving. For all the homage paid to stewardship in recent years, Hirons remains at heart a pioneer bent on opening the wild country. His historical mission is, as scholar Roderick Nash defines the frontiersman, "to bring things to pass." On strictly utilitarian terms, prairies become farms and deer food or clothing. By force of habit, Hirons views trees as lumber. "When I look at a patch of timber, I first start figuring how many loads a day I can get out of it," he says. "Every once in a while I'll see a patch of trees that makes my mouth drool." True to his word, on a drive through the forest he suddenly blurts out, "Look at those legs lying up there on that hill thicker than snot."

In his American travels in the early nineteenth century, Alexis de Tocqueville marveled at the bias against wilderness among those perpetually immersed in it. "You know where I go to get away from people?" Hirons says to me during an official forestry tour staged by local loggers in observance of Earth Day week. "In the middle of a good clear-cut." Urbanites may seek solitude in nature. Hirons fulfills himself in the fruits it and his labor provide. Behold the yeoman farmer whom Thomas Jefferson deified.

At eleven o'clock, the crew breaks for a fifteen-minute lunch. Up in the brush, Stevenson uses his hickory shirt's sleeve to mop his brow and dips his tin hat into a creek trickling past his feet. He awaits his "nose bag," an institutional green tin lunch, missile-shaped bucket made from a .50-caliber ammo—as in ammunition—can with a hinge. It arrives—by Air Express—on a strap hooked in place to the skyline by a simple device loggers call a molly. Down at the landing, the men gobble pairs of sandwiches each prepared the night before. Between bites they make idle chatter. The loud silence of the machinery temporarily shut down allows for natural communication, a refreshing respite to the shouting or the ringing slinger's whistle to which I had grown accustomed.

The forests' relentless industrialization has virtually redefined the American lumberjack. "Once the logger and lumberman found ways to apply energy, from steam to diesel, to the damnedest tasks ever confronted by ordinary men," wrote Ellis Lucia in *The Big Woods*, "and thus save their muscles and increase their comforts, there was no holding them back. What this huge and expensive gear accomplishes today is well beyond their wildest dreams as expressed in the Paul Bunyan tales."

To appreciate the quantum leap achieved, it's worth a trip outside books to meet the venerable personages on whom the timber industry's public-relations specialists based Paul Bunyan. Oscar Nystrom, ninety, has lived in Little Sweden (population, six), another wide place in the road above Mill City, since 1908. His father and mother escaped the real Sweden's military in 1889 to join his uncle in a Wisconsin logging operation. After helping mine that state's green gold, the Nystrom family followed the wave of loggers to the next timber bonanza, in the Northwest. At Little Sweden, they built cabins to house their chokersetters and crew. The migrants from the Great Lakes states and from back East imported some of their old towns' beloved names. In Oregon, up the road from the area the Nystroms homesteaded, they brought in New York's Niagara (at the site of a dribbling waterfall, no less) and Michigan's Detroit. To the east, Massachusetts' Salem and Maine's Portland.

During World War I, at age seventeen, a husky Oscar felled timber and bucked logs alongside his father and brother. A million board feet of wood a day went into barracks, cemetery crosses, and ships. Spruce wound up in planes, precursors to the famed *Spruce Goose*. In the woods, bulls and horses helped skid the logs into chutes and down the hills. "Chainsaws?" Nystrom says. "Never heard of 'em." Oscar and his brother expended sheets of sweat using the massive two-man saws known as "misery whips." The duo devoted the better part of a day to subduing a single giant. A state-of-the-art chainsaw now settles the matter in two minutes. "Some of them took two days. I cut two out at the bull pasture that were nine foot on the stump," Nystrom recalls, "and loaded the logs on the railroad by cutting them into slabs."

Lumberjacks of his breed burned off a Paul Bunyanesque eight thousand calories a day. They lived in logging camps where, in the early years, lumberjacks packed their own bedroll, and a cook came to spray for bedbugs and other unwanted vermin. The Wobblies—the Industrial Workers of the World—later helped clean up camps. "It wasn't uncommon for fellows to eat a dozen eggs and hotcakes for breakfast," Nystrom says. A glint sparkles in the sunken eyes marred by cataracts. A smile may even be taking shape beneath the crevices of his leathery face.

Wilbur Harlan brought his own share of Colossus to its knees. At home in Mill City, the retired, eighty-year-old lumberjack sifts through sepia photos of himself beside logs so big he looks like an infant. He can close his eyes and recall fir and spruce twelve feet in diameter and over two hundred feet high. The chainsaw's high-tech growl has long rendered extinct the warning cries lumberjacks once thundered in the woods' stillness. "Timberrrrr! Down the hillll! Across the hillll!" Harlan singsongs. As the hook tender, his eighteen-man yarding crew's boss, he knew that neither the yells nor luck could always save the best of them. "I had one tree break and snap next to a guy bucking a log. Rammed him right on top," Harlan says. "The foreman didn't ask whether he was okay, but if it got the saw, 'We can replace men anytime, but those saws are hard to find.'"

Like Nystrom, who saw a man's head sliced off, Harlan understood full well the hazards of "highball," hurry-up outfits. In 1950, the worst year on record, ninety lumberjacks in Oregon lost their lives. "Guys got killed on the landing from the rigging. A line once broke from the strain of pulling a tree and took off the whole top of a chaser engineer's head. His brains were hanging all over him," he says. "We cleaned up the rigging and put everything else we could find on the stretcher. Had to stay that night until the coroner came. In the old highball days, a guy would be killed in the morning and be thrown behind a stump until quitting time."

Harlan grips a glass of water awkwardly with stubs that have passed for thumbs since 1959. "I put my hand on a line. The haul block slipped ten feet and cut off my thumbs," he says. "I nearly bled to death on the walk down the hill. Everything was turning green. They brought the stretcher." Harlan kept on logging through his midsixties and still splits firewood with a maul. His face looks like a road map, the curvy lines etched all over. His hooked nose resembles the bottom of an old logging chute.

The octogenarian can draw on forty-six years of experience in the woods to slice through today's overblown rhetoric. "I think there will always be logging," he says. "I don't see how you can stop it. You gotta have paper and wood." And yet on hikes with his grandson he misses the nine-foot-thick trees once so common to those parts. "He and I see lots of little ones now. I'm old enough now it don't matter to say it. I wish they'd leave Opal Creek alone. Pretty places are special places," he says. "It's like people going down to see the California redwoods. When I first heard about them, I couldn't wait to go see for myself."

Reared in Salem, Oregon, Hirons, like legions of youth throughout the Northwest, always aspired to become a logger. At age six, he thumbed through a children's book about the profession's variety of jobs. His favorite illustration showed the most dangerous of all, a high-climber 150 feet up in the air with a crosscut saw top the tree for supporting cable. He dreamed that he, too, would someday touch the clouds. Hirons looked up to the father of his best friend, a logger in the neighborhood who used to take them out into the forests. At the time there were plenty of woods to choose from on the south side of Salem, the sleepy state capital.

By his adolescence, Hirons realized a lumberjack did not have to destroy nature to enjoy it. On weekends he swam and went deer hunting at the Little North Fork, in the vicinity of Opal Creek. As an active member of the Explorer Scouts, he partook in outdoor projects most American boys can only dream about. His post built a cabin at Mount Hood and, at a scouting circus, the first forest watch out in the woods. At the national jamboree in California, Hirons had good reason to feel like a big man for the first time.

Tom's father, Norval, worked for the Oregon Forestry Department, overseeing the main fire cache, a storage place for firefighting tools. The senior Hirons beat into his son's head a healthy awe of fire's fury that would irrevocably shape his attitude toward nature. He devoured a Tom Swift book about a fire lookout. Soon afterward the youth received an award from the Oregon Forestry Department for reporting a small brush fire in the woods.

The real inferno exploded in a fury of flames in late August 1951. As soon as the Sardine Creek fire burst out late at night, Norval Hirons sped down to the cache to remove all the tools. Reaching the blaze at 11:00 P.M. and drenched in sweat from the heat, the eleven-year-old stared wide-eyed at balls of fire bigger than his dad's pickup, jumping across the canyon. The heat was so intense that hemlock trees two feet in diameter snapped like toothpicks and sturdy equipment wilted. Deer had to seek refuge in the cool water. A fire crew abandoned a water pump in operation and raced through the ash-soaked slope in advance of crumbling trees. In late September a torrential downpour finally extinguished the last of the blazes. The incendiary month seared in the impressionable youth's consciousness a moral: If man failed to manage the forest, nature would do so for him—through fire's rapacious regeneration. Even though a careless smoker is believed to have ignited this particular disaster, the Forest Service blames most fires on lightning.

After the Sardine Creek fire, Hirons participated in the Tillamook Burn Reforestation Project. The Tillamook fire, one of the most ferocious the world has ever known, left 300,000 acres in northwestern Oregon charcoal-covered wasteland. From 1949 through 1973, Hirons joined thousands of Oregon schoolchildren planting seedlings and brought 73 million new trees to life.

By the time Hirons appreciated the values his father instilled in him, it was too late to express gratitude. His father had died. Foremost among them was the work ethic. Between ages seven and eight, he picked strawberries in the summer to pay for school clothes—salt-and-pepper cords and navy blue sweaters at a parochial school. On his modest salary, Norval Hirons needed the contribution to help defray the cost of his son's tuition and books. Once his son earned fifty cents for mowing the lawn, the boy expected to be paid for all his chores, from feeding the chicken to taking his grandmother to the store. His father taught him that hard work was its own reward. "An honest day's pay would come with an honest day's work," he told him over and over again. Hirons landed his first job as a newspaper boy for the *Salem Statesman*. Every morning he started work at 4:00 A.M. to deliver to the 147 homes on his seven-mile route. Arriving at school on rainy mornings, the wide cuffs on his unfaded blue jeans—a fashion straight out of a contemporary Dick and Jane book—were caked in mud. In 1952 he saved enough money to buy a ninety-eight-dollar black-and white Schwinn bicycle. However trite his father's maxim may seem now, it infused Hirons with sturdy notions of self-reliance in sharp contrast to the soft values rampant in today's business world.

Nonetheless, a deep wild streak led Tom down a twisted path. Rebelling against the strict discipline of the parochial school his devoutly Catholic mother insisted her son attend, he ran with the wrong crowd from a public high school. Before reaching the age of confirmation, Hirons was already getting drunk on a regular basis, topping off beers with multiple shots till he passed out at parties. In 1959, the year of Oregon's centennial, Hirons enlisted in the Navy to set himself apart from his college-bound classmates and to finance his vague hope of enrolling in forestry school someday. On a Pacific tour, he emerged from a world-class drinking binge with his buddies with a collection of tattoos. Today a rose, USN eagle, and a clipper ship are as much a part of his identity as his logger's hickory shirt.

Despite confirming his mechanical aptitude in the service, Hirons drifted in civilian life. He met Marlene, a sweet farm girl from Iowa, at a dance and, by twenty-one, was married with the first of three babies. With a family to support, Hirons took the long route to degrees in history and forest technology, bouncing around to schools where he could find work. Torn between teaching history and becoming a full-time logger, an odd combination of interests, he chose neither. Short stints as a beer and Coca-Cola truck driver, concrete buster, and insurance salesman deadened his intellectual faculties. The family photo album contains a photo of Tom standing in front of a 1961 Chevrolet Corvair, wearing a flat-top haircut and a melancholy expression.

His preference for defiance over compliance still created a significant stumbling block to career advancement. As a truck driver, Hirons attended a union meeting at which, for fun, he made a motion for the local to withdraw from the Teamsters and join the AFL-CIO (then separate). All he remembered next was being thrown in the air by two heavy-set toughs with a pronounced distaste for "smart-ass kids" and landing on the grass by the street. He had already logged off and on for five years since college when, on the first day of a new job as a choke setter, a beefy old hook tender standing on a stump ordered the crew to pick up the pace. Hirons took just two hours of the abuse. "If you want this to go faster, get your ass down here," Hirons hollered. "Matter of fact, you can handle this all by yourself." He proceeded to walk off. In logging's heyday, men quit left and right. Another job always awaited them down the road.

Hirons realized that the only way he could succeed would be as his own boss. During the two years he and his family lived in the mining camp at Opal Creek, Hirons, with Atiyeh's help, founded North Fork Logging, profiting from the scraps much larger outfits left behind. In 1977, Hirons bought the assets and turned them into Mad Creek Logging, in honor of the brook running by his home. "You know mad, like a pissed-off stream," he tells people who ask him to spell it. In one of his father's final years, Hirons took him and his mother on a day-long tour of a challenging patch of timber on the outskirts of Mill City. At the landing, she feared a log might fall on someone. "I'm careful, Mom," he said, stealing a glance toward his old man. The senior Hirons beamed from the satisfaction of knowing his son had turned into something after all.

Fallers come in pairs like spotted owls, but for reasons of safety rather than biological survival. Each spots for the other as a necessary precaution against unimaginable horrors. At Woodpecker Creek, the Fred Moore Logging Company is clear-cutting a patch of old growth designated in the area as a possible spotted-owl habitat. The chainsaw's whirring teeth chew through thick bark. The Humboldt undercut and top cut form the notch known as the face. The fallers eyeball the lean by looking up toward the crown. Just to be on the safe side, they hold up an ax handle as a plumb bomb. The face they create enables them to drop the big sticks within inches of the desired direction. Their pinpoint precision ensures safety and maximizes profit. Sloppy maneuvers waste wood, possibly spelling the difference between a seven-thousand-dollar piece of top-grade lumber and a thousand dollars' worth of splinters for pulp.

Occupational hazards, to be sure, outweigh economic considerations. In the back of every cutter's mind lurks the fear of a barber chair, a tree that splits down the middle in its plunge, or a barber pole, one bending over another. The chainsaw's sudden jolt can unleash the fatal widow maker by dislodging two trees slanting against each other or a branch hanging above. Over the past few years, some of Mill City's finest have had to be peeled off the forest floor. Small wonder that Hirons did a slow burn when Chris Wallace challenged him about what he thought when cutting down a thousand-year-old tree. "The first thing out of his mouth went straight for my throat," he recalls. "Talk about self-realization. Got that damn chainsaw lined up. Hell, you don't know if it's gonna go the way of the face, backward, or barber-chair in front of you. That ain't no time to be thinking global thoughts."

The dry, crackling sound of splitting wood follows the chainsaw's last snarl. (I have spoken not just to environmentalists, but also loggers, who swear the squeak a mighty fir lets out during its swishing descent is actually a scream.) The earth shudders from a thunderous boom echoing through the canyon. "It is enough to make the hair stand on the neck of the dullest barbarian," wrote Stewart Holbrook, the loggers' Boswell. The giant's crash kicks up a cloud of needles and detritus. Steel and gasoline have undone in ninety seconds what wind and fire could not over centuries.

So far Hirons has politely rebuffed requests to guide me toward fallers in action, for political reasons. He finally relents out of courtesy and to keep me quiet. "Every time I've talked to media, I've been hit. I'm tired of talking to goddamn reporters," he explains. "You can't overcome the visuals. Look at what these motherfuckers are doing. *Prime Time Live* didn't want to look at second growth. Where can we get some pictures of big trees falling? Those guys' minds were made up. If you're looking to sensationalize, it's easy to do."

The long list of subjects inimical to his cause can crimp our conversation. He instructs his aide at the Communities for a Great Oregon (CGO)—the activist group Hirons founded to neutralize environmentalists—to downplay Opal Creek to reporters and glares at me upon learning my book's title. Mill City loggers have strict orders in CGO's yellow newsletter to desist from "owl-bashing" because it backfires. "George," he has told Atiyeh, "as long as the visual is going to be you standing up at Opal Creek with an owl sitting on your shoulder and me standing in the middle of a butt-ugly clear-cut, I lose every time." With environmentalism in vogue, loggers are swimming against the currents of public opinion. The media have presented their economic plight in a sympathetic light and done occasional features on Hirons, giving him a forum to appeal to the public by harping on community stability. But he knows the destruction on the nation's last virgin forests provides the news peg for far more dramatic images.

Hirons is understandably wary of my interrogation as to the age of the trees he is logging. "Is this old growth, Tom? How 'bout this?" I ask him. "I have a hard time calling the stand we're in old growth. It's more like bastard growth," he says, evoking an old loggers' term for immature Douglas fir of lower grade and little use until the better grade was gone. "Old growth is like porno. You know it when you see it. Hell, the only old growth that's left is what the Indians and lightning didn't burn." And, truth be told, what has escaped the lumberjack's saw. According to biologists, much of the blow-down Hirons is logging, but nature brought to earth, does meet the Forest Service's technical definition for old growth. The adjoining patch qualifies as a spotted owl habitat. As part of new guidelines, Hirons must also leave logs behind to replenish the soil.

He insists on leading me on a trip through his career as a

conscientious woodsman. The local back roads' sixty-degree in-
clines impede his pickup's accleration. We sit slumped back in
the seats like astronauts in a space capsule. Most Forest Service
roads contain one lane and no shoulder. Out the door window, I
gaze at the open space of three-hundred-foot drops. Circumstances
remind me that Hirons, a man easily driven to distraction on the
job, has rolled his share of trucks in his day. While answering
his car phone and CB at the same time, he once landed halfway
down a cliff, bottom up. A transfusion administered in the ambulance en route to the hospital saved him from bleeding to death.
Evidently I betray my nervousness while gaping at him navigate
hairpin curves with one hand on the wheel, as he alternates
between drags on a Camel and slugs of coffee from a Thermos
cup. "You're okay, Dave," he assures me.

Starting at Parish Lake in the Detroit district, the tour's highlights seek to demonstrate logged forests' capacity for renewal.
"This is a good stand of reprod," he says, invoking the term—
short for reproductive—the Forest Service applies to trees it plants
in the wake of cutting. "Don't it look good? Coming back like
gangbusters." The uniformly shaped and sized trees are easier on
the eyes than clear-cuts. The successive stages of second growth,
from stubbly saplings poking their heads through the brush to
thirty-foot-high adolescents, date back to his first job, a selective
cut in 1974. "Look, those are my stumps," he exclaims in the
way a hunter might show off antlers; except Hirons considers the
young, healthy vegetation concealing the woody tombstones his
real trophy.

I follow him down the slope, where he recounts how he pulled
the skyline cable straight through a narrow corridor of trees and
yanked the logs out from each side. On jobs calling for selective
cutting instead of clear-cutting, Hirons can avoid bumping standing trees like a city walker on a sidewalk eluding a crowd at rush
hour. "I'm really proud of this. It got my reputation established
on this district. The Forest Service decided it wanted me to log
up here," he says. "Got good production, ten to twelve loads a
day out of it. What's left we didn't cut. See the little ones. You
could drive a tree up the road and never know it had been
logged." At first blush, the lumberjack's success turning a profit
while at the same time sowing the seeds for the woods' next
generation ought to be above reproach.

By contrast, on an aesthetic level, the other half of the story
verges on the obscene. Clear-cutting—the razing of all that nature
has grown in forty- to sixty-acre swaths—has subdivided the forest

into rows of charcoal-black scars. Torching the detritus after the logging, the Forest Service has created vistas akin to a fireplace floor. In 1974, Hirons brought Thurston Twigg-Smith, an Hawaiian-based financier behind Atiyeh and his mining and timber ventures, up to Parish Lake for a glimpse of his work. "Who's responsible for this devastation?" Twigg-Smith asked with a gasp, stepping out of the pickup. His sentiments echoed President Franklin Roosevelt's on a visit to a logging site at Grays Harbor, Washington, in 1937. "I hope the son-of-a-bitch who logged this is roasting in hell!"

Hirons pleaded for his boss's patience until the regeneration in five years. "Hell, a glass eye in a duck's ass can see everything we do here don't look purty," he drawls. "But then again, does what the wood goes for outweigh the visuals? We started cutting in this part of the country right after World War II. Don't forget a lot of it went to make housing for the vets."

The American Dream Hirons has enabled others to build does not come cost-free, lest citizens lose sight of its material origins. "People enjoy a good beefsteak," he says, "but no one wants to go to the slaughterhouse." In an extemporaneous Earth Day speech at one of his alma maters, Hirons reflects on his formidable campaign to bring the urban public, which has migrated from the country over the past five generations, back into touch with the land's harsh realities. "They think milk comes from cartons, beef from the beef case. There's a few of them that think pigs lay bacon," he tells the students. "If you're gonna build a hot tub or a house, a tree is going to fall." Hirons, with homespun eloquence, challenges society to reconcile the trade-off between preserving wilderness and providing lumber.

Still, the primacy of wood in civilization goes only a short way in excusing irreparable harm caused to a wide part of the forest. In his Ford Explorer, we roll over one moonscape after another. Massive rockslides have occurred because the topsoil was too thin and the grade too step. Five thousand feet up a mountainside, where natural conditions render planting trees virtually impossible, permanent bald spots illuminate man's ignorance. Slopes facing the southwest absorb the fiercest sun. Sometimes they can hit 110 degrees, 30 degrees hotter than the other side of the hill. Once logged, southwest slopes stand a good chance of becoming desert. Hirons talks of advanced, scientific forestry's track record and avoiding the mistakes of the past, but admits it all rings a little hollow at the sight of another Sahara the Forest Service has yet to replant within the five-year, legal period. "I take it personally. There are units I logged eighteen years ago that are still bare," he fumes. "It's goddamn forestry we're supposed to be practicing, not logging. It ain't very renewable if there is nothing happening on that ground. That damn reprod is the future." What Hirons and his peers resent is taking the rap for the lax laws governing state and private lands. The clogged creeks and barren vistas on Highway 22, past Mill City, give them a bad name.

At French Creek, on the backside of Stony Ridge, Hirons and I gaze at Opal Lake, a quasi-mirage in the midst of the wasteland. Draped in the dark shadows of two ridges, its night blue shimmers like a big star in the night sky. A few summers ago he and his son fished in it. They threw back all the bony trout. The icy waters tumbling from Opal Lake's outlets give birth to Opal Creek. "I'm inclined to agree with George this should never have been cut the way it's coming back," Hirons says, pointing to the permanent damage from logging on steep, rocky ground. From our vantage point, Opal Creek's sixty-eight-hundred-acre subbasin appears scared and defenseless sitting off by itself under attack from encroaching clear-cuts. The specter of the Forest Service repeating its mistakes gives Hirons pause and Atiyeh fits.

Even if second growth did emerge on the rough terrain—a cloudy prospect at best, judging from what we have seen so far— old growth is irreplaceable. The loss of the last 5 percent of ancient forests in the continental United States forces loggers to grasp its value in terms other than so many thousand board feet. "This is a climax forest. You can see what has happened to the Doug fir. It's old and dying. I'm not saying it should or shouldn't be cut. I am saying you can't preserve it. What's going to happen is eventually going to have a big fire in here," Hirons says, at Lost Shoe pass. He upholds his occupation's traditional view of "decadence," the Forest Service's favorite expression for old growth's wane while in transition. Down the road in Cedar Creek are more snags, broken-topped dead trees, and centuries-old timber. "Rest of that ought to be left alone. The timber ain't worth nothing," he says. "The ground is so broken up, it's going to break when you fall the logs. Some guys would argue with me. It's prime owl habitat. I say let 'em have it." They will, unless, of course, the Forest Service puts up another sale.

The decision to give unprofitable timber to the birds begs the harder question of trees benefiting both mills and wildlife. A mosaic of "big old boys," as Hirons enthuses, and "just shit" could go either way. "We have a finite amount of ground here to grow timber and this stand is deteriorating. It's not putting on new wood," he says. "Let's get rid of it and start over with that piece of ground. In five hundred to six hundred years it will grow back." Given the economic expedience driving the current, sixty-year rotation for cutting second growth, the likelihood of any growth ever reaching a half millennium appears remote. Nor has it been established that, over time, man can restore God's handiwork to its original condition.

The average American, who may have never stepped foot in an ancient forest, could probably enjoy the outdoors as Hirons does in his backyard. "Come on, Haywire," he yells. "Man, you're dumber than a blunt end of a goose turd." The family dog, a mixture of wolf and Norwegian elkhound, frisks behind his master down the hill in the very picture of rural contentment. Our jaunt through Hirons's thirty-two acres presents a catalog of improvements by him and the previous owner. In the meadow, a family of registered steers Marlene bought as an investment now serve as high-priced mowers. The Douglas firs Hirons stuck in the ground ten years ago have risen to Christmas tree height, about fifteen feet. Hirons is in the process of clearing briar around a man-made pond and preventing floods. The dynamite he applied to mud and stick beaver dams barely fazed the residents, who resumed their reconstruction. From the North Santiam's shore, Hirons skips stones over the backs of steelhead released from a hatchery upstream.

We rest atop moss-covered rocks on the gravel bars, enjoying a pair of nesting Canada geese and airborne wood ducks. The absolute serenity drowns out the noise on Highway 22, a few dozen yards away. "I don't need to escape to Opal Creek," Hirons says. "I just sit and hear the traffic, but it doesn't ruin me from having a good experience. It's a different set of values. I'm really fortunate living here. I cut out part of the hillside. Now Marlene and I can see elk out the bedroom window." Academics have termed this blend of wilderness and civilization "the middle landscape." A world away from Opal Creek's forbidding mysteries, Hirons, in his pastoral contentment at home, reflects his domesticated notion of forests at work.

Back at Pamelia Creek, Wes Hirons, Tom's twenty-four-year-old son and a Mad Creek employee since completing a four-year stint in the Navy two years ago, is about to perform perhaps the most breathtaking and dangerous act in American industry. Occasionally, the high-tech tower on a modern yarder meets its match against a mountain's steep grade. Maximum suspension demands a return to the basics of logging from a bygone era. Rigging a spar tree, from which blocks and tackle are hung, allows a log's front end to be lifted over stumps and brush up or down a hill.

The catch is that some soul must be the high climber. "That one's mine and he's paid for," boasts his father, pointing toward his son. In logging's early days the high climber was the logging show's star, often earning ten dollars a day, plus a bonus, for the extra risks he incurred. "We'd go a mile to avoid rigging a spar tree," Tom Hirons says. "What a pain in the ass." Once he lay on the ground, head in hand, for ninety minutes watching an inexperienced six-foot-seven hook tender flounder just twenty feet up a tree. "Big don't make tough," Tom explains.

His son blends the requisite agility and brawn. "Tough as a horse," his proud father boasts. "He doesn't know his own strength." The younger Hirons's frayed, unhemmed jeans are slit a foot above the knee for freedom of movement, revealing trunk-like legs. His bulging arms round out the high climber's ideal physique.

Wes begins the ascent, planting his boots' heavy spikes in the bark. A rope threaded through a safety belt straps him securely to the tree. His twenty-pound chainsaw dangles beneath him. Pulling himself up, he scales the green spire, limbing along the way. "Hey, Wes, what are you gonna do with all that tail? Huh? I just won't ask any more questions," Dad hollers to him, nervously shifting the weight on his feet. "I assume you know what you're doing up there, and I'm down here."

A high climber faces a thousand more perils than his counterpart, a faller, on the ground. At 150 feet up in the air, a high climber has all the room in the world—to kill himself. A sudden wind storm gripping the treetop could catapult him. If the tree splits down the center, the classic "barber chair," his son's safety belt could squeeze his insides out or cleave him in half. Last year, growing tired, Wes decided to use his hands rather than rappel down the tree. The subsequent forty-foot free-fall put him out of work for months.

His perch today amplifies the screaming saw's sound as it notches the undercut and slices through the base of the fir's crown. Off-white puffs of sawdust streak against the lugubrious, overcast sky. Upon the loud pop of breaking sapwood, the tree thrashes about like an uncoiled spring in a maniacal arc across the clouds. "Yoohoo," yells Wes, darting in the air on the trunk like a cowboy bucking a bronco. The thunder of the treetop's tonnage hitting the forest floor ricochets off the opposite ridge. "There she goes. I felt a rush of adrenaline," his father says, with a smile, pounding his heart with a fist. "Damn, Wes. You do that on purpose? Not cut it all the way, so you can get a wild-ass ride out of it?" he asks. "The hell you say," Wes laughs from the heavens. "You need to keep cutting a hair longer," adds the concerned parent.

Wes deliberately makes his way down one spike at a time. On the section of tree Wes just dropped, Tom and I count 150 growth rings, spanning a century and a half. A dark mark in the rings documents a big burn in these woods during Theodore Roosevelt's first administration. Wes lands on the ground one hour after leaving it. He volunteers to be on call for an encore performance later. His father says, glowering, "The kid gets his rocks off topping trees."

Although Hirons can breathe easier for now, danger clings to a lumberjack like the pine pitch coating his jeans and hickory shirt. Every operation is an accident waiting to happen. According to an old logger's saw, if you stay out in the woods long enough, your number is going to come up. Or as Bill Baumgarten, a health and safety logging inspector for Oregon, puts it: "Sooner or later, somewhere, someday, there's a log with your name on it."

Part of the environmentalists' public-relations campaign seeks to debunk the modern logger's classic image of heroic brawn. "These guys try to link themselves to old lumberjacks logging with oxen and cows," sneers Chuck Bennett, a lobbyist for Opal Creek in Salem. "It's like trying to compare logging to coal mining, where they go out in Wyoming and blow up whole sides of mountains." Although the technology has indeed outstripped the resource, as he and Atiyeh argue, it does a disservice to timbermen by denying that death and injury remain constant facts of life in the Northwest.

The numbers paint a grim portrait of the woods. Since 1943, when officials began keeping score, one logger has died, on average, every nine days. Each year, one logger of six is injured or killed in Oregon and Washington State. A logger stands a one-in-three chance of being disabled over the course of his career. Over the last fifteen years in Oregon, the logging industry has averaged 22 deaths per year, totaling 315 in all. According to the U.S. Bureau of Labor Statistics, the industry ranks in the top fifth percentile in the nation—just behind meat packing and fish canning—in injuries causing lost workdays.

The wounds are far from the garden variety. Root wads, widow-makers, and rigging crush bodies beyond recognition. Chainsaws kick back, severing legs and arms. "The danger is what's so exhila-rating. The more scared, the better you are. You can't go out there and be a dumb-ass, you can't go to sleep or you are going to be clipped. You might get away with it a hundred times," Hirons says. "Then the odds grab and beat you up. What's kept me going is the challenge that if I took my mind off the job, I wouldn't be logging for very long." He has the battle wounds to prove it. A log he bucked rolled on him, aggravating an already bad back. On another occasion, during a fall, Hirons caught him-self on an active cable. His work gloves became sucked all the way in. The mishap left him with a common logger's deformity shared by Wilbur Harlan, three truncated fingers on his right hand and two on his left.

The afflicted fill Pastor Aaron Veach's Mill City church on Sundays. "There's a lore of masculinity around here. If you're gonna be a real man, you gotta set chokers and you gotta have a few war wounds," he says. "You gotta have spent some time on crutches. You have to have your body banged up somehow—accidentally, of course."

Mad Creek, the company in which Hirons has invested all his money and dreams, teeters on the edge of a financial abyss. Widespread fears of environmental restrictions have driven up the price of timber bought by competitors and mills. And a slumping market has lowered the demand. Above all, the old growth yarder, standing idle between Atiyeh and him, drains every penny in his name. His outstanding debt on the yarder exceeds two hundred thousand dollars. "It's like having a damn combine with no wheatfields," he says, of his apprehension about imitating the financial ruin of midwestern farmers in the 1980s. "It's a big gamble, but the market is going to go up on these big yarders." At the same time, Hirons grouses about comparable equipment recently selling for fifteen cents on the dollar on the auction block.

A thousand worries hound gyppo loggers trying to eke out a paper-thin profit margin. Jim Morgan, a millowner, pays him only by a thousand board feet (an amount of wood equivalent to a board a foot square and an inch thick; an average house contains about ten thousand board feet of lumber). The average load of second growth fetches up to three thousand dollars on the open market; a single, premium old-growth log, up to three thousand dollars. He can clear a profit between $200 and—on the extremely rare occasion when he can work in an ancient forest—a thousand dollars a day. Time is more than money, it spells survival. Constant glitches with equipment devour the valuable man-hours of his crew while adding to the four thousand dollars it costs him to run his show each day. Half a week into his new job at Pamelia Creek, a nasty sidewash, in which a log catches a stump, topples the rigging the crew has painstakingly set up. In the four hours it takes him to undo the damage, Hirons has lost about four loads and can write off his hard day's work on the wrong end of his balance sheet. "You sure ain't gonna get rich doing this," he says with a shrug.

Only a tobacco fix can soothe his nerves. From a jeans pocket he extracts a can of Copenhagen snuff, or "snoose," thumbs it open with one hand, and sticks a small wad under his upper lip. The damp snuff, once known as galloping dust or Scandihoovian dynamite, is the most powerful chewing tobacco known to mankind. Legend has it a single pinch once floored John L. Sullivan. The champion boxer would surely wonder how Hirons manages to swallow his tobacco juice. For most lumberjacks, spitting out the bilious substance obviates the need for a stomach transplant. As for the smoke, Hirons is just too tightly wound to give a damn. He generally telegraphs his mood swings by the amount of cigarettes he lights up. On an off-day three or more empty Camel packs lie crumpled on his pickup's floor. On days when he should have stayed in bed, Hirons chain-smokes and swallows his snoose juice simultaneously.

The recession in Hirons's business matches his spirits. In a good year, he has earned about sixty-five thousand dollars, roughly the equivalent of recent payments for logging equipment, his biggest investment. "I'm on the verge of bankruptcy," he says. "I'm sure if I showed my books to the accountant he'd show me across the street to the lawyer." Save a one-bedroom condominium in Newport on the Pacific Coast that he and Marlene bought five years ago to serve as a weekend retreat and the electronics that are a staple of most American homes, they live simply, with few extravagances. "When I look at it, we have more stuff than we need. I have no personal plan. I hope I'm going to be able to do this till the day I die. Even if I retire, what the hell am I going to live on?" he muses aloud in his living room. "Marlene and I are damn sure not going to make it on Social Security." Worst of all, he rubs his ego raw agonizing over whether he'll be able to pass on his home and property to Wes and his daughters, Vickie, twenty-eight, and Debbie, twenty-seven.

In the meantime, any move from Mill City to greener pastures would represent a symbolic and literal retreat. "We want to live on this property till we physically can't. People in this canyon opened doors for me that no one opened for me in my life. They gave me my chance at the American Dream," Hirons says. "God, I'm so lucky to have all this stuff. No, not that. All the toys don't matter. I'm lucky to live here. Where can I go? What can I do? I wouldn't want to live in any other place." Do or die, Hirons will stand his ground.

The worst may be yet to come. Hirons's massive old-growth yarder has sunk him in debt too deep to stomach the reminder of Atiyeh's warnings about purchasing it. "I've told him, 'I told you so.' And he gets real bent out of shape," Atiyeh says. "Buying that yarder was one of the dumbest things Tom ever did, next to going after Opal Creek. Now he's really trying to crawl out of a hole."

Five years ago, the Forest Service set sales requiring loggers to move heavy logs beyond the capabilities of the small yarder Hirons owned. Loggers with the right equipment were creaming the high grade, leaving the scraps for Hirons. The last straw came when Hirons's client Jim Morgan hired his main competitor, another contract logger, with a big yarder. "Damn it, Jim! It's one thing when I have to clean up your shit," Hirons snapped, "but when I have to follow another gyppo it's too fucking much."

For all intents and purposes, Hirons had made up his mind by the time he ran the idea by Atiyeh over his kitchen table. Atiyeh had just returned from his first environmental law clinic, at which the heads of top groups plotted their strategy to enforce the full gamut of laws on the books to save ancient forests. "No, Tom. No! Don't do it," Atiyeh pleaded. "The spotted owl is there. The old-growth industry is going to come crashing down."

Nonetheless, Hirons held firm. He reminded them of shrewd equipment deals that had turned handsome profits in the past. This one seemed too good to pass up. At $250,000, a used 208 Washington yarder he priced held the promise of cracking Mill City's big leagues of logging. In hindsight, Hirons might have done business differently. "If I knew now, I wouldn't have bought it," he says. "My lord, it's awful easy for George to say that when he's on the outside. He wasn't sitting at the end of the table getting the short end of the stick."

Before it yanked a single log out of the woods, events were already rendering his Washington obsolete. Two fire seasons, during which the Forest Service shut down logging in hot, dry weather, preceded an early snowfall in the mountains. The eventual thaw generated a short-term bonanza and visions of the financial breakthrough Hirons dreamed about. The boom, however, proved illusory. Mostly the yarder has sat idle. As Atiyeh predicted, environmentalists have choked off the dwindling supply of raw material needed to feed it. "What makes me sick about this," Atiyeh observes, "is there's no solution because we all started too late in addressing the problems."

Far from giving him flexibility, the Washington has saturated Hirons with red ink. Just moving it on a trailer the size of a short city block from its berth in Albany, Oregon, to jobs near Mill City costs five thousand dollars in time and labor. The dollars generated from Hirons's smaller yarder have not begun to cover the big yarder's costs. His unsecured debts have piled high as the 110-foot itself, exceeding two hundred thousand dollars. Hirons knows he would be lucky to fetch twenty cents on the dollar at the regular auction in Medford, Oregon—if he could dump it at all. Rows of white elephants just like his, owned by loggers in equally dire straits, are gathering rust on the block.

All the pressures have exacted a heavy toll on relations between Hirons and his family. Marlene's video store in town now constitutes their principal source of income. Deferring to her to handle his books and payroll, he regards her business talents as superior to his own. "Marlene has managed our checkbook from the time we had fifty cents. And she has a streak of independence. She's done a damn good job running the store, better than I have running my logging company," her husband says. "I'm proud of her for it."

Even so, the role she plays as breadwinner gnaws at his male self-esteem. Lately, the curly, blond fifty-one-year-old's ready smile, complementing her sanguine disposition, has dimmed a bit. One evening a few weeks ago, Marlene finished her biweekly chore of filling out paychecks and doing the books on the kitchen table. She then looked up at her husband to ask him if he was spending too much time at the Communities for Great Oregon office, his political base, and too little on Mad Creek. He came unglued for thirty seconds. "You say stuff you can't take back," he later says. Sitting in the Hirons's living room one evening recounting a story, he suddenly jumps up in the middle of the story to retrieve a rifle and go after a stray cat running around in the yard. "Don't worry, he's a bad shot," says Marlene, without bothering to look up from her newspaper. POP. POP. The terrified creature scurries across the porch, unharmed.

Hirons appears to have lost about five years of his life to the stress. His thick thatch of hair looks as though thinned by a logger in the year since I last saw him. The laugh lines have deteriorated into worry lines on his forehead, deepening like the shallow gulleys his timber leaves being dragged down a hillside. "I used to see him all the time. He used to have animals that go across the street or I'd see him on the road," says Michelle Meader, a neighbor. "You know what's kind of sad? I saw him at the timber rally in Portland after having not seen him for a long time. I didn't recognize him for a minute." Adds her friend Chelsea Stewart: "That wasn't the Tom Hirons I remember." "Tom has aged, hasn't he?" says her grandmother, Marie Stewart, at Stewart's Grocery in Mill City. His friends and neighbors all express profound concern about Hirons's health and well-being.

His battle for solvency is robbing him of his son Wes, whose confidence in his old man is sagging. When he joined Mad Creek, the twenty-four-year-old never thought he would have to make ends meet by building fences down in Salem for $4.50 an hour instead of the logger's $13.00. An agreement they forged together, after he graduated from high school six years ago, rested on the mutual respect fathers and sons treasure over a lifetime. All the senior Hirons wanted was $3,000 a month for life, in return for bequeathing all the equipment and a debt-free company to his son. "No chance of that happening. I've struggled for the past twenty years to have something to leave him. There's not much to give him," Tom says. "Wes was going to be my retirement check. We ain't got nothing else." The son, under the strain of their financial pressures, has stopped talking to his father.

Ironically, Hirons adopts a position strikingly similar to Atiyeh's to probe the nation's distracted psyche. "I feel fortunate that I'm in an industry that provides one of society's three basics, shelter. It's a sad commentary when we hold guys like Donald Trump and T. Boone Pickens up to adulation. They're smart-asses and manipulators," he says. "I believe in entrepreneurship. A guy comes up with a good idea, is able to sell it, and reap the award. He doesn't prey on other people's misfortunes or abuse the system. I bet very few of them have done an honest day's work. The Protestant work ethic is down the tubes." It may be all too easy to dismiss Hirons's sermon as the tendentious pap of a small businessman in trouble, but the rugged individualism Hirons embodies goes to the heart of our national character in refreshing contrast to the herd mentality all too common in today's business world. A self-made man, he has built a satisfying life-style by dint of initiative and determination rather than the blind pursuit of profit.

Anyone along in years who has lost a career when he's least able to adapt can identify with Hirons and his despair. He remains trapped between the frustrations of past successes impossible to repeat and a future too bleak to anticipate. The present is thus a living nightmare. "Sometimes you sit back and wonder why you're doing all this," he broods. "When you gotta jump through hoops like this. It's snapping your guts." To a considerable extent, the ferocity with which he has thrown himself into politics arises from his deflated self-esteem. "You can't be in this business and be a quitter," he declares. "I like a good fight and I'm not a quitter." When all else fails, by that measure, Hirons succeeds in standing up for what he believes.

A snapshot of history in Hirons's logging show at Pamelia Creek one day illustrates his predicament. All work stops on account of the first "three-log load" in two years. Hirons preserves the moment for posterity with a camera he keeps in his pickup, and asks me to pose beside it. The six logs—or four at best—filling a truck's bunk are all that nature usually has left to offer. By a quirk of nature, the blow-down from the storm a few months ago allows Hirons to relive logging's glory days when the motto "Happiness Is a One-Log Load" was still painted on decorative handsaws. He saw his last twenty years ago—an ancient spruce, seventeen feet in diameter, lumberjacks had cut and abandoned forty years earlier.

Loggers today are victims of their own success. The sophisticated yarders and other equipment that have yielded spectacular riches at a record pace have hastened their own obsolescence. They are worth so much scrap metal, absent a supply of old-growth logs. "I don't give a goddam how big the holes are we put in that forest," Hirons says. "The forest is so much goddamn bigger than I am or we are. I say that knowing full well that it reflects the spirit and outlook of generations gone by." The celebration of the rare three-log load encapsulates the cumulative effect of too many holes and dwindling stretches of woods left in which to draw a paycheck or hike.

Hirons falls somewhere between the timber beast of the sensationalist media's creation and the environmentalist he claims to be. As long as there exists a demand for the lumberjacks' product, a staple of our modern economy, Hirons is exactly the sort of man for the job. His sensitivity and professional pride keep damage to a minimum. The proof comes in the painstaking attention to detail and the young woods blooming a generation later. Nevertheless, in his line of work, it only stands to reason that the extraction of natural resource obviously comes at the expense of its preservation. Any distinction between second and old growth is blurred in the utilitarian world Hirons occupies. The homesteader spirit he personifies places the ultimate premium on subduing the earth for man's benefit.

By force of action more than emotionally charged rhetoric, Hirons appears at once a conservationist and a logger. Whereas Atiyeh seeks to save Opal Creek, Hirons strives to avert the extinction of a noble way of life. In his outdoor office beneath the trees Hirons exudes a love of labor's excitement and danger. By and large, the American consumers in cities and suburbs take their yeomen farmers and woodsmen for granted. Were Hirons to stay home from the woods, Trump and Pickens would have no paper to shuffle. Besides friendship, two basics Atiyeh and Hirons provide society—wood and wilderness—bind them together in their competing missions.

IV

At Loggerheads

"What the fuck did you think you were doing today, Hirons?" Atiyeh shouts on the phone. On the night of the Opal Creek hearing Atiyeh still seethes over the personal assault earlier in the day at the Capitol, and knows just whom to blame.

"Yeah? Well, I don't know what the fuck you're talking about," Hirons shoots back. "I ain't responsible for what other people say." There follows a fleeting pause.

"You thought nothing of using my name when we first got started, Hirons," Atiyeh shrieks, "you goddamn name-dropper."

"I've always acknowledged your help," Hirons answers in kind, "so piss off."

Atiyeh's full-throated outburst on the other end of the phone fills the Hirons's living room, as if he were actually sitting there. Marlene, Tom's wife, hears it all. Over the coming months, listening to these frequent phone fights, she becomes attuned to the distinct timbre of Atiyeh's screams—a high-pitched roar—and her husband's holler—a deep, guttural sound. Marlene has had her fill of strife over the past twelve hours down in Salem. Tonight, the slams of the men hanging up on each other every few minutes interfere with the peace and quiet she craves. "Why don't you leave it off the hook?" she begs her husband.

Two weeks later, the phone rings again. "You know, Tom, we're going to put you out of business and you're too fucking dumb to realize that in the long run it's going to be good for you," Atiyeh thunders. "And we're not just going after Opal Creek. We're going after all of it."

"We'll see who the fuck puts who out of business, George," Hirons responds. Turning to his wife, he declares: "By God, if he wants a fight, I'll give it to him."

The Salem hearings bring to a boil months of simmering distrust between two former friends. Hirons had wondered why Atiyeh furtively shut off the computer in his home, where he operates his business, when he dropped in to shoot the breeze over a cup of Atiyeh's strong coffee. It turned out he was guarding his secret strategy to create the Opal Creek Park. Adding insult to injury, Hirons discovered the bill's existence not from Atiyeh, but in the newspapers a few days before the hearings. His colleagues in the timber industry were surprised, and some were suspicious, that he seemed so ignorant of his ex-partner's treachery. In turn, Atiyeh felt personally violated by Hirons's stealthy efforts to help spearhead the log truck caravan.

Fueled by personal rivalry, the feud has developed a lethal velocity. Atiyeh and Hirons used to get along famously precisely because they were so much alike. Both men, of wiry builds, share a monomatic ability to operate at endless stretches on little sleep or food. Their omnivorous appetites for books, a rarity in rural Oregon, where learning often commands less respect than muscle, sparked lively debates deep into the night. Today their mental swagger intensifies the verbal jousting over timber issues. They are not simply vying for a cause, but for rights to Mill City's conscience. Their skills have vaulted Atiyeh and Hirons into leadership roles as spokesmen for their respective camps. The public responsibilities driving them toward extremes appear to dash any hopes of private reconciliation. Perhaps only two men whose mutual affection ran as deep as the closest brothers could turn on each other like Cain and Abel.

Hirons had just graduated from college in Oregon in the spring of 1972 when a friend invited him to Opal Creek for the weekend. Though he had never heard of it, Hirons needed an escape. Bouncing from one school to another, it had taken him far longer than he expected to obtain his degree. Moreover, his father's recent death and a series of unfulfilling jobs whetted his desire, in the parlance of the day, to find himself. From the moment he snowshoed into camp in late spring, Hirons knew he had found the right spot. Within a month, Hirons began spending most of his weekends at Opal Creek.

Atiyeh and Hirons liked one another immediately. "I just liked the SOB right off the bat," Atiyeh recalls. They took a shine to each other's intelligence and mischievous sides, which would spawn a series of ingenious practical jokes over the years. In the summertime, they wiled away lazy afternoons diving into Battle Ax Creek—a few hundred feet from its intersection with Opal Creek—from thirty-foot cliffs overhead. Both men loved to work outdoors with their hands. Atiyeh had plenty of chores for anyone willing to pick up a hammer. Jawbone Flats—the historic mining camp at Opal Creek belonging to the Atiyeh family for 50 years and the battleground against the Forest Service, which had wanted to log in the area—had fallen into disrepair by the time George moved there permanently in 1969 after military service and graduation from the University of Oregon. In August, Hirons scrapped city living and went off to live with his family and three other families, including Atiyeh's, at Opal Creek.

Far from partaking in the hippie back-to-earth fad then so prevalent, Atiyeh and Hirons teamed up to embark on the very career paths that would eventually drive them apart. In 1972, George's uncle, Vic Atiyeh, who had inherited the mining property at Jawbone Flats at Opal Creek from his father three years earlier, decided he wanted to sell it. At the initiation of a friend of George, Vic sold it to Thurston Twigg-Smith, head of Persis Corporation, a newspaper and real-estate conglomerate based in Hawaii.

The philanthropist and venture capitalist agreed to put up the money to restore the old mining camp at Jawbone Flats. The five men living there with their families installed new tin roofs on the dilapidated cabins. To satisfy the wives' demands for minimal creature comforts, they assembled water lines. The toughest challenge involved repairing severe structural damage to the cabins, main lodge, and bridges on the road to camp.

Hirons alone could provide the technical expertise to log for the lumber they needed. He had worked his way through college in the trade for Weyerhaeuser and other timber companies and had recently earned a degree as a forest technician at Chemeketa Community College. He and Atiyeh bought a used yarder and heavy machinery with a tall tower for moving logs, from a lumberman in Mill City for seven hundred dollars and mounted it on the flatbed of a rusting World War II surplus truck. On its very first day in use, the driver assisting them neglected to check the clearance; power lines overhead came raining down.

The chore of training the novices at Jawbone Flats tried Hirons's patience, a virtue he was hardly blessed with in the first place, while overseeing the development of a makeshift operation for cosmetic logging, the surgical removal of trees close to roads or already on the ground. The crew's efforts went smoothly until they ran up against an eighty-foot long monster ideally suited for a half bridge on the road into camp. They found it far easier felling it than yanking it out of the woods. One dynamite stick later all they had for their work was one hunk of wood and piles of short strips for firewood.

As Opal Creek's snowbanks thawed in early spring, Atiyeh and Hirons felt heat from their employer in Hawaii. Nearing the end of the renovation, they were ordered to hatch a means of generating revenue to cover equipment and other expenses. Days of brainstorming focused on marketing the natural resources at hand. Gigantic insects inhabiting the caves could be sold as pets. Fashionable Californians would surely want to be seen drinking bottled water from Opal Creek. Florists always needed moss and ferns, Opal Creek staples. Atiyeh and Hirons were ready to start baling. Unfortunately, none of these ideas projected much cash flow. The men decided it was time to take advantage of the one resource that had primed Oregon's economy for so many generations: timber.

They poured their enormous energy into building a small business for YUM yarding, or Yarding Unmerchantable Material. Today wildlife biologists require lumberjacks to leave a certain number of logs on the ground because such "woody debris" prevents erosion and nourishes the soil, a primary building block for a forest's ecosystem. When Atiyeh and Hirons launched their venture, however, the Forest Service promoted a tidy, good-housekeeping approach to ensure that, after the timber came out, the forest remained as neat and tidy as a golf course. Having removed the cream, loggers complained about being forced to waste man-hours burning the monstrous piles of "cull," worthless logs and woody debris. They never thought twice about letting a couple of young hustlers pick up after them for profit.

As it turned out, Atiyeh and Hirons's woods smarts and good timing created a windfall. They simply moved into logging sites and hauled away scrapwood for pulp without bothering to inform the Forest Service. To avoid the fee at the scaling ramp, they stuffed as much as they could into a Hamm's beer truck Hirons had inherited on an odd job as a delivery man a few years earlier. Slabs of cedar they retrieved went to a small mill built to manufacture shakes, rough shingles used for roofing.

Hirons paid sales calls on the contacts he had developed among

loggers while in school. In contract negotiations with a local mill
for YUM yarding jobs, he demanded an addendum to keep an
extra fifty cents per acre logged. Atiyeh, Hirons, Baumgarten,
and Atiyeh's cousin Tom slapped each other on the back for
driving such a hard bargain. Little did they know that the market
for chips for pulp material would soar from six to twenty-four
dollars a ton in three months. For every load of logs, Atiyeh
and Hirons raked in five hundred dollars for the conglomerate in
Hawaii.

The birth and growth of their company, North Fork Logging,
emboldened them to branch out. Hirons became its president and
Atiyeh the president of Shiny Rock Mining, a company seeking
to extract a few dollars from ore at Opal Creek. The lumber
brokerage they started together for supplying the home-building
business soon generated annual revenues of over twelve million
dollars.

In addition to earning twenty-seven thousand dollars each annually, Atiyeh drew a partial salary for serving as vice president
of North Fork, and Hirons earned the equivalent in the same
capacity for Shiny Rock. Expanding their enterprises, the fledgling
entrepreneurs built a small mill, True Studs. Atiyeh and Hirons
harbored grandiose visions of making a killing as middlemen between North Fork and the Honolulu newspaper empire. All that
was missing to forge a vertically integrated empire was a newspaper mill.

Hirons upheld his end of the deal, and then some. By the
spring of 1974, he had decided to go from YUM yarding into full-
scale logging of second growth and small farmers' patches of timber. He acquired a small, track-mounted yarder designed for easy
setup and portability. It proved especially useful for thinning, the
selective removal of trees in a logging unit, as opposed to
wholesale clear-cuts. Atiyeh and Hirons displayed a sixth sense
in speculating in the timber market through their savvy use of
capital-gains laws. In Hillsboro, Oregon, Hirons bought a 130-
acre patch from a timber company for 25 percent down. Once
the market shot up three years later, he sold it back to the sellers
at a cool $250,000 profit without so much as scraping a tree.
(The windfall went back into North Fork.)

Atiyeh and Hirons sweated over budgets and five-year plans far
into the night in the days leading to the annual meetings with
Persis officials in the lodge at Jawbone Flats and at corporate
headquarters in Hawaii. In 1976 the Persis Corporation summoned them to the retreat of its owner, Thurston Twigg-Smith,

outside Woodstock, Vermont, in a house that once belonged to
Sinclair Lewis and Dorothy Thompson. Wandering the 235 acres
of forest and well-manicured grounds, Hirons wondered if his ambitions dovetailed with those of his employer. An accountant in
Hawaii, incredulous about the cost of a log truck he purchased,
asked him whether it was bigger than a pickup. Hirons refused to
dignify the ignorance with an answer. The founder of the Persis
fortune, Thurston Twigg-Smith, had amassed millions from the
steady revenue of newspapers in a growing market. Logging's year-
to-year volatility defied prediction. "I don't know why you boys
can't find a business we can count on grossing seventeen or eighteen million dollars annually," a Persis director told them.

   While concentrating on the mines, Atiyeh found time to pitch
in at North Fork in an administrative capacity and, on the odd
day, out in the brush. Atiyeh filled in for members of Hirons's
logging crews in emergencies. As head of the truck division he
negotiated the purchase of the first vehicle, a forty-foot long
eighteen-wheeler. "Now that I own the son-of-a-bitch," he told
the seller, "show me how to drive it." A few spins around the
block did not prevent a fitful sleep that night in anticipation of
the next morning's long haul over the top of Mount Hood to the
True Studs mill in North Powder, in eastern Oregon. He had
North Fork's fleet of trucks painted the same color as Mill City's
leading timber company, Young and Morgan, blue and white.
Atiyeh feared that he might run over somebody. On the eight-
hour drives he routinely made over the next year and a half
hauling loads off Hirons's jobs, Atiyeh tried relieving the monot-
ony on straightaways by reading novels, but found himself reread-
ing paragraphs.

   Atiyeh helped repair trucks and other heavy equipment in his
capacity as president of North Fork's log trucking company whenever he could manage to escape his mining duties. He and Hirons
often rubbed greasy elbows together well past midnight, only to
start all over again the next morning. In their labor of love,
neither minded wearing the odd hats of company presidents and
truck mechanics.

   Sawdust never coarsed through Atiyeh's and Hirons's veins in
the same way. Atiyeh hated having to rise from bed before dawn
as part of the traditional predawn logging regimen, while his partner thrived in the mornings and still does. Atiyeh and his ex-
wife Deanne wince recalling Hirons's merry orders at 4:00 A.M.
from his car phone in their driveway for a pot of coffee. Nor did
Atiyeh share Hirons's thrill at conquering nature's tall timber.

The woods struck Atiyeh as even filthier than the mines to which he was accustomed.

Aside from job preferences, Atiyeh experienced flickers of doubt about the direction of his far-flung ventures. He consented to pulling out dead and downed old-growth trees along the roadside in Opal Creek for practical applications such as bridges into camps and mining timber to shore up sagging tunnels. "Remember, we grew up as Oregonians and truly believed those were absolute waste," he explains. "I didn't understand forests were more than just a bunch of trees."

Privately, Atiyeh strained to resolve the contradiction between the preservation of his backyard and the exploitation of the forest. Under Hirons's aggressive management, North Fork delved deeper into old growth so that, at its peak, in 1978, it produced 5.5 million board feet—enough to build 550 houses. "Even when we were cutting old growth," he says, "I'd never let a finger touch Opal Creek. I always loved it because it's so beautiful."

His spiritual odyssey occurred gradually as he took up flying in 1974, first as a hobby then as a local commuter service. Once Atiyeh began piloting his small airplane over Oregon and Washington's mountains, the endless devastation beneath his wingtips jolted him out of his complacency. "I was becoming schizophrenic. I went along with North Fork because I grew up with the mystique left over from our pioneer days that the state is covered with trees. We didn't have any idea that they wouldn't last forever and that we would could cut them all down. There was this idea in Oregon that the forests were so vast it would go on forever," he says. "What changed me was that once I learned how to fly, I noticed clear-cuts as far as the eye could see."

Atiyeh deeply regrets his reluctance to shift North Fork's course more quickly. "I should have bitched my head off, but didn't," he says. Rather than voice his concerns, he deferred to Hirons, whose success solidified his control over the logging end of their venture, and dedicated himself to mastering mines and flight. "At some time in life, everybody has lapses in their principles. Later, you go back and try to understand," he says. "We started cutting old growth about the same time I started getting bent out of shape about what was going on." Echoing Atiyeh's sentiments, management at Persis decided that North Fork violated its company's ecological principles as well. With their assistance, in 1978 Hirons bought North Fork's assets from Persis to form his own company, Mad Creek Logging. Atiyeh washed his hands of logging for good and wished him well in his new venture.

While their professional association ended, their friendship continued to thrive. They, after all, had gone through so much together. "Tom and George were a pair," recalls Atiyeh's ex-wife, Deanne, forty-one. "They had hatched all sorts of mad-hatter ideas together. A lot of them, thank God, I didn't hear about till years later."

All too often, simple domestic chores mushroomed into great adventures. At the ranch home in North Fork that Atiyeh and his wife moved into after leaving Jawbone Flats, he and Hirons bulldozed mountains of dirt to install a septic tank. In celebration, they whipped out a bottle of MacNaughton's Whisky. Two thirds through their refreshment, it dawned on them to check whether a toilet in the house flushed properly. It did not. "Guess we'll have to dig it up," Atiyeh slurred. "Christ, I ain't," Hirons snapped. Against his better judgment, Atiyeh proposed blowing the dirt off with dynamite, of which he owned an ample supply from his mining activities. Hirons egged him on. KABOOM! The tank imploded and caved in. "I can't believe we just did that," Hirons said with a gasp. "Me neither," Atiyeh added. In those days, Marlene Hirons constantly frowned on the boys' liberal use of explosives for logging and sewage. "Somebody had to be an adult," she says now.

In good times and bad, Atiyeh cooked up get-rich-quick schemes for them. "Every time George came over and said, 'I have a great idea,' " Hirons remembers, "I'd cringe." At Atiyeh's urging, Hirons put up money for pinball machines in local taverns. Tom saw the contraptions and his dollars go tilt. They bought a tire shop and service station in Mehama, a town adjoining Mill City. Atiyeh hoped to lease the property back to North Fork. "George, there are such things as laws," Hirons admonished him, regarding the conflict of interest posed by their interest in North Fork. Atiyeh sold it. He and Hirons still remain partners in a small sawmill and yarder purchased together. Hirons, who claims he's yet to see a penny from any of their harebrained investments, still tortures himself for letting his old friend talk him into putting up his hard-earned money so often.

For all their mishaps, Atiyeh and Hirons were willing to put their lives on the line for each other around the clock. "Get up, get up," Marlene nudged Tom one night well past midnight. "What the hell for?" he grumbled. "Somebody's out there," she said. Outside the Hirons's home, dogs howled in a vain attempt to shepherd Marlene's seven-day-old calves, which had mysteriously

games. Business deals as innovative as their husbands' bolstered
the women's own friendship. Marlene, a farm girl born in Iowa
and a 4-H enthusiast, arranged joint ownership of a ram as part
of a venture to generate extra income raising sheep.

Today, both women lead productive lives, entirely independent
of Tom and George, Deanne has custody of the children in their
formative years and, a few years ago, returned to school. She now
performs medical coding in a local hospital to do her part in
supporting them. Marlene runs her own video store in Mill City,
the biggest business to open and thrive in town over the past
decade. Yet neither she nor Deanne can distance themselves emotionally from the conflict engulfing their loved ones.

Just as they enjoyed the rewards of their husbands' past friendship, they now bear the brunt of the breakup. "Marlene is the
type of mom you'd want to have," Deanne says. "I still really like
her, though we haven't spoken in a while. It's almost expected
we're supposed to be angry with them, and I'm not angry per se."
Marlene's equal fondness for Deanne also stops at politics' edge,
owing to the hard logging line she toes with Tom. "In a city you
get along with people, move along, and find somebody else. In
our time together at Opal Creek, we were all very close friends
because we were all we had," she says, raising the desirable but
remote possibility of staging a reunion. "We couldn't do it. It's
too hot and heavy now and we don't get along." The two friends
agree any casual contact between them would have to occur in
Portland or some other venue outside Mill City. Emotions remain
too raw for comfort.

No matter the depth of her convictions, Deanne longs to put
the discord behind them. "Like in a divorce, you've got to see
both sides of the issue. Tom is really in a hurtin' spot and he
doesn't know what to do. Fear is the key word," she says. "The
very worst part of all this is the division of friends. What a waste."
Her unshakable faith in humanity over ideology sustains Deanne's
optimism. "My feelings toward Tom and Marlene have never
changed. It's hard to find good friends, keep them over the years,
and build your lives together and then have something like this
totally tear you apart," she insists. "I'd rather call this a temporary
aberration than a loss in friendship."

At first, both men tried as best they could to overlook the
rumbling. In 1985 Atiyeh presumed he could count on Hirons's
testimony in support of State Scenic River status for Opal Creek.
"What are you asking me to do? You gotta be kidding," Hirons
snapped. "Friendship can go a long way, but not so far as to shoot

yourself in the foot." Had he complied with the request, Hirons claimed he would find himself on a blacklist at Young & Morgan or any other timber company in Mill City for which he logged. In fact, Hirons was swiftly rising up through the ranks of local forces arrayed against environmentalists and Atiyeh.

To counter the environmentalists' campaign, he founded Communities for a Great Oregon (CGO), a "grass roots" group bankrolled by Jim Morgan and fellow timber barons who anointed him president. Nevertheless, on thrice-weekly visits to Atiyeh's home, the two sat on the front porch drinking coffee as Atiyeh's Save Opal Creek Council volunteer staff scurried around stuffing envelopes for Save Opal Creek Council. Hirons pumped Atiyeh for his thoughts on the location of CGO's office on the main highway through town. Atiyeh, who used to operate a small computer business as a sideline, volunteered advice on the type of system Hirons ought to buy for his new undertaking.

Meanwhile, Atiyeh escalated the rhetoric, authoring the lead editorial for the official publication of Oregon Natural Resources Council, an act neighbors considered treason. With a literary flourish characterizing much of his writing and speeches, Atiyeh likened his residency in Mill City to "living in the belly of the beast." "In a lot of ways," he argued, "loggers are like dinosaurs flopping their tails. They are part of a dying industry." When the last tree is cut, he warned, all timber-dependent towns across the Northwest "will wither and die. Maybe it's their own damned fault. It's time for those towns to get off their collective asses and quit blaming the 'preservationists' or the owls for their woes." Atiyeh declared his intention to stop Oregon from being "destroyed by a few greedy millionaire mill owners who don't give a damn about their workers, our land, or Oregon's future. They are not going to get Opal Creek or the rest of Oregon's ancient forest." In a guest opinion in the *Salem Statesman-Journal*, a leading Oregon newspaper, he accused the same villains of "stealing our children's future." His fighting words received an even broader audience on statewide television.

Hirons bristles from the swipes at the integrity of his profession. "I don't suppose he has attacked me personally," he says. "But in attacking what I do, or the industry, which is nothing more than people, he is attacking me. There's no sense in George and I seeing each other. We might talk for five minutes and it generates into a pissing match," he charges. "I don't enjoy that, he doesn't enjoy that. So there's no point. We're better off not doing it."

Atiyeh's intellectual struggle to reconcile his high regard for Hirons the individual and low opinion of Hirons the logger strikes a sincere if hollow note. "I've never attacked him personally," Atiyeh claims. "How can I? Tom has told me he's not a force of darkness. He's not. He's not environmentally insensitive. Only in the context of the times." Hirons's former buddy takes exception to his short view of history. "Logging is not bad per se. But what is right yesterday may not be okay today. The technology is outstripping the resource. We have a moral obligation to check the balance."

Hirons's seeming blindness to the consequences of his own actions torments his former best friend. "Now that we're almost out of the forest, how many Toms can we have out there?" Atiyeh rages. "One time he sat at my kitchen table and admitted it was over, but he was going to keep it up till I stopped him from cutting the last tree. He doesn't want to believe it's over, but he knows it is. He's just forestalling the inevitable day of reckoning. There ain't enough logging out there for five years more."

On the backcountry roads up to Opal Creek, Atiyeh digs into the bag of speeches he has delivered lately to schools around the state. "One of the lines I steal from Sting [the rock singer and environmental crusader] is that most global catastrophes are based on individual choices that seem perfectly reasonable at the time, whether it's the goat herder in northern Africa who's raising his goats on the last shrub because he feels he doesn't have any choice, or guys like Tom Hirons, who's going to cut down the last tree to make payments on equipment because that's the decision life has led him to," Atiyeh muses. "It seems perfectly reasonable for him on a personal basis. It goes back to thinking globally and acting locally."

For all the heartfelt sympathy he expresses for loggers under duress, though, Atiyeh refuses to desist in his crusade until the day they surrender. "It goes to the root of an interesting problem with human beings. They're always afraid of change and think it's the worst thing that's going to happen," he says. "Most people don't go downhill, they can only go up. Even if Tom hit bottom, I believe he'd be better off in ten years if he got out of it. He's so smart. He's wasting his life as a logger."

To no one's surprise, Hirons resents being informed he is squandering his birthright. It may explain why, at times, he has championed, with a ferocity verging on vendetta, the timber industry's strategy to block preservation of Opal Creek. The week of the protest against the state park bill in Salem, Hirons serves notice that the logging truck demonstration represents a mere warning shot. In his testimony, he advocates putting a road into Opal Creek. He later fires off a blistering letter to the *Statesman-Journal* refuting Atiyeh's arguments. His intimacy with Opal Creek provides the grist for claiming the proposal's excessive costs exclude necessary upgrading of rustic trails and accommodations for public rest rooms or RV hookups: "SB500 is a thinly veiled attempt to remove thirty-one thousand acres of national forest from multiple use and lock it up as a scheduled gateway for a select few." The explicit attacks against Atiyeh's elitism seek to sully his altruism. "I believe George does care about people. There isn't a doubt in my mind, either, that he holds all those moral arguments about saving Opal Creek seriously. But over the past few years I have watched his arguments and tactics progress," Hirons says. "George is a very pragmatic person, doing whatever's best for George. I know him better than his shit about Opal Creek as his church and cathedral. He's playing to the media."

Hirons believes the lumberjacks' cause transcends narrow self-interest to fundamental questions of work ethic and economic fairness that society is failing to address. "Yeah, the crazies have that saying: Think globally and act locally. Then why don't they care about us or all the thousands of coal miners? We've seen a constant erosion of the middle class and we're beginning to see a widening gap between rich and poor," he says. "Maybe it's a result of the tremendous affluence and leisure the American Experiment gave us after World War II. We've become so selfish, we don't even care about our kids. We don't want for anything and we don't save. We just go and get it on a piece of plastic. Let our kids pay for it."

Stung by the chainsaw-wielding Judas, Atiyeh agonizes over his own inability to keep him high-minded. "I pleaded with Tom and the others to settle Opal Creek years ago. I have been consistent about my feelings since I was eleven years old. They created this fight," he exclaims. "If someone comes up and hits me in the face, they're in for a fight, goddamn it. I'm not going to quit till this damn thing is settled. How can I, for Christ's sake?"

A healthy dose of rectitude fires Atiyeh's missionary fervor. "Opal Creek is the loggers' downfall. Because of their egos, they took the worst possible place to make a stand," he proclaims. "If anybody should understand the reality, it's Tom. He made a stupid decision. I told him, 'Tom, you lost before you ever started. Nationally people don't give a shit about owls versus jobs. They'll side with the owls every time. Do Tom and all those people around him still believe that the public will choose loggers' jobs versus thousand-year-old trees?" On television and in print, the national media's fixation on the beleaguered owl and bedraggled lumberjacks has accelerated the momentum in Congress for legislation to settle the issue.

The harmless pranks, trademarks of their balmier days, have surrendered to humor cutting an ideological edge. "We can't joke with each other anymore," Hirons laments. "The arguments are taken too seriously." Atiyeh furrows his eyebrows upon hearing that Hirons and logger Randy Moberg jest at the coffee shop about the Communities for a Great Oregon's sponsorship of a booming July Fourth celebration at Opal Creek featuring a busload of five hundred visitors and fireworks to disturb the bucolic setting. (The poker-faced Atiyeh prefers concealing the scant amusement he draws from the latest competition of wit.) After Hirons dubbed his adversary "St. George," on account of his self-righteousness, an environmentalist custom-made a magnetic bumper sticker "St. George of Atiyeh." Its namesake transfers it from his refrigerator to his pickup as a badge of honor.

Hirons strains to find the humor in Atiyeh's gibes. Loggers, for example, adopted yellow ribbons as their stars and stripes before the Persian Gulf War. The Forest Service ties them to trees to demarcate clear-cuts. Communities for Great Oregon, Hirons's political base in Mill City, publishes its newsletter on yellow paper and does a brisk business selling yellow ribbons. The matching Ping-Pong balls on sale there and at Marlene's video store are suitable for attaching to car antennae. Since becoming as ubiquitous on Oregon's roads as bobbing corks in a lake at the start of fishing season, Atiyeh cannot resist taunting Hirons: "See, Tom, you guys have little yellow balls."

The logger's links to Atiyeh compel Hirons to toughen his posture toward him. A whispering campaign in Mill City questions Hirons's own credentials to disarm his old partner. In the back of their minds, even his admirers wonder how he possibly straddles his divided loyalties. "Tom's been plagued by the conflict in his long-standing relationship," says Bert Young, Young & Morgan's well-spoken safety director. "It's to Tom's credit that he's been willing to put his history on the line." Jim Morgan, the mill owner and former friend of Atiyeh and for whom Hirons logs, agrees: "Tom at first wasn't saying much. He and I talked a lot about coming off the fence. The key to the situation is he knew George better than I did. Tom came off the fence swinging." Atiyeh now calls Hirons the "hardest-core son-of-a-bitch on the block." Like a liberal Cold War warrior, Tom flexes his muscles constantly to erase all doubts about where his sympathies lie.

To a larger degree than either cares to admit, they have mortgaged their independence to special interests. In deference to Hirons's ways with words, he heads the activist CGO at the local mill owners' behest. As their point man, he speaks for them in the press. "I don't believe Tom is as nuts as he sounds sometimes or that he can believe in the same things as Jimmy Morgan and the other people he's gotten into bed with. How can Tom be a pawn of the community?" Atiyeh says. "The rhetoric sounds great, but his is still an old-boy network based on economics rather than true friendship. He doesn't have enough balls to flat-out say he's being pressured from doing what he knows is right."

While maintaining a grudging admiration for his rival, Atiyeh believes he's wasting his talent. "Tom is the most articulate guy they have. He doesn't look like a dumb logger. When you get that kind of recognition and people reinforce your ego, you lose sight of who you are. Tom has become exactly what he accuses me of being: a politician. The real Tom I know and love is not some timbering big shot. He's a logger who's a good guy, a real guy, and no more a television star than I am. You'd better be careful you don't start believing your own b.s." Bumping into him at the general store recently, Atiyeh listened to Hirons delivering a harangue about private property and socialism.

Hirons has as hard a time coming to terms with Atiyeh's acqui-escence in the environmentalists' agenda he rails against as sub-versive. "I've got my company and everything I've worked for to lose. Jim has his mill. What the hell does George have to lose? Maybe more than the rest of those assholes supporting him. What the hell are those guys putting on the table, anyway? We can't talk about altruistic crap when you're being asked to negotiate your extinction. George talked about Opal Creek for years, but it never got anywhere," Hirons says. "If Jim and I gave it to him, he wouldn't shut up and go away. George has told me Opal Creek is the flagship of the old-growth movement. It doesn't seem like he can talk about it in a vacuum without talking about the whole thing from Oregon to northern California." Hirons sees no room for compromise unless the other side surrenders its claim to wide swaths of forest.

Compounding the intensity of their philosophical differences,

Hirons carries a profound grudge toward Atiyeh for reinventing his identity for the convenience of the environmentalists' public-relations machinery. Atiyeh cuts an arresting figure in the press and before audiences, casting himself as a former logger who has seen the light. "The biggest argument I got with George and what caused me to lose more respect for him than anything else is that nonsense. Everybody is entitled to a change of heart, but I can't handle the fact that he's trying to pass himself off as a logger. The crazies don't like anything better than a reformed sinner. He used to be a tree mugger and now he's a tree hugger," Hirons says. "He played around the edges. A logger is someone who gets up at 4:00 A.M. in the morning day after day and gets on the crummy [loggers' bus], stays out there no matter what type of goddamn weather it is. Even in the summer when it's hotter than hell. Puts in eight or nine hours. Rides the crummy home too dog tired to eat dinner and falls asleep on the couch. Crawls in bed for a couple of hours and does it again." The affront to his professional pride sears Hirons. At the sight of microphones or notebooks of reporters, he can scarcely restrain himself from setting the record straight.

Ray Weber an ex-employee of Atiyeh's up at the mines and a timber cruiser, or assessor, for Young & Morgan, presents a version of Atiyeh's duplicity more eloquently than most. "George don't know diddly about logging. He may have farted around, but never toiled away," he says. "Just because he cut some trees doesn't mean he knew which way they were falling." Weber and the rest of Atiyeh's detractors try putting Atiyeh on the defensive by training the spotlight on him rather than on the depletion of old growth.

Atiyeh is clearly tired of having to parry the relentless blows. His responses fire off automatically, like a magazine feeding a machine gun. "I don't feel I have to justify anything. I busted my ass. The bottom line is Tom would never have built that logging company without me. I made it happen," Atiyeh says with a growl. "If this is as deep as their argument goes, it stinks. Let's break George's credibility. Then we can discount everything else he says. If they have to attack me instead of the issue, it shows how weak they are."

In their phone fights about his earlier career in logging, Atiyeh raises the rafters in Hirons's home over the matter of the rafters themselves. Visitors enjoy a chuckle with Hirons upon learning that the immense exposed beams above his living room came from Opal Creek. Atiyeh demands credit for doing most of the work.

While constructing his home, Hirons asked Atiyeh for some of the dead and downed trees he was using for mining timber. Atiyeh gladly complied, and participated in the entire phase of the operation—from the actual logging to the purchase of a separate extension for their portable sawmill to meet Hirons's specifications of thirty feet. "I personally logged, cut, and trucked every big beam in his house," Atiyeh claims. "I remember pulling every one off the sawmill and driving them over to his house on a special truck." Atiyeh can accept a lot of intellectual abuse from Hirons. What offends him most is the repudiation of any claim to logging. In effect, it belittles Atiyeh's very contribution to the roof over Hirons's head.

"Tom is going to take it on the chin real hard," Joe Weber says. "He's clinging to the belief that by exposing George in the press, he'll make progress." The scrap between Atiyeh and Hirons strains mutual friends. Weber was so intent on not playing favorites he opted out of the Mill City scene to jump out of airplanes, running a skydiving business in Molalla, twenty-eight miles away.

On the ground, Weber observes events from a unique vantage point. Astute and curious, he authored a history of mining camps in the Opal Creek area to seek protection for Jawbone Flats on the National Register of Historic Places. As Atiyeh's campaign manager in an ill-fated run for the state legislature in 1984, he "put the polishing cloth" on him. He also brought method to his martyrdom. "George is a pretty brilliant person. The whole genius of the Atiyeh technique is to make everyone attack him personally. It saps their energy," Weber says. "It also makes him look great. As much as he wants people to like him, he doesn't shrink from leading the parade."

As long as the character assassins take aim at Atiyeh's self-serving definition of a logger, a parochial diversion to anyone outside Mill City, he can monopolize the debate's morality. His steel-trap intellect already gives him a head start. "He knows more about logging than most loggers," Weber says. "And George's sympathy for them is genuine; the rational sentiment of an intelligent man." A lone voice crying in the wilderness, Atiyeh makes little headway trying to convince the timber industry to prepare for a post–old-growth era.

Dave Alexander, the national forest ranger overseeing Opal Creek, empathizes with Hirons. "George never was a logger. It's a matter of some significance to Hirons, in an industry of people with great pride. They're saying, 'I've been there and gotten my hands dirty," the forester says. "It's kind of like I painted 'DAVE

ALEXANDER TRUCKING' on the side of my pickup and claimed I was the president of a trucking company with a lot of experience. People who do trucking for a living might suspect me. We all have pride in our credentials, and I believe George stepped over the line with loggers."

Had Hirons listened to Atiyeh and him in the first place, Weber is sure Tom could have avoided becoming shackled to outmoded employment and politics. "I've told Tom the timber people are just not clever enough to recognize the extensive damage from doing nothing to regulate themselves," Weber says. He understands Hirons's frustration at the recent spate of television news stories demonizing loggers. "What's worse than being portrayed a villain is that they've never been able to come up with a successful alternative to being portrayed as a villain. What they do really is ugly. I've told Tom if clear-cuts were pretty and loggers weren't stupid, you'd stand a chance." Capturing the essence of his own case, Atiyeh delights in re-peating that line himself.

At the eleventh hour, loggers began jumping aboard the rear end of the green bandwagon. A popular bumper sticker in tim-ber towns proclaims, "EVERY DAY IS EARTH DAY FOR A LOGGER." As in any political war, language is the matériel. Thus Hirons chastises his wife for applying the E word to their adversaries. "Honey, don't call *them* the environmentalists; *we're* the environmentalists," he tells her. "It really bothers me the way the crazies have pulled this off." Loggers have tried to usurp the term for themselves, branding ecologists with the radical-sounding label "preservationists," or among themselves, "crazies." Since they work in the outdoors all day and hunt and fish in it on weekends, loggers believe they have earned the rightful title to husbands of the forests. Weber doesn't buy it. "The 'I'm an envi-ronmentalist, too' act is too late. Like any comedian will tell you, it's timing. They ain't got it," Weber says. "You can have the best argument, but if you're too late, you're fucked." He could have quoted Lenny Bruce: "Comedy is tragedy, plus time."

Detaching the men from their myths at Opal Creek, Weber privately roots for Atiyeh to defeat Hirons. "I don't see any in-credible rationale for continuing to cut down the last of an ecosys-tem," he says. On closer inspection, Atiyeh's sincerity overcomes his occasional bluster. "Opal Creek really is his badge. He marches around the woods whenever he likes it," Weber says. "It's like your old lady. After a couple of years, it may not be as much fun making love anymore, but you still care about her." In this economic predicament, Hirons's heart has abandoned Opal Creek. "If they are at the public table and three votes say cut it and three say don't, which way does Tom go? He would cut it," Weber says. "The only thing that separates the special treasure George is trying to preserve and the special treasure Tom is trying to preserve is a buck. You take the dollar out of the equation, than Tom's argument sounds pretty hollow." Opal Creek isn't worth sacrificing to prolong Hirons's rickety career, he argues. If Weber was willing to leap through the clouds to change his, Hirons has the license to gamble, too, after some imaginative bookkeeping.

Try filling an empty stomach with warm sentiments, cautions Bill Baumgarten. A transplant from Oakland to the original community Atiyeh established at Jawbone Flats while in college in 1970, Baumgarten owes his entrance into manhood to Opal Creek. "It's instant love and part of my roots," he says. "I've told Tom a thousand times I don't want Opal Creek cut. We've reached the saturation point and don't need to put more roads in the valley." Baumgarten, however, breaks ranks with Atiyeh over the potentially high human costs of removing timber from the land base. "I wonder if George had to make a living around here like loggers do, how much he would compromise," Baumgarten says. His two-year stint in Hirons's employ and present job as an inspector for the State Occupational Safety and Health Administration have put Baumgarten in regular contact with loggers. Out in the brush, their legitimate fears of an impending doom weigh heavily on him.

As tensions mount over Opal Creek, Weber doubts the bruised egos will ever heal once, as he anticipates, it is saved. "I expect George to say, 'We fought the good fight. I respect you for what you did and you respect me for what I did. Let's carry on,' " Weber says. "The issue will eventually fall by the wayside, but Tom will never give up the belief that it was George's duplicity that broke him rather than the issue." Hirons is as convinced of the rightness of his cause as Atiyeh is of his. Having been at loggerheads for so long, he will hold one man most responsible for his professional demise.

Yet friendship's enduring strength can withstand life's severest hardships. "I hate the idea of causes, and if I had to choose between betraying my country and betraying my friend," E. M. Forster observed, "I hope I should have the guts to betray my country." Somehow in vicious crossfire, Atiyeh and Hirons still glow from warmer remembrances. "Why do you think he's my best friend?" Atiyeh asks. "Tom is a helluva nice guy. He's basically an intelligent person with a good heart," Atiyeh says with a smile. Hirons needs no prompting to return the compliment: "I've always placed a high value on George's friendship. There aren't many you can bury your soul with. He's a real likeable guy." The volley of venom over the past few years obscures a sad fact: Atiyeh and Hirons sorely miss one another. "I don't blame him for fighting for what he believes, but I still expect him to come over and see me," Atiyeh says wistfully, Hirons waits for the invitation. For now, their positions are too entrenched to effect any rapprochement, political or personal.

The showdown at Opal Creek between two soulmates holding diametrically opposed views crystallizes the stakes in the old-growth controversy. Its outcome turns on basic human values that environmentalists and developers are contesting throughout the nation. A day late and a dollar short, Hirons walks a path to bankruptcy through the dirty sweat of countless hours devoted to building the American Dream. The destruction of the spectacular piece of wilderness Atiyeh strives to save threatens to impoverish him and the nation's natural endowment forever.

V

Trouble in Mill City

Two hours from dawn, on a crisp spring night, darkness cloaks Mill City. Thick mist dripping from a starless sky suspends the promise of sun for the ninth straight day. That's the Pacific Northwest for you. Here on Broadway, the town's older commercial core, Marie and Charley Stewart will open their mom and pop general store at 8:00 A.M. sharp, as they have every day for the past forty-three years, except on Sundays— when the lights go on an hour later—and the big four holidays when they're closed. "If we ain't got it, you don't need it," reads the slogan on Charley's delivery van. He really does sell every item imaginable. Most townspeople will drop by during the day to shop and catch up on gossip.

All is not still at this hour. Down the road, Young and Morgan's plywood mill is bathed in the soaking orange glow of floodlights and plumes of boiler steam. Log trucks on their first runs rumble past the empty storefront once occupied by the Dew Drop Inn Malt Shop. They hook a horseshoe right by the steel bridge carted in sections from Pennsylvania at the turn of the century and inch up the steep hill. A year hardly used to pass without some truck sliding back down and dumping a load. Flatlanders from other parts would be scared helpless, and even Doc Kimmel, a big man around here, once had his car remodeled that way.

Next door to the old railway depot, George Long, the local printer, has already put to bed this week's issue of *The Mill City Enterprise*—circulation, 1,280. An old letterpressman, he is one of the last two printers in the state using offset printing for the timber companies' business cards and stationery. Melting wax and lead perfume the air as he pushes his seventy-year-old linotype machine's pedal to the floor. CLUNK CLUNK. This antique will retire along with George.

The hauls of Mill City's wooden gold keep on coming, trundling down Broadway, past the First Christian Church, where the Pastor Aaron Veach delivers the finest sermons around. On Highway 22, the top timbermen strike deals over breakfast at their favorite hangout, the Dutch End Cafe. They grab pens and pencils from the breast pockets of their plaid shirts to make quick computations. The pancakes at Dutch End are buttermilk, biscuits come with white gravy, and the coffee is drunk black or not at all. Shortly after dawn, students arrive at school by bus or on foot. Just last year, the ultra modern middle school installed a sleek new chemistry lab. Halfway up the hill, renters slip last night's movie through the door of Marlene Hirons's video store. In addition to adventure and romance, her hunting and fishing selections do a brisk business. At the post office around the corner, friends and neighbors don't seem to mind having to pick up mail in person, through the rural delivery system's post office boxes, as it gives them another chance to socialize. Across the street, Girods Hilltop Market unloads fresh shipments of produce. Three years ago Jim Girod established Mill City's first deli department, a radical notion for most customers. Reckoning it sold fancy items, they initially stuck to prepackaged Oscar Mayer cold cuts. Once the idea caught on, though, the deli became one of the store's main attractions.

Mill City is a nice place to call home. Hunkered down in the foothills of the Cascade Range in the heart of North Santiam Canyon, its storybook setting and flavor conjure up a bygone era's flavor. A population of 1,550 enjoys sublime seclusion. Stayton has only three times as many people and is fifteen miles away. Just over 100,000 live in the capital, Salem, thirty-two miles to the northwest. Seventy-five miles to the southeast, 20,000 live in Bend, surrounded by Oregon's High Desert. The sole route to Mill City is east–west, on Highway 22, traversing rolling farmland and forests dotted by the occasional clear-cut. In chilly waters flowing from the mountain's snowcapped peaks, steelhead ply the North Santiam, a fishing line's cast away from Broadway.

In the hamlet's close-knit community people take care of their own in good times and bad. Boys riding their bicycles to the store can park them unlocked outside. They probably learn that from their parents, who leave keys in their cars' ignition while in stores. On warm evenings, families watch television in living rooms with their doors wide open. The television sets splash flickers of light across well-manicured lawns. On July Fourth, the town struts its hospitality by inviting out-of-town guests to delight in fireworks and logging competitions. The fire trucks in the parade belong to the town's crack volunteer fire department, a key part of Mill City's dependable emergency services. The roar of the Life Flight helicopter overhead sends a collective shudder through the canyon—a local logger has been maimed or worse. On a trip from Mill City to Stayton, Sue Moberg recently accompanied a friend who learned her husband, a logger, had been killed on the job. The victim turned out to be someone else with the same name. Death pulls one and all together as tightly as life itself. When Charley Stewart, Jr., a beloved figure in his father's general store and heir to the family business, died in a car accident last summer, the whole town grieved as an extended family at the funeral and at home.

George Long, the *Mill City Enterprise*'s dyspeptic poet laureate, reserves his sentimental side for "It Ain't All Roses," the weekly column he has penned for the past twenty years since buying the paper. Recently, he ran a test to separate the "genuine certified Mill City old-timer" from the newcomer. Herewith a sampling:

1) The pickups in your neighborhood outnumber the cars three to one. 2) You no longer use your turn signals because everyone knows where you are headed. 3) You go out at 10:00 P.M., do the town, and are home by 10:30. 4) Fourth street is the edge of town. 5) You missed church on Sunday and received a get-well card. 6) You've been run off First Street by a chip truck. 7) You forgot your purse (wallet) and didn't discover it until the checker was through with your groceries and they trusted you to come back and pay later. 8) You have received mail addressed something like "the guy who lives four houses south of the post office in Mill City." 9) You drove in to the ditch at least five miles from town and the word got back to town before you did. 10) You have dialed the wrong number but talk for fifteen minutes anyway. 11) Your children have had at least two teachers who also taught you.

Mill City is a small town straight out of the 1950s, beset by 1990s problems. Alcoholism and other social ailments exact financial and human costs. Teenage pregnancy is distressingly high. But all these social maladies pale in comparison these days to the economic disruption sweeping timber-dependent communities with names like Sweet Home, Roseburg, and Humboldt, from northern California to Washington State. Its ultimate impact may dwarf those that occurred in steel and farming country in the 1970s and 1980s. On top of fundamental industrial shifts, the nation is forcing Mill City and its counterparts to grapple with natural resources issues largely beyond their capacity or, for that matter, beyond the comprehension of the "experts" in Washington, D.C.

The latest dip in the traditional boom and bust cycles of timber towns augurs a transition of historical dimensions. Over the past two decades, three national recessions have induced severe housing slumps and lowered demand for lumber, thereby severing the lifelines of the Northwest's local economies. Eighty percent of the Mill City-North Santiam Canyon economy is directly related to the manufacturing of primary wood products. Today's growing sentiment for preserving ancient forests and a dwindling timber supply from years of overcutting may well doom the only way of life most residents have ever known. In the next five years, wood supply will drop in half from historic highs in the 1980s. Asleep, Mill City families writhe in their beds, praying they can make payments to keep the house and the car. In the morning's small hours, they are haunted by nightmares of their town turning into a rural ghetto as bleak as an Appalachian coal town.

Tragically, the fear gripping Mill City is undermining its social foundations. The trust once unifying people has become the first casualty in the quiet civil war now raging. Neighbors turn on each other for insufficient loyalty to the timber industry cause. Schoolteachers and clergymen accustomed to speaking honestly about big issues must mince their words, lest they offend anyone. Business owners dare not resist pressures to post leaflets at their storefronts. A list of "cooperative" merchants circulates around town to deliver an implicit message of boycott to those absent. Hirons has tried squelching it to prevent the rancor from spinning out of control. Meanwhile, Atiyeh has lost all his commuter flying service and a computer business he has run on the side over the past seven years for many of the local businesses, including the logging companies and sawmills—a loss of fifteen thousand in annual income.

At least two different proprietors have felt the strong arm. Bill Anderson owns the Oak Park Motel in Gates—the small town in Mill City's shadow where Atiyeh and Hirons technically live. This motel is the only lodging along the 112 mile stretch between

Salem and Sisters. After purchasing and renovating the motel six years ago, Bill Anderson and his wife, Lina, looked forward to a comfortable living in their sunset years. Given their druthers, Bill and Lina would have preferred to stay free of the ribbons the woodsmen ordered them to fly to prove they, too, had caught yellow fever. "The timber barons. They own everything. They control everything. They run those banks," rasps the jug-eared Air Force veteran. "If it wags its tail, bays at the moon, and barks, it's a dog." Bill's pickup and a dead oak tree outside his motel are among the places around town where the ubiquitous yellow ribbons flap in the breeze. "I told them yes, but I didn't want that," he says, pointing up toward the oak. "I wish I could get that damn thing down."

While interviewing the Andersons in their living room, a brawny young man from Willamette Industries, a timber company, stops by bearing a handful of leaflets for a timber rally in Portland that weekend. "Don't say you're from the newspaper," Bill exclaims to me. "Hurry up. Just put your stuff away." I dutifully slide my microcassette recorder and notepad under the couch. The silver-haired Lina thanks the visitor in her native accent, from the German Alps she compares favorably to the Northwest's mountains. "They want everything from us," she says, following her visitor's departure, "and give us nothing back." Fortunately, the Andersons depend primarily on out-of-towners' patronage.

Ivan Smith paid the price for holding out. Long ago the quaint red wooden store he currently occupies housed a bakery and photography shop. A runaway log truck reduced it to mostly rubble years ago. In 1987 the ex-Portlander converted the dilapidated shack into a successful secondhand store. Smith's informal demeanor and clothes suggest he dips into his stock. His outspokenness in support of old growth and a son, who lived up at Jawbone Flats, raised suspicions. One morning he arrived at work to discover "WE SUPPORT EARTH FIRST!" spray painted on the side of his building. The graffiti tried to tar him to the radical environmental group. "I think we ought to worry about the world or there ain't gonna be nothing left. We've done more damage in the last hundred years than in the last ten thousand," he says. "If we could shut this damn door to save the last tree, we'd do it. I don't worry about those puny little things like my business." For now, the loggers' misfortunes are Smith's gains. After being thrown out of his home, a young millworker down on his luck comes in to pick up a shopworn couch for his new apartment. He leaves his thirty-five-dollar rifle as collateral.

At first, Jim and Cherie Girod presume their solid citizenship will keep them above the fray. After all, he took over his father's Mill City hilltop grocery in 1965. She came from a three-generation logging family in Oregon and has run the Canyon Crisis Center, the only social service outlet in Mill City, since 1987. The last phone call she expects is from a logger threatening to hurl a rock through the store window if her husband fails to festoon her store with yellow ribbons. "Of course we're supporters," she avers.

Then comes the letter. A clerk at the Stayton post office, next door to Mill City, receives five hundred of them with instructions to place one in each of the postal boxes. The fraudulent document bears Atiyeh's forged signature and the letterhead of a nonexistent organization, "Friends of Opal Creek Ancient Forest," intended to sound like the real group, "Save the Opal Creek Council." The letter depicts Jim Girod as a backer of a measure in the state legislature to preserve the block of ancient forest as a park. "The general public must realize as Jim has, that the protection of our environment is more important than the profits of local 'Timber Barons,' " writes the AntiAtiyeh. The provocateur responsible is plotting to scare the supermarket, Mill City's primary retailer and spit-and-whittle spot, into becoming a rallying point against Opal Creek. Although Hirons and Jim Morgan denounce the malevolence, the next day the Girods hand rebuttal letters to their customers at the checkout stands. Yellow hats and yellow balloons for the benefit of logging activists soon pop up in the spirit of a New Year's Eve party. A wide computer printout bearing the slogan "WE SUPPORT THE TIMBER INDUSTRY" is unfurled above the produce section.

Atiyeh moves swiftly to clear the market owner's good name. "While I wish the Girods were supporters of our efforts, THEY ARE NOT. The Girods have steadfastly supported the timber industry during this entire controversy. I respect that position," Atiyeh writes to the *Mill City Enterprise*. "I love my State and community, that is why I have spent my entire life here. I may disagree with you but I will defend to the death your opinion and I expect no less from all Oregonians." He offers a five-hundred-dollar reward for information leading to the arrest and conviction of the perpetrator. The regional chief inspector's office for the U.S. Postal Service doubts the letters could be traced to their sender. It hardly matters, in view of the episode's chilling effect on debate in Mill City.

An old saw in small towns cautions never to mess with the man who owns the ink. In the *Mill City Enterprise*, George Long shifts his usual voice of a cracker-barrel curmudgeon to an irate polemicist in his paper's nonstop campaign to keep the log trucks rolling by his office:

> If you didn't know it before you probably are at least suspecting it by now. We are at war. Oregon's farmers, loggers and mill workers are under attack. The preservationists use the protection of the environment as their pompous shield and the legal and political system as their sword. They are ruthless fighters that have backed the timber and agriculture industries into a corner. The fight that will ensue indeed will be a big one. It will create national attention and may ultimately bring to an end our way of life.

In *The Stayton Mail*, fifteen miles west of Mill City, a headline reads, "Couple Says Forest Issues Draw Parallels to Marxism." Marlene and Tom Drynan, a private detective and ex-state sheriff who arrested Atiyeh in 1970 at Opal Creek for assaulting an officer and Forest Service official with a dangerous weapon, are "taking their story to the people" about the "protectionist" views at local venues such as the Chamber of Commerce. Neither Long nor the Drynans have to mention the object of their ire by name; the neighbors know he's Atiyeh.

That the mere invocation of Atiyeh's name, like some evil talisman, should fire such passions is proof of his notoriety. A homegrown environmentalist, he bears a special burden. Many woodsmen besides Hirons have worked, fished, and hunted with him since he first moved from Portland twenty years ago. They are already chafing at the hordes of journalists and politicians invading their fair town. These natives attack the environmentalists as outside agitators. But the unkindest cut of all is aimed at Atiyeh for alleged betrayal.

He has trained the national spotlight on the area through the campaign he wages to lock up the timber in Opal Creek as the flagship in the campaign to save old growth. "In our town we like to know the facts about everybody," Thornton Wilder observed. And so it is on the rumor mill one Mill City resident terms the jungle tom-tom. Word goes out to treat Atiyeh as a pariah. At coffee shops and store the locals curse his name under their breaths. His public appearances can silence a conversation and freeze a glance. Good, decent people wrestling with their fractured consciences are unable to face him.

They charge Atiyeh with stealing their meal ticket. Kevin Long, the heavyset son of George Long and head of Mill City's Chamber of Commerce, eagerly defends the interests he represents and for whom he has lobbied. "Our chamber must do whatever it can to assist the three timber companies here. If we can save even the smallest one, Frank Lumber," he says in a small office adjoining the state police department on Highway 22, "then we have done more than twenty years of tourism." His asymmetrical face appears to be of dissimilar parts, like a watercolor overlaid on an oil portrait. Sad, drooping eyes convey a basset hound's hangdog look.

Until recently, he believed otherwise, writing a sympathetic story about Opal Creek in his father's paper and working in the ill-fated campaign Atiyeh waged for the Oregon State House to save ancient forest. Long attributes his erroneous viewpoint then to callowness. "I was young and got duped," he explains. Under the logging companies' influence, he discovered the real Atiyeh. "George is a very calculating, crafty individual," he says. "I believe he has exaggerated the chastising he has received in this community." The soothing words, still moist from his tongue, fall suddenly like a load off a log truck. "If you had two hours I could sit down with you and show you four pages of Atiyeh's lies," Long adds. "He will stop at nothing to save Opal Creek."

Atiyeh flicks off the fighting words as those of an opportunist. "Kevin is a two-faced, cheap timber whore," he says. Indeed, Atiyeh almost seems to relish squaring off against his adversary, particularly on television. Long's brooding appearance on NBC's *Today* with Jane Pauley required Hirons to step in as the industry's chief spokesman. "It was as if they opened up the local hospital and let him out," Atiyeh says. "Put a camera on Tom, he looks okay. Put a camera on Kevin, he looks like a Mongoloid. There's genetic defects in Mill City."

Impartial observers warn that Atiyeh's days are numbered. "He is not a very welcome person in this town," Pastor Aaron Veach says. "He is the one who has the albatross hung around his neck." In his capacity as a humanities teacher at the high school, Ross Miller knows Atiyeh and his three children well. Miller is also exposed to the enmity parents and pupils heap on Mill City's *persona non grata.* "I say, 'George, these aren't your friends.' They accuse you of creating your own personal paradise," Miller explains. "They are going to shoot you. Why are you doing this?"

The obvious answer—principle—defies human nature. Beneath Atiyeh's honorable exterior bubbles an unreconstruced daredevil. "Oh, boy, when you're him, isn't it fun being right?" chuckles friend Joe Weber. "It goes with the righteousness." Atiyeh's defense of Opal Creek allows him to revel in the ostracism he must endure.

His behavior verges on a macho-martyr complex. The one-man shock troop cuts an almost bizarre figure cruising around Mill City in a pickup emblazoned with a bumper sticker "ENVIRONMENTALIST FROM HELL." "George has more angles than a cold tablet," says the junk shop owner, Ivan Smith, of his talent for giving opponents headaches. "How's it going?" acquaintances sarcastically ask in town. "Hell, it ain't easy, man," Atiyeh retorts, "putting fifty-five thousand people out of work." He may be giving himself too much credit. Economists put the highest estimate of the loggers' job loss at about half that.

Meddlesome politicians and conservationists from Washington, D.C., call on him to serve as their tour guide. "People who hate George really hate him," says Michelle Meader, the seventeen-year-old daughter of a millworker and girlfriend of Atiyeh's son. "He lives around here, so it's easy to attack him."

While actively campaigning for his park bill in the state legislature, he has the gumption to show his face in the Dutch End Cafe. Restless natives just stare and glare. Finally, Atiyeh jumps atop a stool. "Fuck you, all you guys!" he erupts, then sits down and orders breakfast. Pretty soon a few of them warm their cold shoulders enough to come by. "You may be an environmental asshole, but you are a crazy bastard and maybe not so bad after all," one assures him. By refusing to lie down in front of them, Atiyeh earns his nemises' grudging respect.

Atiyeh's missionary zeal steels him against abuse for the time being. He expects Mill City to welcome him back later for doing what is right now. "I wouldn't stand up and take the ridicule if I didn't believe my community's way of life has to change," he says. "The world goes on." During the 1950s and 1960s, southern society went through protracted convulsions in coming to terms with racial integration. Today, social tensions in Mill City and its sister cities throughout Oregon, Washington State, and northern California are veering perilously close to reaching the upheavals of Liberty, Mississippi, circa 1964. Thirty years later, the Old Northwest lags behind the New South in coming to terms with its future. "There's a good possibility of violence breaking out here, as long as people have nothing but despair and no hope,"

Atiyeh says. In such a climate, he is as much a villain to them as a hero to conservationists. "The trees are the Negroes. I'm just a freedom rider coming in from the North," he adds, at the risk of overtaxing the metaphor. "Except I come right out of the community. That's worse." The moral certitude Atiyeh exudes gives ex-friends scant reason for breaking their pledge never to speak to him again.

Being an island unto oneself, however, would try any man's soul. It pains Atiyeh, a good sport with an exceedingly gregarious nature, not only to have lost virtually all his friends, but also to find his status drop to that of an untouchable. Even the small circle of acquaintances who quietly agree with him are afraid to be seen publicly in Atiyeh's company. At his son's football games, he sits by himself in the stands, as though in the middle of a clear-cut. "I've told George he's gone past the point of return," says Dave Alexander, the U.S. Forest Services's local district ranger. "I mean, how much crap are you going to take?" For all the swagger, Atiyeh betrays real hurt. "I'd like to have my friends back," he insists. "I don't know if it will happen. It depends on them."

Woodsmen have so far refrained from any of the physical abuse once common to the South. Rather, Atiyeh is hounded by turned backs and flagrant intimidation. A log truck tries running him off the road. After putting away a few beers, it becomes a favorite pastime to call from tavern telephones with death threats. At the height of hostilities, Atiyeh averages three death threats per day. "We're gonna get you, so you'd better shut up," growls his typical harasser. Growing tired of the routine, he screens incoming calls through his answering machine: "Hi, this is George. If you have a death threat, you probably haven't done it before and are very nervous. Please relax and take a deep breath. And leave your name, address, and telephone number."

A millworker on a fund-raising drive for the high school pays Atiyeh a visit at home. He informs him, perhaps in jest, that word of a five-hundred-dollar bounty is out on the street. "I've cost them a helluva lot more than that," Atiyeh jokes. "They're treating me like they treat you guys. They never pay you what you're worth."

Although Atiyeh worries most about some young kid on drugs or booze potshotting him, he holds Rob Freres, a mill owner, accountable as a ringleader. At the outbreak of hostilities, he dials his number to put him on notice. "Robby, I don't know if you're behind this goddamn thing, but I'm gonna tell you something," Atiyeh booms. "If you guys decide to shoot me, you'd better make the first shot count. I'm gonna come after every one of you and I know where you live."

At first blush, such tales appear to strain credulity. Among his detractors, Atiyeh's brilliant flair for the dramatic embellishes both his arguments and autobiography. Yet in dozens of conversations I have had in Mill City and points west, south, and north, it becomes obvious that George's antagonists bear chief responsibility for creating a larger-than-life celebrity through character assassination. The ferocity and frequency with which his blackened name pops up—in the absence of any prodding—leave me squeamish. From muscle-flexing loggers to indignant Forest Service bureaucrats, a line has formed to take aim at him.

Atiyeh has company, too. The controversy's fallout extends, in Oregon, from Albany to Portland, where veteran newspaper reporters on the timber beat have had to contend with death threats aimed at them. While leaving work one night in Salem, an editor dove to the ground to avoid a log truck headed straight toward him. A restaurant owner in Detroit, above Mill City, is warned by timbermen in a log truck caravan to retract fairly unobjectionable—at least to neutral eyes—comments reported in a paper or else they would burn her eatery to the ground. She complies. Not suprisingly, then, Atiyeh speaks of lying low for a while. Still, he refuses to surrender his ground. "I'm too damned stubborn to move."

Atiyeh can take care of himself. "I'm not real big. But I'm not a wimpy guy and I'm not passive. If someone takes a swing, they're going to have a real fight," he vows. "If people thought they could beat the hell out of me, they would have done it." To complement his fists, he keeps a .357 Magnum stashed in the bedroom dresser. "If I was George, I'd have two," says Bill Baumgarten, a friend and safety inspector with Oregon OSHA. In his bedroom Atiyeh fondles his piece. Spinning the barrel, to my urban astonishment, he reveals ammunition in the chamber. "Whadya expect?" he asks, "An empty gun's like a limp dick. It ain't worth shit."

A framed membership certificate in the National Rifle Association sits atop his desk. On errands, Atiyeh sometimes brings his other weapon he calls his "loaded gun." Cody has four legs. The equine Doberman pinscher is a delightful companion, provided you remain on his better side. Taunting Atiyeh at Mill City's auto parts store, a timberman playfully grabs him. The "damn preservationist's" best friend bares his teeth and growls.

The sole regret Atiyeh may harbor about his crusade concerns his family. It saddens even the staunchest protimber adults to watch their wrath trickle down to the impressionable children. The handsome strapping Atiyeh boys, Aziz, eighteen, and Arin, sixteen (all the clan's names are Arabic), prefer taking girls to Giovanni's pizza parlor on Highway 22 to being teased by their classmates. Aziz flares his dad's cockiness to keep potential critics at bay. Translated from Arabic, the name means beloved. His girlfriend, a millworker's daughter, proves just how much romance transcends all. Arin's sensitivity puts him on dangerous footing. When a bruiser disparages him as a "tree-hugger" at Girods' grocery, he shot back "forest raper." He proudly shows me the B he received for writing a well-balanced paper on the old-growth issue. "They've all had a hard time," the father says. "I worry about him a lot. A local logger didn't want his nephew playing with Arin. I told him to go to hell."

The meaning of Aniese, innocence, fits the sandy-blond, freckle-faced daughter's gentle demeanor. In the Audubon Society documentary *Rage over Trees*, the three Atiyeh children's wholesome, striking features on a hike with their father through Opal Creek present a picture-perfect human backdrop. In the night scenes, the campfire bathes their faces in a pure, red glow. At school a gang of classmates scream "environmentalist" at the thirteen-year-old and try tying yellow ribbons around her wrists. She comes home in tears. "That's like making a Jew wear a Nazi symbol," her father says, steaming. During a surprise visit to the middle school, Aziz and Arin warn Aniese's diminutive tormentors to back off or else.

Their mother bristles just thinking about it. "Don't mess with the she-bear," George says. Her tall, reedy physique is set off by a dandelion top and an infectious smile. On a trip up to Opal Creek, Baumgarten and I stop by to say hello. In the driveway she casually discloses that her car's tires have just been slashed, as though describing an oil change. The vandalism only hardens her attitudes. Shedding her sweet nature, Deanne lashes back at her neighbors. "I say not another damn old-growth tree for logging," she says in the living room after dinner with the whole Atiyeh family. "They don't see this as an opportunity to grow professionally. It's like saying I never want to leave the house and work. I just want to sit home and eat bonbons all day. The reality is you get off your back and do something with your life." True to her word, she returned to school and learned medical coding at a local hospital.

Fragments of her old friendships still surface through the animosity. At the Christmas bazaar in Stayton, near Mill City, the wife of Jim Morgan, Mill City's top timber baron, put her arms around Deanne Atiyeh. Jim patted her on the arm and smiled. Nobody felt obliged to utter a word about better times past. "George and I've had some drinking times and doping times together," Morgan says. "We've been together on fishing trips. It's a sad thing he's so close to Tom. It's a sad thing for all our families." Deanne concurs. "I'm basically a private person," she says. "It's almost expected that we're supposed to be angry with them." For the time being, politics negates social decency.

George sits back on the sofa, basking in his ex-wife's inner strength. Two years ago personal differences resulted in a painful, if amiable, divorce. He has always been married to his labor of love, reveling in the adulation his good works and good looks kindle. Yet since environmental activities sucked the younger Atiyehs into the fray, their parents are converging again for their sake. The domestic discord that drove them apart shrinks in comparison to the challenges they face sheltering Aziz, Arin, and Aniese from grown-up cruelties they are too young to grasp fully.

Deanne and George fear seeing any of the three robbed of their adolescence. Aziz's facility with his hands and affinity for the woods are pulling him toward a life as a logger. His father—who reiterates his respect for the profession—gently counsels him to try it for two years, but beware of the trade's long-term risk of being over the hill at thirty-five. "My kid would be a good logging company owner. My fear is he will marry his girl, start logging and start having babies, and have no way out," his father says. "He sees a kid hopping off the school bus and on to the crummy earning twelve dollars an hour, with a new pickup. Ten years later, he's just stuck with no future and no retirement, just looking at the other loggers busted up. It's too easy to go work in the mills, but I want my kids to make the choice for themselves." Arin is considering a move to live at his grandparents' home in Portland, where he can attend school free of the distractions. Aniese is about to venture out on her first date.

I go to Mill City fearing an icy reception. For two years timber towns have railed against the elite eastern media stock I personify. Lately, the *Prime Time Live* piece and others on national television have come down clearly on the spotted owls' side. *Life*, the sister publication of *Time*, at which I work, runs a cover package extolling the virtues of trees. Northwest woodsmen denounce it as sappy propaganda. Fortunately, before I arrive, Hirons issues an oral letter of introduction to all his neighbors and friends, instructing them to treat me like royalty. The instant I set foot in town, his phone rings off the hook, through the jungle tom-tom. Tom vouches for my trustworthiness.

His crew chief, Jack Stevenson, resists taking any chances. "The guys on the crew think you're a spy and are going to write a story for the environmental news. It just don't look like no best-seller to me," he tells me. "I don't care. It don't make no difference what you do as long as you don't fuck me around. Then I'll look for you." I hope he's joking. His long, straight hair and fiery eyes and drooping mustache lend him the appearance of an old western outlaw. Stevenson has earned his sobriquet "Mad Jack" from Hirons for the mordant humor Stevenson employs to defuse tense situations in the brush.

My initial trepidation in Mill City proves absolutely groundless. "You're not one of them environmentalists who's going to stir up trouble," glowers the female super at Fir Grove apartments when I come looking for a place to rent. "We have a retired logger living here." That man, Charlie Belleck, soon becomes a good neighbor and friend before being jailed for shooting our next-door neighbor in a heated argument. "Well, we haven't tarred and feathered you yet," jokes a grim-faced Marie at Stewart's Grocery. The delightful woman and her equally amiable husband, Charley, invite me to their home after work for pan-fried fish and vanilla ice cream doused in Hershey's chocolate sauce. A competition arises for my presence at local dinner tables. At the home of the Girods, the proprietors the Hilltop Market, I'm beneficiary of Jim's talents as a gourmet cook. By the end of my stay, my midsection is bulging from a surfeit of delicious home-cooked meals.

"I've been using your name in vain," warns Verl Moberg, a logging company owner, on the sidewalk outside Stewart's. I brace for the inevitable. As it turns out, his son Randy wants to take me out on a predawn fishing trip. At the first jerk on Randy's line, he selflessly hands me his own rod to reel in a feisty steelhead. Though the fish escapes and we are skunked on that frigid morning, my fond memories of all the good people of Mill City will always remain. I rack up a big long-distance phone bill keeping in touch with them. In all my travels throughout the United States, I have yet to meet a more gracious lot than these down-home, honest Northwesterners. I can pay no better tribute to their hospitality than urge my own parents to visit Mill City on their next vacation.

All these people ask for is a fair shake. "Hell, I've told you all along I've never trusted the media," says Jim Morgan, vice president and co-owner of Young and Morgan, the largest mill in town, crystallizing the common suspicions of the fourth estate. "The minute it starts being unfair is the minute I'm going to railroad you." He dodges none of my soft or hard questions.

At the center of town, Stewart's cracker-barreled sensibilities teeter between old-fashioned service and an uncertain future. From cradle to coffin, a human being could fill virtually every need imaginable from beneath the fifty-six-hundred-square-foot building's roof. The store's patriarch can keep anyone happy. "Every time the door opens, you have a new boss," he says, standing on a wooden floor polished with wear. His six employees are local. In the back of a store, the stocky sixty-three-year-old, after wiping his hands on the bloodied white apron draped around his waist, mans the butcher block. As a big-game cutter, he has few peers in the Northwest. In the fall, hunters bring in their elk to be aged and slabbed by an electric circle saw. It takes Charley a whole day to cut six hundred pounds, at a cost of about two hundred dollars. A family with a deep freezer can stretch the meat till next hunting season. In the mornings, the busiest time at Stewart's, Marie, Charley's friendly-faced wife of forty-four years, handles the cash register near the front door. She sells half a dozen packets of Big Red, Apple Jack, Work Horse, or Beech Nut chewing tobacco by noon. The Stewarts always stock at least ten thousand dollars' worth of cigarettes.

The clothing and shoe departments alone at Stewart's are worth a tourist's detour. In the boot room, footwear is shoehorned into floor-to-ceiling racks. What red-blooded man could pass up a pair of Gorilla brand boots? Conservationists will be pleased to learn that no inventory is ever thrown away: It stays in the store until sold. "One shoe went out of style, then it came back," says the gentle-eyed brunette Marie. She must be excluding the ballooned, thick-heeled shoes that men wore in the midseventies and that surely rank as one of her least salable "dead items." I did, however, purchase cuffed, twill trousers older than I am for $5.98, their original price; they are still serviceable after a brisk dusting.

Stewart's immutable fashions are as timeless in style as an old tree. "We can outfit a logger from hard hat right on down," Charley says. "I know what it takes for everything he wears and eats." He buys loggers' hickory shirts by the case to satisfy constant demand. Gray wool socks, ringed in bright orange at the top and toe, fly off the shelves in the seasons the tall timber falls. At a cost of $245 per pair, Stewart ensures that West Coast-brand calked boots, with spiked soles critical for gripping the slippery logs, fit just right. The vital supply of sixty-six-inch-long spare laces keeps the boots tied to the loggers and the loggers tied to Charley Stewart.

The indomitable work ethic Charley Stewart embodies through seven-day workweeks is largely rooted in his spare upbringing in windswept western Texas, where living comes hard. The gritty winds whipping across the prairie blew the grocery and feed store his family operated in hardscrabble country straight up to the Northwest's pastures of plenty. From the moment he opened Stewart's in Mill City in 1949, Charley's ceaseless toil became his play. The milk-bottle-thick glasses he wears accentuate the slight bags under his eyes from arriving early at the store and leaving late. A prominent mole dots the side of Stewart's face above a soft chin melting into his face. The roundness of his nose and Santa Claus cheeks blend into the happy smile radiating from his face.

He recalls a scrap of wisdom his father bequeathed him. "You better find some fun in your work," Charley says in an accent still drenched in a Lone Star drawl, " 'cause you got a lot of it to do." The younger Stewart also picked up from his dad the business and humanitarian value of extending clients a helping hand. A new arrival to Mill City can count on his generosity. "Charley says, 'if you ain't worth twenty dollars,' " notes Hirons, " 'you ain't worth a damn.' "

Stewart's symbiotic relationship with the timber industry reinforces their mutual dependence. Upon arriving in the canyon, a new woodsman's first stop is at the store. Charley calls the logging company to secure advance money for boots, hickory shirts, and the rest of the logger's uniform through "wage consignments." The total is deducted from the worker's paycheck. Most of Stewart's customers are willing to pay somewhat higher prices for groceries for the luxury of credit purchases. In the glass-enclosed office next to the butcher section, Marie keeps tabs on the McCaskey Account System, a huge, battleship-gray metal card holder from the turn of the century. Stretching up to three hundred dollars, a credit line can carry a logger's family through winter's seasonal unemployment. By spring, Stewart's accounts receivable drop only 15 percent, to ninety-eight thousand dollars. A young man Charley has known since he first walked buys a hair dryer with a white credit check. "I've dealt with him for twenty years. His father was killed on a Cat," Charley whispers. "These are not fly-by-night people."

Mill City's merchants wince when contemplating the impact of impending timber cutbacks on the local economy. "We live out of the workingman's lunch box. When he gets needy, we're not selling. They are dependent on us and we are dependent on them," Charley says. "When they have hard times, we have hard times. We are tied that close together. They need to be helped." The century-long partnership between business owners and timber raises doubts about the viability of new industries such as tourism. "We see trees here every day. When people come from out of state, we take them for granted," he adds. "You cannot enjoy beauty for long on an empty stomach." Yet, it seems that the indigenous population had better begin marketing its natural treasures intact or it will go hungry once they vanish.

By definition, Mill City earned its name from mills. The town's continuing existence bolsters its entrenched traditions. Its stillbirth in 1887 and repeated ups and downs since then provide apt parallels to today's travails. Legend has it that in the 1870s, a lone widow and grandmother—by the name of Hennessy—mounted on a pinto, rode into the woods along the roaring Santiam River. One look at the virgin Doug fir enveloping the Cascade Range's foothills convinced her to buy a tract of eighty acres for a home. "The forest was so thick homesteaders had to cut down trees to get space for a cabin," noted a contemporary observer. Lumber to build her log cabin came piece by piece from a jerry-built sawmill constructed for the job. In 1886 she sold some of her land to four men from Stayton, fifteen miles away. It took them many months to haul heavy machinery by wagon from Salem. The Santiam Lumber Company's founding on the river's northern bank spawned a grocery store, restaurant, hotel, blacksmith shop, and saloon. Heads of commerce gathered downtown to decide on a name for the post office before petitioning the government. "Well, we have a mill . . . Mill City," ventured one. There were three other post offices by that name in the United States. The only one in the entire world left of any significance is now in Oregon.

Early reports of the town's death proved premature. Within a year after the mill turned out its first wood, a newspaper account eulogized: "Mill City . . . is deserted. Everyone has moved away except the ranchers. The sawmill has closed down as no one is there to buy any lumber. John Sorbin has boxed up his saloon as the patrons are all gone. The place will . . . someday spring up again." It did, just as quickly as it mysteriously collapsed. Two dozen men worked in the mill and the bordering forest. Oxen dragged the felled trees to a mammoth wooden flume on which the logs sped a mile down to the mill on a bed of water. The construction of the Oregon-Pacific Railroad line hooked commerce into international ports on the Pacific. From a shantytown, Mill City bloomed into a booming frontier community. By the turn of the century, the population—consisting mostly of immigrant laborers in the woods, mills, and nearby mines—soared past two hundred. To house them, accommodations popped up in town and in surrounding logging camps. Known as the Bulgarian Hotel, the Russian Hotel, the Japanese Hotel, and the Greek Hotel, they produced the Northwest's own version of the melting pot.

In 1909, the sale of the sawmill and most of Mill City to A. B. Hammond ushered in the era of the company town. Hell bent on expanding across the Northwest and beyond, the timber magnate from San Francisco viewed the town and profits as synonymous. "Here is the seat of a busy industry where the Hammond Lumber Company is zealously turning out lumber for the commercial world at the rate of over 250,000 feet daily. The Hammond mill at Mill City is the largest institution of its kind in the Willamette Valley," declared the 1916 Mill City School yearbook. "No mill in the state is better equipped and few on the coast are adapted to make lumber for the finest retail businesses. The machinery is all modern in both the saw and planing mill."

Throughout its twenty-one-year reign, the Hammond Lumber Company suffused every fiber of Mill City's political, economic, and political being. At the outset, the primitive conditions meant no electricity or running water. Hammond quickly brought the town into the twentieth century. First it rigged the mill's stream turbines to power a light and water plant. The shacks that blighted most mill communities came down. On the Santiam's southern bank, Hammond laid out twenty-five neatly trimmed blocks. Families took up residence in the thirty-two modern, comfortable homes, replete with lawns and gardens (most are still standing). Half the crew boarded in the company hotel. In the early teens, a guest plunked down $4.50 a week for board and a double bed, two men to a room. The fine meals were served family-style, all you can eat. Conversation, in a melody of foreign languages, dwelled on their employer's fringe benefits. Private health insurance gave peace of mind. For 75 cents a month, workers enjoyed the services of Doc Ransom on contract with Hammond at his residence-*cum*-hospital across the road from the company's horse barn.

Six days a week, at dawn, the mill's wake-up whistle shrieked for breakfast. The coffee had barely cooled before the final whistle blew at seven o'clock. For the next eleven hours, including a sixty-minute lunch break, a common laborer brought home two dollars, mostly in gold. (A dollar then was roughly the equivalent of eleven today.) The head sawyer, the top man in the mill, earned five dollars a day. Exclaimed a local boy: "Someday I am going to take time off to look at a man who makes that much money." The work was as long as it was hard. Men stacked lumber by hand onto two-wheel carts. Until Model T Fords were modified as tractor units, the men relied on a horse with a long chain fastened to a tree for motor power. When the Santiam crested in the spring, "river rats" rafted the logs down the river, keeping their balance with the finesse of a gymnast on a spinning top. One slip was all it took to be crushed or drowned. On the days when the mill exceeded its target, Hammond passed out free cigars. (The ungrateful recipients complained they came from the company's store's unsold inventory and were too dry even to chew.) Not surprisingly, turnover was heavy. It was said the mill had three crews: "one working, one coming, and one going."

In return for the job security and basic creature comforts, the town submitted absolutely to the company's autocracy. What was good for Hammond was good for Mill City. All lights had to be out in homes from 8:00 P.M. to 5:00 A.M. to preserve power at the mill. Electric ranges and refrigerators were prohibited for the same reason. This being the great Northwest, wood had always been as free as the wind. Yet once Hammond gobbled up 90 percent of the private land around Mill City and put timber off-limits to cutting, it charged whatever it pleased for the main source of fuel and heat. The company store, a prehistoric Stewart's filled with dark wooden and glass cases, sold everything under the sun and then some, from fifteen-cent-a-pound meat—"an old milk cow that had been milked to death . . . and was so tough you couldn't shoot through it"—to seventy-five-cent overalls. Customers made purchases in company-issued script rather than money. Hammond automatically deducted the amount, plus rent and utilities, from paychecks.

Half the year, the bookkeeper's hardbound ledger heaved from the weight of unsettled accounts. From November through March the snows shut down the mill, along with employees' income. In an age before unemployment compensation and welfare benefits, families had to charge groceries all winter long. By the time they finally cleared their credit in July, the long, vicious cycle was four

months away from beginning anew. Workers were broke and had
to work the next month just to survive.

The monopoly guaranteed that Mill City owed its soul to the
company store. The efforts of small entrepreneurs to break off a
small piece of business met unhappy fates. Hammond employees
caught leaving the upstarts received pink slips the next day. To
bring home the message, the company cut off the power supply to
an upstart grocer's lights, thereby forcing him to sell. Patronizing
businesses elsewhere was virtually impossible for lack of time off
and modern transportation.

Hammond owned the railroad, Mill City's sole link to the outside world. The wood-fired *Skunk Train,* so named for the stink
it created, arrived from Albany at 10:00 A.M., no sooner or later,
occasioning such a social affair that most of the local women
dressed up in their Sunday finery to greet it in case someone
important happened to be aboard. Many of the passengers had to
scrub the pitch off their hands from helping the tired rail crew
toss cordwood in the tender every few miles. One Sunday in the
first August after Hammond took over the Skunk, workers and
their families dug into their hard-earned savings for a special com-
pany-arranged excursion. From Yaquina Bay on the coast, a ferry
took passengers to Newport Beach. Though disposable income
was tight and the long round trip cut into the fun in the sun,
the seats were full.

No price probably seemed too high to escape Mill City's stifling
isolation for a few hours. Day to day, before used Studebakers
and Model T's became affordable in the late 1920s, the horizons
reached as far as people's feet carried them. When Walter Witt's
appendix burst, his uncle and other relatives had to carry him all
the way down the hill to Doc Ransom. By contrast, Mrs. Bill
Beatram passed away of an unknown illness. The mill suspended
operations on the day of her funeral to allow the whole work
force to attend. In the procession from her house following the
service, the only two autos were the hearse and the car for the
next of kin. The rest of the mourners walked the three miles to
the cemetery.

Hammond's tightfisted attention to the bottom line kept it remarkably depression proof. When the bottom fell out of the lumber market in 1929, the company's patriarch wanted to close Mill
City's operation. His plant manager convinced him that it could
remain profitable simply by slashing wages. A series of 10 percent
cuts over a number of weeks finally lapped up 70 percent of total
pay. The mill dropped to two six-hour shifts per week. At 20

cents an hour, workers ended up averaging $2.50 a week by 1933, about what they earned a day twenty years earlier, when Hammond first arrived on the scene. At least they had jobs. In 1934 the final whistle wailed, not out of deference to the green eyeshaders, but because old man Hammond died. An internecine quarrel among his heirs prompted stockholders back East to send a new man to take over the presidency. He moved swiftly—and, some think in retrospect, unwisely—to liquidate assets. "The mill of the Hammond Lumber Company, which made Mill City, is being dismantled," reported the *Oregonian* in October 1935, "and as this was the only reason for the town's existence it will not be long until there will be no town there at all." A mass exodus ensued among young loggers.

That winter, panic struck the neighbors left behind. Overnight, Hammond had orphaned employees with families and unpaid mortgages. Houses commanded fire-sale prices—from two hundred dollars to five hundred dollars for a well-built house. "When Hammond closed down, everybody thought Mill City was going to be a ghost town," the retired logger Wilbur Harlan recalls. "Boy, they said it would be nothing." Weaned on Hammond's quasi-benevolent despotism, an entire populace suddenly had to fend for itself.

The prospect of perishing concentrated minds wonderfully. Townspeople called a meeting and fifty men, with the help of a Salem lawyer, scraped together eleven thousand dollars to launch a small, cooperative mill. They bought the log pond from Hammond and equipment from Clatskanie, another terminally ill timber town. Since Hammond had logged off most of the timber within reach of three strung-out donkies (steam engines used for skidding and loading logs), Mill City Manufacturing, the new firm, had to settle for turning out about half of Hammond's top volume. Production peaked at a hundred thousand board feet during World War II, about the same time the doomsayers' predictions about overcutting came true. With private lands already depleted, the timber supply was on the verge of running out.

The nation's peacetime construction boom proved a godsend. Washington, D.C.'s, decision to open the national forests for logging presented a new source of timber and gave birth to dozens of new sawmills and logging companies throughout the North Santiam Canyon. Mill City had one more reason to believe that its feline inclination toward multiple lives would last forever.

For nearly a decade, talk of moribund timber towns always comes back to the sad tale of Valsetz. To woodsmen it represents what Pompeii was for Rome—the death of a small but vibrant civilization. For sixty-two years, Boise Cascade ran Valsetz—Oregon's rainiest community—much like Hammond once did Mill City, except that Boise Cascade owned every square inch of land. On February 24, 1984, however, business was far from usual for the 150 residents tucked away in the heavily forested Coast Ranges, forty miles west of Salem. Valsetz's two streets, Main Street and Cadillac Avenue, bustled with the sluggish foot traffic of heavyhearted locals on their way to and from the post office, cafe, and general store and houses belonging to the company. On this day, Boise Cascade commenced implementing a plan to recoup four straight years of losses by converting Valsetz into a tree farm.

The company went about methodically erasing Valsetz—man, beast, and abode—from the face of the earth. "That's big business," shrugged Cecelia Hutchinson, forty-seven, a cook and waitress at the cafe. "A person's a number now, not a person." Bulldozer's first plowed through the veneer mill's front entrance, reducing the twenty-five-year-old structure to rubble. A lighted match finished off the job. By April, more than a third of the town's sixty houses were pounded into heaps of shattered glass, rafters, and abandoned possessions before succumbing to the torch.

The balance remained standing for the families with children still in school. They had until mid-June, after the term ended, to vacate the premises. "Time will help to ease the bitterness that once flowed so feverishly through our hearts," Anthony Johnson, the eighteen-year-old valedictorian, told his graduating class of nine. "Time is a great healer. In order to survive in this everchanging world, we cannot let hatred control us." Two weeks later the Valsetz post office made its final delivery and hung a sign on the front door reading "Closed Forever." On her home's garage, Dana Reckard, an eleven-year-old girl in Valsetz's last family to move out, spray-painted the message "Boise Cascade—Hope Your Proud." By the summer, Valsetz had vanished without a trace.

Perhaps only a sentimentalist could blame a conglomerate for ridding itself of an unprofitable venture, oblivious to the sensitivities of faceless victims. The free-enterprise system abounds with comparable tragedies before and since Boise Cascade drew the final curtain on the era of this company's town. Americans, after all, pride themselves on their rootless mobility. Nonetheless, the antiseptic disposal of a home to hundreds of employees and their families for more than half a century—like so many leaf piles in autumn—still sends chills across the Northwest. Timbermen in Mill City and elsewhere speak of their towns "drying up and blowing away like Valsetz," a specter terrifying enough to convert eleven-year-olds into cynics.

"I think Mill City will be like Valsetz," says Chelsea Stewart, a sixteen-year-old junior in Ross Miller's humanities class at the Santiam High School, which incorporates Mill City and nearby Gates. The teacher has invited me to meet the cream of the student body. On a break from their advanced course in history, literature, and philosophy, they have a lot more on their minds today than Homer. Virtually all of the teenagers' fathers work either in the mills or the woods, as their fathers and grandfathers once did. Economics and environmentalism may deprive the fourth generation of the opportunity to follow in their footsteps. Graduates will no longer have the luxury of heading into the mills or the woods. "We have to do our damnedest to make sure kids leave," Miller says. "The huge majority will."

Education, the surest escape, has traditionally ranked as a low priority. Out of this year's senior class, twenty-five, only four will stretch themselves at a four-year college rather than a two-year junior school. Rarely do any of them actually complete the four years. Many in Miller's class admit that after twelve years of school, they lack the motivation to tough out the work load at an institution such as Oregon State, which has raised its grade-point average requirement to almost a B level. From their vantage point on campus, home remains where their hearts are; Mill City doesn't seem so bad after all. "It's a cultural thing," says a peach-fuzzed sophomore. "You don't have the drive. You're just satisfied to be who you are." Parents, few of whom attended college themselves, refrain from exerting pressure.

Students toying with the notion of higher education view a business degree, or its vocation equivalent, as a preferable stepping-stone to a career rather than a liberal arts degree. I, a history and English major, am asked my salary. The students are surprised to learn that, as a journalist with a bachelor's degree in English and history from Georgetown University in Washington, D.C., I earn hardly more income than their fathers in a good year in the mills or woods. Nevertheless, college-educated Americans in general outearn workers with just a high-school diploma by up to forty percent.

In practical terms, the average male adolescent in Mill City can hop from the school bus to crummy on the day of graduation.

Four male seniors, out of about fifteen in this year's class, are unable to wait that long and simply drop out. "College is the ultimate deferred gratification," Miller says. With diplomas fresh in hand from the previous year, many male graduates still hang around the high school, showing off their gainful employment's material rewards, after work or during winter downtime. The nineteen-year-old loggers swagger in the fringy and unhemmed jeans, wool socks, and—the uniform's most macho accessory—hickory shirts begging for a needle and thread. Their wheels are high-rider pickups, twelve feet off the ground. These status symbols announce to the world that they have made it. The schoolboy still collecting small change feels small standing in the shadow of woodsmen raking in twelve dollars an hour. The intense peer pressure blinds him to twenty-six-year-olds with bad backs or thirty-year-olds hobbling about on crutches.

He takes solace from a good woman standing by him. A lot of the coeds become premature adults. Nearly half the seniors this year are pregnant. Within the cultural milieu, it is perfectly acceptable for a seventeen-year-old to bring her baby to school. She, like the father in the pickup, enjoys being the center of attention at school. "The babies come to the baseball games," Stewart says. "I don't understand at all what possesses them to do it." A fourteen-year-old too young to marry her ex-love, a millworker ten years her senior, lets Mom and Grandmom take care of the baby while she struggles to attend classes. The parents look the other way, as they do in small towns and urban ghettos nationwide. In logging country, the young couples who do wed and have three or four children by their midtwenties must scramble to support them. "We have kids who go away to college and kids who get married and stay," says Pastor Veach, "but the ones that get married and stay, stay in the timber industry."

In Oregon, the educational system is ill equipped for the transition away from its principal source of funding. The U.S. Forest Service returns 25 percent of the revenues from its timber sales to counties within national forests. The counties keep three fourths of the money and give the rest to schools. Portions of timber sales from the federal Bureau of Land Management forests go to counties to offset property taxes for schools and services. Dave Alexander, the ranger in the Detroit District of the U.S. Forest Service, is quick to point this out on a forestry tour he and Hirons lead to observe Earth Day.

Naturally, the Mill City high school eschews any pretense of evenhandedness toward the logging crisis. On the Friday of a massive rally orchestrated by the timber industry in support of the cause, students are given the choice of attending it or classes. The administrators offer to provide the schools' own buses for transportation. The industry appreciates the offer but has already rented a fleet and easily fills it with backers of all ages. The young receive strong encouragement from their parents to take the ride. Atiyeh is furious upon discovering that his mischievous son Aziz has seized the opportunity to skip classes that day.

King timber remains writ large on the blackboards. Three months after the spotted owl's listing as a threatened species, marking the beginning of the end of the timber era as Mill City knows it, Santiam High begins the first forestry class ever, the brainchild of Carol Cree. The pleasant and earnest substitute teacher in the district leads the class. Cree is married to a logging company owner and worked in Hirons's CGO office until recently. "Why?" Miller says he asked her. "It doesn't make any sense. Industry got real excited at first, except when it came time to foot the bill." The funds came out of arts and other courses.

The class amounts to a symbolic gesture of solidarity with the timber companies' faded glory. Cree defends the curriculum, from tree identification to logging skills, that she and Hirons have developed as solid vocational training. "There will always be forests and logging," Cree insists, even while acknowledging that there will be fewer jobs. In the classroom a "How a Tree Grows" poster hangs alone, surrounded by posters of yarders and chainsaws.

Outside, fourteen students—all boys, most of whom have fathers in the timber trade—prepare for the past. At the corner of the football field, they throw axes and saw mammoth logs by hand in a scene as surrealistic as blacksmiths fitting horseshoes in a Ford factory. "I want to be out in the brush," says Jeremy Timey, the fifteen-year-old son of a foreman for a local logging company, "but I'm probably going into the service. I'd rather be a farmer. Right now I'm worried about my parents not having a job."

The high school's emblem, the wolverine, stares in paint from the football grandstand. One of the last reported sightings of this animal—quick, strong, and about the size of a bear cub—occurred in Opal Creek in the mid-1980s. Coincidentally, the grizzly bear, featured in the foreground of California's official seal, is now extinct in that state, as it's believed to be in Oregon and Washington State. Some friends of Atiyeh in an agency task force at Yellowstone National Park have suggested putting a few of the endangered bears in Opal Creek on the sly, shutting down logging cold.

The learning business, like the grocery store, will suffer the effects of Mill City's contraction. The other English teacher's seniority jeapordizes Miller's career. "It's a personal tragedy for me because I want to stay. I can live with the redneck punks. The pay is crappy, twenty-nine thousand dollars at the top of the scale. In Salem, they're making thirty-five thousand dollars," Miller says. "I choose to live here. There are certain values, the primacy of beauty and freedom. I hate to portray it as a dying town, but as industry goes down, the few professionals here are going to move out." Lately, Miller has been updating his résumé.

Following Miller's class, Chelsea Stewart and Michelle Meader invite me on their daily cruise through town. Stewart, a tall, long-haired brunette decked out in a Portland Trailblazer's jacket, is the granddaughter of Charley and Marie Stewart. Michelle Meader, a petite, short-cropped blonde in powder-blue shorts and sneakers, is the daughter of a millworker. Her godfather is Jim Morgan of Young and Morgan, and her boyfriend is Aziz Atiyeh. Some afternoons and weekends the girls pop over to Stayton or Salem for a movie or a jaunt through the shopping malls. Mostly, the young kill time doing the aimless "loop." In the seventeen-year-old Stewart's Datsun stick shift, we climb a rocky, windy road to Sheapard's Hill, the teenage hideaway perched above town. A few beer bottles scattered among a clear-cut are left over from Friday and Saturday nights. Mill City rests comfortably below, in the valley's cradle. "There is no other place to go," says Meader. "There isn't anything to do here. Things get boring here. It rains a lot."

The two best friends strain to express their identities under the straitjacket of conformity. Stewart chuckles recalling the odd reaction they elicited for requesting mixed flavors in their pint of ice cream. "Two wacky girls," said the fountain jerk. We grab a quick bite at Giovanni's Pizzaria on Highway 22. All roads lead back to bucolic Mill City. "You know, I never stopped to think about it," Stewart says, "but it sure is pretty here."

While both betray restlessness, neither of the girls gives it wings. They dream of renting a studio in Los Angeles. "California is clean and pretty," Meader says, proving she hasn't seen all of it. "No Betty Crocker for us," Stewart insists, of her professional ambitions. But she and Meader show signs of wavering, if a hypothetical suitor carried them across the threshold back to Mill City. "I would laugh at him," Stewart says. "I don't know," Meader interjects. Stewart takes a long, deep breath: "My dad didn't think he would be back, either, but decided to return to become America's grocer." Time and again, Mill City's warm homesteads draw its young back to the fold.

Chelsea Stewart vacillates between wanting to make a break for it and settling down to the comfortable life her grandfather has set up for her. On summer evenings after work Charley Stewart visits a cherished plot on a hill above Highway 22. He has rejected offers to sell the 150,000 board feet of timber on it worth about seventy-five thousand dollars, preferring to hand it down to his family. The chores of filling in the swamp and grading the muddy road have given him a new hobby. "Grandpa shoves the dirt back and forth," his granddaughter says. "He's real proud of that little patch and wants me to live on it." Wherever she may go, the land in Mill City awaits her.

On the verge of adulthood, Meader is reevaluating for the first time the axioms she accepted as absolutes growing up. Her forty-six-year-old father, a hot press operator at Young and Morgan's veneer mill, may have to quit the only work he has known since graduating from high school. "I don't think he could do anything but work in the mill," says the smoky-voiced girl. "We have a big house and a lot of property and he's afraid of losing it." The car rolls past it, across the road from the Hironses. Cows graze on lush, rolling hills, next to a clear pond teeming with fish. No sane man could possibly leave a home this pleasant without a fight.

Two years ago, the costs of saving it began to dawn on Michelle. "The logs are getting smaller. A lot of them are cull," she says. "There was a one-log-load this morning for the first time in a long time. I saw a lot more three-log-loads when I was a kid." Industry, Michelle is coming to realize, is exhausting the timber supply allowing her father to pay his bills.

Since taking up with Aziz Atiyeh, Michelle has found George Atiyeh's influence rubbing off on her. "George doesn't really seem like he's preaching," she says. On her first trip up in his plane, perfect visibility afforded her a vista straight to Mount St. Helens. None of the horseback rides she took with her father in wilderness areas or television news stories she has watched lately prepared her for the shocking scenes below. "There were a lot of clear-cuts down there. All my life I've seen forests and forests, and always thought there were billions of trees," Meader says. "I figured the stuff on TV wasn't even here. That's not in Oregon. But it is. You get a different perspective from the sky." At the dinner table the night of her flight, she fixed her innocent gaze on the man at head of the table and asked for an explanation. Between bites, he softly reiterated his industry's claim to environmentalism. She backed off from pressing him further. "I guess I'm scared for Dad," she says. "I feel bad about saying anything because of him." Meader's fidelity to her father, however, bumps against her growing awareness of the stakes involved. "I guess I want to save Opal Creek," she says softly. "I'm hoping there's someplace to go."

At lunchtime, Hirons, straight from his logging show at Pamelia Creek, skids to a stop in the Chamber of Commerce's graveled parking lot. The Oregon Economic Development Department has convened a brainstorming session for a report titled "Review of Strengths, Weaknesses, Opportunities, and Threats for the Transition Communities." Above the thud of technocratese, the emergency program, better known as SWOT, sounds an alarm to nineteen mill towns in Oregon. Either they cure themselves of the timber habit or perish. The National Association of Counties has put the Santiam Canyon, and Mill City in particular, on the endangered community list. The state and federal governments' thin resources mean the initiative must come up from the local level. Help will arrive for those who help themselves. "Mill City could be described as a community ADRIFT," a voluminous SWOT report concludes. "As is the case throughout many rural communities, there is considerable reluctance to change. Some believe that the area will MUDDLE through much as it has in the past." That "some" are actually officials in Salem, who are decidedly pessimistic about Mill City's prospects for crossing the Rubicon into the next stage of its history. For their part, the townspeople feel the bureaucrats in the state capital look down their nose at the hicks out in the sticks.

At a set of tables pushed together, most of the dignitaries from the banks and City Hall chew over local pizza and Mill City's future. The foremost challenge is to prepare for the spiraling downturn in the wood products industry over the long term. Regardless of environmental restrictions, the fact remains that technological improvements will enable the mills to produce the same amount or more timber with fewer workers. "It's a given that we're going to lose forty to fifty percent of the employment. You fight it tooth and nail, but it's a given," Hirons says, smiling thinly. "I was retrained once as a forest technician. It's my own damn fault that I'm still a logger." In his dirt-caked clothes and

Greek fisherman's cap, Hirons strikes an odd contrast to the genial woman from OED, Maryln Johnston, leading the discussion.

"Tomorrow I'm meeting with the dean of the University of Oregon's Business School. I'm going to tell him my community is going to hell in a handbasket," Hirons says between bites of pizza and to the nodding agreement of other lunchers. "I think our best bet is secondary manufacturing." He is referring to the standard products—window frames, wood molding for the do-it-yourself market, prefabricated housing and components, furniture components, and structural wood goods (laminated beams and trusses)—touted as the answer to the Northwest's prayers. Elsewhere, well outside the earshot of Johnston, Hirons has railed at SWOT's emphasis on "cottage industry" niche products—chopsticks, tongue depressors, Popsicle sticks—for little towns. It clearly deflates his ego imagining the big sticks he logs ending up on a Good Humor ice cream pop.

The problem with any fiber processed into so-called value-added products besides lumber or plywood concerns logistics. According to textbook finance, manufacturers reap more profit from transporting logs and lumber from woodlands to factories near or in population centers for conversion to finished goods than in moving cumbersome finished items produced near their source of supply to big cities. Nevertheless, Mill City and other timber towns from northern California to Washington State stand to harvest a cash crop from products for the Northwest's housing boom. Any location in the United States, of course, offers a closer market than Japan, Korea, and China, where a quarter of the whole logs cut in Oregon and Washington State have been shipped in recent years.

No one at the lunch table likes discussing the social upheaval paralleling the economic transition taking place. Cheaper rents have led social service departments in Salem and in Linn County to send welfare recipients to Mill City to live, turning it and other similar small towns into dumping grounds for the poor. Mexican immigrants who have taken advantage of liberal amnesty laws toil long hours on ranches in the Willamette Valley and the mills. "We got a lot of Mexicans. They're good workers and we don't have to put up with no guff from them," says Jim Morgan, vice president of Young and Morgan. "There's resentment to them moving in here. Hey, we need them." Their influence permeates the culture. Second-grade school children in Mill City are learning the Pledge of Allegiance in Spanish. Natives have come to calling the adjacent town of Gates "Little Tijuana" due to the ethnic origns of the millworkers and transient residents moving there.

At the same time, an invasion from the nation's most populous state, California, is overrunning the Northwest. "Mill City may be around, but it won't be the same," Hirons says. "It's conceivable to me this could end up a 100 percent retirement community from California." Over the past year, newcomers, 70 percent of whom are California retirees, have been buying homes locally at a record rate of more than four a month. Most of the so-called equity émigrés cash in on greatly appreciated property in Los Angeles or other large cities, and then spend only a fraction of the proceeds to snap up a comparable or better home in an Oregon timber town. In 1991 the average price of a home rose in Mill City to sixty thousand dollars from forty-five thousand dollars. Diane Quinlan, a local realtor, has sold fifty homes over the past year—mostly to California retirees, but some small-business owners and bedroom commuters—almost twice as many homes as she sold the previous year. "We're seeing the changes right now," she says, "but none of the mills have gone."

An influx of transplants, primarily from California, has been pouring across the Pacific Northwest's alluring frontiers by the tens of thousands. The onrush into booming areas such as Seattle and Portland is citifying a rural hinterland and fueling the region's already simmering debate over local growth. *Seattle Times* columnist Emmett Watson regularly exhorts readers to "fight Californication" and has founded a "Lesser Seattle" club aimed at keeping the "bastards out" by harping on the city's infamous rainfall and other faults. The group's motto is "Have a Nice Day—Somewhere Else!" In the past year Washington State has gained a hundred thousand new residents.

Oregon, where fewer settlers have moved, has laid its thin welcome mat out since Governor Tom McCall's invitation in the 1970s to the outside world to visit—but not stay. The state's Tourism Division spends $2.5 million annually on promotion to entice travelers. A billboard in downtown San Francisco recently showed a pair of deer on a forested road and the slogan "Oregon Gridlock." By the turn of the century, demographers predict Oregon's population will rise from 2.85 million to well over 3 million, as swelling hordes of Californian urbanites seek refuge from crime and grime.

Mill City's transition toward a resting spot for Californians and a bedroom community for workers commuting to nearby larger cities is certain to wreak social havoc. The locals chafe under the new arrivals' antipathy toward the timber companies whose clear-cuts in the surrounding hills mar the scenery that attracted the newcomers in the first place. The retirees balk at paying taxes for schools and other services they don't need.

The real-estate boom poses added logistical challenges to Mill City. A serious housing shortage threatens to bump up property values and taxes beyond the reach of the average timber family. The last new house was built in Mill City six years ago. Serious infrastructure problems impede industrial and residential development. In the past, sites for major lumber mills were often situated in low-lying floodplain areas unsuitable for other uses. Today's floodplain and wetland regulations cut into the number of new marketable sites. Moreover, costly water, sewer, and street improvements must be made before a business can commit to locating in the area.

Any developer seeking to capitalize on commuters' and retirees' affinity for rural living would have the field to himself in the Santiam Canyon. I discovered the opportunity for construction of rental and single-family housing for myself as soon as I shifted from Oak Park Motel in Gates to Fir Grove Apartments in Mill City as a modest economy move. (All that remains of groves of firs are a few stumps.) At three hundred dollars a month—about the price of a parking space in my native New York—I applauded myself for a good bargain at the no-frills, L-shaped complex of apartments that were built to accommodate workers at the Detroit Dam up the road in the late 1940s. The roar of heavy machinery and log trucks from Young and Morgan's log yard bordering the property certainly provided a timber town's ambience.

What I saved in rent, however, I lost in such amenities as a working refrigerator and shower. Both would have come in handy after I finally finished tidying up my quarters. I subsequently learned that Linn County Building and Health Department officials threatened to shut down my landlord, a double-chinned ex-trucker partial to sleeveless T-shirts, for operating an outlaw mobile-home village behind Fir Grove. The county claimed that none of the twelve units satisfied zoning, electrical, woodstove, or septic requirements—inconveniences his tenants, whom he describes as "poor working folks," put up with for the sake of shelter. The landlord evicted them to keep his electricity from being turned off at the rest of Fir Grove.

While the prospects for turning mill communities into Silicon Valleys appear dim, hope springs eternal through technology.

Kevin Long has been negotiating lately to bring in a high-tech firm that would employ a hundred workers. From telemarketing and consulting to mail order and desktop publishing firms, "foot-loose service companies," as the SWOT reports define them, are not confined to any particular geographical area. The electronics revolution affords a well-funded entrepreneur the luxury of country living. It may mean a one-man operation running a computer business out of a garage (or in George Atiyeh's case, an airplane hangar), or an organic foods company employing fifty people. "Because of our natural resources, Mill City hasn't had to work for anything," Long admits. "It's lived on easy street forever."

One creative solution stares Mill City in the face seventy miles southeast, on the highway at Sisters, in central Oregon's High Desert. In the early 1960s, with the shutdown of the last of its five mills and a slump in agriculture, Sisters reached a dead end. A decade later, the City Council and merchants teamed up with a consulting firm to give storefronts a facelift befitting its birth at the turn of the century as a frontier outpost. The style of architecture, as mandated under comprehensive guidelines, restored the luster of Sisters Hotel and other original structures. Low-interest loans ensured that new shops—from clothing to antiques—blended in. Strolling about, a visitor feels the fascination of happening upon the set of a John Ford film. When the Forest Service planned an aesthetically offensive timber sale in the sight of visitors, the community formed a committee of recreation, retail, and real-estate interests to negotiate with the agency and save the trees.

Against the backdrop of Three Sisters Mountains—once named Faith, Hope and Charity—the town has pounced on every conceivable niche in the year-round tourist trade. Through aggressive marketing, it draws throngs for golfing, sightseeing, sailing, fishing, hiking, boating, camping, swimming, climbing, rafting, and horseback riding during the summer, hunting in the fall, and snowmobiling and downhill and cross-country skiing in the winter. Thanks to the Chamber of Commerce's indefatigable sponsorship, Sisters has become synonymous with a June rodeo, October harvest festival, and a host of other seasonal promotions. On weekends, waves of urbanites from Salem and Portland descend on Black Bute, one of five ranches in the Sisters area.

Today, life could hardly be finer for the population of seven hundred. "Sisters was a scuzzy logging town that made Mill City look like a thriving metropolis. The people just got together and pulled themselves up by their bootstraps," says Atiyeh while driving through. "What does this place have that Mill City doesn't? A few false storefronts. Sure the weather is better, but not in the summer. It's just a spot in the middle of the forest. The choice for Mill City is Valsetz or Sisters. Do we change our ways or continue to stick our heads in the sand until we're gone? I wouldn't stand up and take the abuse and ridicule if I didn't believe it. My community and our way of life have to change. The world goes on."

Tourists rarely see the other side of Sisters outside the commercial district. In his pickup, Dave Moyer, a U.S. Forest Service employee and mayor, takes me on a tour of a half loop a few strikes away from the new bowling alley, Memory Lanes. We pass a thriving cabinet shop, a pillow and vest company, an auto body shop that just expanded, and a log home manufacturer. Just ten acres of space remain in the industrial park for future companies to occupy. "Light industry keeps this town going," Moyer says. That is by design. Sisters' Planning Commission has worked hand in hand with small businesses, cutting county red tape for water and sewer lines, not to mention laying down new streets and sidewalks. The town is clearly content to leave laissez-faire to the Northwest's Mill Cities.

The same spirit behind Sisters' reincarnation put Leavenworth, Washington, back on the map, farther north up the Cascade Range, one hundred twenty miles east of Seattle. In the 1920s it served as a major railway hub and home to one of the largest sawmills in the state. By the Great Depression, the railroad had closed its switching yard, and the mill, no longer able to haul timber by river drives, had unloaded its land holdings. It also sold the mill machinery and razed its sawmill buildings. During the late 1950s, two dozen empty storefronts in the commercial core were strewn with broken windows and rubble. The state's condemnation of the old high school touched off a heated feud among neighbors over the location of a new school.

Leavenworth might well have sunk without a trace had Project Alpine not taken flight. Merchants and building owners hatched various ideas for reviving the economy, from the establishment of a vodka factory to a Gay Nineties theme, before finally opting to exploit the mountain setting. The transformation proved so spectacular that *Look* magazine named Leavenworth the All-American City of 1967 "for pulling itself out of a serious economic slump." Today, drawing a million tourists from all over the Northwest each year, its Swiss Bavarian architecture mingles half-timbered stucco walls, overhanging roofs, balconies, flower-filled window boxes, and wrought iron signs. Hoelgaard's Bakery, the Susswaren candy shop, and all the other buildings—even the Chevron gas station—share the identical motif. From the moment visitors enter past an immense sign—*Willkommen zu Leavenworth*—they are immersed in the authentic Bavarian culture of costumes, music, and food. The shops sell German nutcrackers and cuckoo clocks. In the beer halls men dressed in lederhosen hoist imported beers. Marlin Handbells, a musical choir of fourteen dirndl-clad women, chimes away. Nobody seems to mind that its favorite, "Danny-Boy," hails from another tradition. The zeitgeist rings just as true.

Leavenworth understands that its two cash crops—the logging and forest products on which its economy still heavily depends, and its scenery—can coexist harmoniously. "In the Northwest we are particularly lucky to have incredible wilderness in our backyard," proclaims the *Sonnenschein*, the local newspaper, in the course of quoting John Muir. "These areas provide a variety of wilderness experiences from an afternoon's walk along the trail among the giants of the forest to a weeklong backpack trip amid sparkling lakes, lush meadows, and snow-covered peaks." Mill City treats Atiyeh as an alien for preaching a comparable wilderness gospel.

For all the wholesome appeal, recreation and tourism come far short of offering the Northwest a panacea. "We should not waste time looking for a pie in the sky," Hirons cautions the SWOT lunchers. Average wages in tourism jobs tend to be lower than those in the mills and are mostly seasonal and part-time positions. After all, how many tour guides or waiters take home twelve dollars an hour like a Mad Creek choker-setter? Beyond the financial considerations, it rubs cultural sensibilities raw to convert a logger into a Royal Bavarian hawker of gnarly corkscrews. Maybe some white-shoe lawyer from the Environmental Protection Agency in Washington, D.C., would be willing to come out and help clear tables at the Little Beaver Cafe.

Yet, as Sisters' and Leavenworth's attractions demonstrate, recreation holds the potential of underpinning diversification programs. That part of the labor force comprised of students, working parents, and retirees can match part-time positions with their lifestyles. The recreation industry also remains fertile ground for the small businessman sowing entrepreneurial seeds. In coming decades, the swelling ranks of retirees who have high disposable incomes, and baby boomers with families, will doubtless latch on to easygoing outdoor pastimes. In 1990, the latest year for which figures are available, tourism in Oregon created more than 46,000 jobs, a 24 percent increase since 1987. The industry's employees earned $520 million, a 63 percent jump over the same time span.

Idaho's boom has covered all the bases. Ten years ago rock-bottom prices for silver and wood matched the barren vistas of dreary, polluted towns scarring the state's northern section. Then food-processing plants and high-tech firms doubled their sales abroad and their work forces at home. Regions rich in natural resources have spawned small manufacturing enterprises along with tourist attractions. In Kellogg, a ski resort has supplanted the smelter. Coeur d'Alene, a retreat and convention center tucked away in the mountains, is attracting visitors worldwide. Sandpoint, an old mill community, saw a bathing suit factory open and flourish. From 1979 to 1989, Idaho's employment rose by 10 percent.

Mill City's own ideological stranglehold has kept it pinned to the past. "The owl's going to be listed. That's a fact," Atiyeh says. "You're talking about hitching a wagon to a falling star." The timber industry's *ancien régime* continues to resist diversification, the mantra of urban environmentalists and economists. Stories abound of the frigid receptions newcomers have encountered in threatening to disturb the status quo. The timber industry tried blocking a local golf course's upgrade, fearing it would attract clientele at odds with noisy logging trucks and unsightly clearcuts. "We're worried about tourism," Long says, acknowledging his own ambivalence. "The community doesn't want to change." Natives rue the outsiders overrunning their favorite childhood swimming holes and coffee shops. They resent their trash and human waste. The new elderly require medical services the town is ill equipped to provide.

Whether the vested interests like it or not, Mill City's economic metamorphosis is already occurring on Highway 22. The state Transportation Department's construction crews are out every day widening the thoroughfare through town to accommodate all the traffic. Girods' Sports Center retails bait and ammunition to locals and visiting sportsmen. At Panache Additions, the solder and stained glass Jay Swanson melds highlight nature themes. The oil paintings and sculptures sell well, too. If he had to depend on Mill City, Swanson admits, he would go under. "These things like Giovanni's Pizza exist because of the timber economy," Long says of the food he and the rest of us are enjoying at the SWOT lunch. Well, not quite. Since its opening three years ago by a young, attractive husband-and-wife team, business has exceeded their expectations four times over, and almost, they say, half of it comes from tourists. Giovanni's may represent the ideal enterprise, crossing over both markets. And, when eating there, Mill Citians prime the local pumps through the self-interest Jim Girod describes as the "circulating dollar concept."

Progress it is as inevitable as the rainbows ornamenting the Willamette Valley sky after a soaking spring rain. Traffic on Highway 22, already one of the busiest roads in Oregon, is expected to double by the year 2000. As a gateway to some of the most glorious landscape in the Northwest, Mill City will keep on grabbing weekenders and vacationers. Their destinations include Detroit Lake, a three-thousand acre play place for anglers and boaters. The North Santiam ranks at the top of the region's steelhead rivers, although dams and drift nets have depleted fish runs in the past few years. Rafters and kayakers ply its waters, pulling out at the landing in Mill City besides the old railroad bridge. In the fall, the hunters bag their big trophies. In the winter, skiers kick up snow in such ski areas as Hoodoo Bowl and Mount Bachelor. In winter, backpackers hike the Mount Jefferson wilderness area's trailheads in snowshoes, and in summer, in shorts.

Mill City enjoys golden opportunities to satisfy consumers' fluid appetites. For starters, a quality restaurant is in order. At the Frontier, parakeets flutter about as part of the live-bird exhibit to entertain diners during their meals. From my own informal survey, the experience is an acquired taste. ("Never eat the clam chowder," goes the joke around town. Hirons, for one, eats in another room.) A franchise along the lines of Denny's stands a good chance of packing in crowds. Mill City still lacks any motel lodging, although I cannot complain about paying $14.50 a night at Bill Anderson's small roadside motel in nearby Gates. A Best Western, or, better yet, a family-run bed and breakfast, might thrive if situated on the river. One woman in Mill City has hit on the idea of a laundry drop-off on Friday for a Sunday pickup, or a kennel. Venture capitalists call these "sleeper opportunities."

While Mill City must content itself primarily with commerce passing through en route to somewhere else, there exists enormous potential for repackaging it as a destination unto itself. For starters, it enjoys a monopoly on its name. Day to day, the town remains a living tribute to an exciting chapter in U.S. history, the pioneer and taming of the West. Mill City would do well to build on its popular logging competition featured in its July Fourth celebration by staging it regularly. On television, ABC's *Wide World of Sports* and ESPN have drawn wide audiences for such programs. Brawny men hurling axes and rigging spar trees rivals the rodeo in outdoor theater.

Mill City already boasts a collection of historic pieces it could dust off as attractions. On Evergreen between Fourth and Seventh Streets still sit company homes constructed under the decade-long reign of Curtis Lumber, Hammond's predecessor at the turn of the century. Their pyramidal roofs—popping up in four directions, and flat on top—radiate a cupcake charm. But they are in sore need of repairs. The quaint, historic wood frame buildings in Mill City's downtown, such as Stewart's, also harken back to the company town era when they served as recreation halls. At the deep bend off the highway, the sturdy white edifice with "Welcome to Mill City" painted in black once housed the Hammond store. Currently it sits mostly vacant. Any town's beautification begins at its front door; something as simple as an uncluttered sign on the highway could beckon visitors to Mill City.

At the end of Kimmel Park abutting the log pond in which Mill City's cooperative splashed its logs rest the carcasses of an old water tower and wigwam, the towering, upside-down ice-cream cone-shaped receptacles for burning woody debris before environmental restrictions closed them down in the 1960s. The three mills in town today might pool contributions to restore their relics as part of a logging museum showcasing antique logging equipment.

Upon hearing Wilbur Harlan's name bandied about at the SWOT lunch as an example of Mill City's model cottage industries, I pay him a visit. The eighty-year-old native personifies the kind of national treasure his town would do well to spotlight. Besides regaling me with stories of his life as a logger for half a century, he steeps himself in Mill City's memories, painting its history. Seven years ago, he followed his wife, Ev, into her art class out of curiosity. "I did not think I would ever paint," he recalls. "Good God, I cannot even paint the outside of a house."

While his classmates were applying their brushes to canvas, Harlan was pounding his old saws into artistic plowshares. His folk art originates from tole-painting, or painting on tin, in Norway and Sweden. The Harlans have painted objects as odd as washboards, water pumps, and plow blades, but primarily apply their paintbrushes to sandblasted bucking crosscut saws, circular saws, and buzzsaws.

At an early arts and craft show, his highbrow peers frowned on his creations as just "crafts," so he quit the guild. He ended up winning $150 at the 1989 Oregon State Fair for one of his saws, and has taken home the judges' choice award for the past three years. Today he sells about sixty a year at prices from thirty-five dollars to six hundred dollars. The couple has earned enough income from their work—eight thousand dollars last year—to pay for trips to the islands of Bora-Bora and Grand Cayman. His logging scenes, comprising about 80 percent of his portfolio, have won him imitators. One female classmate, in obvious admiration of his subjects and sales, depicted two fallers dropping a tree near eight men. "Nobody comes that close to the cutters," Mill City's Michelangelo advised her. "You'd better paint a couple of guys coming with a stretcher."

In a puckish moment, I commission Wilbur to paint for me not just any old rigging slinger or coyote, but the bane of loggers' existence. While doing his share of wildlife, since timber folks— as opposed to environmentalists—are his best customers, he has hardly been besieged by requests for the northern spotted owl. Of course, it takes a certain gumption to undertake the project in the first place. Joyce Trout, Harlan's only competition in town and a talented saw painter in her own right, politely declines. Two months after sending him my collection of magazine photos and the balance of sixty-five dollars, I receive the finest artistic rendition of the little big bird I've seen (including a *Time* magazine cover). The letter I write Harlan telling him so, emboldens him to do a second, for the state fair. "I see you have one of those damned spotted owls," growls a logger, pointing to the hole in the center of the saw and tree on which the endangered species was perched. "I see you missed him with the 30./30." Since I bought that one, too, from him, on my next trip, Harlan plans another.

Mill City's natural resources probably preclude it from ever becoming history like Valsetz. "The tree-covered mountains, the fast-flowing river, the salmon leaping over the dam were all things so new to me I considered Mill City a paradise," rhapsodized Otto Witt, in the town's centennial memoirs, of his arrival from Germany in 1909. Witt was no John Muir devotee, merely a Hammond millworker rejoicing in his divine fortune. Even if most of those mountains have been scraped bare from logging and some have grown back as second growth, Mill City remains beautiful.

Time and again, in the past, events forced moribund Mill City to raise itself from the ashes. A dose of the civic spirit that created the cooperative after Hammond closed during the Great Depression is just what it needs today. A generation later, with the dust still settling from World War II, the Chamber of Commerce hedged its bets. A brochure touting Mill City as "Oregon's Mountain Wonderland" devoted most of its text and photos to recreation. "There are no closed seasons on fun and relaxation for those who know this picturesque country," it declared. Aside from glorifying its easy access to prime old-growth fir for plywood, it lists among "POTENTIALITIES, wood toy and novelty manufacturing, furniture (plenty of alder and maple), cedar products (shingles, battery separators, etc.)." Well before it fell victim to its own success in logging old growth, Mill City was already looking beyond a one-horse economy.

Timber towns' fates hinge on their degree of self-sufficiency. Even under Bill Clinton, bare coffers in Washington, D.C., and Salem foreclose the possibility of much financial aid, except, perhaps, in the reverse form of such tax relief measures as enterprise zones and instructional programs outlined by SWOT. In the end, the responsibility for sinking or swimming lies with Mill City itself.

In coming decades, the greening of the Northwest's economy promises to cut into traditional development of its abundant raw materials. Ed Whitelaw, a University of Oregon economics professor and advisor to the state's governor, Barbara Roberts, has invented the popular "two paycheck" theory to describe the phenomenon. If Americans followed the highest wages, we would all live in New York and California. In fact, we choose to live in an area because of the environmental, cultural, and educational opportunities it also affords. "Every worker in Oregon receives, in effect, two paychecks," he argues, "one dominated in dollars and the other in the state's clean air, clear streams, scenic vasts, publicly owned beaches, and forested mountains." Such resources translate into more jobs and tourism and recreation. The Northwest's billion-dollar salmon industry, with sixty thousand employees, depends on water unpolluted by logging.

In 1991 the Institute for Southern Studies, a nonprofit group based in Durham, North Carolina, rated Oregon the top state in the United States in its "Green Index." It based the ranking on environmental conditions and legislative policies in such areas as air and water pollution, toxic and waste disposal, land use, and recreational opportunities.

Damage to these assets drive workers away. At the same time, it reduces the state's economic competitiveness by lowering the standard of living for those who remain. "It's the conflict between old and new engines driving the economy," adds Atiyeh. "The old is timber and the new is livability. People may be greedy and want material wealth. But they also want clean air and clean water." Opal Creek's intact watershed, for example, ensures crystal-clear water; once a pristine and free resource for nearby timber towns. They are now having to install costly water treatment plants to mitigate siltation from logging. "Those guys," Atiyeh says, "are peeing in the pot."

He remains convinced that one day his Mill City neighbors will thank him for doing them a favor. "It's the dumbest, damnedest thing I've seen. In ten years, when Opal Creek becomes a significant part of the economy and people are loving it, you watch the revisionism. I've seen this with [federal] wilderness areas and the forest," Atiyeh says. "This community will recognize Opal Creek is the best thing they have for their long-range plans. Just think of an 'Ancient Forest National Monument.' "

Oregon's appealing environment, in effect, socks away money in the bank. Whitelaw has sought to tabulate the account's balance by using earlier studies to identify fringe benefits, such as museums and symphonies, and social factors, including the crime rate. After calculating these cultural and community-service pluses or minuses, most of the researchers have concluded that the residential benefit of environmental amenities equals 3.5 percent of monetary wages currently paid in western states. In the late 1980s Oregon's personal income from all sources averaged $40 billion annually. At 3.5 percent of this total, the dividend comes to about $1.4 billion, or roughly $500 per Oregonian. The figure represents more than one quarter of the entire payroll of all manufacturing firms in the state, $5 billion, and almost as much as the entire payroll, $1.75 billion, of the lumber and wood-products industry.

For the Northwest to keep issuing second paychecks, it must maintain the inheritance California has partially retained. New businesses entering from the Golden State base their decisions to come precisely on those aspects of quality of life that scattershot profits threaten. "If Oregon allows widespread air pollution from field burning, degraded streams, diminished fishing from logging, congested highways from poorly planned urban development, and nasty surprises from business that generates hazardous waste," Whitelaw contends, "it is unlikely to realize rapid growth in such potentially important sectors as high-tech manufacturing, international trade, and health services."

Mill City's regeneration frightens a lot of natives. Change usually does. The town is more than a wide place in the road tourists blow by en route to Sisters and Bend. Its tightly knit community breathes the family values of a bygone era. Fifty-seven couples have lived in town and been married for at least fifty years, a remarkable statistic in light of Americans' migratory habits. Mill City's immutable sense of place should survive the continuing influx of newcomers. The elderly, commuters, and entrepreneurs will have to adapt to its quiet tempo more than the town will adapt to them. That's why these new people come in the first place.

It probably will hurt the mossbacks to recognize that the most enduring treasure anchoring Mill City's future is the one with which they are least comfortable. A way of life geared toward the appreciation rather than extraction of natural resources augurs a dramatic change in life-style. Over the past twenty years, the loss of steel and coal industries has left towns in the Midwest and Appalachia grasping for straws in the wind. By contrast, the breathtaking scenery draped around Mill City features one of the biggest pieces of intact virgin forest left in the United States. Properly marketed, it could become a tourist mecca approaching the redwoods and sequoias in northern California. The short-term political gratification of beating George Atiyeh could cost his antagonists dearly for generations. Better that they preserve Opal Creek as a testament to their own foresight than log it to spite their own faces.

VI

Wing 'Em in the Knee

To reach Opal Creek from anywhere in the United States, first fly to Portland International Airport. If you prefer stopping in San Francisco, the ten-hour drive affords appealing views of northern California and southern Oregon's rugged landscape. Either way, take Interstate 5 to Salem, Oregon, forty-five miles from Opal Creek. Then head east on Highway 22 toward Mill City, past a series of clear-cuts. Signs for Newport point westward to Oregon's coast; that's the wrong way. About a half mile past Mehama, stop at a flashing light at the Swiss Village Restaurant. Turn left onto Little North Fork Santiam Road. Go straight, past Mill City, and you will have to hazard Gates Hill, the road from hell, where you might bend fenders with Tom or George.

Continue on Little North Fork, which turns to gravel, for about twenty miles. When Atiyeh was a boy in the 1950s and the road was unpaved, it took his family three times longer to make the trip from their home in Beaverton, outside Portland—over five hours—than it does today. At the Willamette National Forest Boundary, follow Forest Service Road 2207, the kind of artery that Hirons takes to jobs. Beware of the sporadic log truck on workdays. About three miles farther, hang a left onto Forest Service Road 2209.

The six miles on 2209 provide an ideal introduction to Opal Creek's wonders. The single-lane road lacks guard rails, so drive carefully—the better to enjoy the entrance into the sixty-eight-hundred acre basin. In the early Miocene and Pliocene epochs, from twenty-three million to seven million years ago, nature gouged and creased the earth to form the seventy-five-degree crevices hundreds of feet deep and thousands of feet across, creating these magnificent vistas. Ten thousand years ago Douglas fir coated the valley from the top of its walls, whose contours the road follows, to its floors below. The Northwest's temperate rain forests are kind to this V-shaped dimensional canvas. Puffs of white fog dance against the blue and green fir background like clouds in the heavens of a Romantic's landscape painting.

The drive along 2209 is bittersweet for Atiyeh. He can recall its sharp turns once striking considerably more fear in his heart— a dizzying possibility to imagine for any motorist today. For nearly half a century, the road of his childhood had remained a tribute to industrious Welsh miners, who had hand-carved it from a forest trail winding back and forth up these canyons with nothing more than mules, horses, picks, and sweat. On their beasts of burden, they ferried their heavy machinery, explosive powder, food, and other supplies up the mountains. When the Welshmen hit a stream, they merely cut down small trees to bridge it. Some of the narrower stretches were just wide enough to accommodate a horse, but not a wagon's four wheels. The miners snubbed the wagon with ropes around a tree, so the horse could swing it. While the two inside wheels teetered on the road's hairpin curves, the other pair hung in the air three hundred feet above the ridge's bottom.

On the old mining road of Atiyeh's youth, he sat fingers crossed in the rear seat of a big, old Plymouth station wagon as it teetered around the cliffs and corners. The driver—usually his Uncle Vic—kept his foot on the clutch the entire route. Craning his neck above the door handle, he saw only open space. For a child, the sensation was akin to going airborne.

Opal Creek probably would have been logged long ago were it not for Jim "Grandpa" Hewitt's hard-nosed visionary. He was the grandfather of George's cousin Tom and de facto grandfather of George after his had died. For four decades, Hewitt had used an old and soft law to keep title to the land and resources on it, including timber and minerals. He called the small mining camp he built in the cozy hollow amid Opal Creek's mountains "Jawbone Flats," and intended to amass a huge fortune from its underground riches one day. Viewing him as an obstacle in its path to control of the land, the Forest Service sought to wear down Hewitt into submission. With his resolve stiffening by the day, the

miner gained an unshakable respect for Opal Creek's scenic wonder, which he never expected the Forest Service to share.

Following in Grandpa's footsteps, Atiyeh continued his strategy
to defend Opal Creek. As long as the Forest Service had designs
on the trees, he would beat it at its own game. In exploiting
prodevelopment laws for mining to foil the agency's logging, he
has exposed the hypocrisy of the federal government's rampant
abuse of the nation's natural resources. The mounting pressure to
cut Opal Creek ultimately obliterated the friendship nurtured by
Atiyeh and Hirons during their two years together at Jawbone
Flats. So far the loss of his best friend, above all the financial
and personal prices Atiyeh has paid, overshadows any of the successes he can savor.

The Forest Service waited until the summer of 1964, while
Hewitt was away in Mexico, on one of his rare excursions from
Opal Creek, to exact revenge. He returned two months later to
find a long stretch of the familiar route he had helped thread
through the mountains four decades earlier bulldozed into obliv-
ion. Over the next two years, the Forest Service's scar came
within three terrifying miles of his home. The Forest Service had
announced its intention to extend the new road, for log trucks
or as a conventional highway, through the camp's guts by cutting
a tract across Cedar Creek, in Opal Creek's upper basin.

In the Forest Service's haste to punch its way toward Opal
Creek, it violated sound engineering principles. Atiyeh's employees at the mining camp must still clear persistent rockslides from
the heaving of deep freezes' relentless expansion and contraction,
the twenty-five-year-old echoes of engineers' misbegotten dynamite sticks. The government's maintenance leaves a lot to be
desired, since 2209 is—as long as Atiyeh can help it—an inactive
logging road. "This thing is a damned scar. What a monstrosity,"
Atiyeh says, behind the wheel of his Bronco. Hirons, who knows
the local highways and byways as well as anyone in the Willamette, concurs: "It's one of the worst roads ever engineered. The
Forest Service said, 'Let's just do it, the hell with the consequences.' It doesn't make any common sense. An absolute abortion." At $200,000 a mile, he estimates the road cost $1 million.
The first road's remnants, overgrown with weeds, jut out from
cliffs. Any log truck willing to risk it would undoubtedly have
taken its last haul.

Fortunately, the Forest Service's handiwork stops short of Opal
Creek. There is plenty of parking at the end of the six-mile
stretch of 2209, near a large green gate dominating Mill City

conversation. The Forest Service erected the first gate over half a century ago to prevent trespassing on the mining claims at Opal Creek. Today loggers seize on the triangular barrier of galvanized steel as the infamous symbol of Atiyeh's privileged dominion over the woods. But for the beginning or advanced hiker the gate amounts to a gateway to a magical journey a thousand years into the past. Most of the public experiences Opal Creek's wonders through the ninety-minute, three-mile hike along the original mining road the Forest Service left alone.

That peculiar juxtaposition is only fitting. For, above all, the route highlights the delicate symbiosis between man and the natural world. Except for the intermittent vehicle driven by a Forest Service worker, Atiyeh, or his staff, the road serves primarily as a foot trail. The inability of Shiny Rock's graders to smooth out the rocky rut yields in authenticity whatever it subtracts from shock aborbers and shoe soles. The stumbles occur with a frequency surpassed only by the surprises around each bend.

A mere two hundred yards past the gate, below the road to the right, stands the quintessence of old growth: the Governor "Guts" Gibbs tree, honoring Governor Addison C. Gibbs, who located a mining claim on Webfoot (now Whetstone) Mountain, a few miles away, while in office. Guts Gibbs earned his nickname for the intestinal fortitude he displayed keeping Oregon out of the Civil War. In 1865, he called the legislature into special session to ratify the thirteenth amendment to the U.S. Constitution, abolishing slavery. After receiving the caucus nomination for the U.S. Senate the following year, he lost the election by one vote.

The Gibbs tree shares with its namesake an uncommon strength the world all too often takes for granted until it's too late. The road envisioned by the Forest Service would have grazed the stately Douglas fir. At the peak of Gibbs's career, this spectacular Douglas fir is believed to have already reached a thousand years in age. (Biologists can determine a tree's age by boring a small, harmless hole in the trunk and counting the rings on the dowel-shaped sample.) Long before there even existed a United States, the tree had joined the class of ancients. It had seen five centuries in the years when Michaelangelo painted the ceiling of the Sistine Chapel. This Douglas fir had grown larger than a sapling in 1066, at the time William the Conqueror landed in England.

The sheer grandeur overwhelms any human beneath it. In size the Douglas fir ranks second only to California sequoias. This exemplary trunk bulges twice as wide as a six-foot-man's height. It takes a good half minute to walk the full circle at an average clip, past bark, as the venerable forester George Sudworth noted at the turn of the century, "which is often very rough with deep, wide furrows and great ridges." The tree shoots through the air the equivalent of a skyscraper's twenty-five stories; so high it's impossible to find its penthouse, the pyramid-pointed crown. The long shadows cast in odd directions play gyroscopic tricks with daylight. Fifty feet overhead, the understory's latticework of boughs and pine needles imitates the geometric patterns of a snowflake under a microscope.

A short distance beyond Gold Creek, the mining road leads down to the little North Santiam River and the Santiam No. 1 Claim. Two foreboding tunnels bracketing the river penetrate the landmark Lotts-Larson mine. In the late 1920s, miners dug out copper ore and processed it through a large mill right above the tunnel on the north bank. Nearby, there remains a boarded-up wooden door and an empty ore car on two rusting rails.

The mines at Opal Creek present a living history of a young nation on the run to the continent's farthest corners. The California gold rush sent droves of Oregonians spilling into their neighboring state in the hope of striking it rich. Bigger finds and homesickness drew them back to Oregon in the 1850s. The great wagon trains of settlers who had crossed the Plains soon led a reverse migration back home to the Willamette Valley, quadrupling the population to forty thousand in five years. Availing themselves of free land and farming, these frontiersmen planted their crops in the spring and harvested them in the autumn. During the hot summers, they headed up to the mountain mines. In 1859, when Oregon achieved statehood, the discovery of gold near Opal Creek afforded them the chance to live in their own backyards. The first claim that year is believed to have been near Jawbone Flats.

From 1860 through 1865, a total of 155 prospectors filed mining claims in the area. Among them were yeoman farmers, itinerant miners, and diehard optimists—a hearty lot eager for high adventure. Gutts Gibbs was one of many historical figures to make his mark here. In the Yakima Indian War of 1855 General Stephen Coffin led the Portland Volunteers on a daring rescue mission at the first battle in the Cascades. A well-trained cavalry and scouting patrol under his command guarded settlers on their way West. James Webster Perrit Huntington, President Abraham Lincoln's superintendent of Indian affairs for Oregon, launched his career in mining at age eighteen in 1849 when he joined a consortium of forty-three young, bold adventurers who invested in a ship and packed it with mining equipment back East. They sailed around Cape Horn to the port of Yerba Buena in San Francisco, later spawning one of the first mining companies in the heart of Jawbone Flats. Over the next century a procession of small-time miners continued to carve a living out of the extreme conditions in the mountains there.

The road meandering to the left leads to Whetstone Mountain and Gold Creek trails, a mineral buff's mecca. Early one Saturday morning, Bill Baumgarten, a mutual friend of Atiyeh and Hirons for the past twenty years and a frequent visitor to Opal Creek, leads the way. At the Eureka 13 Mine three miles up, we slide feet-first down a manhole-size hole into the rocky "adit," a nearly horizontal passage from the mine's surface. The old Welsh miners had single-jacked these marvels of engineering by hand, leaving just enough room for a man to carry out a load on his back. Our hiking shoes sink in mud the consistency of soup. Baumgarten rues the flickering battery-operated lamp helmets we took instead of the trustworthy antique carbide models stashed away somewhere in camp. They keep going on the blink, forcing us to feel our way along the slimy walls. Baumgarten hammers away with a pick at a spot he remembers as especially fruitful. Through a cloud of chips, we grab miniature lumps of ore, whose splendor remains a mystery in the dark. Once our eyes adjust in the midday glare outside, we gape at the treasure. On each specimen, dozens of icy quartz crystals leap toward the sun out of a metamorphic core speckled with zinc, copper, and gold—fool's and real—in a hand-held light show. Thanks to Baumgarten's perseverance, we come to appreciate Opal Creek's two faces, from the tall trees spanking the clouds to the earth's womb underground.

On the way down the Gold Creek trail, we notice fresh yellow ribbons fastened to trees and flapping in the breeze, the Forest Service's tools for demarcating a clear-cut. The agency recently decided to grant a logging permit for a sixty-six-acre private holding belonging to The Times Mirror Company. The Los Angeles-based company, which obtained the land through a series of transactions long ago, has had to decide whether to face the political controversy from selling or cutting valuable lumber or donating the parcel to conservationists. Atiyeh has sought to sway Times Mirror to work with him and the Nature Conservancy. Should the area, so close to Opal Creek, be logged, it would severely compromise the integrity of Atiyeh's proposal for a twenty-five-thousand acre park that Atiyeh is trying to resurrect since its legislative demise in Oregon's capital.

Back on the mining road into camp, a walk across the extraordinary half bridges provides a lesson in the ingenuity of backwoods engineering. The cliff was too steep to blast a platform for a full suspension bridge, so in the 1930s the miners, aided by mule and horse, crafted half a bridge from logs and dirt to span this seventy-five-foot ravine. The present structure, built by Hirons and Atiyeh, is a faithful reproduction of the original.

The Forest Service trails peeking out of the woods owe their birth in the 1930s to the Civilian Conservation Corps (CCC), Franklin Roosevelt's favorite program and perhaps his most critically acclaimed. At the Great Depression's peak, the president strove to employ able young men to conserve America's natural heritage. From southern pines to northwestern firs, 2.5 million men earned a dollar a day protecting and restoring woods, beaches, rivers, and parks, building wildlife shelters, preventing forest fires, and providing flood control. The CCC did half of all the forest planting, public and private, in U.S. history. A half million enrollees in Roosevelt's Tree Army lived in camps, including a sizable contingent at Opal Creek; they took over and rehabilitated some of the first cabins built at the site at the turn of the century. At the hillside's edge, a skein of underbrush partially conceals crumbling red brick fireplaces and mulching gray boards, the ruins of a bunkhouse and cookhouse slumping into the ground. Listen to the haunting wind, to the youths still inhabiting the ghost town.

The CCC's fire-fighting skills met the challenge handed out by the Industrial Workers of the World (IWW), in yet another historical chapter writ large in these mountains. In their organizing campaigns, the IWW, or Wobblies, fomented unrest across the Northwest as they attempted to provide miners and loggers with decent working conditions. To achieve its end, the outlaw union resorted to tree-spiking, a form of sabotage that caused mayhem in the mills. In recent years, it has found favor among certain elements of the environmental terrorist group Earth First! When the Wobblies instigated cookhouse fights at Jawbone Flats, Hewitt ran them off with a shotgun. Three days later, a mysterious fire swept through the upper camp and jumped the creek to the forest beyond. The CCC and miners rushed out to douse the flames.

The next highlight on the tour is a walk through the Bertha E. Hewitt Memorial Grove. The absence of dense undergrowth and the road's slight incline offer a panorama of ancient trees, a nineteenth-century master's landscape brought to life. It matched Jim Hewitt's generous spirit to have dedicated one of Opal Creek's crown jewels to his wife rather than appropriate it as his own monument. The patron saint of Jawbone Flats inspired the movement his nephew carries on today.

The special breed of American adventurer James P. Hewitt personified has long since disappeared. Fighting on Europe's front lines in World War I, Lieutenant Hewitt contracted emphysema from mustard gas. He returned to his native Florida to build houses at the peak of the 1920s real-estate boom. A gambler at heart, Hewitt then decided that the Sunshine State promised a mere fraction of the riches available elsewhere. On a map he drew a line from Florida to just about the farthest points north and west. In early 1925, the thirty-nine-year-old Hewitt and his wife, Bertha, headed West to strike it rich.

In Portland he hooked up with a contractor, A. W. Dawes, who personally introduced him to the gold, silver, copper, lead, and zinc mines at Opal Creek. Hewitt considered the mine an golden business opportunity, and agreed to work for Dawes as a superintendent. By dint of his intelligence and will, he managed to merge the mines in a single venture and, within a few years, pooled resources and capital to launch Jawbone Flats' first major mining company. Over time, Hewitt would end up owning it all and outlasting everyone. "His interest in the mines was making money. His vision was to build a mining empire in the canyon," recalls his daughter Thelma. "They don't make his kind anymore. There aren't many men that dream like he did. He stuck to it. He was not one to expect somebody else to do it for him. He was a dreamer and a promoter, a real good one."

Hewitt's first enterprise, Amalgamated Mines, proved an instant success. From 1929 through 1934, six dozen miners kept the zinc and copper operations running full blast seven days a week. Most of his laborers were hiding from the law in one way or another, allowing Hewitt to pay them low wages or in stock until they struck pay dirt. In keeping with his eternal optimism, he believed the mother lode lay under every hill and rock. One-lane roads twisting among the mountains led to scores of claims he staked hither and yon. As the ore piled up in the mine shafts and at the mills, most of the profits were poured back into improving production. Slack periods late in the Great Depression ended at the outset of World War II. High demand for metals to feed the nation's military machine yielded a bonanza for Hewitt. Deep into the nights, the ore mills loudly crushed the rock. Through the Reconstruction Finance Act, Amalgamated received an infusion of money to speed up the big steam engines that turned mill wheels and compressors, sending ore along a conveyor belt into crushers and on its way to market. Hewitt owned the largest operating mill in this region of the Cascades.

His daughter Thelma Hewitt Bowman considered her three years at the mines from 1947 through 1950 paradise. Her husband, Bill, caught wild brown trout in the Little North Fork for dinner or breakfast long before hatchery fish appeared in the county. "One of the good things up there was the wild blackberries. Oh, man, we'd pick those blackberries; nothing like them for pie," Thelma related to Cherie Copeland in *The Santiam Legend*, a newsletter of local history and genealogy. "We picked huckleberries, too." She enjoyed watching cougars and bobcats frisking in and out of the brush. The bears' occasional visits particularly thrilled her.

One winter it snowed for three months steady—twenty-two feet altogether. Her husband, Bill, shirtless in the sun, kept busy all day just keeping the roofs and the windows clear to avoid cave-ins and allow light in the darkening cabins. The tunnel walkway he maintained exceeded his six-foot-seven frame and the full length of his shovel. On the radio's nightly news, the couple heard a bulletin aired by her sister's husband in town assuring them help was on the way. "We needed rescuing like we needed a hole in the head. We were happy. We made our own bread and stuff like that. We had all the staples we needed," Thelma says. "We didn't care whether we were left up there or not. I actually resented it and I think Bill did, too. There we were, snug as a bug, really." Bill hardly seemed to mind at all being coldcocked by a block of ice from a hundred feet above. He awakened one day on a path he had dug out in a befuddled stupor. The bomb nature dropped lay beside him on the ground. But for a hat on his head, Bill might have been history. "It was the most beautiful territory in the winter. We lived in this winter wonderland. We would snowshoe all over," Thelma says. "We stayed so healthy as long as nobody came from town. We never had colds or anything. It was the good life. It's lovely being snowbound, it's so quiet, just lovely."

Over the following two decades of peacetime economy, nature snuffed out Amalgamated's shrinking business. The abundance of scrap metal from the war depressed prices. Hewitt continued to bide his time, thanking the gods in the spring for putting him through another harsh mountain winter. In 1948 his luck turned. A big snow in the Cascades struck with shipwrecking vengeance. Five big miners who had crawled atop the ore shed could not shovel fast enough through the blinding waves of snow to prevent the roof from caving in. They escaped, but Amalgamated never completely recovered from the financial loss. By law, each year Amalgamated had to invest just a hundred dollars in upgrading to keep its claim active. It spent most of the time retimbering the mines and doing exploratory work. The rough roads remained in perpetual need of repair. Hewitt clung to the hope his ore would reach profitable levels again.

To stay afloat, Hewitt tried branching out into new ventures, such as the Santiam Copper Mine. Two hundred fifty shares of stock of dubious value went on sale for a hundred dollars apiece. Miners received it in lieu of hard wages. Down in Mill City over stiff drinks, Hewitt regaled friends with tales of the mother lode he was sure he sat atop at North Fork. He could find few takers for the tailings in the shafts waiting to be refined.

Then the Blizzard of '64 whipped through Jawbone Flats on a deadlier rampage than the last, lifting the snow like a curtain above the cabin windows. Half the 220 inches of snowfall from January 1 through spring came down during the first three weeks of March. Late that month, a relief party dug through to bring the Hewitts supplies. E. Nazwood Billy, Hewitt's assistant, had attempted to drive out two days earlier. After five miles on the mining road, he broke his truck's axles in an aborted effort to crash through the heavy snow. Billy hiked the last eight miles to the nearest home, that of Louis Myers. "I'm getting tired of it—son-of-a-gun," he said of the weather. Myers and Mehama timberman Bud Johnson hopped into a four-wheel pickup equipped with shovel and chains. Starting at 9:00 A.M., for three harrowing hours they bucked over the icy mountain track to pack in grubstake—supplies furnished a prospector on the loose promise of a piece of the discoveries—to Jawbone Flats' snowbound residents. Hewitt and his wife, Bertha, had run low on fresh food, gasoline to power their generators, and news from the outside world. They learned that their son-in-law, State Representative Vic Atiyeh, had filed for the State Senate.

The boyish insouciance the seventy-six-year-old conveyed to his company about Amalgamated's prospects proved illusory. "We have quite a lot of ore blocked out. All we need to do is to get the road fixed and get a concentrating mill here," Hewitt assured his company. A few weeks later, an Indian summer turned winter's excess into spring's flood. Hewitt's ore, valued by him at $1 million in processed form, washed down the canyon along with all his aspirations for financial success. Through the rest of his lean years, he sustained himself on Social Security checks and Opal Creek's precious beauty.

Even disasters never dampened Hewitt's enthusiasm for the wilderness experience he scratched out of Opal Creek. In the lean years, when Amalgamated bled red, he could have blown away 90 percent of the mountainside to extract 5 percent of it, just as the larger operations did, or converted to an open-pit operation. After all, his own daughter spoke of his burning ambition to amass a mining empire. But he also knew bulldozing the dirt back into place, as the law required in later years, would have restored the land to its original state no more than a tree farm approximates an old-growth forest. Hewitt instilled in his grandson Tom Atiyeh and in Tom's cousin George an enduring respect for nature.

On the trails he helped whittle through the mountains, Hewitt taught them to appreciate their surroundings' singular beauty and serenity. The wild shock of silver hair atop his long, craggy face fluttered in the breeze as he scampered through the woods dispensing wisdom. In the evenings they would gather in the Big House crafted from downed trees to hear him spin yarns about Jawbone Flats' heyday. Hewitt's luxuriously appointed home bedazzled the boys. From the 1920s until it burned down in 1977 in a fire ignited by a propane heater, the spectacular furnishings remained as reassuringly constant as Opal Creek's sunrises. The Big House was impeccably appointed with a baby grand piano that came around the Horn; gorgeous oriental rugs; overstuffed couches; tortoiseshell lamps; leaded bookcases; kerosene lamps; crushed red velvet curtains; wind-up Victrolas; wicker chairs; brass transits and scales; little black, speckled pots and pans; tin plates; and amethyst glasses. In the house's resemblance to a museum's period room, time seemed to stand still much in the way nature does amid Opal Creek's ancient forests.

In an expansive mood before dinner, Hewitt sipped "old socks," his homemade firewater, so named because it dripped from a still through socks with the toes removed, or J. W. Dant Bourbon and branch water flavored by the mountain streams. On the nights when mossy sediment turned it cloudy, he admonished the boys for riding the flume, the three-foot-wide and one-half-mile-long wooden channel funneling branch water into the kitchen faucets, instead of the creeks' natural slides. The boys felt important sitting at Grandpa's feet. "Never forget, we're the mountain people," he counseled them. "Don't trust the flatlanders."

Hewitt, an entrepreneurial Henry David Thoreau, looked back

at the self-reliance he had personified in his own Walden Pond as the ideal antidote to materialism and the rest of civilization's maladies. Survival in these parts distilled life's true essence. Though he never struck pay dirt in his sunset years, Hewitt was able to bequeath priceless values to his progeny. He found a receptive disciple in his grandson Tom Atiyeh and Tom's cousin George, whose own grandfather died the year he was born, 1948. Little George eagerly adopted Hewitt as his own grandpa.

With maturity, it began to dawn on Atiyeh that Hewitt's courtly demeanor and whiskey-sweet southern drawl masked the soul of a warrior. From the instant he first moved into Jawbone Flats till the day he left forty-three years later, Hewitt and the U.S. Forest Service waged a cold war against one another over its control. The federal government deemed it its prerogative to maintain full access to Opal Creek, lock, stock and barrel. When cool persuasion failed, it tried hounding Hewitt out of his beloved camp.

Since Gifford Pinchot first created the Forest Service in 1905, the green gold growing aboveground and yellow gold beneath it have pitted lumberman against miners. Periodically, the Forest Service, under pressure from northwestern politicians trying to keep the cut high, levels charges of an immense "timber grab" by claim stakers on thousands of acres. According to a law from the nineteenth century, patents on the lands give miners full title to all resources, including the timber.

The Forest Service fired the first shot in the summer of 1933. It informed Hewitt of plans to take over the mining operations and turn them into a public thoroughfare, at risk to Jawbone Flats' private properties as well as its extensive mining and milling operation. Hewitt had spent thousands of dollars on the original road across established mining claims and always kept it open to the Forest Service. At the very least, he was due some compensation or else he would continue to "resist the confiscation," Hewitt wrote Henry Wallace, the secretary of agriculture (which oversees the Forest Service), in 1939. Six years earlier Hewitt had upbraided the forest supervisor over this "matter of justice." Years later the agency welshed on its agreements to pay Hewitt $50,000 and grant him easements on mill sites.

The Forest Service never bargained for Hewitt's fury. Like Hank Stamper, Sr., the noble curmudgeon in Ken Kesey's northwestern epic *Sometimes a Great Notion*, Hewitt "never gave an inch." "Grandpa used to put a rock in the road," Atiyeh recalls. "By the time the Forest Service moved it, there were two others in its place." His legal tactics gave the bureaucrats fits. Hewitt, the master of mining law's intricacies, held them at bay until they had to retreat in advance of winter's snow. "You never want to kill them, boy," he advised Atiyeh. "Just wing 'em in the knee." Atiyeh was dimly aware that the philosophy he was absorbing sprung from a man well ahead of his times. Hewitt became an activist before the term came into vogue, not as a career move or political fashion statement but out of devotion to a place he devoutly believed was worth conserving.

By 1969, Hewitt's wife had already passed away when he broke his hip in a fall outside the cabins. His family put him in a nursing home to ensure that he received proper care. Two years later, with the end nearing, Hewitt pleaded to see his mountains one final time. His family thought the trip would put too much strain on the frail eighty-five-year-old. George's fear of shouldering the family's blame if an accident happened tempered his desire to grant Grandpa's last wish. Hewitt died within a few months, adrift from the spot on earth he most cherished. Atiyeh still ranks his timidity as one of his life's biggest regrets. In Grandpa Hewitt's memory, Atiyeh took up the battle cry "wing 'em in the knee" to keep the crusade alive.

"ENTERING JAWBONE FLATS, POPULATION 8." Around the turn of a bend, the hand-painted sign is nailed to a tree. The road suddenly dissolves into a clearing straight out of a movie set. Ankle-high log fences and stones trim impeccably manicured lawns. On both sides of the road, a collection of modest grayish weather-beaten houses with steep tin roofs and spacious front porches stands at the end of graveled paths. The total sensation is of stepping back into time in the old, old, West. Despite modernizing these alpine cabins inside with creature comforts and repairing foundations over the past two decades, Atiyeh and company retained the original exteriors. The smattering of new buildings have all been constructed from the same rough-sawn, native materials used in the historic buildings. The designs are characteristic of the Cascade vernacular, a rustic style that blends into the woods. "I'll tell you what's so unique about Opal Creek," Hirons concedes. "Jawbone Flats, the mining camp, and history behind it. The whole damn thing."

Please sign the guest book as five thousand have at last count. The barking dogs summon Tin Cup from the cabin to welcome you. What better symbol of this fairyland in the woods than this bearded, elfin man, the spitting image of a troll? Don't be afraid. Paul, or Tin Cup, as he prefers to be known, works for Shiny

Rock on weekends and in Jawbone Flats' cluster of mines at other times. A friendly, outgoing sort, he is a fount of knowledge of Opal Creek's highlights and history. If you are lucky, you may hear him sing one of the mining ditties he's penned: "Jawbone miners dig the muck/Jawbone miners don't give a . . ."

Jawbone Flats sits in a hollow sculpted by glaciers and volcanic eruptions ten thousand years ago. It sits at an elevation of 2,050 feet, rimmed by cozy mountain walls cuffing the clouds 5,000 feet above. The Little North Santiam River's headwater tributaries feed into the confluence of Battle Ax Creek and Opal Creek, presenting an aquatic serenade's perennial murmur. In the night's stillness, beneath the glistening galaxy overhead, the dulcet sounds keep a person company.

Jawbone Flats, the last intact and operating mining town in the Cascades, still survives largely for the same reasons its old growth does—a location too remote for scavengers. Built in the early 1930s under Hewitt's supervision, it served as a residence for married miners. Hewitt segregated the rowdy bachelors in the upper camp. Legend has it that the constant chatter between husbands and wives gave Jawbone its name.

In its heyday more than sixty years ago, twenty-seven separate structures comprised the flourishing town of Jawbone Flats. There was a cookhouse to feed the miners, a community hall to raise a little hell, bunkhouses to sleep it off, and showerhouses to remove occupational grime. Business at the infirmary picked up after periodic gunfights. The town also boasted a sawmill, commissary, paymaster's office, and scores of cabins. Covered walkways between the buildings in the lower and upper camps and the mines allowed workers to stay indoors from waking to sleeping in all sorts of inclement weather, particularly the harsh winters.

Of all the individuals to exemplify Jawbone Flats' rough-and-tumble values, E. Nazwood Billy stands alone. The Navajo Indian had served as a B-29 tail gunner in raids on Japan in World War II. Out of the Air Force, he supported himself in warm seasons operating his own sheep, goat, and cattle ranch in northwestern Arizona and touring the rodeo circuit as a bareback rider. Billy honed his bronco-bucking skills in his cabin on a saddled barrel strung from the rafters by rope. On and off the job, Hewitt's wintertime aide from 1955 through 1968 remained in perpetual motion, loping through camp on the balls of his feet like a little antelope. The Indian's quirks and steadfast allegiance to Jawbone Flats forever enchanted a young Atiyeh, imbuing him with an abiding interest in the Native American as a quasi-archetypal natural man. He invited a group of them to bless Opal Creek to observe the twentieth anniversary of the first Earth Day.

In the winter of 1968, with Billy gone and Hewitt away, twenty feet of snow fell at Jawbone Flats. Upon finishing college and meeting his obligations in the military, Atiyeh had felt Opal Creek's familiar pull. His foreign travel plans were put on hold. Instead, he tried rushing to the defense of his favorite place on earth, to pick up where Grandpa Hewitt had left off, in a seamless succession of familial duty.

Atiyeh had to wait six months for the thaw, marking the longest vacancy at the camp since Hewitt first arrived in the 1920s. It took four weeks for Atiyeh to cut his way through the blowdown to the camp. The snow had leveled a quarter of the buildings—crushing roofs, snapping rafters, and cracking two-by-six joists. Atiyeh used a Caterpillar to push the wall back in Hewitt's Big House. He lived alone for six months pondering his next move until his hippie acquaintances joined him to do crude assessment work in the mines so they could stake a legal claim to remain there.

In the early spring of 1970, Atiyeh had decided to come down from the mountains to scout college campuses, then the center of the hippie revolution, and bring back a wife. All he had to his name were his pack and his dog. The woodsy Lothario auditioned women each weekend up in the mountains. Deanne fell completely under the spell. One evening he came home to find his house clean, the curtains sewed, and dinner served. Following their wedding on December 5, the newlyweds scrounged up three hundred dollars to buy canned food—enough to sustain them through a winter at Opal Creek on a prolonged, glorious honeymoon.

Atiyeh's enthusiasm for restoring Jawbone Flats rose almost in direct proportion to his family's flagging interest in keeping it. Although the commotion had subsided since the altercation with the Forest Service and the State Police, Vic Atiyeh, who had become executor of Hewitt's estate on his death, wanted to appease his wife by unloading the property they now owned. The social desolation Hewitt's daughter had to endure as a child living among crusty old miners far from girls her age soured her on the place early on. The small mountain of debt Hewitt had accumulated simplified Vic Atiyeh's decision to come up with a buyer. His son Tom and nephew George realized a financial angel had to be found fast, lest Opal Creek soon fall into the wrong hands.

Acting on Vic's behalf, they turned down four offers because the buyers viewed the property with only dollar signs in their eyes.

From the mines, Tom Atiyeh dashed off a letter to Rick Schaefer, a fraternity brother and housemate of his and George's at the University of Oregon, and a native of Hawaii. The correspondence proved auspicious. Schaefer is the godson of Thurston Twigg-Smith, the great-great-grandson of the missionaries Reverend Asa Thurston and his wife, Lucy Thurston. They and their inspirational voyage from New England with a pioneer missionary company in 1820 inspired the fictitious Abner Hale family in James Michener's historical novel *Hawaii*.

Twigg-Smith has dominated the island's society as a presslord since taking over the family-owned *Advertiser* in 1961. On paper, Twigg-Smith possessed all the right attributes for assuming control of Jawbone Flats. His publishing and real-estate empire in Hawaii put him in the upper echelon of American magnates. An eager philanthropist, for most of his life he has tithed to various charities supporting the arts. (In 1992 he donated his stamp collection, worth $8.2 million, to Yale.) Twigg-Smith's interest in conservation had led him recently to acquire scenic real estate on the mainland, in New England, and he was shopping for more. His godson, Schaefer, sang the Northwest's praises to him. Most importantly, Twigg-Smith, a Yale graduate (class of 1942), had the brains to outwit the Forest Service in tandem with George Atiyeh.

On July Fourth, 1972, only four days after being approached by Schaefer, Twigg-Smith and his brother David hopped on a plane to Oregon to spend the weekend at Jawbone Flats. Tom Atiyeh picked them up at the airport in a four-wheel-drive. Riding up the mining road, Twigg-Smith fell in love at first sight even before the Atiyehs led him on a regal tour. In Eugene, he learned from the Willamette Forest's regional supervisor, Zane Grey Smith, that the status of Opal Creek's timber remained in limbo. Twigg-Smith did not even have to return to Hawaii to think it over. The place absolutely bowled him over. "It's such a gorgeous spot. You walk in there and fall in love," the tycoon says. "You feel the majesty and romance of those giant trees standing when Columbus landed on the other side of the continent. I'd seen the giant redwoods back in the 1930s. There's nothing really like those. Still, Opal Creek is much more of a primitive, untouched area. The big Doug fir there, they are really the wild ones, different from the stands of redwoods in parks."

Before the weekend was out, Twigg-Smith and Vic Atiyeh huddled in Atiyeh's Portland living room and set the price on a yellow legal pad. "My father's an Arab and will be insulted if you don't negotiate," Tom Atiyeh told the Hawaiian. He asked for more than $1 million, whereupon Twigg-Smith offered $60,000.

Jawbone Flats changed hands for $101,000. Advertiser Publishing Corporation (the Honolulu-based company was subsequently reorganized as Persis) now owned the mining claims on three thousand acres, equipment, buildings, fixtures, oriental rugs, and furniture. The extra $1,000 paid for Hewitt's baby grand piano.

George Atiyeh urged him to return to Jawbone Flats' basics. The mining operation's revival would fulfill dreams he had nursed since sitting at Grandpa Hewitt's knee. Underneath filial fidelity Atiyeh admitted ulterior motives. While college classmates studied revolutionary politics or skipped classes altogether, he had been immersing himself in economics and geology in his second education at Portland State on the way to becoming a certified miner. On his own, he devoured bookshelves of dusty old mining books in the Big House. In the course of his research, Atiyeh mastered the ins and outs of a relatively obscure legal statute Grandpa Hewitt had talked about. Under the General Mining Law of 1872, patented claims on public land can be converted into private property for as little as $2.50 an acre, depending on the quality of the deposits. The antiquated law was aimed at speeding settlement of the West.

As long as there stood a fair chance of the claim paying out, Twigg-Smith could keep title to the land at Jawbone Flats, plus the minerals and timber on it. The government can challenge miners of unpatented claims if it has proof there has been no discovery of minerals sufficient to justify "a prudent man" in spending time and money for further development. Atiyeh has rarely prided himself on his "prudence" when Opal Creek is on the line. With an ironic flourish, he intended to stand a prodevelopment law on its head to preserve the environment instead of exploiting it.

Twigg-Smith wholeheartedly endorsed Atiyeh's plan, thus spawning Shiny Rock Mining Corporation, a subsidiary of Persis. "All throughout this conflict, our intent has been to preserve Opal Creek and turn it over to the United States for public use," he says. "We weren't being greatly noble." He thanked George's cousin Tom by sending him a gift, a book on wise land stewardship. Twigg-Smith, a corporate heir to Grandpa Hewitt, has backed his words with money to the tune of more than $6 million pumped into the mining venture. That includes $400,000 in 1978 for sixty acres of old-growth forest on Stony Ridge. The land was bought from Cascadia Lumber Company and would be worth $2 million today if cut. Young and Morgan tried to buy it first. "Are we buying timber or a lawsuit?" Vern Morgan, the mill's owner, asked. "A lawsuit," Atiyeh said. Persis has also picked up about $750,000 in the legal fees Atiyeh has rolled up contesting the Forest Service. The whole property, including the mines and timber, has been appraised at about $13 million.

Twigg-Smith's second investment through Persis, following the initial purchase through Persis, may pay the richest dividends over the long run. He put five families on the payroll for $150 a month plus food, clothing for the children, and medical coverage, to serve as caretakers at Opal Creek. George and Deanne Atiyeh, Tom and Marlene Hirons, Tom and Pat Atiyeh, and the families of friends Bill Baumgarten and Mike Broili leaped at the chance to spend the prime of their lives in paradise breathing the pure mountain air rippling through big, ancient trees.

Hirons had snowshoed up to Jawbone Flats with Broili in the winter and swam there in the summer. Tired of odd-job-hopping after finally acquiring sufficient credits for a college degree, he had reached a crossroads in his life. The strain of fatherhood at a young age had driven him to walk out on his family for a year. He figured Atiyeh's invitation might give him a new lease on life. The two men hit it off from the day Hirons first hiked into camp. "Let's go be hippies and live up in the mines to find out who you and I are," he told Marlene, chomping at the bit to remake a home for his wife, children, and himself. Hirons forever savors the memory of leading his family at night into camp without a flashlight. Little starlight permeated the narrow bowl in the mountains. Striking matches to find his cabin with only the sense of touch as his guard, he fumbled around in the darkest dark he had ever seen.

Jawbone Flats' lost and found generation from 1972 through 1973 shared a dream pure and simple. The creation of a commune, the rage within the counterculture then, was the farthest notion from their minds. Rather, the will burned in these young refugees from civilization to commune with nature and to escape from American society's bustling tempo and shallow values. All they sought was to live alone and be left alone in their own version of the country's back-to-the-land craze. Their utopian aspirations at Opal Creek were at a blissful distance from what Thoreau described in the nineteenth century as the "commercial spirit" infecting the nation. Stepping back in time in the heart of wilderness, they learned life's true meaning. Since man cannot exist in an island unto himself, even deep in the woods, Atiyeh spelled out an uncomplicated political agenda to his compatriots: Take full advantage of Jawbone Flats so the Forest Service would not.

Shiny Rock's first order of business was for the men to repair the dilapidated infrastructure. Each morning, after chopping wood to stoke the wood stoves, they gathered on a porch to set the day's plan of action. From dawn to dusk, the tip-tap of hammers installing new, tin roofs echoed throughout Jawbone's ravine. The cabin walls and holes were stuffed with insulation. Butter knives came in handy for the thinner cracks. Vacant for three decades, the Hirons's humble abode saw its attic converted into a children's bedroom. Hirons whipped the neophytes into bona fide loggers who could lift downed logs to rebuild the half bridges on the mining roads. His skills meshed well with Atiyeh's in mining as they shoveled out the rotten wood and retimbered mines.

Countless snowfalls had collapsed the flume line that once supplied the camp's electricity. They had to depend on a small gas generator for juice. Atiyeh launched an intensive project to provide power from water collected at the same dam site. In one of the first environmental impact statements filed on the Willamette, covering the biological repercussions of aquatic diversion for insects and fish, he kept the Forest Service off-balance by quoting Zen philosophy. A plastic pipe, the new flume line, funnels water downhill to a shed in the upper camp, turning a Pelton wheel and cannonading water through a pencil-thick nozzle before falling to Battle Ax Creek seventy-five feet below on its merry way back to nature. The plant generates twenty-five kilowatts of power—more than enough to power the light bulbs, videocassette recorder, and various appliances used by Jawbone Flats' present community.

The denizens now live luxuriously, compared to those first two winters. In cold weather, the pioneer women learned to chop wood during the day to keep the wood stoves well stoked. The conveniences suburban housewives take for granted with the flick of a wall switch demanded intensive labor. Laundry had to be handwashed in water piped in from springs and boiled atop the wood stoves. The clothes then dried on lines outside or inside from the wood fires' hot, dry heat. The temperature plummeted to fourteen degrees below in the first winter. With the pipes frozen over, in the mornings the men took the tractors they had bought through Persis to break Opal Creek's two-foot-solid surface for water. Crowded together, the ladies selflessly shared creature comforts. Drawing stove-heated water from a thirty-gallon tank, showers had to be limited to just half a minute. The grim visage on a Nixon poster hanging in one of the outhouses (visited only in emergencies today) reflected the discomfort of visits there on frigid February mornings.

Food presented far more challenges than a quick trip to the supermarket by station wagon. The women planned supplies for six months, in case they were trapped by snow. It took two trucks to bring in all of them in bulk from Portland. Dozens of cases of canned bacon, ham, and hundred-pound sacks of raw sugar and flour were stacked on the commissary porch. More than a ton of dog food satiated the canine population. The ladies bustled about swapping coffee for sugar and white flour for whole wheat as though in an Arab bazaar. A deep freezer chest preserved perishables, including a whole side of beef. To conserve electricity, it was only opened once a week, on meat days, Wednesdays. Marlene Hirons prepared powdered eggs for the first six weeks. "Honey, I'm pooping plastic," her husband announced. Pretty soon the wives elevated scratch cooking to an art form. The aroma of freshly baked bread and cake wafted through camp, driving the men to distraction during their chores. Each morning, Marlene's incomparable pancakes summoned Baumgarten and Broili to the Hirons's breakfast table like a bugle's reveille.

To combat cabin fever, the men—or boys, in the eyes of their spouses—were seldom short of ways to amuse themselves. In the hallowed memory of Grandpa, they rigged up a new old-socks still with hosiery and a pressure cooker. The batches of white lightning came from blueberries, raw sugar, or just about anything else lying around. The night Hirons got into the stuff during a poker game he prayed for salvation to deliver him from his misery the next morning. In hindsight, he would rather have dipped into the dreaded "horse piss," the camp's stash of fifty cases of Old English Malt Liquor, whose chief selling point was its rock-bottom price. In the winter the snowy, all-male touch football games, in which the players wore gray long johns, inevitably degenerated into tackle. On July Fourth at 8:00 A.M., while the rest of the camp slept, the boys proved their patriotism by launching a fifty-five-gallon steel drum loaded with sticks of dynamite at the site of the new ore mill. The sound of rattling windows and sight of their sleepy-eyed, stark-naked wives running outside to check the carnage capped the celebration. The women's own fling with pyrotechnics came the day of a lottery for the chance to blow up a tree leaning across the road. After drawing straws, the lucky winner depressed the handle fused to the tree a hundred feet away, to the accompaniment of the losers' cheers.

At nighttime the families did the best they could to overcome the still of wilderness. Kerosene lamps and lanterns, the only sources of light in camp, projected the eerie shadows of a horror movie against the walls as the children heard their bedtime stories. When the weather was right, they could pick up the distant tunes of Jimi Hendrix and Steppenwolf on Portland radio. They read voraciously—novels, history, the Bible, cookbooks, or just about any printed matter within reach. Hirons, who needs little sleep, stayed awake late turning pages with one hand and holding a flashlight with the other. It shone on a continual procession of mice climbing across the wall. One night he could no longer take the unwelcome visitors. Reaching for his .22 under the bed, Hirons unloaded. POP, POP, POP—missing by a country mile. Marlene levitated from the bed, unable to enjoy sound sleep in the camp again for a month.

Life at Opal Creek tightened the bonds between the Hironses and their children as never before. Marlene took advantage of Oregon's liberal home-school laws to pick up books from the Detroit School Board, a two-hour drive away, and become the principal teacher of Wes, six; Debbie, nine; and Vickie, ten. The students received their mother's instruction in spelling and reading from 9:00 A.M. until noon six days a week. In the evenings the men put their college studies to good use. The Hironses' father taught history; Baumgarten, math; and George, science. They and their wives framed their setting at Jawbone Flats through the wild West's exciting history. On the long hikes they enjoyed together through Opal Creek, Atiyeh and Hirons left the pencils and chalkboards behind to teach the children nature's wonders up close in outdoor classrooms.

Holidays at Jawbone Flats excited grown-ups and youngsters alike. Once a year, down in Salem, the Hironses bought party supplies matched to dates checked off a complete calender. On Halloween the women dipped into a steamer trunk containing the vintage clothes Grandpa Hewitt's three daughters wore long ago. Trying on the western dresses with big black polka dots and puffy sleeves, Marlene and Deanne fancied themselves as Miss Kitty from *Gunsmoke*. The long formals and two-layered, beaded flapper's dresses harked back to the Jazz Age. On the crisp, clear night, Marlene led her brood past Tom Atiyeh, decked out for the occasion as a troll under the bridge. The children received candy from Mike Broili, dragging a ball and chain in his cabin.

Knocking on George's door, they heard no answer. Suddenly he leapt out of the dark toward the porch in the full regalia of an Indian. Hot cider and apple-dunking in the Hironses' cabin helped soothe the little ones' nerves.

For the tooth fairy, all the adults scraped their pockets for loose change. Coins—or any money, for that matter—were virtually nonexistent in camp because there was nothing to buy. During their eighteen months at Opal Creek the Hironses somehow managed to sock away nine hundred dollars in spite of their meager salary. Even if they had saved nothing, the Hironses would have valued their time in the company of each other and the other couples. "In a city you don't get along with someone, you just move along. We were all very close friends because we were all we had," Marlene recalls. "Maybe the best part was being united as a family. We had to stay together." Teamwork spelled the difference between surviving and perishing in the wilderness. The mutual dependence back then sustains the close relationship today between Marlene and her married, grown-up daughters, who vacation together and are frequent fixtures in her Mill City video store.

Jawbone Flats' seclusion freed the homesteaders to follow their own drummer. Marlene protected her daughters from the peer pressure she found so corrosive in public schools, in keeping with the community's tolerant mores. If *Webster's* contained photos, Deanne or Marlene's could come under the entry "flower-children." Their hair hung low south of their waistlines—kept trim from the strenuous hikes and housework. Marlene's pair of pigtails dangled with the grace of tassels. The men did not look a whole lot different, save for the long, bushy mustaches. Standing side by side in cowboy hats on the edge of a bluff, they effected the appearance and sometimes the demeanor of Butch Cassidy and the Sundance Kid. The Hirons family album contains a photo of Tom's austere mother on a visit to the camp. The pained expression she wears says a thousand words of disapproval.

The mountains, like the Swiss Alps, formed a natural barrier to the outside world. Leaving caused as much physical and emotional strain as did entering. The camp was not primitive, just wonderfully isolated. Civilization was something to be avoided at all costs, other than emergency runs for supplies. Even then, not a soul volunteered to forfeit their Arcadian pleasures for the town's disruption. On a trip to Salem, amplified noise and dizzying movement from people and traffic gave Marlene a headache. She could hardly wait to go home to Jawbone Flats' bucolic confines. Atiyeh, as friendly as a hermit happening upon civilization, went around yelling "Howdy" to complete strangers.

In the creeks, bathing suits were not *de rigueur*. Atiyeh still holds them in about the same regard as he does tree plantations. "I have a real adversity to swimwear. It's the most absurd thing I've heard of in my life. Why would you have to put on clothing to jump in the water?" he asks. "When we were little kids, we'd take our clothes off to jump in the river. When we grew up, we did it as big kids, too. Even Forest Service district rangers do it, for God's sake." Baumgarten, a dropout from Berkeley and Oakland's mean streets, took to going *au naturel* like a duck to water. One afternoon he returned to camp from skinny-dipping dressed only on head, cowboy hat, and toe, boots. A lost family happened to bump into him. The mother waved her children away. As the father asked for directions, his sight never fell below Baumgarten's eyes.

Although the Hole-in-the-Wall Gang, as Tom Atiyeh dubbed the camp, kept the firearms under wraps, it still suffered from an image problem of hippie outlaws on civilized society's fringes. Tom printed postcards and affixed stamps with checkoffs for visitors to mail to the Forest Service indicating how well they were treated. "It was our PR move to prove to them we weren't tying up, raping, and pillaging all the hikers who came through," Tom Atiyeh remembers. Mike Broili, however, proved a star-crossed choice to greet guests as a well-wisher. Outfitted in an old leather cap and outsized star-shaped badge found in camp, he deputized himself sheriff. Intruders did not dare ask for credentials. "Badges, we don't need no stinking badges," he was fond of quoting from the movie *Treasure of the Sierra Madre*. Depending on his read of visitors, he either welcomed the friendly or sent home the hostile. For the latter, Broili updated Hewitt's motto "wing 'em in the knee"—"the more people we meet, the more bullets we need."

The camp had to maintain a constant state of high alert for intruders. Hikers came and went up the mining road. Hunters roamed the woods. Dangerous motorcycle gangs had set fires in the past. If Jawbone Flats' residents were not the law in this part of the wild West, far from the nearest sheriff, then no one was. In this era of bad feelings, an adolescent gang that had repeatedly vandalized a Caterpillar parked near the gate had the misfortune to be caught. Three campers—Mike Broili, Bill Baumgarten, and McDonald (before leaving for good)—gave them the third degree. One of the youths cursed McDonald under his breath. "Hey, Larry, he just called you an asshole," Baumgarten said. "What do you say we shoot them?" McDonald replied before whipping a .357 Magnum out and shooting it in the air. Baumgarten and Broili bent over while plugging their ears with their fingers. The terrified intruders left unharmed.

One evening in the dead of winter, the campers were about to prepare a fire in the Big House, Hewitt's central lodge, when a loud bang reverberated from across the road. Peering out the window, Atiyeh spotted a red Dodge pickup, the first sign of trouble because only the Forest Service and Shiny Rock had keys to pass through the gate at the top of the mining road. A motley band of ruffians had shot off the lock and was now taking aim at the commissary. Grabbing their guns, Atiyeh dashed out the front doors while his cohorts exited through the rear. Atiyeh marched head-on to the leader of the pack. "You gonna shoot me, kid?" he asked while moving toward him and fiddling with his .30/.30 at the same time. The click of cocked rifles wielded by the Shiny Rock crew announced their emergence from the bushes. "Looks like we got the drop on you," Hirons piped up from the side. After helping disarm the gate-crashers, Tom Atiyeh called the police on the camp's ham radio. The police thanked him for capturing escaped convicts from San Quentin.

Shiny Rock's employees could ill afford to let their guard down because peace seemed so elusive. By geographical circumstance and the political reputation preceding it, Opal Creek's fate has hung in a precarious balance for the past half century. The government's taste for its timber and the suspicions of its occupants have fired unending hostilities. It appeared next to impossible to go there without becoming caught in the crossfire.

On a quiet Thanksgiving weekend, Twigg-Smith decided to unwind from the business pressures in Hawaii at his new retreat. He and his brother David stood before the Big House's fireplace, soaking in the orange glow. The serenity gradually dimmed as the clatter of an approaching National Guard helicopter rose. It landed on a clearing above camp. Out leapt a SWAT team clad in fatigues to join a small militia that had surrounded the camp. "What the hell is going on?" Tom Hirons asked, gasping. The Treasury agents and State Police officers stormed cabins looking for a college friend of Atiyeh—on the lam—whom he hadn't seen in years. They presented neither explanation nor warrants. "I'm not ready," Marlene bellowed to a commando in her doorway. "I haven't cleaned yet."

Lest a few of the more abrasive paramilitary types persist in overstepping their lawful bounds, Tom Atiyeh dropped the name of his father, then an influential state senator, and called the state's attorney general. Tom also apprised them of his benefactor's clout as a big-time newspaper publisher and friend of officials in high places at the U.S. Justice Department. The authorities' jaws dropped a foot. Five hours after launching the invasion, the force faded back into the woods. Twigg-Smith, amused and astonished at the same time, sat down to muse about the mess he landed into by purchasing the camp.

With the days growing shorter and colder in the fall of 1973, Jawbone Flats' campers prepared to brace themselves for another harsh winter. The Hironses had second thoughts about continuing their employment at Shiny Rock. They were in the best physical shape of their lives from the exercise. Happiness and good health had reunited the family, a paramount objective in going there in the first place. "It was like a vacation," remembers Marlene. Unfortunately, all vacations provide at best a temporary flight from reality. She expressed bittersweet reluctance to her husband about remaining in log cabins their whole lives. The washer, dryer, refrigerator, and all the other appliances sold before moving to the mountains would have to be replaced. They would start life anew in the valley close to schools and movie theaters.

Tom, emboldened by the professional and parental maturity he had attained, readily consented to seek fresh challenges. "My dad had his doubts. But I knew when I went up to the mines it was going to lead to something good," he recalls. "I just wasn't sure what." The call of the woods beckoned him finally to parlay his contacts in the logging industry into North Fork Logging. On their final day at Jawbone Flats, the Hironses packed their belongings into his pickup and her little Toyota clear to the top. She hopped in the driver's seat and turned around—only to realize in her haste that she had forgotten to leave room for the children. On the ride, daughter Debbie straddled the gearshift.

In his third winter, Atiyeh weighed his own priorities. One bone-chilling morning he spied Deanne in the distance walking across the Little North Fork and carrying a splitting maul and a laundry basket. Sneaking up, George observed his wife beating a hole and washing diapers on her hands and knees. Their first child, Aziz, was two and a half, and number two, Arin, was on the way. For her sake, George felt compelled to ease the hardships of mountain motherhood.

For his own sake, he knew he had to move on as well. Every single day of the past three years had felt like a living dream. Food, shelter, and wood for the stove provided all the subsistence anyone could possibly need. He dwelled in the idyllc and—when not invaded—peaceful place of his choice with his loved ones. One hundred years ago, he might have kept relishing the luxury of his solitude. To his eternal regret, twentieth-century America has overtaken it. "Maybe I was fooling myself about the traditional goal-oriented garbage," Atiyeh says today of his itch then to join Hirons in the business world. To protect Opal Creek, he also had to come down from the mountains closer to the political action. Atiyeh struck a Faustian bargain with himself, forsaking Opal Creek on a permanent basis in exchange for the hope of saving it.

Toward that end, he threw himself into Shiny Rock. For two decades, thanks to his single-minded perseverence, its operation as a legitimate business has prevented the Forest Service from cutting Opal Creek. One of the many ironies of Atiyeh's venture centers on the striking similarities between mining and logging. "They are a lot alike. You're getting a few more feet underground and facing the mystery of what you're going to do every time you drill. Fire that round and go back and see if you have good ore from it," he says. "It opens up, you shine your light on it. It's like looking at a gem collection. Everything is shiny, sparkling. I do love mining. People think I'm crazy. It's something I've been doing for a long time." Atiyeh still savors the exhilaration many explosions ago of a round he and his crew fired on the fifth level of the Ruth mine. Slashed open, the vein revealed a glittering lode of lead, copper, zinc, and silver. In celebration, the miners sung, hugged one another, and danced little jigs on the platforms and tunnels.

Atiyeh has steeped himself in the lore of local mining to keep Shiny Rock steered on a true course. In his student days he tapped seasoned miners' brains all he could for valuable tips. Atiyeh was at once reverential toward the scruffy codger's affinity for the earth's bowels and curious about the wild streak they etched aboveground. The museum-quality collection of mining and drilling tools housed in the dusty old blacksmith's shop ranks as one of the finest in the Cascades.

Atiyeh's last brush with miners from the primitive school occurred a few years ago. Before the market's bottom fell out, Shiny Rock had contracted for a crew of drillers from California to stay at Jawbone Flats to drill for copper. On payday they spent their checks—with the ink still wet on the stubs—on refreshments in town. Atiyeh recalls them coming into camp bearing the cuts and bruises of a particularly savage evening. Rip-roaring drunk at the

Old Fish Hatchery Tavern in Mehama, the drillers wound up in a spirited debate with loggers over their respective talents for savaging the environment. The loggers boasted of ripping up trails and mountains. The drillers insisted their true mission was to find black gold. Once it started gushing, they vowed to let the oil pour down the mountainside. The debaters finally resorted to fisticuffs to settle the matter.

In a peculiar paradox, the Ruth mine's approaches own the distinction of being Opal Creek's ugliest spot by far. Decades of mining have left about ten acres of wasteland. Pale, gray tailings and rock litter the landscape abutting the embankment of a flowing stream. "No, I'm not proud of it," Atiyeh allows. In his raw mining days, Atiyeh recklessly flushed out sediment into the creek. The employees and wives were swimming downstream at the moment the water clouded up from the gunk. Their fury turned Atiyeh red with shame. He closed the mines until he could afford expensive pumps to filter the water. The spent mines soon became repositories for tailings. Cement seals prevent the waste from leaking acid into streams. He admits—usually in a fit of pique—to spraying cyanide solution, a highly toxic solution, for a month to keep the fool's gold from floating. Recent orders from the Environmental Protection Agency to clean up the waste site further sharpen the controversy over whether Atiyeh's end—safeguarding Opal Creek—justifies his sometimes ecologically impure means.

The troubled miner has wrestled with the contradiction between mining and preservation ever since prying into his first mountain. "We are all consumers of the planet," he argues. "Since we're all using metals, driving cars, somebody has to mine that from the ground. We're not going to shut down and go back to living in caves and beat animals over the head." Hirons cannot help but laugh hearing his friend's testy defensiveness. The rhetoric Atiyeh has adopted bears a carbon-copy resemblance to his own about houses and the multitude of necessities logging provides.

Atiyeh deflects the charge of hypocrisy by letting his environmental sensitivities take precedence over boardroom considerations. "Twigg-Smith bought this property because it was beautiful. You don't buy a work of art and destroy it. We've always had a conservation ethic," he says. "If we were traditional miners, the idea would have been to rip the side out of the mountain as fast as we could, take the money, and get out like the Forest Service does. Donald Trump would take the $6 million, which is what the Ruth mine is worth, and get the hell out in two years."

Atiyeh has struck a shrewd balance between political and economic goals. It behooves him to measure the impact of his activities so that Opal Creek's pristine condition ensures its potential eligibility for classification as a federally protected wilderness area. "We made a conscious decision to only extract from the land what we needed for as long as possible," he insists. At their peak, the mines' modest production, backed by Persis' largesse, has covered the annual two-hundred-thousand-dollar budget for Shiny Rock's crew's (five in summer and three in winter) overhead, and Atiyeh's own forty-thousand-dollar annual salary. "In his life," says parachute jumper and former Shiny Rock worker Joe Weber, "George has never bought high and sold low." It remains a tribute to Atiyeh's political and business savvy to have kept Shiny Rock going for so long by his own wits.

He believes spiritual forces prohibit him from digging and running, even were he so inclined. "Every time I thought about doing that the mountain actually sensed it. I said I was going to expand the mining operation," Atiyeh says. "Then the Cat wouldn't work and other stuff started breaking. There was something fighting against me." In the late 1940s, the Merten Lumber Company at Jawbone Flats, where the steam capstan from the battleship *Oregon* sits at the entrance to the camp, had to close down after losing two log trucks off the precarious mining road and over the mountainside. Nature had struck back.

Over the years, Atiyeh has seen more crashes than the Indianapolis 500. When the road gave out, a Caterpillar hung off the edge of a cliff over Gold Creek. Upon calling the insurance company, he learned it would have cost more to tow it out than to replace it. Atiyeh took the money and went to town where he bought equipment so his crew could winch it up themselves. He and Hirons then had two Cats, new and used, for the price of one. After hitting a rock while hooked up to a tree with a winch-line, another truck occupied by Atiyeh dangled over the edge of a cliff. "Nobody move!" Atiyeh said with a gasp from the inside. "Huh? I'm getting the hell out of here," shrieked an employee, whereupon he climbed over Atiyeh out the side door. Obviously, Atiyeh survived. A bridge collapsed under a backhoe, rolling the driver down a hill and knocking him unconscious. He awoke in a deep bed of moss and flowers, convinced he had gone to heaven. It may have been the mountains sending him a message.

Atiyeh's ironic embrace of mining positions him in a sort of no-man's-land in an environmental dispute now raging throughout the West. "It's not a completely conscious thing. I've actually been a miner, but I'm the one who has used the mining law as a lever to help us preserve the forest at the same time," he explains. "That law is a horrible thing. They ought to change it." The rising value of precious metals and new technologies that can profitably process low-grade ore have sent waves of prospectors back to the hills. In the 1980s the number of open mines in the United States grew by 300 percent. Five hundred gold mines operate largely as a result of the 1872 Federal Mining Law giving title for as little as $2.50 per acre if the claims show legitimate potential of paying out.

As holy in the West as God and guns, this outmoded law has led to cut-rate sales of federal lands for a fraction of their worth. Thousands of squatters, many with a geology degree, and recreational miners with bulldozers and portable dredges are profiteering to the tune of millions of dollars and to the detriment of a natural heritage. From Alaska to Utah, they are stripping mountains bare and leaching hazardous waste into streams. In late 1992 the U.S. Senate, under pressure from mining interests, rebuffed efforts to toughen the 1872 law. In a sharp departure from the philosophy that has guided the government's commodity-oriented philosophy toward its public lands for the past century, Interior Secretary Bruce Babbitt is asking Congress to amend the law by charging a royalty on the value of the extracted minerals.

Downhill from the Ruth mine, the Starvation ore mill sits at the upper end of the camp. Like the new buildings at Jawbone Flats, it's constructed from native wood. For the hardware, Atiyeh hired an old mining engineer from Reno, Nevada, to teach him the ropes. He took Atiyeh on a tour of antique mills across Nevada. Back home, the incorrigible tinker cannibalized parts from scrap piles lying around in camp. Atiyeh found a generator from a World War II radar set and had it baked and varnished for the Pelton wheel supplying the camp's power.

Shiny Rock's ore mill can process about thirty-five tons of lead, zinc, silver, and copper ore a day, about a tenth of Jawbone's mining capacity were Shiny Rock to go full blast with mobile, high-tech equipment. A truck dumps the ore through a bin. Water spilling over the top separates fine material from the coarse, which goes through a jaw crusher to ground particles smaller than a dime. A series of conveyer belts drops the ore into a bin before depositing it into a mill. Once there, cannon balls rolling around inside pulverize the minerals into the consistency of flour. A vat filled with a frothy shake of water and a variety of solutions attaches metals to bubbles. What rises to the surface is skimmed off the mix's top and dried into a cake.

After loading it into barrels, Shiny Rock has shipped its final concentrate to domestic and foreign markets, fetching, in a bullish market, between $150 and $500 per ton. "Does it look like a fake mining operation? The Forest Service has argued we really weren't mining," growls Atiyeh, standing astride an empty barrel on its side. "I don't know anyone who would do this shit—all that retimbering, build an entire mill—for fun. It's so stupid, it's scary. The timber industry will never understand. They figure there's gotta be an ulterior motive. They can't understand people doing something just because it's the right thing to do."

Since 1981, the Forest Service has fought to prove him wrong by mounting sweeping challenges against the economic viability of Atiyeh's mining claims. On technical grounds, it invoked the Surface Rights Act to defend its right to manage vegetation and timber the way it saw fit at the same time it proposed timber sales in Opal Creek. In their campaign to downplay Jawbone Flat's historical uniqueness, officials hinted at razing it.

On a personal level, Atiyeh came under repeated attacks in court and in the media for engaging in mock mineral sales and overstating the extent of mining activities. To gather evidence for its case, the federal government conducted years of surveillance at Shiny Rock. Forest Service workers spent thousands of man-hours observing employees up close and took hundreds of photos in an effort to wrest control of the land from Atiyeh. "We had our guys take pictures," says Dave Alexander, whose tenure as the Detroit district ranger in the Willamette National Forest—from 1981 through 1990—coincided with the start and close of the legal feud. "They were telling me that George's operation was a facade, there is no ore being hauled."

Hirons seethes at the sham he says Atiyeh has put over. "Environmental miner. Oh, that's all hype. The last time I was over there, there were fifty-gallon drums of concentrate behind the house," he says. "If Shiny Rock were not subsidized by Persis, there's no way that thing could stand on its own based on the Ruth mine's revenues. There's no way they could ever get the goddamn money out of the ground to pay the patent attorneys. What a bunch of bullshit the way they got patent. I was sitting there when the strategy was first designed. George said, 'We'll go on the offensive, get that mine operating to get the Forest Service off our ass.' George played the paper game and played it right."

Hirons now dares to think the unthinkable aloud in the political maelstrom—logging Opal Creek. Not long ago, he adamantly opposed the U.S. Forest Service's plans to cut it. By all accounts, including his own, pressure from Mill City's timber barons, for whom he logs, and a certain measure of personal resentment toward his past partner's environmentalism precipitated the change of heart almost as dramatic as Atiyeh's love loss with their logging venture. "I have a soft spot for Opal Creek and always have. I'm NOT sure Opal Creek should be logged. Its heaviest emphasis should probably be on recreation, research, and wildlife because that's what the public wants there. If it's cut, I'd like to see it done very, very carefully as part of a salvage—a big burn or big insect infestation," he says. "That's going to happen someday. I have seen places up there with hellacious lightning storms."

The concept of salvaging, central to the loggers' case for removing dead timber (either standing or on the ground), presents ancient forests as potential waste, better suited to man's immediate needs than nature's timeless cycles. The most recent science requires loggers to leave the decay of dead and downed trees behind to replenish the soil for future growth.

Biology aside, Hirons's pronouncements strike Atiyeh as sheer heresy in view of their two years together at Jawbone Flats. "Tom and I have grown so close and gone through so much together, it's shocking. He was supportive for a very long time. Friends of ours and I have a very hard time figuring out how Tom justifies it. I understand his professional trap. But why Opal Creek?" Atiyeh cries. "Is he willing to sacrifice Opal Creek after it has given him so much? I have never really believed in my heart that if it came down to it, Tom would stand by and let Opal Creek be cut. But maybe he would because he's so wrapped up in his position."

Atiyeh has his willing, if guarded, alibis. Deanne jokes about her ex-husband's "science fair" project, an echo of Hirons's description of it as a "pilot mill." Twigg-Smith renders the ultimate verdict. "Shiny Rock has never turned a profit. Never. Never," he says. "But the mining experts have always testified it was a prudent investment. It's been totally legitimate."

As a prime architect of Shiny Rock's strategy while in its employ at the heat of the court battle, Joe Weber claims partial credit for embellishing George's profile. "We had the polishing cloth on him for years. I'd tell him, 'Here's the audience and it plays in Peoria.' The gentleman miner, the environmentalist miner," Weber says with a chuckle. "He's up there with deer feeding out of his hands living Gifford Pinchot's dream." Weber takes pains, though, to point out Atiyeh's high-minded objectives:

"Sometimes you end up sacrificing the truth a bit if you feel strongly and time is running out. Then the end justifies the means."

Regardless of Shiny Rock's murky ledger sheet, Weber blames the Forest Service for its attempt to divert attention from cut-and-slash policies. "No, the mining never actually supplied George's income. A capitalist, Thurston wanted to save trees all along. He paid George's bills and gave him the free time to do whatever he needed to do. It was a good move for the Hawaiians to protect the cool historical place," says Weber, whose authoritative history of mining in the Cascades provided the intellectual backbone of an adroit but futile effort to gain designation for Jawbone Flats in the National Register of Historic Places. "I'm proud to have helped George, too. The historic holistic values of a neat-looking camp in the old-growth forest, of all places. A responsible forest manager would save it."

In the courts, where the only fight that matters is waged, Atiyeh has compiled a perfect record against the Forest Service. A federal judge ruled in 1987 that the potential for developing a profitable mining operation justified the awarding of patents on six of Shiny Rock's claims. Three years later Atiyeh won the decisive round in the contest when a federal appeals board ruled that valuable mineral deposits exist on four claims, clearing the way for patents on them and on three other related parcels at Jawbone Flats. Shiny Rock thus gained ownership of ninety-five acres in the heart of Opal Creek. In the end, a single headstrong environmentalist, represented by one persuasive lawyer, had humbled the federal government.

Atiyeh's resemblance to David slaying Goliath, like all myths, contains various shades of truth. The guile and cunning he has exhibited are marks of a conservationist possessed about defending his turf—even under the guise of a profession ostensibly at odds with his high-minded ends. The modern mining methods across the West may cause more harm to the landscape than even logging, owing to the lingering harm of toxic waste. By contrast, Atiyeh's type of mining belongs to a gentler era. In the age of the pioneer, prospecters from Guts Gibbs to Elijah Smith barely scratched the earth's surface, extracting only what they needed to supplement their livelihoods during the rest of the year down in the valley. Through almost fifty years of boom and mostly bust, Grandpa Hewitt drew his and Bertha's existence from the mines at minimal cost to the mountains he worshiped.

For the past two decades his spiritual heir has emulated him straight down to the equipment salvaged from the original mill. Atiyeh's master stroke has been keeping his mining operation small in scale and low in impact while at the same time meeting the Forest Service's every acid test. Twigg-Smith's role as a financial angel surely simplifies the challenge. But were Shiny Rock to depend completely on his largess, which is not the case, Twigg-Smith's philanthropy would still testify to enlightened capitalism in the vein of Carnegie giving the gift of learning. Appropriately, the latest solution he and Atiyeh propose to resolve the conflict would emulate the Nature Conservancy, an exemplary land trust and an organization comparable to Atiyeh's Friends of Opal Creek. The Nature Conservancy has saved millions of acres of wilderness soley through the private initiative of public-spirited citizens.

Atiyeh's string of victories has bred wild suspicion of hidden agendas. Hirons, who knows him better than anyone else, ascribes his behavior to the ego trip he enjoys from control of the gate into camp. In fact, neither the salary Atiyeh draws from Shiny Rock nor the swelled head from standing in the spotlight account for most of his actions. The true method to Atiyeh's madness springs from Hirons's own understanding of Jawbone Flats' novelty as a reflection of the historic West, writ large and living. The Hironses radiate a glow thumbing through the family's photo album and telling stories of their Opal Creek experience. Up in the mountains, they came of age together.

Any objective visitor to Jawbone Flats will likely come away believing Atiyeh is sincere about doing the right thing. The obsession of loggers, many of whom have never set foot there, with Atiyeh's ulterior motives founders on some self-evident truths. Opal Creek and Jawbone Flats fire the imagination. The complete package of the last operating mining camp in the Cascades nestled in one of the last absolute spots of ancient forest constitutes a national treasure. In the course of my stay in Oregon, it draws me back each weekend. At the risk of abusing my hosts' hospitality, Jawbone Flats' small community in the cabins, I invariably overstay my welcome. In man and nature's timeless abeyance, my stay in this western Shangri-la ends the moment I turn the key of my car's ignition outside the gate.

VII

The Last American Cowboys

D ave Birdwell, at the wheel of a log truck hauling Hirons's eighty-thousand-pound payload from the job at Pamelia Creek, babies his rig down the tortuous Forest Service road in low gear at just seven miles per hour. Safety comes before speed in his occupation, a reassuring rule of the road to the thirty-three-year-old's wife and two children. A blown front tire would sail us over the mountainside. A slip into the roadbank could send a log through the cab, shearing off our heads. Needless to say, a loaded truck always has the right-of-way.

On the road, "Super Dave," as his handle goes, talks the time away on the CB with a colleague who inquires why he's driving so carefully. "Harvey, I gotta behave. I got someone with me," Birdwell replies through the airwaves' static.

"Shit, Dave, ask who he's for. If he's for Opal Creek and George up there, we'll see if we can't educate him," rings the voice from the other end. "But if he's not taking a log hauler's job and is on the loggers' side, tell him to stop by and some pretty good ol' boys will buy him a beer."

Birdwell briefs me on his radiomate. "Harvey's known for roughhousing in bar brawls. He's settled down since Young and Morgan [the Mill City timber company] dried him out. He's a helluva nice guy, but not someone you're looking to cross. He loves to fight and knows how. If you're looking for trouble, you'll find it with him."

One group in these parts lately would top Harvey Spears's

enemy list even beyond Atiyeh. The band of ecoterrorists Earth First! has been destroying logging machinery and staging civil disobedience to block operations. "I think if he knew he could get away with it, Harvey would kill them all with his bare hands. I don't think he'd have it any other way," Birdwell muses. "I'm serious. No gun. He'd beat every one of them to death, not that he isn't a gun collector. He has all kinds of guns. He'd just get some enjoyment doing it by hand."

Harvey Spears packs such a lethal and lightning-quick punch that when he unloads, all of Mill City feels it. As a boxer in the army, only his feet ever touched the canvas. In 1971, the year he started logging, it was nothing for three outfits to bring in their crews to see who was toughest. Spears was. Outside a saloon, one man's eye popped out from the patented Harvey hit. Spears complied with the bartender's wish for him to take his business elsewhere. Scrapping from two to five times a night, Spears was spending more time at the courthouse than at home. He considered himself a throwback to an earlier era documented by the logging historian Stewart Holbrook in his book, *Holy Old Mackinaw*:

> In the lumberjack's trinity of entertainment, Battle undoubtedly ranked a close third to Booze and Bawds. Their fighting was crude stuff and often cruel, but there was little animosity in it. Loggers fought for the sheer delight of it and to see who was "best man." Gun play in these affairs was extremely rare; so was knifing. The gouging of eyes was rather common and ear-chewing was highly thought of. It was a man's right, when he had an opponent down, to jump upon him with both feet and puncture his hide with calked boots. This was called "putting the boots to him" and it usually left the boot-ee in bad shape.

Spears's friends warned him repeatedly that he was going to hit somebody so hard one day that the poor soul might never get up. Then it happened on a night Spears has regretted ever since. The man went down and bounced his head on the blacktop. He died three days later from pressure swelling in his brain. Spears beat the manslaughter charge only because his victim had pulled a knife on him.

With Spears's reputation growing to Jesse James proportions, challengers came all over with knives, guns, and whatever else they could carry to dethrone him. This being the hinterlands, a shortage of cops on corners usually meant Spears had to fend for himself. He occasionally found himself dodging flying bullets and oncoming automobiles. A defeated opponent would return with his brother or cousin, only to have Spears dispose of the lot. Spears clobbered an angry Mexican colder than a cucumber at Lefty's in Mill City and a blackjack fell out. In their next meeting, Spears's foe brandished a golf club. It proved irrelevant, as did six accomplices swinging baseball bats and cue sticks. Two of them hit the floor while Ellen Spears took away their clubs. The remaining four had her husband pinned down until the police finally arrived.

In person, Spears, forty-one, appears straight out of central casting for *Seven Brides for Seven Brothers*. He is as burly as he is bearded—sporting a thick, dark forest of hair on his face and thick chest, which he displays through a hickory shirt kept unzipped in all kinds of weather halfway down to the jeans. The furry face and broad shoulders exude the aura of a grizzly bear. His legs and arms jut out of this tree-trunk mass like hardwood limbs. Yet, in the mold of Hirons's son Wes, Spears is no plodding hulk. His well-proportioned physique, resembling a football running back's, affords him the agility to perform all the athletic tasks demanded in the brush when not behind the wheel.

Spears and his family live in Lyons, on Mill City's outskirts to the east, in a trailer that has seen better days. On a cool evening, we finish coffee atop the folded-down door of Spears's open pickup. "Go get your daddy some more snoose," he says, punctuating his comments with streams of juice into a paper cup. "I've never been scared of nothing in my whole life. I've feared no man in this canyon. I used to get drunk a lot and fight a lot in this country. I whooped 90 percent of the assholes around here, and some of them are my best friends," he says. "But I'm scared shitless now. I have a sixth-grade education and been in timber since I was sixteen. Don't know nothing else and what the hell else I can do. It's on my mind all the time."

So is one man in Mill City, George Atiyeh. Spears recalls climbing out of bed in the middle of the night to help pull Atiyeh out of a mud hole in the days of North Fork Logging. "I'll tell you something, my fighting days would probably come back if I can catch that son-of-a-bitch in town. I wouldn't just deck him. I'd try to provoke him. I'd want it to be a fair fight as much as I could possibly make it. If I thought it would make me look better, I'd hit him first and then I'd kill him," Spears says. "George Atiyeh is full of shit in more ways than one. All he's doing right now is for his personal gain. He's wanting to keep that mountain for himself."

The fury in Spears's voice, leavened by fright, echoes throughout the North Santiam Canyon and the Northwest. Dwindling supplies of timber from decades of overcutting and mill automation and other technological changes have cost fifteen thousand jobs since 1978. Saving the northern spotted owl from extinction could slash timber production by one third on federal lands, which account for a third of the cut. By some estimates, the resulting set-asides of land could eliminate ten thousand to twenty-eight thousand jobs in the mills and woods by the end of the decade.

Timbermen are traumatized by the painful truth that the conservation of their outdoor workplaces may doom the only livelihood they have ever known. Bracing for the tough times ahead, they struggle to ease the stress on their families and themselves. Some even pray they won't strike their loved ones. Many confront the prospect of tumbling down the slippery slope of midwestern farmers who failed to meet their mortgage payments and fell into foreclosure, or eastern steelworkers left destitute and adrift when their plants turned silent. Timberworkers may actually have more in common with coal miners trapped in poverty largely because of public concern over air quality. Recent federal legislation shifting emphasis to cleaner forms of energy will deal another blow to the Appalachian coal country, an area already in severe distress. The tumult there and in the Northwest, caused as much by the sudden lurch in federal policies as by market processes, raises fundamental questions about society's obligations to the workaday folk caught in the clash between economic and environmental values. In the political arena, timber interests claw at the forces arrayed against logging as though their bread and butter depended on it. And they do.

In the Northwest, the closing of the last frontier spells the end of a way of life as vital to the American landscape as the forest itself. As a cultural icon, the logger, like the cowboy, roamed free beneath the open sky, defying natural and human obstacles with reckless aplomb. In reality, both tussled to survive under harsh conditions at barely subsistence levels. "The lumberjack and the cowboy followed many of the same basic economic and ecological patterns. They achieved a balance if they were broke at the end of the year," writes Norman Maclean in A River Runs Through It. "If they were lucky and hadn't been sick or anything like that, they had made enough to get drunk three or four times, and to buy their clothes."

Since the conquest of the New World, it has taken mighty men and, later, mightier machines to level 95 percent of the native forest once covering the continental United States. The legend of Paul Bunyan, the frontier hero who helped settle and develop the United States, transcended his incredible muscle and logging feats. In a children's book glorifying him, the stalwart lumberjack symbolizes the American genius for getting things done.

> He was taller than the trees of the forest. He had such strength in his huge arms that they say he could take the tallest pine tree and break it into two with his bare hands. They tell of his mighty deeds and strange adventures from Maine to California. He could outrun the swiftest deer and cross the widest river in one great stride! Even today lumberjacks who work in the woods find small lakes and point them out, saying: "Those are the footprints of Paul Bunyan that have been filled with water."
> A giant logger was Paul, and he chopped down whole forests in a single day. And he and his woodsmen logged off North Dakota in a single month! His ax was as wide as a barn door and had a great oak tree for a handle. It took six full-grown men to lift it!
> When Paul Bunyan had cut down all the trees in the Red River Country, he called his men together. "Tomorrow we go into the North Woods where no white man has ever gone before. It is to the west and north near the Great Lakes. And it is the largest forest in the world. The Indians say that the trees grow so large it takes all afternoon to walk around one.

In the era when Paul Bunyan built his reputation for fortitude, know-how, and bravado, half the land's tall trees still beckoned farther west. By the time his peers reached "Oregon County" he was ready to put down his ax to take Babe the Blue Ox and go up into the mountains, where he could hunt and fish with his faithful dog. Bunyan had hit on the twentieth-century concept of multiple use in the forests.

Had the modern timber industry followed his example and stretched out its supply, it might have averted the present shortfall. The end of cutting old growth represents as much a psychological as an economic setback. Paul Bunyan, after all, did not stake his fame on puny second growth, three feet in diameter. But from now on, Mill City and its counterparts will have to settle for fewer employees handling second-growth timber to satisfy the nation's economy. Most timber barons are clinging to the illusion that their entrenched interests remain impervious to the environmental revolution sweeping the United States.

In spite of the spotted owl, the lumberjack's mystique will forever hold its grip on the Northwest's imagination. His image graces the myriad trinkets, from coffee mugs to key chains, sold in gift shops everywhere. Timber Radio KTBR from Douglas County, Oregon, entertains timber towns from the Cascades to the Coast. Cigarette butts drop into glazed ashtrays ornamented with miniature chainsaws, ammo can lunch buckets, and calked boots. Cheerleaders at high-school sporting events fire up crowds with the chainsaw's rhythmic revs. The logo of the Portland Timbers, a professional soccer team in the 1970s and 1980s, consisted of an ax framed against a wooden circle. The mascot, Timber Jim, wore a plaid shirt, corked boots, stagged pants, and heavy wool socks—almost a dead ringer for a Mad Creek crew member. Timber Jim celebrated his team's goals by bucking a slab off a mammoth log and climbing a spar pole. At one point stadium operators considered banning him, as they had air horns, to reduce noise; Timber Jim prevailed. If San Diego could have a chicken, Portland deserved a lumberjack.

Since its inception in 1956, Mill City's small-town Fourth of July celebration has presented elaborate parades. For the past ten years the main attraction has been the Loggers' Games. The rare truck filled with a three-log load, compared with the old average of six, serves as a reminder of the forest's past cornucopia. Spectators oohed and aahed at the scratchless, dentless, brand-new yarder Al Ward showed off in one parade. In the float competition, an anointed "princess" being run through a make-believe mill edges out the Forest Service's Smoky the Bear. Squaring off with their teammates in the "Powder Puff Bucking" event for young women, Hirons's daughters, Vicky and Debbie, coax their crosscut saw through a downed log. In the adult version, "the Jack and Jill contest," Harvey and Ellen Spears take first-place gold trophies four years running.

South of Mill City, Albany's festival, one of Oregon's oldest, goes back about half a century and routinely draws crowds of forty thousand. The five-day competition, often televised on ABC's *Wide World of Sports* and ESPN, pits hundreds of athletic contestants against one another, rope-skipping on floating logs, handsawing, and chopping. Recently the big show has reflected the industry's troubled times. In years past, Willamette Industries has donated a pair of 125-foot Douglas firs from one of its tree farms for spar poles, the ramrod-straight trunk planted firmly in the ground for the toppers and speed climbers. A week after the spotted owl's listing, the carnival president announces that the sawyers will cut detachable, reusable wooden blocks fastened to the original spars. The diminishing supply of big timber calls for a new look at recycling.

Ironically, few of the entrants in the competition are full-time loggers anymore. The advent of steel yarders and similar modern machinery has thinned the ranks of adept high climbers like Wes Hirons. Except for performing for neighbors at gala events like Mill City's, sane woodsmen prefer to leave their work behind in the forests. In Albany, professional competitors from as far away as New Zealand vie for the generous prize money. Store clerks, construction workers, and other would be loggers from the cities and suburbs polish their skills year-round. Their nostalgia for the pioneer experience accounts, in large part, for the carnival's success. Its popularity comes close to rivaling that of the rodeo, another event starring an endangered western icon.

Harvey Spears spits sawdust. He was reared in northern California logging and mill camps by timber workers on both sides of his parents' families. After dropping out of high school, his first job, in a mill, lasted only a few months. "That's inside work," he says. "I've always been an outside boy." Spears has performed every job out in the brush. Hirons fired and hired him three times when he worked for North Fork. "Tom is the best friend I've got," Spears says in appreciation of his former boss's willingness to forgive a wayward worker with a weakness for drink. Fifteen years ago, Spears's chainsaw kicked back, slicing through his knee. Spears subsequently sought refuge in the loader's safer confines. "If my legs would come back, I'd rather be out there in the brush, but it's a young man's occupation. God, there's so many damn things that can cripple you," he says. "There's really no reward other than living." Lately, with loading jobs fewer and farther between, Spears has been filling in as a log truck driver to make ends meet.

He sees the good life—for which he has busted his bones—slowly coming apart at the seams. For a quarter century, Spears has been willing to put up with rising at 3:00 A.M., playing father to his children only at dinnertime, and collapsing into bed at 7:00 P.M. from complete exhaustion. He is too spent on weekends to do much of anything but catch up on sleep. In Spears's top years he has provided for his family on thirty thousand dollars, a princely sum in these parts. This year he will count his blessings to earn twenty thousand dollars. The creaky mobile home occupied by the Spears awaits structural repairs. "Right now we're going to just exist in the SOB until things level out so I can buy a new place," Spears says with a shrug. The new pickup may go back to the dealer. In austerity measures, the Spears have forgone dinner out and replacement shoes for their five boys. Since selling off a few head of cattle they owned for extra cash two years ago, the family has seldom tasted meat.

Were the Spearses simply passive victims buffeted by events, their predicament would provoke sympathy. Yet their resolute commitment to Mill City borders on the tragic. The logging roots of Ellen, his wife, a comely platinum blonde, stretch back to the turn of the century. Her grandfather served as the first Detroit district ranger in the national forest near Mill City. A few years ago, reaffirming their faith in the community, the couple funneled their entire life savings—save $3,500 for retirement—into the beauty salon a block down Broadway from Stewart's General Store. The $20,000 investment in Guys and Dolls seemed better than money in the bank prior to the timber crisis. With women streaming past the front window, embroidered by painted logging scenes, for shampoo sets twice a week, the Spears saw many a $175 day in their first year. Last week, a $100 day occasioned a raucous celebration. Today's $58 take, doubling yesterday's, will make a small dent in covering the salon's utilities, telephone bill, and taxes. The peeling and cracking building, crumbling toward condemnation, could use about $10,000 in repairs. They know it would only be pouring good money after bad. "It's falling down around our feet. We're afraid to do anything," Ellen says. "The timber industry the way it is, we can't afford to. We bought paint, but don't even know how many gallons it would take." Since Linn County has already assessed the taxes at $4,800, they fear a fresh coat might raise rates another $1,000.

If the government ever establishes tax-free enterprise zones in timber towns, Guys and Dolls should qualify as ground zero. A cornerstone of Bill Clinton's campaign was to offer a 50 percent tax exclusion to small businesses and entrepreneurs who take risks by making long-term investments in new ventures.

The Spearses' investment in Mill City's future and their own has saddled them with debts as painful as those Hirons has accumulated from his yarder. "I'll just bet you we don't recover a dime of all our life savings stuck in this damn business," he laments. "Everybody is anticipating the crunch. Everybody, like me, is looking for the worst and hoping for the best. If I thought I could get my money out of it today, I'd sell it. Why even pay $15 to $20 to list it when nobody is going to take it?" Plop goes another gob of snoose juice into the cup.

Spears's short résumé, beginning and ending with one career, exacerbates a terrifying midlife crisis. Loggers in general lack a college degree and even a high-school diploma. Many are approaching fifty years of age and have had experience in only one job. "Christ, it's just like starting over again, the only thing is I got half-grown kids. I'm still a young man, forty-one, but only twenty-five years away from retirement. Everything I've done falls back on timber. How the hell are they going to teach me something that's going to help?" he thinks aloud. "I'm not so old I can't find another job. If this lingers on for another four or five years, then goes down, then I'll be forty-five or forty-six in that age bracket where they won't hire me." Among his options, construction holds little appeal, and beating the highway blacktop as a truck driver puts him away from his family for long stretches. And any education for marketable skills would cost him the paychecks he needs to support his family.

Only two years ago, this talented lumberjack received half a dozen calls in winter requesting his services for hire. Today he waits in vain for the phone to ring. "I did some dumb things in life, it took me a lot longer to grow up. All that fighting was totally uncalled for," he allows. "I'm stupid in the sense that people around me can change occupations and it don't bother them. Well, I'm so damn stupid that I'm afraid to change my occupation." The professional futility wounds the psyches of Spears and thousands of other loggers. And the downturn in the trade they have plied so long drains them of self-esteem.

Opportunistic industry officials, and the politicians in their pocket, tend to mistake much of their rank-and-file's modest education for ignorance. (In a meeting at *Time* magazine in New York convened at the request of timber interests upset about the magazine's spotted owl cover, one hired gun protested pairing a "professional, smooth-talking environmentalist" with "just" a timber faller—exactly the sort of elitist notion the Sierra Club allegedly harbors.) The semiliterate Spears's poor spelling does not cloud his clear judgment about shortsighted practices leading to today's debacle. While he favors cutting decadent old growth and castigates Atiyeh, he questions the wisdom of turning Opal Creek into a litmus test. "There's timber in this country that needs to be harvested, let's do it. But look, I don't want to see Opal Creek cut. There's places that don't need to be," he says. "It's one of the most pretty spots in Oregon. Let's keep it."

A number of loggers grouse, both privately and publicly, to me about the pell-mell rush to wring profits from private woodlands too close to home. The NIMBY (Not in My Backyard) syndrome accounts for only part of their anger. It simply defies common sense to compound their breed's image problem. "I don't think they should log by the highway. Know what I hate? You see this mountain right yonder?" Spears says in his backyard, pointing toward the scalped bump against the darkening sky. "You see how that's been clear-cut and raped? That was one of the nicest stands of small timber you'd ever seen in your life. Now people will look at it because it's an eyesore. They've logged that whole hillside up there and ruint it for the people here. We love a beautiful view as much as anyone does." I wonder just who the "they" is whom Spears and other woodsmen are disparaging.

Men like him are wise to the widening divergence of interests between themselves and the timber magnates who write their paychecks. Spears's gratitude toward Jim Morgan, an owner of Young and Morgan, for taking him under his wing during alcohol rehab and befriending him on countless other occasions through small gestures of kindness ends at the bank vault. "Jim probably has a little more feeling for the little people than Freres [another mill owner in town] or the rest of them. If I needed something, I'd call Jim on the phone and I'd get it. There's no doubt in my mind," Spears insists. "But when it comes right down to it, it's for Jim Morgan. The more money you got, the more power you got, the more greed you got." With every man for himself, loggers are looking toward management for more rewards from their toil than handshakes and promises.

Spears reserves his deepest scorn for the megacorporations bent on exporting logs to Japan. "I say stop. Let's mill that SOB. Let's plane it. Let's put it in the form that it belongs in for building a home. Let's don't ship nothing out of here," he says, echoing sentiments of all the loggers I spoke to. "Let's mill the stuff to keep those people working. I don't think we should totally destroy our forests because we want to ship uncut logs to Japan and get rich. I think they can have their share, we can have ours, and we can all live happily after."

It may mark the height of gall for big business to raise howls of anguish about the spotted owl's deleterious effect on their workers as it bids *bon voyage* to jobs by shipping "raw" logs overseas. The Asians' first taste of the Northwest's finest came from the extensive blow-down following the Columbus Day storm in 1962, leading the United States to seek new markets to absorb its excess of timber. By 1988 and 1989, according to U.S. Forest Service figures, 3.6 billion board feet of raw logs were exported from state and private lands in Oregon and Washington State to Japan, Korea, and China, about a quarter of the timber cut in the Northwest and 80 percent of the total unprocessed timber nationally. Those logs never saw the inside of an American mill. This astronomical amount comes close to equaling the whole timber output of the national forests in the Douglas fir region. Or to put it into another perspective, it's enough to fill log trucks and park them end to end from New York to San Francisco and back again.

The export of unprocessed whole logs has sharply reduced local employment. Developing nations are belittled as "banana republics" for exporting their raw materials for the benefit of other countries, which turn them into lucrative, finished goods. Yet Thailand and Indonesia, whose GNPs are a fraction of the United States' prohibit unprocessed logs from leaving their docks. This restriction enabled Indonesia to build 126 plywood plants in the mid-1980s, boosting its share of the Japanese market from 1 to 18 percent.

On the Northwest's shores, Weyerhaeuser and ITT Rayonier cram vessels to the brim with raw logs bound for Asia. Most of it comes from private and, up to 1990, state lands, but exporters have been adept at exploiting loopholes to sell abroad hundreds of millions of board feet that come off federal lands. Weyerhaeuser ranks as the Babe Ruth of exports, at over a $1 billion. At docks and log-storage yards the endless vistas of stacks of 350-year-old logs are enough to cause environmentalists and millworkers alike to weep in frustration. In 1989, by a nine-to-one landslide, Oregon voters sounded an alarm by approving a constitutional amendment banning the export of whole logs from state-owned lands.

Small, independent mills have long sought a ban on the export of state timber because, unlike the giants, they rely exclusively on public sales in the national forests for their raw product rather than vast tracts of private land. Nonetheless, their protests against the big-time competition ring fairly hollow in view of their own liberal interpretation of export laws. The cants—rough-cut, squared-off logs—slabbed at their mills and shipped to Asia require minimum manufacturing. Watchdog groups find it hard to track shipments to verify whether mill owners actually send only 2 percent in cant form, as they claim. Any amount is too much as far as woodworkers are concerned. "Why send it at all?" pleads a logger who workers for one of the Mill City companies involved in cants. "They go through a deck of logs in a day like you wouldn't believe. Why don't you make lumber out of it?"

If American mills' rhetoric about jobs matched their true concern, they would be extracting the maximum value of timber through finished lumber before the wood left the nation. "They are exporting the bridge to second growth to Japan," Atiyeh says of the employment opportunities secondary manufacturing presents over the next fifteen years.

In 1990 George Bush finally signed into law federal restrictions on log exports in an attempt to offset job losses expected to result from the protection of the spotted owl. The impetus came almost entirely from Congress's northwestern delegation. The law is aimed at shoring up timber supply for domestic purposes by halting 600 million board feet in exports of whole logs from most state-owned lands in the West, including 350 million from Oregon and 100 million from Washington State. Moreover, the law belatedly narrows certain loopholes that enabled timber companies to ship federal logs abroad. Critics complain it still permits the export of cants, wood chips and pulp.

Next on the agenda for Congress is to enable states to enforce their own restrictions on private lands, or to offer tax inducements for landholders to sell their logs to local rather than foreign markets as part of comprehensive conservation of ancient forests. If the stick proves mightier than the carrot, Congress could tax log exports outright. New sources of revenue would not only emerge to boost the stock of second growth for mills but also defray the costs of enlarging the national forests. At the very least, the Clinton administration should end export subsidies for timber sold abroad, which allow big companies to reap profits away from home.

Spears shudders leaving his fate to treacherous public officials. "I think we got too many damned politicians playing games with our lives. That's all there is to it," he fumes. "Win, lose, or draw, those SOBs are going to survive." He welcomes the change at the White House. "I told them when they voted for that SOB, he wasn't going to do nothing for the state," Spears says. "Ol' Bush, I'd like to get him by the nuts. I really have no trust in none of them politicians, they're screwing us."

He figures he will have to go it alone. Pride prevents him from relying on special favors from Jim Morgan or government-sponsored retraining, an idea most loggers equate with handouts. "I don't think society owes me nothing. I've always been able to make a living in this community without having to ask," he boasts. "I've never had welfare in my life. I've never had food stamps in my life but once, and that's when I got thrown in jail. I've never had to ask for that kind of help." Neither a lender nor a borrower, Spears draws inward for salvation.

At the Canyon Crisis Center, between the Dutch End Cafe and Santiam Valley Bank, Cherie Girod's case log bulges. The only social service outlet for a thousand square miles treats an epidemic of distraught loggers and millworkers. The number of emergency calls on the twenty-four hour crisis hot line patched through on 911 has increased by 59 percent over the past year, from 253 to 403. Cherie, the crisis center's coordinator and wife of Jim, owner of Girods' Hilltop Supermarket in Mill City, attributes half the incidents of drug, alcohol, suicide, and child abuse to the timber crisis. She and a staff of twelve trained volunteers hold the hands of strong men in need. Anxiety over designation of the spotted owl as a threatened species stretches their nerves like coiled springs. Timber wives, as they are officially called, require their own support group. "Up and down the whole county, there's so much fighting among people, some of them I've known all my life. It's a chain reaction," Cherie says of the woodworkers who call. "They say, 'I come home. I'm all tired and frustrated. I kick the dogs, wife, and kids.' "

Elisabeth Kubler-Ross's theories on death and dying are receiving a thorough workout among pop psychologists. The emotional trauma afflicting timber workers follows the series of stages undergone by terminally ill patients and persons suffering any form of radical loss or profound change, such as divorce. Faced with the traumatic and inexplicable predicament, deep-seated denial precedes anger. Then extreme depression sets in at the thought of saying good-bye to everything and everyone. Finally, acceptance, based on a sense of detachment, sparks a glimmer of hope.

Unfortunately, the Northwest is ill equipped to cope with the social woes plaguing its timber towns. Most of them lack any remedial programs. For all its good intentions, the Canyon Crisis Center runs a makeshift operation, funded by the largess of local mills and a hodgepodge of public grants. Girod spends a lot of her time hustling for funding. "Salem is four times farther from Mill City than Mill City is from Salem," goes the local saw. Country folk who trudge from the country to the city for public assistance often feel like fish on land. They chafe under the condescension of paper-pushers eager to engage in debate about the environment at the drop of a form.

The hand-holding Girod uses to comfort patients bears the mark of her own father and brother's lifetime in the brush. While she was growing up in the area, logging dominated conversation in the home. Her father had cautioned her brother about the occupational hazards, but he headed into the brush anyway. Together father and son would share years of breaks and bruises. "It's almost like an inborn moral tradition handed down," she observes. "My dad and grandpa were all loggers. I wanted to be one, too."

She realizes that her counseling rises in proportion to Mill City's desperation. Until last year, most of the individuals affected by the timber industry's flux believed that the crisis center administered exclusively to battered women and children. Many still never visit in person, fearing that their personal travails will provide grist for the local gossip mills. Calls still come only as a last resort from men in their forties and fifties desperately seeking information about education, unemployment compensation, and retraining. "A lot of callers take it as an affront. This is their way of life. They don't tell anybody else how to live. They pay their taxes, pay their bills, and don't live on welfare," Girod says. "They don't like the way they are being treated and they want to know how responsible government is going to be." These lumberjacks—rough-talking, rugged individualists—are reaching out for the first time.

A preponderance of urban and suburban Americans probably have trouble relating to loggers' resistance to moving. Our continent's roominess nourishes the freedom to move. Conversely, Girod understands her people's innate attraction to the rural northwestern life-style. "When you grow up with so much space and big blue sky you feel like a wild animal with no fences. These guys grew up being able to fish where they want, they can go to a lake or a river. They can wander these hills from one end to another," she says. "They know how to survive out in the woods. They don't point toward the ocean or city, they point to the mountains," she adds, shifting from couch to soapbox. "We're the best stewards of the land. Why would anyone think we would want to destroy it? This is our heritage."

An inherent paradox aggravates logging's social maladies. The very rough-and-tumble qualities at the root of the culture leave loggers vulnerable to spiraling stress. While all the nation suffers from its share of alcoholism, perhaps none has desperately embraced the bottle as in the Northwest. As they are wont to admit since "taking the cure," Spears and Hirons hailed from a long line of lumberjacks afflicted by delusion of invincibility through inebriation.

It has gone with the territory from time immortal. After dismal months in the wet back country, lumberjacks headed into town to let off steam. Roving bachelors, they lived for the moment and thought nothing of blowing a month's pay on broads and booze. Their destination was skid road, a central gathering point in every logging town for men to drink, debauch, and duke it out. In the old days the term (otherwise known as skid row) applied to the route over which oxen pulled logs. Soon Portland's skid row emerged as the West's answer to New York's Bowery, the most violent district of all.

The Northwest's weather can drive any sane man to drink. The price for its temperate rain forest is unrelenting wet and gloomy weather. The western side of the Cascade Range is one of the wettest parts of the conterminous forty-eight states. Weeks go by in the fall and winter when the sun never shines. "The moisture," wrote Ken Kesey in *Sometimes a Great Notion*. "It's certainly no wonder that this area has two or three natives a month that take that one-way dip—it's either drown your blasted self or rot."

The numbing boredom of the mills and the nerve-racking danger in the forests have always enhanced the allure of intoxicants. Mill City's residents are known to refer facetiously to AA meetings on Saturday nights in Gates as "the great social event in town." The crisis center estimates that more than half of Mill City attends.

Charlie Belleck, a living case in point, crash-lands before my eyes. At Fir Grove Apartments outside Mill City, we become neighbors and friends. All Belleck, sixty-two, has left of a log truck business he once owned are memories and a little log truck etched in a wooden nameplate beside his front door. He supports himself driving for Young and Morgan.

My neighborly visits for utensils and the like conceal my true aim. Belleck's homeric skills are the stuff of legend in Mill City. He has few equals for spinning a yarn and turning a phrase. His description of the wife of a crew member: "Nice, but not the prettiest thing. Her teeth were so bucked, she could eat the corn off a cob through a barbed-wire fence." A good quip sparkles eyes otherwise stuck in a hollow look. At breakfast he sits at the kitchen table, staring off into space and tossing down vodka and milk, a common mixture for alcoholics. His breath could light a kerosene. lamp.

A family of rambunctious huskies, belonging to the neighbor

residing in the apartment between Belleck and me, is all it takes
to set him off. Delaine "Dee" Hicks, whom I occasionally bump
into at night, is a tall, muscular fifty-one-year-old construction
worker. He has paid the apartment manager to look after his dogs
while away from home on odd jobs. Belleck jokes about strapping
them to sleds for a trip to Alaska. He is less amused listening to
them bay at the moon deep into the night, when he needs his
rest for long hauls at first light.

On a Sunday in spring, the two neighbors become embroiled
in an argument over whether the dogs are trampling on Belleck's
garden. The larger Hicks charges him, whereupon Belleck pulls
out a nine-shot revolver from his back pocket and puts a bullet
in the man's heart. Boasts Belleck in a videotaped confession: "I
dusted him."

Belleck's apparent remorselessness flies in the face of the gentle
disposition I had known. Tests reveal an alcohol content well
above the legal limit. At the trial, two mental health experts
attribute his evil deportment to brain damage caused by chronic
heavy drinking and age. "[He is] unoriginal in his thinking, and
inflexible in his problem-solving," explains a psychologist. "He
tends to be rather rigid in his orientation and approach to life."
From interviews with Belleck and his family, a psychiatrist diagno-
ses a personality change over the past four years. "Alcoholism,
aging, besides the hard wear and tear that guys out in the woods
get have affected his mind," he concludes. Belleck is ordered to
spend a minimum of ten years in prison without possibility of
parole, work release, or temporary leave.

At the First Christian Church, a modest white building occu-
pying a spacious grass-carpeted lot a few doors down from Stewart's, Pastor Aaron Veach, Mill City's preeminent religious figure,
summons a higher power. A blue needlepoint behind the desk in
his office simply says "Jesus." Each Sunday morning his pews overflow with lumberjacks, millworkers, and their families. All five
elders on the church's board have ties to timber. "You have to
be with the people to know why they are hurting and how they
are hurting," Veach says. "How a person could live out a frustrated dream." Veach, forty, a tall man with a high forehead and
long, narrow face and thick mustache, is handling a heavy case-
load from stress.

Veach understands the symptoms from growing up in Roseburg,
a timber town in southern Oregon, and spending off-hours in a
logging truck on its rounds to Mill City. "I've picked up more
seriousness. I asked a real good friend of mine in the Forest Ser-

vice if this was the beginning of the end or just another bump in the road," Veach says. "He said it was a combination of both. A lot of the things were going to have to change. We've been cutting more than we can sustain." The other day a logging company owner who stands to lose a lot from conservation admitted to the pastor that the amount cut in the federal forests near Mill City amounted to logging sixteen months of timber in one year.

The yellow ribbons flapping from his car in a show of solidarity belie the pastor's true sentiments. A serene man of the cloth in quieter times, he preaches fire and brimstone on the question of moderation. "Anybody in the timber industry with more than a pea brain will readily admit that we've overcut. The industry, to a point, has shot itself in the foot by doing that and yet the environmentalists are shooting themselves in the foot by making clear from the start they want to shut down all timber harvesting," he says. "You have timber barons on one side, saying anything that grows more than six inches we'll cut and make lumber out of it. Earth Firsters! [the radical environmentalists], on the other extreme, say you won't cut another twig. Somewhere in the middle is where most people are."

Leaving aside his own dependence on the timber economy to keep the First Christian Church operating, Veach asks his hundred-strong flock to look beyond material concerns. "What's your trust in? Your bank account or your God? Unfortunately, most people only trust in their payday," he says. "I'm not saying God is going to write a check against the National Bank of Heaven. Regardless of where it comes from, the Scripture says the earth is the Lord and fullness. He gives it to us."

When asked about the spotted owl, Veach ponders the possibility of delivering a future sermon on man's role in the environment. "It's like asking wolves to guard the sheep. I don't think for a moment we have the right to eliminate a species. The Scripture teaches us in Genesis to be fruitful, multiply, and have dominion over the earth," he says. "It does not say anything about destroying any part of it."

Indeed, religion, and the Judeo-Christian tradition in particular, have lengthened humans' distance from nature by giving God's blessing to conquering the earth for their exclusive benefit. The injunction from the first chapter of Genesis, to which Veach refers, is unambiguous about nature's inferiority to man: "Be fruitful and multiply, and replenish the earth and subdue it: and have dominion over the fish of the sea, and over the fowl of the air, and over every living thing that moveth upon the earth." As

Roderick Nash, dean of wilderness historians, notes, the Old Testament contains hundreds of references equating wilderness with "desert" and "waste," an arid wasteland verging on hell. The snake, an evil creature in the natural world, tempts Adam and Eve to eat the forbidden fruit in the Garden of Eden. Consequently, the first couple must forsake its paradise for a "desolate wilderness" of "thorns and thistles." The Puritans, beholden to their Bibles in the New World, exalted a city on a hill over the cursed frontier. Michael Wigglesworth, summing up the prevailing view, warned the first New Englanders of "a waste and howling wilderness,/Where none inhabited/But hellish fiends, and brutish men/That Devils worshiped."

In their heyday, loggers lauded themselves for subduing the ancient forests they called "green desert" and for "letting a little daylight into the swamp." Such prejudices continue to infuse their literature with a missionary zeal. A story in *American Timberman and Truck* immodestly titled "The Day Oregon Closed Down" blesses a well-attended loggers' rally in Portland and arrogates to timbermen the role of wilderness's savior. "The logger is the best environmentalist on earth. He was created to be God's steward of the forests"; it proclaims, "to harvest, replant and to care for wildlife."

The conceit of improving upon nature, prevalent among timbermen, ought to strike both creationists and secularists as heresy. Devotees of clear-cuts stress the quicker growth of Douglas fir in sunlight and the better foraging opportunities for game, debatable assertions refuted by the latest forest science. At any rate, man's stab at playing God in old-growth forests have fallen far short of nature's perfection. The "decadence" loggers carry on about to justify themselves is merely the earth's way of stretching out its seasons so that dying trees replenish the ecosystem like leaves mulching a suburban lawn in autumn. To presume otherwise reeks of human chauvinism. Nature, after all, has not jeopardized its own creatures or 95 percent of its native forests. In Mill City an exasperated logger snaps to me: "Hell, the sun is going to burn out in two million years anyway." At their pell-mell rate of destruction, humans will have long since left the scene.

The conservationist David Brower employs the six days of Genesis as a metaphor to describe the world's creation in four billion years. A day equals about six hundred sixty-six million years, he reasons. After organic wholeness develops, life begins on Tuesday. Four days later, when the redwoods appeared at 9:00 P.M. on Saturday, the big reptiles had already disappeared. Man appeared at 11:57 P.M., and Christ at one fourth of a second before midnight. At one fortieth of a second before midnight, the Industrial Revolution began. "We are surrounded with people," Brower says, "who think that what we have been doing for that one fifth of a second can go on indefinitely."

To varying degrees, loggers like Spears reap the mixed rewards of their industry's evolution. A mere fifty years ago, primitive technology and disagreeable weather relegated their forebears to the status of itinerant laborers. Wages ceased at the edge of steep cliffs and during blizzards. Like leaves in the wind, lumberjacks and their families scattered in logging camps at the mercy of circumstances beyond their control. In winter they eked out existence by drawing on what meager resources they had squirreled away and by grabbing part-time work wherever they could.

Heavy, modern machinery laughs at the seasons. Today's lumberjacks can settle down alongside their wives, kids, and pickups. The welfare state looks after them for a few months of seasonal unemployment in the harsher winters or hot fire seasons until they can return to the woods. Lately, however, the scarcity of work due to overcutting and environmental restrictions has driven them farther afield for their livelihood. Cheap motels have become the equivalent of the old camps. Lumberjacks remain on the public dole for longer stretches, wondering when their safety net will be yanked from under them.

On a black Friday, the heaviest downpour in two years drenches Sweet Home, a mill town at the edge of the Cascade Range thirty miles southwest of Mill City as the spotted owl flies. The tempest raging sets the historical tone at noon. The Midway Veneer Plant will shut down, terminating employment for thirty-eight workers here and at Sweet Home Plywood, which forms its product from veneer. A contagion of closures has spread throughout the midvalley. In Lebanon, White Plywood, which totaled about $16 million in sales the previous year, sent home 180 employees for good. In Philomath, 80 employees of Leading Plywood will work a final shift. White Plywood and Leading Plywood both candidly cite sagging wholesale orders and swelling stockpiles of unsold inventory as reasons for layoffs. Fears of impending timber set-asides for the spotted owl have boosted the wholesalers' prices so high that retailers have held off buying. But the root cause, economists argue, stem from fundamental shifts in the nature of the industry unrelated to the spotted owl, particularly the automation of mills.

At the Midway plant, officials of Willamette Industries, a

publicly traded forest products company listed in the top two thirds of the *Fortune* 500, put their own spin on the shutdown. The intensive public-relations campaign waged by Willamette Industries, Georgia-Pacific, Weyerhaeuser, and other megacorporations seldom attributes cutbacks to market forces. The "fact sheet" Willamette distributes to the media at the plant stresses the links between "reduced timber availability," a codephrase for conservation, and dozens of "terminated" employees. Many of those pink-slipped know better. In their own, uncensored voices they quietly voice displeasure at being pawns in the political game.

Life in Sweet Home has soured of late. This mill town in the foothills of the Cascades never completely recovered from the recession of the early 1980s. Over the past two years, the total number of employees in lumber and wood products in Linn County has fallen 15 percent, from 4,890 to 4,170. Scores of them worked for Willamette's old-growth sawmill and the Griggs plywood factory until both ceased running in recent years. Willamette operates four plants in Sweet Home, employing 425 people. Midway's closing reduces the local work force another 10 percent. With 9,730 employees nationwide, 3,000 of them in Oregon, Willamette is unlikely to notice.

In an office above the Midway mill, John Davis, general manager of western timber and logging for Willamette, insists on presenting his case above the din of constant thumping downstairs. Tall, silver-haired, and bespectacled, he looks the part of the corporate executive. Davis, a Southern California native, betrays a certain defensiveness about the credentials he brings to the debate. "I'm a forester with a metropolitan upbringing," he says. "My experience doesn't satisfy the great unwashed." Pitching the party line about old growth's death and rot, his genial demeanor turns grim reciting familiar litany of wilderness areas, spotted owl habitat, and regulations removing raw material from production. "Wind, bugs, and fire. Eventually nature is going to do her thing," Davis says. "Locking up old growth for the wine and cheese set will not keep old growth in the equation. We have to intensify management on lands to have lumber for houses for people forever."

Sniping at the "wine and cheese set" diverts attention from the true economic picture. "We cannot log at any price just to keep our mills running," Davis says of the decision to close Midway. "At today's cost, the profit margins are thin." In fact, headquarters in Portland have seen to it that black ink runs deep. Two weeks ago Willamette reported a robust 6 percent increase in profits in the first quarter, in the wake of record earnings of $191 million the year before. Industry sawmills in Oregon and eleven other western states took orders for 5.5 billion board feet in the first quarter of 1990 preceding Midway's demise, slightly less than the record high demand in 1987.

Willamette has not enjoyed unprecedented growth by keeping outmoded facilities running. By its estimates Midway needs $15 million worth of renovations—an investment the white shirts in the boardroom have calculated would be better made elsewhere. In 1987 such modernization accounted for the ten plywood plants in Sweet Home producing 30 percent more volume than the thirteen plants did in 1980. "We've lowered our labor and production costs," the annual report boasted the previous year. Or, put another way, Willamette can earn more money at fewer plants paying fewer workers.

It can reap greater profits, too, by beating the high costs of wood manufacturing in the Northwest. The South's lower labor costs and accessible tree plantations on flat ground have beckoned the seven largest lumber and plywood manufacturers, including Willamette. Between 1978 and 1990, these firms lowered their capacity in the Northwest by 34 percent while boosting it in southern states by 121 percent. Smaller northwestern entrepreneurs have bought facilities at low prices to continue producing lumber and plywood.

Meanwhile, Willamette has already seen the future, through diversification, and it works. Having helped consume 90 percent of the Northwest's old-growth forests in its mills, the company is moving on to alternative products. Particle board and medium-density fiberboard (MDF) are made of residual shavings from mills and other cheap materials pressed together to form panels. Willamette is adroitly tapping the value-added market by coating its composite board with water repellents and colored overlays in wood-grain patterns for furniture and cabinets. The new products possess sufficient strength to serve as substitutes for plywood in flooring and similar applications. Last year Oregon plywood accounted for just a quarter of the national market in structural panels. The trend has continued steadily downward since the 1970s, when the state produced 65 percent.

A puny second-growth log drops from the conveyer belt into a bin en route to its afterlife as plywood. Failing to meet requirements for size, the system rejects it. The previous log, of the grand old-growth variety, receives the honor of being the last log.

Midway thus goes out with a bang, not a wimper. "That's all she wrote," Davis intones. A few moments later, the final whistle blows a period on his sentence. All activity comes to a halt. In the eerie silence, employees and onlookers, after removing hard hats and earplugs, can hear themselves think for the first time since their final workday started.

The workers drift about in a daze, seemingly oblivious to the phalanx of local print and television media closing in on them from the plant's entrance. Fifteen minutes ago, Duane Winslow ran a drum chipper, his last job in wood products after twenty-two years. He plans to look for a job with a utility company. "They say it's the spotted owl, but the owl is a scapegoat," the thin forty-two-year-old steams, stroking his beard. "The whole place has been making money right and left the past two years and now they decide to shut down. It's just a bunch of political and corporate politics. The guys out back in the mill feel that."

Capitalism's tragedy takes on an ugly edge in the search for culprits. In modern history, the scene has recurred at numerous automobile and steel factories across the nation's Rust Belt. "GOOD LUCK MIDWAY VENEER," urges a banner hanging limply above. Employees, wearing the long-drawn faces of the condemned on death row, are handed their parting paychecks. Tears roll down the cheeks of a female superintendent reading the names aloud. Relationships forged over years of camaraderie at the workplace will end or assume abbreviated forms. "I guess the spotted owl has had another victory, but we can't let it get to us. But I can't blame the environmentalists, either," says a foreman, trying to cover his tracks as the cameras roll. "I've worked in wood all my life and you've worked in the mill all your life and I don't think there's anyone who likes the forest more than we do. I've enjoyed working with you guys." A dutiful applause trickles from the humid air. Loyal workers receive notepads and penholders bearing Willamette's logo from a catalog of company-sanctioned trinkets. Nary a gold watch in sight. The chosen few are tossed yellow CGO baseball caps emblazoned with the inscription "Communities Together Means Timber Forever."

Standing off to the side, Mike Gross collects nothing other than his earnings. The forklift driver refuses to don the political paraphernalia at crew meetings or participate in the letter-writing campaign Willamette has orchestrated against the preservation of ancient forests. On the contrary, he has kept his own correspondence running with Congress members opposing his employer's policies. More than two decades ago, he ran away from home to work in the mills, where he has remained ever since, including twelve years at Midway. At forty-one, the slightly built man sporting a dark beard and brown jacket has reached a crossroads in his life. "I don't see any reason to cut down every old-growth tree to save my job for another five years," he says. "There's nothing that I know that makes me the most important thing in the world."

Gross is no ingrate about the creature comforts Willamette has provided. Last year's nineteen-thousand-dollar salary from steady work covered all his bills. "Willamette has treated us very well," says the father of two. "You have really good working conditions here. The mill is clean, pretty, and brightly lit. It's got plenty of room." The new forklift purchased two years ago simplified Gross's job.

Something rotten in Sweet Home, however, tempers his appreciation. In the argot of Wall Street, it appears that Willamette is downsizing to maximize profit. "I took a 15 percent pay cut three years ago for this job at the same time that there were record profits," he fumes. "There are politics going on here that we're not supposed to know." The local paper reports that Willamette has offered Midway's workers jobs in nearby mills with a 30 percent cut in pay, at the bottom of the scale, and loss of all benefits.

In excoriating corporate America's sellout of its labor force, Gross articulates the sentiments of legions of workers. "You may have noticed Willamette has never said a word about the export of raw logs. The amount of logs exported in one year, according to my figures, could run this mill for three hundred years," he says. "It's like your savings account. You have one earning interest, which is trees growing, and you take your principal out and sell it to the point where your interest is not keeping pace with your withdrawals. You have a net loss. That's what's happening here. If we weren't selling 3.6 billion board feet to Japan every year, we wouldn't have to cut so much. The timber could grow a little bigger. There would be plenty for everybody and we could still have old-growth stands."

He tugs the brim of a black baseball cap. "I think you have to save the owl, like saving the whales. For sure, we may never walk more than a mile into a wilderness area or pet a whale, but I certainly have hopes of doing so."

Gross is the rare bird in his field to understand that both the human and owl's fates hinge on reformed forest practices. "It really saddens me to see all the old growth cut down. It is not renewable. I don't think we need to turn the entire Northwest into tree farms," he says. "I think, in contradiction to what Dave [the foreman, who spoke] just said, old growth is valuable. I'm in favor of keeping what hasn't been cut and then managing the rest. Industry is plundering to some extent." Driving through this morning's predawn dark and deluge on the way to Midway, the millworker fretted about the deteriorating water quality in rivers muddied by the runoff from clear-cuts, a logging practice he roundly condemns. His lungs have felt the sting of woody debris being burned after logging for the exclusive economic benefit, he believes, of timber companies.

His sixth sense about the Northwest's future inspires his next career move. "I think the Willamette Valley is going to boom over the next ten years as California moves here," he predicts, "it's so beautiful." By then, the ex-millworker expects to have exploited the expanding demand for greenery by cornering Sweet Home's nursery business. A recent letter to the Forest Service about seedlings shows promise of taking root. "I just really like plants," he says, beaming. "I just love watching things grow."

The foreman, eyeing him warily from a distance, yells for Gross to join the gathering. At a crowded picnic table Midway's former employees pick at an anticlimactic buffet lunch of fried chicken, fried potato wedges, and coleslaw. Topping the potluck desserts their wives prepared are sinfully good fresh banana cream pie and dark chocolate cake. The *pièce de résistance*—in size, if not taste— is an immense creation from Molly's Bakery, in Sweet Home. On a canvas of white icing blanketing the angel food cake alights the bird of the hour atop an evergreen. "SAVE A [sic] OWL, GET A LOGGER." "Don't look at that owl," implores Willamette's Davis. "We're trying to discourage that."

Gross ambles over for a slice. "I find that repulsive," he says with a snarl. "I'll eat a tree, but won't touch the owl." With all the time in the world now to indulge their sweet teeth, most of the men prefer to shake hands and promptly leave Midway, out the door and into the driving rain.

While mills may be closing in Sweet Home, fortunately, for Hirons's sake, they continue to operate in Mill City. He races down a Forest Service road on the heels of a log truck hauling his morning's toil to the profit center in Idanha, a two-store town twenty miles east of Mill City, in the Cascades. As Jim Morgan of Young and Morgan, the town's biggest employer, and Hirons haggle over the price of his logs, I'm treated to a tour of Green

Veneer Mill, a Y and M property. Mill owners, like proud captains, glory in showing off their cruise ships.

I had already developed a soft spot for this mill while making the rounds with Hirons. In a foreman's booth beside a muddy runway, a wag has made sport of environmentalists and loggers. On the wall is posted a letter written in a schoolchild's crude penmanship:

Dear Sir:
You are right about wildlife using the snags [dead standing trees]. Almost every snag my dad cuts down is full of birds and squirrels. We try to kill the little bastards with our shovels so they won't shit on our wood.
Your friend,
Gregory

Green Veneer, a study in contrasts, encapsulates the wood business's past and future. It employs 115 employees on a payroll of $3.2 million. In 1959, Bob Young and Vern Morgan, young Mill City entrepreneurs, bought this property where an old lumber company had been situated primarily for the creek-fed mill pond and the mill's empty shell. The obsolete plant has long since been retrofitted, but the pond, about the size of one and a half football fields, remains a functioning anachronism.

Once upon a time in Oregon, every mill used these small bodies of water, an excellent preservative, to store and move logs. Pond men, descendants of the river rats—the intrepid lumberjacks leading the drives—collected logs in the water and floated them to the gangway connected to the mill, or cut wood on the spot using pond saws. They jumped around the wet, round rafts of loose logs until the health and safety mandarins from Salem stopped them for good. Then the Department of Environmental Quality (DEQ) entered the scene to stanch the detritus overflowing from the ponds. Last spring, Young and Morgan complied with the DEQ's wishes by filling in its other pond at Lyons, near Mill City. The conventional cold-deck system it erected in its place combines modern efficiency and good economics. Whereas the single layer of logs a pond can handle often get scrambled, cold decks can accommodate dozens of neat stacks for sorting and grading. Driving through Mill City's back roads, past the three major logging companies, the full decks resemble a small city skyline stretching for blocks on end.

Young and Morgan is wisely waiting for the plywood market to shake out before committing itself to scrapping its mill pond, one of the last in Oregon, and installing a cold deck. Meanwhile, a miniature, diesel-powered tug boat performs the job "pond men" once did. Struggling to keep his feet dry, the skipper cramped inside a cab resembling a floating toll booth nudges the sticks. He earned his nickname, Jacques Cousteau, for hitting a "sinker," a moisture-laden hemlock and pine submerged under the surface, and capsizing. Today Cousteau is wearing a life vest.

From the moment a log leaves its aquatic home on a conveyor belt, it enters a high-tech world. First, spiked metal fingers grab the logs' ends and skin off the bark. Saws buck the cylinder into eight-foot blocks, the uniform length for plywood. The excess wood circles falling off—called lily pads because they used to go back into the ponds where they were scooped up—are stashed away for later use. The automatic charger lifts the wood block on spindles and hands it to the lathe. At the computer console in a small control room, the head lathe operator reads data processed from a laser measuring for diameter and adds or subtracts for knots and splits—thus ensuring, in the trade's parlance, "maximum recovery" and eliminating the costly guesswork that once enraged sawmillers who lost precious seconds and wood.

Two four-and-a-half-foot-long knives, tapered down to razor-blade sharpness, reach up from a carriage to peel the logs into ribbons of veneer. Laid out flat like a map, we scan the growth rings spanning the ages from Hirons's logging job a few days ago to George Washington chopping down his father's cherry tree. Millworkers liken plywood production to unwinding rolls of toilet paper. Two clippers, sitting atop each other, drop with the resounding finality of guillotines, chopping the sheets—some stretching out 157 feet into 103-inch-long, 54-inch-wide pieces. Men pulling the green chain, a term referring to the unripe wood, create stack after head-high stack. It usually takes five veneers, glued together, to form one plywood panel. If the single sheets produced over an hour were attached lengthwise, they would stretch four miles. Two eight-hour shifts a day devour hundreds of trees, unfurling a ribbon that could reach from Washington, D.C., to Baltimore. For every Midway Veneer in Sweet Home closing down, dozens of mills from Albany, Oregon, to Aberdeen, Washington, race ahead of nature's timeless cycles.

Man must scramble just to keep pace with himself. Industry's feeble attempts to downplay the effects of automation, overcutting, and export skirt the truth. Production continues to outstrip raw materials. As early as 1976, "the Beuter Report" from Oregon State University's Forest Research Laboratory warned of a 22 per-

George Atiyeh pays the price of ostracism in Mill City for fighting to save Opal Creek in the Cascade Range, a magnificent vestige of the virgin woods that once blanketed North America. *Photo by David Falconer*

As owner of Mad Creek Logging in Mill City, Tom Hirons, a conservationist in his own right, strives to conserve a proud way of life rooted in the frontier soil. *Photo by David Falconer*

Wider than a man is tall, Opal Creek's green spires are the last living links to the early Middle Ages, centuries before white settlers stepped foot in the New World. *Photo by David Falconer*

On a hike through Opal Creek, a preeminent forest scientist has insisted that he has seen bigger trees and older trees, but never so many big, old trees in one place. *Photo by David Falconer*

With the number of visitors to Opal Creek doubling each year, to more than 10,000, its fame has soared — at risk to the careers of bureaucrats and politicians who dare to talk of logging it. *Photo by David Falconer*

From its alpine headwaters, Opal Creek cascades through dozens of waterfalls, up to 240-feet high, while providing some of the world's purest drinking water for millions of people. *Photo by the author*

Rows of yarders, including Hirons's, are so many white elephants gathering rust on the auction block for lack of old growth, shattering his and other loggers' middle class American Dreams. *Photo by David Falconer*

Old-growth logs like these waiting to be peeled, in a process millworkers compare to unwinding rolls of toilet paper, make the finest plywood because they're tight-grained and knot-free. *Photo by the author*

The sheets of veneer from ancient trees that will be glued together to form plywood disturb critics who liken the waste to turning Carrara marble into limedust for garden trim. *Photo by David Falconer*

The Northwest timber industry, particularly such anachronistic mills as Young and Morgan's Green Veneer, is realizing that to stay afloat it must produce more lumber in its final form. *Photo by David Falconer*

Fewer log trucks hauling their wooden gold augur a transition of historical dimensions for timber towns, perhaps dwarfing those that have recently occurred in steel and farming country. *Photo by David Falconer*

At the turn of this century, lumberjacks such as these atop a Douglas fir stump in Clearlake, WA, first felled the most accessible and gigantic trees growing in the fertile lowlands. *Forest History Society*

Using two-man saws known as "misery whips," a pair of loggers might spend most of a day subduing a single behemoth such as this nine-foot fir in Snoqualmie, WA, and burn off a Paul Bunyanesque 8,000 calories a day. *Weyerhaeuser Sales Company*

Even before the chainsaw's advent in the 1950s, these loggers perched on antiquated "spring boards" above the thicket of debris were running out of very big trees to cut. *Forest History Society*

Most people of Mill City view the clear cuts in the foothills of the Cascades surrounding their town as progress, but to prosper they must preserve as well as exploit their natural resources. *Photo by David Falconer*

In the heart of Mill City, the crackerbarreled sensibilities at Charley and Marie Stewart's well stocked general store teeter between old-fashioned, family service and an uncertain future. *Photo by David Falconer*

Pastor Veach believes that if staunch environmentalists were to come into Mill City and open the kind of grass roots political office Hirons has, it would probably be fire bombed. *Photo by David Falconer*

The total sensation of going to Jawbone Flats, the last intact mining town in the Cascades, is one of stepping back into the old west or onto the movie set of a John Ford film. *Photo by David Falconer*

Atiyeh, at Jawbone Flats, has never lost a legal appeal protecting Opal Creek, largely by exploiting pro-development laws for mining to foil the U.S. Forest Service's attempts to log it. *Photo by David Falconer*

Atiyeh and his employee, "Tin Cup," are not alone in believing that the package of historic Jawbone Flats nestled in the perfect spot of ancient forest constitutes a national treasure. *Photo by David Falconer*

After sanctifying Opal Creek, Calvin Hecocta, a Paiute Indian, and Wilmer Stampede-Mesteth, a Sioux medicine man from North Dakota, claim that logging it would amount to defiling a church. *Photo by David Falconer*

Highlighted by snow, a fresh, jarring clear cut on the opposite ridge of the gateway to Opal Creek reminds visitors of the ancient forests' tenuous fate. *Photo by the author*

Hecocta: "The animals and birds cannot be here to tell you about fears of losing their homes. Teach it to your children. Teach them about love for God's earth and each other." *Photo by David Falconer*

cent decline in Oregon's harvest as a result of the land's depletion by the year 2000. From another vantage point, between 1977 and 1988 lumber production in Oregon and Washington State jumped 17 percent, from 11.5 billion to 13.5 billion board feet per year. At the same time, industry employment dropped by 19 percent, to 108,000. Eight workers could thus produce 1 million board feet annually that once took the work of ten. According to a Forest Service study, technological change and the exhaustion of private lands will reduce the number of woodworkers in the Douglas fir region of Oregon and Washington State to 64,000 by the year 2000, a whopping 52 percent decrease from 134,000 in 1979. Although the General Accounting Office reports that the national timber yield will soar by more than half during the next half century nationwide, based on the Forest Services's own data, it projects the disappearance of one in four industry jobs because of greater efficiency in milling.

Any of these projections exceed the twenty-eight thousand "victims" the Forest Service's worst-case scenario estimates will fall prey to set-asides for the spotted owl. State economist Paul Warner has documented a 20 percent decline in Oregon's wood products industry over the past decade. "The main reason is improved productivity from automation and new technology," he says. "The output is the same." Many loggers are doomed to follow the small farmer's free fall, whether or not national timber sales remain at today's high levels.

Apologists for cutting the last ancient forest are apt to quote Mark Twain's admonition—"There are three kinds of lies: lies, damned lies, and statistics"—whenever economics bolsters their adversaries' arguments. So, turning off the calculator for a moment, an in-person visit to the issues clarifies them considerably. After all, a higher output from fewer workers ranks as modern industry's crowning achievement. The continuing technological revolution is wiping out jobs everywhere. "It's very much a production line process that lends itself to automation," admits Willamette's Davis. Had his company kept Midway Veneer operating in Sweet Home, he adds, it would have substituted automatic stackers for people pulling the green chain. Dave Barnhardt, a twenty-six-year-veteran of Young and Morgan's brain trust in Mill City, informs me that the company has doubled its production per person over the past ten years in the mills and woods, thanks to advanced machinery. Green Veneer, a state-of-the-art mill, presents unambiguous lessons on the causes of the current crisis in the woods. During its early years, the mill had two men using end hooks feed the lathe and spot the blocks. Automatic chargers have long since replaced them—just as the pond boat took pond men's job.

In this century of progress, occupational dislocation and technological innovation go hand in hand. "We're all in danger of losing our jobs. Our economy constantly changes, whether it's an autoworker or a magazine worker. Look how carriage workers went to work in automobile plants," Atiyeh notes. "Who says the most adaptable animals on earth, *Homo sapiens*, can't adapt to change here?"

Today far fewer lumberjacks are needed to bring home the big timber. "I've seen so many changes, so much damn equipment— hydraulic loaders and all that," recalls Wilbur Harlan, an eighty-year-old retired logger in Mill City. "My dad insisted those damn chainsaws would never replace the handsaw."

Years ago about 60 percent of the crew worked as fallers. It would probably require a few dozen of them at both ends of a misery whip to keep up with one faller today using a powersaw. A pair of modern cutters can easily buck the five trees that seventy-five men used to break their backs on. The feller-buncher, a relatively recent invention, opens its steel claws and jaws to grasp a forty-year-old tree seventy-five feet high, bite it off, then move it into a pile for loading onto a truck—in one fell swoop, like a hand grabbing strands of uncooked spaghetti, breaking them in half, and dropping them into a pot. Add an automatic delimbing machine, and one driver in a cab eliminates the livelihoods of an eight-man crew.

To mill operators, the mother milk of plywood evokes ecstasy as intense as a naturalist feels traipsing through the forest. At least 99 percent of what runs through the knives at Green Veneer is Douglas fir. Twenty-four hours before sliding down the green chain, the former trees lay still on a hillside at Pamelia Creek, awaiting Hirons's crew. In their processed form, many of them will make the best plywood money can buy—tight-grained and knot-free as only near-eternity can yield. Old growth's grain, starting from the decay in the core, becomes "white sand," smooth and brown, halfway through the log; and, finally, clear and crisp in its outermost peel. Nearly half of Green Veneer's plywood meets the highest grade because it has three knots or fewer per piece. A builder's dream, it is lightweight and resilient yet rigid and strong. Fine plywood's resistance to warping and twisting makes it ideally suited for floors, roofing, and a host of daily applications. Chances are the average American wakes up on it in the morning, sees it in road signs en route to work, and leans elbows on it in the office.

Plywood's practical popularity, however, obscures the aesthetic sin of exploiting a natural gem for so functional a purpose. "There're trees standing for four hundred years before Columbus and yet we're talking about turning them into plywood or pulp," notes Chuck Bennett, a Salem-based lobbyist for Opal Creek. "It's like going into a Carrara marble quarry and turning it into limedust for garden trim."

The United States' pragmatic impulse, it often seems, takes for granted infinite food, fuel, and space. By contrast, Japan wiped out its forests ages ago. Its coolness toward conventional plywood from Green Veneer—or from any American mill, for that matter—stems from an abiding appreciation of old growth's exquisite patterns on bare beams and trim. "The Japanese live on top of one another. Within thirty or forty miles of Tokyo there are about 40 million people. Conductors jam people on the subway until the door closes. The joke is you could have a heart attack in Tokyo and wouldn't know until the train stops, the door opens, and you fall out," says Rick Schaefer, a Portland-based West Gulf lumber broker. "I think beautiful, natural wood is a balance to this crowding. In Japanese city homes, they're used to having everything perfect, and that means a lot more quality wood exposed."

On a late Friday evening, the air hangs heavy and still over Vancouver, Washington, a major northwestern port across the Columbia River from Portland. Schaefer guides his car past the security gate. In another example of the smallness of the continent's corner, the Hawaiian-born Schaefer is the godson of Thurston Twigg-Smith, the owner of Shiny Rock, the mining company at Opal Creek. Schaefer founded the brokerage end of North Fork with Atiyeh and Hirons sixteen years ago. For the past eight years, Schaefer has served as a buffer between northwestern mills and foreign customers, handling export functions such as marketing and customer relations once the lumber leaves the yard.

Hirons and I accompany Schaefer across the sea of blacktop as he shares the secret to generating more American jobs per tree in the international market. Acre upon acre of old growth, constituting about 1 million board feet of lumber, stacked far above our heads, wait to be loaded onto a break-bulk vessel almost two football fields long—700 feet—and 100 feet wide. It takes about fifteen days for the ship to make Tokyo or Osaka. At any give time, Tokyo's docks contain 120 million board feet, enough to build twelve thousand houses. "Whoa, look at these damn beams," Hirons exclaims upon seeing his wood shipped from this port for the first time.

As meticulously as diamond cutters, Japanese mills slice the Douglas fir in five-inch clear, vertical-grained overlays on plywood, shoji rice paper doors, or a multitude of other items on the high end. "There's nowhere else in the world where they're going to get the fibers they get out of here," Schaefer says. China and Korea don't mind buying the less aesthetically pleasing second growth. The denuded nations have little choice and it costs less. Over the next two decades, Schaefer plans on selling the wood, cut to their exact specifications, as a product finished on U.S. shores. "Our company is going to be a survivor. We're getting out at the front of this thing as far as we can," he adds. "We're going to be more and more into finished products like windows and doors. That's where the market is going to be. There will be less timber and it will be more expensive." The Japanese, in particular, have generated a large enough GNP to enjoy a standard of living that showcases premium wood.

Schaefer and Jim Morgan, co-owner of Young and Morgan in Mill City, recently returned from a two-week mission to Japan to join the growing ranks of businessmen selling lumber in its final form to the export market. Vanport Manufacturing in Boring, Oregon, began cutting wood to metric dimensions favored in Japan and built a traditional Japanese guesthouse to attract buyers. Sales soared. Weyerhaeuser and the Bank of Tokyo joined forces in a new plant in Aberdeen, Washington, to manufacture plywood fashioned to Japanese taste. Young and Morgan has custom-cut complete screen doors and is talking with builders of prefabricated homes about manufacturing them on a regular basis as soon as it retools its Mill City plant. A paperweight-size cube of veneer glued together so that it shows clear, vertical grain on all four sides sits atop Morgan's desk. To look at it fires a mill owner's inspiration.

Morgan is beginning to realize that to stay afloat he must squeeze the value, from domestic or foreign markets, from a dwindling number of trees. Born and bred on the outskirts of Mill City, Morgan, a wealthy but unassuming timber baron, prefers a good hunting trip to a vacation in Europe, which he has never seen. On his first trip to Japan recently, however, Morgan gladly put up with the exotic culture. He found the quarters cramped and the diet disagreeable. "I couldn't hack the slimy oysters, and the squid tasted like shoe leather," he grouses. Schaefer's diplomatic skills and modest proficiency in Japanese helped smooth out the social wrinkles. "Doing the things Jim does in value-added, you gotta work downstream," Schaefer says. "That is where the industry is going to have to go, spotted owl or no spotted owl."

The Forest Service reports that milling finished lumber "provides at least three times as much employment as exporting logs; fabricating plywood or veneer, four times as much." According to an Oregon State University study, processing all northwestern timber within the region could generate ten thousand to fifteen thousand jobs.

Conservation makes as much sense as secondary manufacturing. "Every time something happens, these guys scream bloody murder. How many times do the walls come down like Jericho?" Atiyeh asks. "It's much ado about nothing. I heard this about losing jobs when I was a little kid in the early 1960s." Generations ago, merely a third of the tree was actually used, while the rest was left in the woods or burned as rubbish at the mills. Today, nothing goes to waste. More than half a tree is now turned into pulpwood for paper. Douglas fir makes superb newsprint and noble fir high-quality office paper. Scientists, proving the extent to which necessity mothers invention, have devised ways of transforming bark into insulating material, mulch, and fertilizer for lawns. Sawdust and shavings are compressed into fuel logs and briquettes. Wood chips and shavings go into making paper and packaging. At both Green Veneer and Willamette Industries, my tour guides, according to the gospel of maximum recovery, demonstrate how the last dregs of bark and mill waste fire modern hogged fuel boilers.

Environmentalism pays off. New, cleaner technology provides countless opportunities for future profits. The enactment of the world's toughest laws protecting air, water, land, and public health improved the efficiency of plants while spawning the cleanup industry, one of the nation's most dynamic. According to the Department of Commerce, 65,000 to 70,000 companies in this business employ nearly 1 million workers and had sales in 1991 of $130 billion. For every $1 billion spent to control air pollution, the EPA estimates up to 20,000 jobs are created in industries producing new technologies. In the meantime, manufacturers from Monsanto to Dow Chemical have lowered their production costs and waste disposal by installing state-of-the-art equipment. "If the theory is correct that the way to create jobs is trash the environment, you would think Eastern Europe would be economic leaders of the world," says Vice President Al Gore. "You would also think that Japan and Germany would be struggling Third World nations."

"Nah, too high. Maybe, get back to him later," grunts Jim Morgan in his office at North Plywood, headquarters of Young and Morgan. Wheeling and dealing in the wood market, he glances at figures on scraps of paper furnished by lieutenants. Hirons slugs down his umpteenth cup of coffee and drags his umpteenth Camel. Morgan, along with his father, Vern, and his uncle Bob Young, presides over the operation. Young and Morgan, Mill City's largest employer, runs a plywood plant, a veneer plant, a timber-cutting subsidiary, and a trucking company—with a total of 450 workers. About 300 draw their paychecks from Freres Lumber Company, which owns three veneer plants and a sawmill. Frank Lumber Company employs 150 workers. The Big Three dominate the Mill City scene as thoroughly as Andrew Carnegie once did Pittsburgh.

Over the past three decades, hundreds of Mill City families have owed their comfortable homes and full dinner pails to the Big Three. About 80 percent of the community, in one form or another, currently enjoys the wages and benefits of the Big Three. In return, the saw-wielding serfs and the merchant class pledge their absolute loyalty to Mill City's feudal system. In many ways, the millocracy is a throwback to a simpler era of unbridled capitalism.

Environmentalists try to tar Jim, or "Jimmy," as his cronies call Morgan, forty, a timber baron. Yet his demeanor and appearance defy one environmentalist's depiction of him as a "nice Donald Trump." For one thing, Morgan's dress—blue jeans and denim shirts—complements his down-home beard. It runs against his nature to put on airs, assuming he had any in the first place. "I know him personally. Bought booze for him before he was old enough to buy it for himself," Harvey Spears says. "He's never been treated like the boss's son. Jim has rolled around in the mud with us. He's been more on our level." The flesh folds over Morgan's eyes show the wear and tear of hard living at both ends of the day. He routinely works thirteen-hour days, starting at 6:00 A.M. His voice often crackles on the company CB long before dawn. In Hirons's truck I hear Morgan requesting paint and wire. The hands-on administrator even talks to telephone salesmen on their calls.

Morgan's unassuming air reflects his own style and cultural mores. Northwesterners make a point of not flaunting their affluence, a tradition dating back to such early settlers as William S.

Ladd. On his rise to becoming Portland's preeminent businessman, Ladd never abandoned his Yankee thrift. He still answered
his letters personally by turning letters sent to him upside down
and writing between the lines. Oregon may have less Mercedes
per capita than any other state in the country. "When people got
stuff," Morgan says, "they don't have to brag about it." Hirons
has observed Bob Young outside the mills in overalls, grease-
monkeying equipment. "You never would think of him as a millionaire two or three times over," Hirons marveled. "He's as common as dirt."

Morgan radiates an affability so sincere I can think of few good
ol' boys in Mill City I would rather join on one of their weeklong hunting trips in autumn. "I'm a grass-rooter, down-to-earth
person who grew up in this canyon," Morgan drawls in his rural
twang, thick as pine pitch. "We're honest people. I'm not going
to feed you a line of bullshit. I'm not industry or a politician, but
I get dumped in the same bucket as Boise Cascade."

As Mill City legend has it, Young and Morgan refused to lay
off a worker during the twenty-six-month-long recession in the
early 1980s. Actually, Young and Morgan Lumber, according to
its official company history, did shut down for a year, from late
1981 to 1982. And most of its employees outside the lumber
division gratefully accepted a 20 percent pay cut to stay working.
"This canyon has a history of operating when no one else does,"
Morgan says. "These are family-owned and family-run companies.
We just don't pick up and say 'so long.' "

Young and Morgan's devotion to its extended family of workers
starts at home. In 1946 Vern Morgan, Jim's father, and Bob
Young, his mother's brother, made a beeline from military service
to the Oregon woods. Unable to compete head to head with Boise
Cascade and other big corporations, the landless entrepreneurs
scraped together enough money to buy a few private woodlots and
buy into federal sales of old growth. As luck would have it, the
Forest Service had just begun selling off its land on easy, negotia-
ble terms. At only seven dollars per thousand board feet, Young
and Morgan found the seeds of their fortune. Morgan displayed
a cutthroat instinct for business. Among the cheap secondhand
equipment his partner, a mechanical genius, turned into gold was
a Model A truck that gave them a serviceable log hauler. When
Hirons once asked if he had any hobbies, Young replied, "Yeah,
building mills."

In addition to eyeing future deals, Morgan and Bud Johnson,
the head of the trucking division, ogled each other's wife. Instead

of a duel, they agreed to a trade. A sheepish inquiry about Jim Morgan's pedigree elicits a forgiving smile. "My folks divorced when I was twelve and ended up in a swaperoo," he says. "My brother is a product of that swaperoo. That's why his name is Johnson. He's a half brother." In another sign of intermingling between the various families at Young and Morgan, Jim volunteers that John Bishop, a top wood seller for the company, is his son-in-law. His sister and brother-in-law run a local Ford dealership. Nepotism suiting British royalty keeps the reins tight on the empire.

Try as he might to break free, Jim Morgan belongs squarely in his relatives' orbit. He matriculated at Oregon State and studied business and forestry. In his sophomore year, Morgan came up against the liberal arts requirement. "They told me I had to take history and all that crap," he recalls, "so I got pissed off at the system and quit." He decided to return to Mill City to learn the wood trade from his father. Vern Morgan, a stern taskmaster, can melt underlings with his piercing gaze. The septuagenarian patriarch and his son, perhaps settling ancient scores, make the Atiyeh-Hirons flap look tame by comparison. Jim has tooled around town in a pickup with a kicked-in door, courtesy of Vern. Their ferocious shouting matches have competed with the din of the mills, terrifying employees. All that separates the office they now share is a sliding glass door. "Working with your father in a family business is not all peaches and cream," Jim Morgan says with a smile. Finally, the two combatants agreed to cool it, lest their emotions lead to patricide or infanticide. While Hirons was plying the backroads one day, his ears were singed from a Morgan melee on CB radio, the canyon's electric billboard. He crept up to a familiar pickup, only to discover Vern and Jim sitting in the front seat, passing the microphone back and forth and laughing. The younger Morgan harbors few regrets about his career choice. "Ten or fifteen years ago I seriously considered doing something else," he says. "I decided that rather than going out and building my own mountain I'd just as soon build on top of their mountain."

Atiyeh, an old friend of Jim Morgan, measures his words carefully in evaluating Mill City's social stratum. "Tom Hirons has a small logging company that employs eight guys and gives them a reasonable living. He hasn't taken out much more than he needs. A little bit, but not much more. He hasn't been a major exploiter of the planet, even though he cuts down forests. On a scale of wealth measuring what the two of us have accumulated, we're probably pretty much the same. How can I judge him? I probably have more than I need, too. I got my toys, like my airplane. I used to do real well making money flying," Atiyeh says. "Jimmy, on the other hand, through no fault of his own, was born into a system in which his worth as a human being was measured by how much money he made. Look, I love him. He's a real guy, not at all pretentious. But, even though he has worked goddamn hard for it, his consumption is beyond what he needs. Philosophically, what he's operating under isn't good for humanity as a whole. Jim doesn't need millions of dollars and to move from a big house to another just for a wife and one kid."

Atiyeh doesn't even bother inviting Jim Morgan or other timber barons up to Opal Creek in the hope of converting them. "None of these people are that in touch with themselves in a deeper sense to sit around and analyze why they do what they do," he says. "They just do what they've always done. It's tough talking New Age philosophy with these guys. Happiness is a four-wheel-drive pickup and a new boat."

Jim Morgan is a millionaire many times over. "It depends on how you consider the company's assets and their worth. When I turn in a statement at the bank, yes," Morgan allows, in a refreshing display of candor. "My income is good. I like spending money as good as anyone." As the logging dollars evaporate, timber barons are branching out into new ventures to keep their coffers full. Employees accuse Young and Morgan of investing in gold and tin mines throughout the West and Southwest; a paving company in Salt Lake City; and tents for fairs and various outdoor events. Other than the Stayton Ford dealership, a local auto parts store, and a ranch in eastern Oregon, Morgan insists that 90 percent of his company's stake remains in timber. He neglects to mention a Chevrolet dealership, Marion Forks Lodge above Mill City in the Cascades, and a good deal of rental housing.

Even so, he has yet to silence the grumbling among neighbors about mill owners making hay while the sun shines. "You watch Vern. They take care of themselves. They've diversified with every bit of profit they've made," says Jay Swanson, owner of Pastiche gift shop in Mill City, echoing the sentiments of fellow merchants. "If that mill goes under, their life-style ain't gonna change one bit. They'll still live as high on the hog as ever because they're in business everywhere else. They won't look back." Adds Pastor Veach, "It wouldn't surprise me if Jim Morgan had sixty-three companies."

Part of the suspicion rests on past examples of the barons' narrow concept of public interests. Like the monopolistic railroad and oil moguls from the turn of the century, they have tended to believe, as Gore Vidal puts it in another context, "in a unique society in which we have free enterprise for the poor and socialism for the rich." It has always galled them to have to pay the feds for lands at their own doorstep ever since railroad grants in the last century permitted forebears to take it free. Since the forests, national or not, belonged to the people locally, the mill owners reasoned, the revenues ought to be recycled through their hands back to the community. Two decades ago, they sat down together at a coffee shop in Detroit, above Mill City, to hatch a plot. Between slurps of liquid caffeine these magnates of commerce divvied up the spoils at upcoming timber auctions. In 1975, a federal judge convicted Robert Freres and Vern Morgan and their companies of conspiring to rig bids on five national forest sales at the Detroit Ranger District in 1971 and early 1972. The defendants denied any willful wrongdoing. The last of Mill City's Big Three, Frank Lumber, was acquitted. The U.S. Supreme Court refused to hear the case on appeal.

The Antitrust Division of the U.S. Justice Department, which prosecuted the case, claimed the conspiracy covered more than one hundred sales between 1967 and 1972, costing the U.S. Treasury $17.3 million. Oregon, demanding its 25 percent cut (as the law entitles counties encompassing federal lands), sued. "Freres and Morgan are wealthy men, owners of profitable firms, whose incomes were greatly enhanced by this offense," argued U.S. Attorney Sidney Lezak. "Their only purpose was to save themselves millions of dollars, money which rightfully belonged to the U.S. government and to local governments and people of the counties in which they operated." The statute of limitations for the period and the state's bungling of its civil suit allowed the defendants to cough up just $105,000 in corporate and personal fines. "Who says crime doesn't pay?" Atiyeh asks till this day.

The tragic codependence between the mill owners and the seven hundred workers in their thrall manifested itself in the court drama's final act, in 1981. The judge reduced the defendants' sixty days' confinement in community service centers to sixty days' probation on the humane grounds that it would distract them from coping with a one-year ban imposed on them by the U.S. Forest Service. Pressure from politicians and community leaders, who worried about the harm to mill towns, forced the Forest Service to back off from its original proposal for a two-year ban. Companies had only to sit out auctions for a year during a slow season when few sales were in the pipeline anyway.

Washington, D.C., tried turning Morgan and Freres into national examples. Their case triggered a far-reaching Justice Department investigation into comparable abuses of other national forests in the West. Congress, bearing the defendants in mind, inserted a provision in the 1976 National Forest Management Act mandating the Forest Service to sell its timber through sealed bids to avoid a repeat of the price-fixing in the traditional oral auctions. The new restriction lasted all of six months before the forest products industry, flexing its mighty political muscle, put an end to it. The uproar was understandable. Sealed bids drove up the price of timber.

The conspiracy seems quaint by current, cutthroat standards. The average price that northwestern mill operators are paying for scarce, federal Douglas fir and hemlock has more than tripled in the past four years. Mill City's Big Three blame each other for overpaying.

In Mill City, the siege mentality culminated in 1989 as the politics of labor unrest and the Opal Creek state park bill intersected. The Morgans resolved to block a union whose acceptance had already become the norm at Willamette and much of the industry. Mill City's timber barons have regarded unions as foreign as Marx's *Communist Manifesto*. Workers had primarily petitioned to restore wages and in some cases medical benefits lost during the recession in the early 1980s. At the eleventh hour, just prior to the union vote, Jim Morgan announced he would have to shut down, in accordance with prior notification laws, and pinned the blame on logging cutbacks from the spotted owl and Atiyeh's crusade. Mill City workers feared for their livelihoods.

No sooner had management won the election and beaten the union than Morgan announced that, by sheer coincidence, market conditions had improved sufficiently to keep the mills open. "We would never have signed [on] the dotted line. If people come and ask I'll do anything, but if they come and dictate, I'm going to tell them to get fucked," Morgan says. "If they'd picketed us, we'd have gone ahead and hired scab labor. We believe the people can do as much for themselves as the unions." It may be of interest to such rank-and-file people as Spears to recognize the virtue of self-reliance, an American truism on the order of what's good for Young and Morgan is good for Mill City.

The company's long-term responsibility to employees commands a modicum of its attention. "We're not out there to screw people," Morgan avers. "We're out there to get the best job we can out of them." Workers earn $10.00 an hour, about the industry average, and receive basic health coverage. They are encouraged to earn extra income working overtime. Although there is no profit sharing, Young and Morgan chips in to a modest 401K pension plan. Employees' children receive preferential treatment for part-time jobs at the mills during vacation and summertime. For instance, Michelle Meader, a seventeen-year-old neighbor of Hirons, earns $4.60 an hour roaming the mills on the lookout for fires. As for the future, Young and Morgan's veterans, many of whom have put in twenty-five years, receive vague assurance of retraining for whatever new equipment that may come along in secondary manufacturing.

The pillars of Mill City grouse about industry violating its end of social contract to the community. "I have nothing against Young and Morgan. They are sharp men and good at finances," says Pastor Veach, pointing to a Christmas card one logging company owner graciously sent him, inviting the Veach family to stay at his condo on the Oregon coast. "When you talk about the Morgans, Franks, and Freres, they have bucks. The reason is that they haven't let them loose. It's time they did." Growing up in a timber town, Veach recalls the generous scholarships the mills once sponsored for high-school seniors entering the forestry field. His pet proposal: establishment of a "Young and Morgan Scholarship" to study practical subjects in today's market, such as engineering or accounting. "I'd like to see the companies go back to basics. They've been rolling back wages and stopped providing insurance. Some of them still have paid vacations, but not to the same extent as before," Veach says. "The mill owners make the money. We need to retool those workers." For timber barons to decry environmentalists' insensitivity to the plight of their workers while doing so little for them of their own accord smacks of sheer hypocrisy.

True to himself, Morgan flicks off the challenge with homespun wisdom bouyed by past success. "We are going to be a decider until we decide to quit, and we've no intention of quitting. I believe it's a given there's always going to be timber harvested in this state. We want as much as we can get," he says. "You heard the story about the two hunters in the tent while a grizzly bear was circling outside? One guy was dressing up, putting on all his heavy clothes. Another guy was putting on his jogging shoes. They were friends. One guy says to the other, 'That bear is going to get you and you have nothing to protect you.' The other says, 'I don't have to worry about that 'cause all I gotta do is outrun you.' " I hadn't heard this story. "The point is," Morgan explains for my benefit, "we're gonna be out there on the leading edge to survive."

Once upon a time, he and Atiyeh leaned on each other in work and play. "We were close and we were friends," Morgan recalls. They hunted together and went sightseeing together with their spouses and the Hironses in Canada on a crosscontinent train ride. In Atiyeh's early days at Jawbone Flats, a Land Rover containing a drum of gasoline veered off a bridge. Morgan immediately drove up his Caterpillar to fish it out before an explosion could occur. Atiyeh thanked him for pulling off a "miracle."

Since the environmental fracas has driven a deep wedge between them, however, Atiyeh holds Morgan responsible for inciting the rank and file against him and all environmentalists. "I vilify industry for hiding the ball. The government is wrong for letting it do what it does, blaming the environmentalists and people who want to save ancient forests rather than looking for solutions," Atiyeh fumes. "I'm bitter about them for being so stupid, shortsighted, and caring so little about their communities. They will say anything or do anything to perpetuate a system that's doomed. Then they have the gall to turn around and blame me."

All across the Northwest, longtime logging families fear they are looking at deadends. Few are as proud and tightly knit as the Mobergs, owners of Fred Moore Logging in Mill City, a contract company about twice the size of Hirons's Mad Creek. Whether on the job in the woods or on vacation, they seldom stray apart. On one of my last visits last year, three of the men posed together for a photograph spanning their respective generations. A Grant Wood image, beautifully captured by a *Time* photographer, of the family standing side by side celebrates the honorable yeomen of the northwestern woods. Fred Moore, seventy-seven, the patriarch, holds the rusted crosscut saw he used horse-logging in Mill City half a century ago; his son-in-law Verl Moberg, fifty-six, an early chainsaw half as large as a man; and Gary Moberg, thirty-four; the sleek modern model common today. (Gary's brother Randy, thirty-five, is out in the woods running a log loader.) Their lumberjack garb and intent gazes seem to fuse them into a solitary being. A few months later Fred Moore passed away in Randy's arms on the very site where the picture was taken.

Fred Moore's memory lingers in the sturdy presence of Verl and Sue Moberg. A shirt she bought her husband proclaims "ON THE EIGHTH DAY GOD CREATED A LOGGER." The family's American logging lineage dates back to the turn of the century in Minnesota, by way of Sweden. Reared by his father, a logging engineer, in a one-room cabin at Little Sweden above Mill City, Verl grew up calling the logger Oscar Nystrom "Uncle Oscar." "My family is a *true* fourth-generation logging family," Verl boasts. "I've been in timber all my life." His wife shoots him a sympathetic glance. "There's a lot of mad people in this state who don't want to see timber locked up," she says. "It's going to be a long, hot summer."

Sue Moberg subscribes to a tortured conspiracy theory gaining currency around town. "You may think I'm off-base and a McCarthyite. I think this is Communist-based control of public lands. I think Earth First! is Communist-based. They've got people in the Audubon Society and the Wilderness Society. I don't mean Communist like Russian. I mean the communistic idea. They've been doing this for twenty years. They would like zero population growth. They want to go back to the fifteenth century," she snaps. "Let's face it. I just think it's an absolute fact. An elite group wants control of all public property." Loggers have prospered for so long off national forests they tend to regard their comfortable arrangement as an entitlement.

Randy mulls over his mother's random thoughts about applying his construction and managerial skills to a new trade if logging goes down. Fresh from the shower after a long day operating the yarder, water drips from his hair onto the floor of his new, well-appointed home. It pains him to consider uprooting his family. "I love rural America here. It's like going back twenty-five years. We have an awful lot at stake, our whole way of life," he says. "It's like they talk about how you can't move the spotted owl. You take some of the loggers and their families here and shove them in the suburbs, they are going to die from the transplant. People are scared. I guess I am, too."

The continuity between the father and his sons has united them in their past toil and present agony. The uncanny resemblance between them is strikingly clear in their look and gestures. Their voices' rising inflection accompanies furrowed eyebrows and nodding heads in a single motion. Three or four generations comprise more than a half century—a short stretch, some cynical environmentalists claim. Yet these skeptics are at a loss to answer how many occupations exceed two generations in a nation filled with people migrating into and out of professions. The lumberjack qualifies as the last of a dying breed.

Gary Moberg, Randy's younger brother, would sooner surrender his family homestead, down the road from Atiyeh's, than his birthright to log. "I started logging when I was eighteen. Why should I throw away sixteen years for nothing? We didn't destroy the country," Moberg says. "I don't want my kid to go into logging. How many people are they talking about losing their jobs, thirty thousand? But don't get me wrong. I would be proud. Logging's in our family's blood. We're farmers, it's just a different crop."

His claim to the green mantle would probably leave the average environmentalist speechless. "We work in there every day and we go up there to play. We love the woods. We love the trees," he avers. "Nothing smells better than a fresh-cut log. I love it." At first glance, his proposal for shifting the present rotation for cutting trees from sixty to eighty years to four hundred to five hundred appears above reproach, were there evidence that man could actually duplicate the old-growth forests for fortieth-generation loggers to cut. "Why can't we plan that far ahead?" he demands. The Forest Service experiences difficulty mapping out its five-year plans, let alone five hundred. Gary's concern for the animal kingdom's welfare covers all corners. "You think it's hard on wildlife now. Put people out of work with nothing to buy. They will eat anything that moves," he warns. "Everybody hunts and fishes. I'd go into the woods to shoot squirrels." If the good-ol'-boy argument holds true, the northern spotted owl may have company on the endangered species list.

A mischievous gleam in his eye shines as Moberg unveils his designs on Opal Creek. "It's a sensitive area. Don't go hog wild and let three hundred trucks a day go out there. No logging on three-day weekends like Labor Day," he adds. "I wouldn't be against putting restrictions on it. No logging on weekends or during the week of July Fourth."

Of course, the visitors would probably stay away, since they come to Opal Creek to enjoy their trees in an upright position. "George has no control over those other guys [Earth First! members and other extremists]. He's just a henchman," Moberg says. "You give them Opal Creek, they're not going to be satisfied with that. They're going to want the rest of it anyway." According to the domino theory, an article of faith in Mill City, if the best-known stand of old growth falls under the preservationists' domination, the adjoining fragments of forest would follow, as a row of dominoes would topple end to end.

The Moberg family once counted Atiyeh among its dearest friends. The two brothers joined George on fishing trips to Canada in Atiyeh's plane. Their father reserved a soft spot for him and Opal Creek ever since he helped to plow roads through snow and washouts to bring Grandpa Hewitt supplies at Jawbone Flats in the 1960s. In 1980 Atiyeh took Hirons, Jim Morgan, and Moberg on flights over a smoldering Mount St. Helens. Above the red zone Atiyeh invoked the name of his uncle, then Oregon's chief executive, by identifying his party to the air traffic controller as "Governor Atiyeh's Task Force on Volcanoes."

Today they hold Atiyeh accountable for robbing future Mobergs of the chance to carry on the family tradition. Their terrific row at the hearings on the Opal Creek park bill in Salem raised neighbors' eyebrows. In the last contact between Gary and Atiyeh at the Circle K convenience store, both pretended not to notice the other through their cars' downed windows. "I don't know if we can still be friends," Gary says, "the way George has stabbed this whole community."

The image of Atiyeh conspiring with the lunatic fringe remains indelibly etched in brother Randy's mind. "That day the Earth First!ers were hanging around at the Capitol. Their hair was long and dirty and they were on George's side," Randy says of the support marshaled for the Opal Creek park. "Earth First! and George were saying yes, yes, and everybody else was saying no, no. Pretty soon everybody saw beads hanging on George. And he had a suit on." Moberg expects Atiyeh and himself to grow apart steadily. "The wounds have festered. I will never trust him again. I would never sit down with George and spill my guts buddy, buddy," he says. "Not like Tom might."

In their sunset years, the senior Mobergs will see Atiyeh's face each time a grandchild splinters off from Mill City to seek work unrelated to wood. "George is the one who brought this down on us," says Sue. Adds her husband, Verl: "I honestly feel he did stab us in the back. It would be awfully hard to have relationships with him. He could care less about the whole community suffering. This sure could be the end of the line for the Mobergs."

At the east end of Mill City's Kimmel Park, Atiyeh surveys the remains of his town's cooperative mill. A cloudy log pond has sat stagnant for at least a generation. The men who stoked the fires and fished the timber out had to find new work, just as their descendants up the road will in coming years. "The owl's listed. That's fact. Deny it and you're talking about hitching your wagon to a falling star. It's not the loggers' fault. I have tremendous empathy for them. They were told they would have trees forever, a promise that could never have been kept," he says. "It's not nice when my kids come home and are upset because their friends are moving away." But Atiyeh hardly becomes misty-eyed at the dinnertable listening to tales of his neighbors' misfortunes. The bigger picture overrides such concerns. "How can these guys be as insecure as they are about their jobs? A lot of people lose their jobs four or five times. Nobody has tenure. We can all lose our jobs for economic reasons or anything else," he says. "If I'm going to lose my job over something, I'd much rather it be protecting a species than the cash flow of a big corporation. At least you're giving up your job for something that is worthwhile, not because your corporation is being taken over by some corporate raider."

He maintains that short-term disruption to wood workers justifies the eternal benefits to the earth. "I think it's important for people to understand that these things have to happen, whether it's toxic waste or smokestacks that burn high-sulfur coal. They're going to be making cleaner cars. It's all going to have social costs and put people out of work temporarily," Atiyeh observes. "Hey, we gotta do it or the alternative is death of our species and all the ones that go with it. We'll start down the road and get scared. If we don't do it, then what the hell have we got left?"

At Pamelia Creek, Tom Hirons navigates the slippery bark of a thumper lying in the ground. The thought of being cast as the guinea pig in his ex-friend's social experiment raises the bark on his neck. "The whole environment movement is anti-people regardless of the platitudes you here about doing this to save humanity," he snarls when confronted with the nation's seeming indifference toward human suffering in recent years.

In a speech later delivered at his alma mater during Earth Week, the logger reflects on the global implications of failing to square conservation with economics. "Poverty is the leading cause of environmental degradation. You can't blame some poor native Brazilian for cutting down rain forests when the only thing he's thinking about is putting food on his family's table," Hirons says. "You can't blame some poor worker in Mill City for working in the woods when all he's thinking about is putting food on his table for his family. And you certainly can't deny that in this country the gap is widening between the rich and the poor."

For the moment Hirons is loath to await Big Brother's outstretched hand in Washington, D.C. "Retraining is a cruel hoax. It holds out little promise for families trying to bring home livable income or the promise of good roads and good sidewalks," he says in speeches delivered around the state and in Washington, D.C. "What kind of businesses are we going to attract? We can only diversify our communities when they are based on a sound social infrastructure." Hirons laments the transition from an industrial to a service economy as a refutation of his own gritty career producing one of society's basic materials. "Maybe my thinking is getting jaded, but we can't piecemeal shut down communities like Mill City," he says. "Hell, we can't all make a living doing each other's washing. It's gotten to the point where there'll be no one to buy a loaf of bread from."

To a worse extent than he cares to acknowledge, the world may be passing his breed by. According to Oregon's employment division, about 90 percent of all new jobs created in the next decade will be in service industries. Workers in manufacturing, including the eighty-five hundred in lumber and wood products expected to lose their jobs in the next decade, primarily from automation, must master new skills geared toward new technologies or continue on the same economic roller coaster.

Hirons is certain the lofty sentiments his nemesis espouses will feed few families. In this century's second half, the forgotten man, as Franklin Roosevelt once dubbed him, has lost a great deal of job opportunities in farming, steel, and auto manufacturing. Stripped of the chance to provide for loved ones by plying the trades their fathers and grandfathers had before them, many have fallen through threadbare safety nets. With the government abdicating its responsibilities during the past decade, the economy's victims find themselves adrift. According to a national study of blue-collar workers displaced during the early 1980s, it took them almost half a year to find new jobs, and often at lower wages. Harvey Spears needs more than a politician's campaign pledge to launch a second career and retire the debts incurred from having the courage to invest in his community.

The nation owes its loggers. Verl Moberg's upset about the government's further intrusion into his life betrays a certain lapse of memory. Washington, D.C., bears singular responsibility for weaning generations of workers on cheap, abundant federal timber to satisfy the postwar housing boom. Displaced workers in the steel or auto industries have largely fallen victim to natural market forces such as changes in production techniques, drops in demand, and corporate belt-tightening. Their counterparts in the Northwest are sustaining the added hardship of a sudden jerk in federal policy.

The federal government is not short of tools to cushion the blow. For starters, in 1990 it imposed a belated ban on whole-log exports from national and state lands, easing log shortages to local mills and helping stem the decline in jobs. Restrictions on wood from private lands raise constitutional issues. Still, a special tax on exported logs from these sources could generate funds for retraining and compensating mill towns for lost revenue.

The timber barons are due for a dose of behavior modification. Bill Clinton campaigned on a pledge to require every employer to spend 1.5 percent of payroll for continuing education and training for all workers, who would be able to choose advanced-skills training and the chance to earn a high-school diploma. Tougher laws requiring advance notice of layoffs mitigate the disruption in the lives of those laid off. A year after closing a mill in Albany, Oregon, Simpson Timber has found new jobs for 63 employees through a federally funded program in partnership with the company and the plywood workers' union. They and 117 other workers have received classroom and on-the-job instruction in writing résumés, in interviews, and in computer skills. The new jobs the employees obtained through the program include clerk, welder, food processor, carpenter's helper, and landscaper. The average hourly wage, $8.31, is a little more than 20 percent less than what mills once paid. So while the families survive, the standard of living has slipped. Still, it beats unemployment.

The finest features of state and federal proposals recognize that timber workers deserve to be treated as an investment rather than as welfare recipients. The rapid depletion of savings, need for assistance from family or friends, and unemployment compensation compound the need for relief. It must go to whole families, including oft-neglected spouses. The duration of financial aid must be linked to education or training programs to ensure that money woes do not force the worker or spouse to drop out of programs at a community college or vocational school. Given the mobility of American families and Oregon's growing economy, training programs ought to be geared toward the specific requirements of industries in and outside their local communities. Toward that end, legislation gaining backers in Washington, D.C., would defray moving costs.

Most of the beneficiaries, as University of Oregon economics professor Ed Whitelaw notes, carry little of the risk posed by clients in existing programs designed to address chronic poverty and unemployment. Woodworkers' work ethic and high aspirations have already benefited the state through the investment they have made in their homes and community, backbones of the state's economy. Where loans are available in lieu of outright

grants, the high probability of workers returning to work lowers
the chance of default.

Even under the worst-case scenario, at least half of the industry's jobs will still exist by decade's end. Logging will then resume
in the Northwest, when vast tracts of second growth come on
line for cutting. But at that juncture, by some estimates, the yield
will be four to six log trucks of timber per acre, compared to old
growth's ten to twelve. Meanwhile, the maximum number of jobs
per trees can be achieved with the new logs remaining in the
United States. Lumber commands higher value than logs, flooring
more than lumber, and furniture tops them all. Free traders among
industry officials argue that removing barriers to the export market
in finished products alone could boost it by $2 billion by 1994,
the equivalent of twenty thousand jobs or two thirds of the total
expected to disappear from saving the spotted owl.

Of course, secondary manufacturing depends on a primary
source of wood. Oregon and Washington State contain 4 million
acres of so-called nonindustrial private forestland. Their lower
elevations and gentler topography allow trees to grow faster than
on national forests. Washington, D.C., ought to restore programs
dismantled in the Reagan era to provide small landowners with
technical counsel and incentives to proceed with the intensive
management of tree farms. Western Oregon's nonindustrial forests, encompassing the North Santiam Canyon, may well hold
the potential of a fourfold increase in timber production. During
the next fifty years, the suburban sprawl around Seattle, Portland,
and other cities threatens to swallow up another 1 million acres
of private and state forestland. Voters will likely approve the same
bond measures to conserve it as they do to curb the subdivision
of farmland. What urbanite or forester would not choose a partially logged forest over a shopping mall?

New forestry practices offer the best of all possible worlds to
lumberjacks and the ecosystem. The Forest Service would cease
its usual method of forty- to sixty-acre-wide clear-cuts. Under
scientist Jerry Franklin's new techniques, live trees, snags, and
woody debris remain in the logged-over swaths to replenish the
landscape and harbor wildlife. He advocates treating second and
third growth with equal ecological sensitivity. Hirons has had
tastes of sustainable forestry on the occasional selective cuts in
sensitive areas. The compliments from the Forest Service and
vibrant healthy woods left in Hirons's wake presage the rising
demand for the special set of skills he has developed for years to
come. With the days of relatively cheap and easy old growth

nearing the end, the least versatile loggers will fall by the wayside. But Hirons and his crew stand a golden chance of naming their price on labor-intensive jobs demanding more than just a chain-saw and yarder.

The shift of cultural values invariably creates victims. The Cold War's end has resulted in the layoffs of about half a million defense workers over the past four years. "Defense conversion," as Bill Clinton envisions it, would ensure that the communities and their workers in defense industries would be guided toward using their skills and technologies to help rebuild America into advanced communications networks and for research and schools. The government ought to take stock of a "green conversion" to move beyond environmentally unsound enterprises it has subsidized, such as logging in unprofitable federal lands. The money could then be invested putting the displaced back to work renovating roads, bridges, and railroads; or even, among new environmental technologies, recycling plants and modern water and sewage systems.

Congress passed the Clean Air Act, hastening the switch from high-sulfur coal from Appalachia to the cleaner-burning, low-sulfur variety from Montana and Wyoming. "We as legislators have a responsibility to try to alleviate the pain and suffering of our own acts," proclaimed Robert Byrd, West Virginia's senior senator. "Have we looked into the eyes of a hungry coal miner's child?" He pleaded for assistance to the five thousand coal miners doomed to join the unemployment lines.

The timber conflict presents the nation with an ideal test case for softening the economic shocks of environmental crises. Congress has already set useful precedents. A federal aid package Byrd successfully incorporated in the Clean Air Act provides $250 million worth of income assistance and retraining to coal miners over five years. Congress agreed to pay the full salaries for up to six years to twenty-nine hundred workers dislocated by the expansion in 1978 of the Redwood National Park in northern California. The next workers that congressional legislation will probably displace will likely be victims of improved automobile fuel-economy standards. Sound investment in the affected workers and their communities clears the most difficult political impediments to executing national policy based on good science and safeguarding everyone's well-being.

It surely amounts to small consolation for Hirons to play martyr in Atiyeh's morality play. The loss of a job to the preservation of the spotted owl rends the heart. Yet a detour in the career of a coal miner for the sake of a cause as noble as clean air joins them to humanity's higher calling. Down to the last logger in the Northwest, intact old-growth forests will remain an equal-opportunity provider of intangible assets beyond income. Pristine rivers, scenic beauty, and biological diversity in the public domain belong to all people, including loggers themselves.

VIII

Waterloos and Watersheds

Late Thursday, the sun begins drooping over the Cascade Range, taking with it the hint of warmth in the air. Clusters of guests at the Breitenbush Hot Springs Retreat and Conference Center, a New Age community and resort, feel the winter chill brace their bare skin from head to toe. They shed their clothes in mixed company, as is the custom, to dip into the natural, rock-lined pools formed at the end of geothermal rivers and streams flowing through faults and folds in the layers deep below the earth's surface. For millennia, Native Americans and settlers have flocked to these hot waters for their legendary curative powers. Visitors can bathe in and drink twenty-seven different minerals, more than most other hot springs. The waters, sprinkled about a sloping alpine meadow in the heart of an ancient forest, yield psychological as well as physical benefits. This afternoon they reach 106 degrees, about 70 degrees warmer than the mountain cold. The clouds of steam floating above the hot water wrap the bathers in a misty blanket.

Most of the guests are weary urbanites stepping from mean streets into an idyllic world. Breitenbush ranks as one of the Northwest's biggest tourist attractions. At the start of Easter weekend, one of three busiest at Breitenbush all year, they meditate on matters large and small. A variety of New Age workshops offer "happenings," among them "Expanding Your Inner Light" and "Elisabeth Kubler-Ross: Life, Death, and Transition" (which a few loggers in the area could stand to attend). "Tens of thousands of people have found Breitenbush offers a unique blend of creature comfort and intimacy with nature that promotes healing, renewal, and spiritual growth," notes Breitenbush's marketing director, Peter Moore. Guests discover inner peace in a pyramid-shaped chapel or, better yet, a stroll through the old-growth forest. The glaciers of Mount Jefferson, Oregon's second-highest peak at 10,500 feet, and forest springs combine to feed the Breitenbush River on its raucous trip past 250 foot-high, 800-year-old trees.

Suddenly all hell breaks loose in paradise. The community's permanent residents scurry about on the hard dirt footpaths, commiserating. Breitenbush's general manager has just received a phone call from the U.S. Forest Service informing him that the timber sale at North Roaring Devil's Ridge would commence tomorrow. "What the hell?" gasps Michael Donnelly, down in Salem upon learning the shocking turn of events. "That's outrageous." Donnelly, vice president of Oregon Natural Resources Council and president of Friends of the Breitenbush Cascades, serves as a plaintiff in a long-standing lawsuit challenging the timber management practices in the Willamette National Forest.

He and other environmentalists have been caught with their guard down. They had been operating on the erroneous assumption, based on the advice of a careless lawyer, that they still had an injunction in force at the sixty-three-acre site near Breitenbush because the timber sale would do irreparable harm to the terrain and endanger a northern spotted owl habitat. They were unaware that behind the scenes the Forest Service has been working hand in hand with Bugaboo Timber, a subsidiary of Young and Morgan, to ensure that the sale, on which it holds contract, would proceed as planned. Stretching undisturbed from the Mount Jefferson Wilderness area to the Breitenbush community, North Roaring Devil's Ridge measures up to its Dickensian name in the pristine, massive trees and symbolic importance it has assumed in the fight over old growth. In their rustic alpine cabins at Breitenbush, residents and guests sleep fitfully tonight.

At dawn's first blush on Good Friday, fourteen hours after the fateful phone call, Forest Service employees and Young and Morgan's loggers roar through the forest near Breitenbush on snowmobiles. Within a few hours, the centuries-old trees fall gently on a pillow of snow, at the rate of about one every two minutes. (As if the gods are grimacing, on this Good Friday the *Exxon Valdez* oil spill occurs in Alaska.) Later in the morning Donnelly and his colitigants ask U.S. District Court judge James Burns in Portland for an emergency temporary restraining order while waiting to present their case for injunction. Burns defers a decision on granting such an order until Tuesday.

But by then it will be too late. The damage already done to the forest will render the request moot. Moreover, none of the environmentalists place much faith in Burns. An ally of industry, he had ruled against environmentalists three years earlier, only to be directed by an appeals court to issue a restraining order preventing the logging until the Forest Service met certain requirements concerning its effect on water quality and spotted owl habitat. He allowed one twenty-eight-acre patch in dispute to be cut. Last month, Breitenbush and the Oregon Natural Resources Council filed a request for a hearing on the North Roaring Devil's Ridge Timber sale in response to Young and Morgan's stated intentions to start logging as soon as the weather permitted. Burns never ruled on the request.

Jim Morgan has chosen North Roaring Devil's Ridge for his blitzkrieg to teach a lesson to the preservationists standing between him and his business. He's pulling out all the stops to prove Bugaboo is anything but an imaginary object of fear under *Webster's* definition. Snow logging, a fairly recent development in the woods, requires him to bring special equipment to the mountains for the job. Donnelly charges him with cutting trees he cannot even haul out for a month. Extra fallers are even hired to do the cut quickly and beat the environmentalists in court. On top of that, Morgan plans to log through the snowy weekend, from Good Friday through Easter Sunday. By the admission of an assistant forest ranger at the scene, it is extraordinary for logging crews to work on a holiday.

Young and Morgan has yet to recover from a self-inflicted black eye from the last cut at Halloween time three years ago. A home video they produced for themselves haunts them like Nixon's tapes. "Helluva splash," shouts a cutter preening before the camera as he falls a tree, on the order of six-hundred years old, into a creek. While constructing a temporary dirt and gravel bridge over a creek, a tractor gets stuck in the mud. Rather than retrieving a Caterpillar to free it, the workers break the dam, dumping silt and sediment into the creek downstream. The water turns cloudy. "Oh, we're polluting the river," says a worker sheepishly, eyeing the crowd uphill. "Look at the news media taking pictures of that." Bootleg copies of the video documenting their complicity circulate in Mill City, compounding the loggers' public image problems.

On Easter Sunday, Morgan confronts opponents of an entirely

different stripe than those in court. The band of militants Earth First! has issued an all-points bulletin throughout the state. Forty of them show up with their infamous reputations for monkey-wrenching, the damaging of equipment, and driving spikes into trees, a deadly hazard for fallers cutting them. The loggers arrive for work to discover protesters blocking the U.S. Forest Service road. A bonfire Earth First! has set rages at its entrance. About a mile farther up the road it has built a three-foot-high barricade of rocks in which one demonstrator sits, buried to his neck. After engaging the Earth First! members in cordial debate about whether the old growth should be cut, the loggers turn around and go home to observe Easter with their families. After they leave, the police charge thirteen of the protesters, including an extremely hairy man identifying himself as Woody Debris, with disorderly conduct. The national media jump on the story.

Having underestimated the other side's resolve, Atiyeh girds for the next blow at Opal Creek. He had pleaded with Morgan to keep his chainsaws away from Breitenbush. The mill owner held off, then figured he had to show them. Morgan boasts of his moral victory when the two friends run into each other in town. Atiyeh throws down the gauntlet. "When it comes down to Opal Creek, I ain't one of those damn hippies you slam-dunked, Jimmy," Atiyeh reminds him. "You don't want to get into it with me."

The Breitenbush community goes on alert. Three years ago, a number of Breitenbush's residents were arrested for aiding and abetting Earth First! "Your ass is grass if you do that again," Breitenbush's lawyer warns its directors. They could be setting themselves up for enormous liability. As Peter Moore reflects in the *Breitenbush Newsletter*:

> The Breitenbush community wants to live as a good neighbor. The disregard some protesters showed towards the logging community has left bad feelings toward environmentalists in the Santiam Valley. But beyond political pragmatism, we also feel an ethical imperative. We understand [the loggers'] desire to be left alone to get their work done and support their families. Our quarrel is with the Forest Service. We profoundly hope in future battles the environmentalist side will carry on its struggle with a Gandhian respect for the people we must confront if we are finally to change the policy we oppose.

One hundred guests and residents of Breitenbush stream into North Roaring Devil's Ridge to bear witness to the federal government's violation of the law's spirit. Their contributions to an ad hoc legal fund total two thousand dollars, less than one tenth of what Breitenbush racks up in legal fees.

Morgan vows not to let Earth First! gain the upper hand again. Over the next five days, before first light, he and Hirons hold briefings at the Hitching Post coffee shop in Detroit, fifteen miles east of Mill City in the Cascades, plotting the next moves of Earth First! "They're probably going to jump in front of your damn face and probably going to spit on you and say all sorts of shit to provoke you into doing something," Hirons says between slurps of coffee. "Just remember there is going to be a media guy jumping from behind a tree with a camera if you do retaliate. We don't give a damn if they ruin your saws. We'll buy you new ones." Hirons hauls cutting crews on snowmobiles himself, just in case he must play peacemaker. He also knows he must calm Morgan's nerves. Their affinity for each other extends beyond the typical relationship established between a contract logger and a mill owner. As close friends, they have drunk and dried out together. Hirons knows how to keep a lid on Morgan's explosive temper.

Plenty of volunteers step forward to restore order the wild West way. One cutter, a mountain of a man and avid fisherman, is a legend around town for sinking a boatful of adolescents drifting too close by hurling boulders through the hull's inside. At the last protest at Breitenbush two years ago, he cut trees near Earth First! tree-sitters, the heartiest demonstrators of all, who climbed the firs to build temporary shelters aloft. The timber brushed the support branches on its descent. This time he wants to put a bigger scare in them. "Hey, are you a few sticks short of a full load?" Atiyeh asks him. "You're going to jail. At the very least, they'll take away your drift boat and pickup." Mill City's finest, Harvey Spears, can barely control his itchy knuckles. "If I found one of the Earth First!ers chained to a shovel and I was on the landing," he volunteers, "I'd probably dump him pretty good." Morgan asks him to stay home.

The one-day interruption ends abruptly. A battery of Forest Service employees, state troopers, and county officers escorts the cutters into North Roaring Devil's Ridge. Their convoy of snowmobiles, dump trucks, and a front-end loader crashes through makeshift roadblocks and rock walls erected by the protesters. The addition of a bulldozer and a road grader expedites the Forest Service's job. A human barricade has to be treated more gingerly. Five protesters have chained themselves together at the neck around one of the trees on death row with Kryptonites, supposedly indestructible steel alloy bicycle locks. Deputies break one lock and summon a locksmith from Salem to unlock the other four. Officers haul the five away in a paddy wagon.

Pairs of demonstrators lock arms and fall down in the path of Hirons's snowmobile, forcing him to veer into a ditch to avoid them. A dozen others mill about in groups, breaking out into bizarre gospel and folk songs. The bloodcurdling wolf howls they yelp rival the growl of chainsaws reverberating through the forest. Loggers, within twenty yards of their tormentors, go about segmenting the logs and trimming the limbs. Five of their wives stand nearby in a show of support for their husbands' work. The antipathy between the two camps erupts into a shouting match. Hirons is amazed to see the clash remain verbal.

The security forces clearly have their hands full. Earth First! has delivered on its threat to do monkey-wrenching. The Forest Service finds the air released from the tires of a road grader and a number of other vehicles. A fire extinguisher's contents have also been emptied into the grader's crankcase. Loggers routinely hide equipment at a site to avoid carrying it back and forth. This is one week they wish they hadn't. Three of their chainsaws, costing about two thousand dollars apiece, have been beaten with axes, and another is missing. Young and Morgan has hired Tom Drynan, the ex-state cop and current private investigator who busted Atiyeh and McDonald at the mines, to help coordinate law-enforcement activities. A female Forest Service agent Hirons has never seen before runs around packing a .357 Magnum on her hip. "Whoa," he exclaims to a cutter beside him on a snowmobile, "that's some no-nonsense bitch." The number of arrests reaches thirty-four.

Hirons's efforts to soothe Morgan's beastly side founder. The mill owner becomes understandably overwrought dodging spit flying from the mouths of Earth First! members while trying to ignore the media circus. Baited by a sitter a hundred feet up in cedar, he rubs the butt of a chainsaw against the tree and cuts a notch in it for fun. He also hammers an ax against the trunk to send a vibration straight up. The maneuver has the twin advantages of relieving his tension and depriving the tree-sitter of sleep.

With the television cameras running, a comely young blonde sporting Rapunzelesque pig tails below her waist uses the cutters as a prop to tell the world her story. She might as well have waved a red flag in a bull's face.

"Hey!" Morgan thunders, lumbering his wide body toward her

up the road. A cluster of people by the road scramble out of his way.

"There's a lot of old trees in this whole forest," she preaches, her certitude crumbling with every step he takes.

Onward Morgan marches, kicking up dust on his march.

"There's a lot of spotted owls," she pleads. "I saw some spotted owls' nest up here." He looks not up, only at her.

The flushed-faced Morgan grows incoherent. "So have I. I grew up in this canyon. I lived this whole, this whole life in this canyon." He continues barreling toward her.

The object of his ire backpedals as fast as her thin legs can move. "Yeah. Hmm. Your posture is kind of aggressive?" she squeaks, lilting her voice on the high note of fear.

"So's yours. Why don't you go back to wherever you came from."

She beats a hasty retreat.

In the days following Easter, the old giants keep hitting the ground. After hearing arguments for an emergency injunction, Judge Burns says he needs time to mull them over, even if his uninspiring track record in environmental cases, overturned by appeals courts numerous times, foretells this decision. The next day he rejects the injunction. A member of Earth First! declares an "all-out war" on the U.S. Forest Service.

The profits Morgan reaps from the North Roaring Devil's Ridge Timber sale defray much of his security expense and aggravation. Over the past three years he reportedly has had to pay more than $30,000 for damaged equipment and security agents to remove protesters. The fight against his opponents' appeals in court has cost him $75,000 in legal fees. For the sale's $1.6 million purchase price, Bugaboo Timber has brought home a staggering 3.2 million board feet of prime old growth—enough to build 320 houses. This dense volume of timber per acre equals a record. Throughout Easter weekend, a series of trucks, needing only two or three gargantuan logs to fill their bunks, pull out of the woods, leaving in their wake stumps three to eight feet in diameter.

In retrospect, Steven Benham's survivors probably wish Judge Burns had slowed down the pace of logging during that frantic period. Before starting his eighth day of work at North Roaring Devil's Ridge, Benham, a reliable and skilled thirty-four-year-old employee of Young and Morgan's XL Timber, holds tailgate safety meetings for his five-man rigging crew. As hook tender, he works alongside them while serving as their supervisor. The crew is setting chokers on logs being yarded about 600 feet uphill to a

landing and loading area off the U.S. Forest Service road traversing Devil's Ridge. At 9:30 A.M., Benham and a coworker retreat
into a buffer strip of dead, leaning, and damaged trees. Upon
Benham's signal to go ahead, a load on the skyline accidentally
knocks a 106-foot-high, uprooted hemlock ajar 100 feet away from
them. The hemlock strikes a dead standing tree, snapping its top
third off. Benham and his crewman dive for cover to avoid a
piece several times larger than themselves on its meteoric descent
from 80 feet above. Benham's head is pushed into his ears by the
worst object known to loggers, a widow maker. These hair-trigger
branches high up drop on contact. His men immediately adminis-
ter first aid prior to moving him to the landing. By the time
ambulance medics rush to the scene, they confirm the absence of
all life signs. Moments later, Hirons and Morgan arrive to find
nothing more than a pink splotch in the snow.

Oregon's Occupational Safety and Health division launches a
protracted investigation. It cites Young and Morgan for failing to
fell "unstable danger trees' in close proximity to the crew before
Benham and his crew began yarding. The company's detractors
infer from that allegation that loggers succumbed to pressure to
haul too much timber too quickly out of the woods. A year after
the accident and a series of hearings, the company is cleared of
complicity. The deceased and his coworker are held responsible
in "an isolated incident of poor judgment." OSHA inspectors and
loggers themselves still wonder what went awry on the watch of
Young and Morgan, normally a stickler for safety, on that fateful
day of the Easter Massacre.

Benham's death kindles Mill City's hysteria. Rumors race
through town of a card Earth First! has sent to his family calling
him an "EARTH DESTROYER." A sign on Highway 22 reads
"GOD TAKES RETRIBUTION." It hardly matters that there
appears scant evidence of either. Anxiety mounts in town under
assault from two fronts, from Atiyeh boring from within and from
ecoterrorists invading from afar. Behind Charlie Stewart's meat
counter, he and Marie frame and hang a news clip from the *Salem
Statesman-Journal* picturing a crazed female member of Earth First!
being dragged away from the U.S. Forest Service's nearby headquarters.

The Easter Massacre marks the culmination of the crusade to
save ancient forests. While losing in court and the woods, environmentalists win in the domain of public opinion. In Washington, D.C., groups such as the Wilderness Society find a hot
button issue to fire up their membership across the United States.

Newsmagazines and network television run prominent stories romanticizing an odd assortment of green rebels living up in trees beside an equally exotic creature known as the northern spotted owl. The ensuing outcry prompts Congress to call the first hearings ever on old growth's disappearance.

Meanwhile, environmentalists are poised to take a quantum leap. They have devised and perfected legal tactics. Thanks to intense lobbying, the state legislature in Salem considers measures to put wide swaths of timber out of loggers' reach permanently. Yet along with conservationists' rising influence comes internecine turmoil. Earth First! operates on the law's fringes against the masters of the inside game, working the courts and capital. The two factions compete for the conservation movement's soul. In advancing the cause toward society's mainstream, moderate conservationists must measure their success against the concessions made to achieve it.

My new friends in Mill City caution me to keep a safe distance from the Breitenbush retreat. They've heard from friends up in Detroit, a town on its outskirts, of people going to visit the "naked, hippie, voodoo, devil-worshiping cult," never to return. At the very least, I hear there may be communicable diseases in the hot springs. On a hunch, I drive up anyway to join the community, as a spectator, in observing the first anniversary of the Easter Massacre.

As soon as a guest finishes an invigorating dip in the hot springs atop the mountain, he notices the unusual assortment of people who will be neighbors for a while. The experience comes close to entering into a 1960s time warp. Psychedelic incense burns near tables laden with crystals. The men wear their hair long and women theirs short. They have names like Walking Deer, Wind Song, and Mahogany. "Glorious moment in eternal life," says a dead ringer for Jesus, when a simple hello would suffice. Michael Donnelly, my well-grounded escort and ex-Breitenbush resident, rolls his eyes. Donnelly's intense gaze, beamed through a wide forehead above his beard, matches the convictions of his firm mouth.

A decade ago, Breitenbush's spectacular setting inspired utopian visions peculiar to the American countryside. In the midnineteenth century, transcendentalists at Brook Farm strove to pioneer the ideal community. In rural New England, intellectuals in the short-lived venture were required to do some manual labor while learning to inoculate themselves against industrialism's evils. Passing up the invitations to join them, Henry David Thoreau and Ralph Waldo Emerson deemed the venture too impractical.

After graduating from Life Spring, a human potential course and offspring of est, Alex Beamer decided to put $250,000 he had inherited to good use. "Poor people who lived in the cities were cheated. I had a dream," he says. "I wanted them coming and experiencing a healthy way of life through interconnectedness to nature and spirit. We would form a place to live in the woods and have available the most exciting minds of scientists and channelers." Beamer bought Breitenbush, a popular resort built in the 1920s that had been out of business for ten years. The egalitarian self-sufficiency he first envisaged asked people to give what they had and take only what they needed for themselves from the earth. The community draws its heat and energy from hydroelectricity and geothermal lakes, both renewable resources, and fertilizes its gardens with organic refuse. Reverence for life precludes all hunting and fishing on the property. "Worker-owners" earn profit-sharing after one year, though Breitenbush has yet to turn a profit.

Even if much of the original experiment has suffered the sad fate of all of its utopian predecessors, Breitenbush still retains the ambience of a low-key commune. Beamer quickly corrects me when I use that loaded term suggesting Rajneeshpuram, the sinister commune exported from India to Oregon in the 1980s, and accused of brainwashing the red-robed followers of an Indian guru. "We're an intentional community of people living and working together," he says, "as opposed to an unintentional community." Employees residing here as part of the cooperative corporation no longer bicker among themselves about sacrificing their individual interests to reach consensus on all decisions. "The results are both comic and exasperating as the group labors to birth a collective mind," notes Marketing Director Peter Moore. They do support each other in the essential chores, from preparing the vegetarian fare to maintaining the trails. Security is always a concern. Breitenbush attracts all sorts of oddballs, by dint of its reputation. One morning Donnelly discovered a madman running naked around the forest, throwing matches. The intruder proceeded into the mountain lodge's mess hall during breakfast, *sans* clothing, donned an apron, and announced he was ready to serve. Donnelly helped escort him out. On another occasion, a group of naked lesbian bathers caught Japanese tourists in the bushes taking pictures of them. They stormed into the business office to complain to a bemused Donnelly.

Breitenbush is living down its image as an asylum for unrecon-structed hippies in favor of one for well-heeled yuppies. The secret lies not in the Paul Winter concerts it has staged for New Age clientele but in the shrewd salesmanship of its natural assets. "We're a glorified hotel-restaurant business," Moore says, "that just happens to be in the perfect spot." Business has tripled over the past three years, to twenty thousand guests per year. As the timber industry declines, Mill City, which catches some of the traffic on its way through, might wish to take note from the long-hairs about capitalizing on this growing market. Guests seeking an uplifting experience like their springs hot and their woods wooded. Clear-cuts are a downer.

Breitenbush's uneasy coexistence with the timber towns on its outskirts rests on more than contrasting life-styles. The commu-nity and loggers covet the same ancient trees on adjoining na-tional forestland for different reasons. "Once cut, these last whispers of antiquity will never be seen again," notes Michael Donnelly. "In twenty to thirty years Breitenbush Hot Springs will have gone from an idyllic haven to an outpost in a factory forest of spindle trees, brush fields, and rocky screes [debris strewn on a slope]."

Throughout the 1980s, the area bore the brunt of the U.S. Forest Service's designs on timber. In the Breitenbush Watershed, more than six hundred acres—one square mile—per year have been logged over the past decade. The North Fork-Breitenbush River's southern bank is almost completely denuded. The commu-nity's residents complain of runoffs caused by the bare hillsides eroding the riverbank. During the 1981 Christmas season, on the heels of a two-hundred-acre clear-cut along the North Fork, a flood swept away parts of a nearby Roman Catholic retreat center, Villa Maria.

In 1986, Breitenbush Hot Springs could still claim arguably the biggest stand of old growth left in Oregon. Then, early one morn-ing, in a prelude to the Easter Massacre, the emergency bell rocked Breitenbush from its sleep. Guests and residents of all ages came by horse, bike, and foot to watch Bugaboo Timber Company at work.

Soon 150 fellow travelers from Breitenbush joined Earth First! in singing New Age hymns under ancient trees. When a tree-sitter who had been up in the air too long imagined hearing chainsaws, they hugged his tree and reassured the Earth First! member. They smuggled the demonstrators sacks of food and helped them block roads. Four Breitenbushers were arrested as accomplices of Earth

First! Like a trophy, a sign removed from the woods still hangs on the wall of a cabin: "CLOSED AREA. IT IS PROHIBITED TO GO INTO THE AREA AND THE ROADS BEHIND THIS SIGN. VIOLATION IS SUBJECT TO $500 FINE OR 6 MONTHS IN JAIL OR BOTH." The front-page stories on Bugaboo Timber drew early attention to the loss of twenty-eight acres of ancient forest.

The contest over the remaining blocks of trees at North Roaring Devil's Ridge touches off the Easter Massacre. One year to the day, a group from Breitenbush invites me on a special hike to heal the wounds from the black holiday. We take "The Spotted Owl Trail," so named by the community. The trip through old growth takes us on an odyssey in tactics from the Earth First! underground to the legal system above. While sprucing up this trail one day, a family of spotted owls swooped down like gifts from heaven, enabling Breitenbush to stop seven sales. The community then rerouted the trail to bypass a nest housing two juveniles. "This is where the road and landing would go," says Donnelly. "This was going to be cut." The grove of ancient trees is as fine as any I have seen outside Opal Creek. "These are vertical and alive, not on the ground," says Moore, unlike those in North Roaring Devil's Ridge. "An ugly, awful scar on what had been a beautiful area."

Toward the hike's end, we run straight into the famous Devil's Creek. The men disrobe to take the plunge. Bowing to peer pressure, I follow suit. The baptism is pure pain in the forty-five-degree snow-melt. "You are now officially an arch-Druid," Donnelly and Moore declare in unison. The Druids, an ancient Celtic priesthood, are remembered mostly for worshiping trees.

To round out Easter weekend, I pay Jim Morgan a call at North Santiam Plywood. In the quiet comfort of his office away from his office, a Ford Bronco beneath second-growth firs, he reflects on the events that Moore aptly describes as "Waterloos and watersheds." By all accounts, his Pyrrhic victory helped put the issue on the map for the media and congress. "No, I have no regrets about Breitenbush. If I had to do it over again, I'd deck that son-of-a-bitch that spit in my face. And that Earth First!er buried in the rocks? I wanted to piss on him," Morgan says. "The tree-sitter? There is some truth to rubbing the butt of the chainsaw against the tree. We didn't fall his tree, but I'm not sure I didn't saw into it. Hey, I took an ax and beat on the SOB to keep that guy awake."

In retrospect, abstinence might have been the better part of valor. A one-day respite would have at least preempted his foes of the moral high ground forever known as the Easter Massacre. Morgan is not one to waste a good workday for the Sabbath's sake. "I ain't religious at all, so it doesn't mean much to me. I don't believe in God, but I'm not an atheist," he hastens to explain. "I don't believe in churches, either. If there is a God, you can preach just as well in this pickup right underneath this tree."

For all his bravado, Morgan betrays the anxiety of a general still fighting the last war. He cannot conceive of ever surrendering North Roaring Devil's Ridge to the enemy. "Why didn't I ignore it? You mean start something and walk away?" he fumes. "We had all the right in the world to be there. Breitenbush is just another special interest like Opal Creek." Even so, Morgan now shies away from again appearing as the heavy on the nightly news. "We've learned a lot about Earth First! and how you deal with them," he says, referring to a recent encounter south of Breitenbush. "We just turned around and went home, then told the Forest Sevice to go clean it up."

Springing up in 1980, Earth First! presented itself as an eco-guerrilla fringe set on torpedoing the best-laid plans of developers, loggers, and other interests it regards as anticonservationist. To these environmentalists, the ends justify their notorious means. Its preferred methods of "direct action" range from high-profile civil disobedience to vandalism, or "ecotage," as they term it. It exhorted terminally ill people to embark on suicide missions by blowing up hydroelectric dams and power lines.

Some fifteen thousand members, most of whom keep their names strictly confidential, are thought to belong to a network of fifty chapters worldwide. As a movement, as opposed to an organization, Earth First! prides itself on its aversion to hierarchy. "There is no card-carrying member," Atiyeh explains. "It's impossible to keep track of groups that are so anarchistic. One time they held a 'Stumps Suck' rally. The FBI launched an investigation into Stumps Suck."

In the Northwest, Earth First! members have declared war on virtually all logging interests. In Breitenbush and elsewhere they have lived in treetops for prolonged periods to stop the trees from being felled, and they have lain in roads to block bulldozers. The most radical fringe resorts to tree-spiking and "decommissioning" heavy-duty equipment. The group's credo is "NO COMPROMISE IN DEFENSE OF MOTHER EARTH," and its logo is a clenched green fist. Almost to a man and woman, the activists effect the scruffy, unkempt look consistent with the crude caricature main-stream conservationists are trying to dispel.

No single element in Mill City has inflamed such passions as the Earth First! members. A local paper runs a toll-free number to report acts of monkey-wrenching: 1-800-SABOTAG. Randy Moberg, a principal in his family's company, Fred Moore Logging, and a rational individual by any measure, bumps into Hirons and me one morning downing coffee at a restaurant in Marion Forks in the Opal Creek area. "I told my guys that if you see one to beat him to a pulp," Moberg steams, gripping his glass of Coca-Cola close to the breaking point. "We're not talking virtue here. This means war!"

Two years ago, cutters on a Moberg job discovered a spike in a log. Verl didn't think of calling the Forest Service or the papers to give Earth First! any free publicity. He has a plan for protesters chained to machinery: "Put bear juice on them for the yellow jackets. Or smear them with jelly. I'm serious. They're a cancer. One of these days an Earth First!er is going to meet some logger and there's going to be some thumping. And I know on my crew there'd be some. I know a few loggers who'd be glad to do it. They're tired of getting pushed out of jobs and out of work. Us loggers have never been ones to sit back and take a bunch of guff." Adds his son Randy after his outburst at the restaurant: "Earth First! is a bomb waiting to blow, and it will blow."

In truth, the environmental absolutists have inflicted consider-able financial and mental damage, costing industry untold millions in lost workdays and damaged equipment, though the companies refrain from revealing the exact amount to deny the opposition the satisfaction. Earth First! preys on every woodworker's fear of losing life and limb as well as livelihood. Shrapnel can fly when a cutter in the woods or a saw operator in the mills comes across a spike buried in a log. Yet the only documented case of this tactic ever being used, in which a northern California millworker was severly injured several years ago, was not linked to Earth First! The spike may have been left over from a saboteur belonging to the Industrial Workers of the World, a renegade union that fa-vored the same sort of booby-trapping earlier in this century.

Oregon Earth First!'s renunciation of the tactic is small consola-tion to potential victims if the leaderless movement cannot force members to abide by the majority's edict. On his desk, a timber staff officer at the Forest Service ranger station closest to Mill City displays a hunk of wood with a spike sticking out from a timber sale on a ridge above Opal Lake—courtesy of a logging company in town whose sawmill equipment was destroyed. The keepsake captures local anxieties.

Hirons, ever the hard-bitten realist, has a hard time taking Earth First! seriously. "If any of those crazies had a brain, they'd take it out and play with it," he jokes. "I mean, how can anybody in their right mind buy off on that shit?" In his CGO office he shows me an article about Earth First! in *Smithsonian* magazine. Dave Foreman, the group's cofounder and dean of direct action, effectively calls for reducing the world population to 100 million people. Hirons cannot resist passing up such ripe material in an Earth Week speech he delivers at his alma mater: "I'm tempted to give him a gun and say, 'You go first.' "

On a profounder note, Hirons demands that moderate environmentalists come clean about their zealous breathren. "Nobody wants to claim them," Hirons says, "but everybody wants to endorse them." The wild and woolly shock troops confer legitimacy on the moderates' shift from the political spectrums' center. "Martin Luther King had his Malcolm X. King then had an opportunity to say to the white power structure, 'You want to deal with me,' " says Andy Kerr, conservation director of the mainstream Oregon Natural Resources Council. "Civil disobedience has its role in saving the forest. It's not ONRC's style, but we need more people in the woods getting arrested. It has to become as socially acceptable as marching through Selma."

To the degree that logging road-sitters take their cues from lunch-counter sitters of three decades ago, Earth First! has succeeded in stoking public outrage at events unknown to most Americans. Its masterful manipulation of the media first brought the issues into American living rooms and kept them alive long after the gimmick of throwing themselves in front of log trucks turned stale. Atiyeh, a grudging admirer, savors the time the activists in Portland scampered about affixing Earth First! stickers on a Forest Service building and pricking pins in Smoky the Bear dolls outside the glass windows. Inside, the employees appeared to twitch and writhe from the voodooism. My favorite personal piece of guerrilla theater featured five demonstrators dressed as owls, a bear, and a bat who stormed the office of Senator Mark Hatfield (R., Ore.) in Salem and sat on nests of Douglas fir boughs they brought with them to draw attention to Hatfield's protimber stance.

At the Alton Baker Park in Eugene, a steady drizzle soaks the information and food booths of a fair celebrating Earth Day's twentieth anniversary. Karen Wood is preoccupied with the unen-

viable task of drumming up enthusiasm for the direct action beginning in the woods outside Eugene at this very moment. This
spring and summer Earth First! is staging a series of last "last
stands" for the ancient forest. On the surface, Wood, a twenty-
nine-year-old part-time bookkeeper, conveys a wholesome middle-
American look anchored in her neat right-angle bangs—until she
runs down her rap sheet, including three arrests for interfering
with logging sites, as if it were a badge of honor.

Her speech has the ring of desperation. "The forests are coming
down fast and furious out there. If all of us came out there, they
wouldn't be able to do this," she cries. "What's stopping us?
What's stopping you? Nothing can stop us now. Take a day. Take
a week. Take a little time out of your life and make a statement
for the forest. Get out there. We're going to do something till it
stops." The audience appears more interested in finding a dry spot
out of the rain. "I'll either call you," Wood tells me afterward,
"or if I'm in jail have someone else call." Considering all the
sensational press clips on the infamous ecoterrorists, my first brush
with Earth First! members proves anticlimactic.

I drive over to the Blue River in the national forest fifty-five
miles from Eugene to check on the foot soldiers taking their last
stand. It turns out to be a poor showing. The ill-clad and ill-
groomed protesters rotate their hands over a campfire, looking
perfectly wretched trying to ward off the cold damp. Heaps of
soda and beer cans lie beside them. A smiling sheriff, delighting
in their misery, drives up in a patrol car to ask how they are.
The long-awaited occupation of public lands a few weeks later
fizzles as well. A half dozen demonstrators chain themselves to a
yarder and loader, and their accomplices block the road with
chunks of wood. By noon, a locksmith arrives to enable law-
enforcement officials to clear the human detritus the Forest Service brands "scraggly counterculture types." Local newspapers and
television stations, in search of fresher stories, ignore them.

In fact, the sole media members still covering the stale story
are east of the Hudson River. From their studios and newsrooms,
editors view civil disobedience as ready-made drama featuring
photogenic characters and supercharged dialogue. "Under a cloak
of darkness, small bands of men and women [Earth First! mem-
bers] begin an arduous hike over a steep ridge, their flashlights
dimmed with blue filters to elude the timber company's security
men," writes a breathless reporter in a six-page story for the Sunday magazine of The New York Times, the nation's paper of record.
"In all, there are more than 70 intruders in ragtag camouflage

fatigues." On television's 60 *Minutes* and NBC *Nightly News* they receive star treatment.

The national media just refuse to let go of a dramatic story even after it becomes yesterday's news. This myopia stems partly from the Twin Peaks syndrome, a fixation on the eccentrics populating the nation's far corner. Reporters are thus spared the gritty chore of venturing out to meet the workingman in the woods to understand his take on the situation. Nor must they do the serious legwork involved in covering the courts, boardrooms, and bargaining tables where the real action is taking place.

Sixty-five miles away from the protesters' encampment at Blue River, Charlotte Levinson joins George Atiyeh in a quiet, weekend-long observation of Earth Day at Opal Creek. Her evolution from outlaw activist to moderate environmentalist presents a telling lesson in the ecoguerrillas' rise and fall. Once upon a time, Levinson, thirty-eight, was as Earth First! as they come. She earned a politically correct livelihood in a soy foods cooperative, working as a tofumaker—"a righteous product, organic, and healthy—plus you got to take home all you can eat." In her spare time, the transplanted New Yorker boned up on the philosophy of nonviolence.

The third time Levinson occupied a logging road she was arrested. In her company were her two small children, Suntara Loba, and Robin Liberty Tree. (They had decided, after their mother's divorce, to take new names she suggested.) "I went to jail, a little closet in a dinky, horrible, windowless place. A big black woman with no shirt on walked back and forth spraying air freshener. You would have died. I said, 'I can't take this anymore.' She growled, 'What are you here for?' " recalls Levinson. "I thought to myself, 'This isn't going well. I should say, "murder." ' I told her 'I'm here because I stopped a logging truck.' She put down her air can and looked at me: 'It's all right, I like the political girls.' "

Perched on a cliff above Jawbone Flats on Earth Day weekend, Levinson's soft face and light curls glimmer in the sun. "Once you get into jail," she says, "you're suddenly in a whole other political context." On top of being called a "common criminal" (as opposed to an uncommon criminal), Levinson suffered the indignity of having to pay Willamette Industries ten thousand dollars she had recently received as an inheritance, after losing a civil suit. At least her children enjoyed themselves. "The kids thought it was great when I was arrested," she adds. "My daughter is a total Earth First!er. She protests everything, and is now into animal rights." Suntara declines comment.

In addition to her personal anguish, Levinson has outgrown Earth First! politically. "It's attracting younger groupies because it's much more leftist," she says of the trend on campus. Levinson now serves as president of the Oregon Natural Resources Council (ONRC), the driving force behind the fight to save old growth. "ONRC actually has had an impact. What you have to do is get in their face, tie them up in courts, appeal decisions, do administrative work, call meetings," she explains, sounding less the terrorist than the technocrat. "Earth First! broke the issue. But you can't be constantly drawing new attention when its a familiar issue. There's no question that litigation drove the law. If we hadn't won the lawsuits, everything Earth First! did wouldn't have amounted to anything." Although Levinson now spends her time behind a desk instead of bars, she is innocent of selling out. "I'm the person industry loves to hate. I'm Jewish, from New York, and I don't give a damn about timber supply," Levinson says. "Everything wrapped up in one stereotype and nightmare."

Events have simply passed Earth First! by. Having trained the spotlight on the pillaging of forests, it is unequipped to carry the campaign to the next step by lobbying legislatures and drafting legislation. Martin Luther King, Jr., masterfully parlayed sympathy for his protest marches into the Civil Rights Act of 1965. Earth First! just keeps marching and marching, relegating itself to a footnote in history.

In his salad days at Opal Creek, Atiyeh could have qualified as a founding member of Earth First! After all, he and Larry McDonald engaged in clandestine missions against logging equipment at Opal Creek a decade before today's radicals resorted to ecotage. Since then, Atiyeh has maintained mostly sentimental attachments to radicals. "Earth First! has more than its share of lunatics. But all political agendas are moved by extremes. Earth First! exists because issues are not being addressed within the system. Personally, I wouldn't spike trees. But it's not the environmentalist's job to compromise. We lose credibility. How do you compromise the extinction of a species, the end of a genetic code, or destruction of wetlands?"

Atiyeh's fertile imagination runs wild at a notion of Armageddon he has obviously thought through over the years. "I'd do nonviolent protest to stop [the loggers], but if they continued, I'd probably climb on top of the Cat [tractor], drive the guy off, and kick the shit out of him. And I'd clobber and take a chainsaw away from a guy cutting a tree a thousand years old to protect something that precious. That's just self-defense. It's like someone with a gun shooting a burglar with reasonable force," he says. "If it came down to destroying Opal Creek and the individual was not defenseless, I'd have an equal right to defend Opal Creek— even if it means fighting him to death. I couldn't see sneaking through the bushes with a high-powered rifle. I could see approaching him directly, making a fair fight of it, and betting his life against mine. I'd probably know him and he'd probably know me. He wouldn't respect me unless I did."

It appears a distinct possibility that the hypothetical "he" with whom Atiyeh contemplates being locked in mortal combat would be his former best friend, Tom Hirons—were Jim Morgan to buy the timber and hire his number one logger to do the job. "I don't know if I could kill Tom," Atiyeh says. "He'd have to kill me or get into a physical fight. I'd lay down my life for Tom, too."

Faced with the all-too-real prospect of loggers punching through the forest primeval he has fought so long to save, Atiyeh is poised to call out the troops. "If industry ever tried cutting Opal Creek, I'll guarantee we'd have five thousand people out there in the greatest demonstration you ever saw," he says. "It wouldn't just be Earth First!ers, either. It would be middle-class Americans and old women, some of whom have never even gotten parking tickets. We won't have enough jails in Oregon to keep all the people. It would be insane for the Forest Service to allow it."

Atiyeh keeps that option stored in the back of his mind even as he acts the consummate insider. "I could never join Earth First! My strategy is to stay within the process," he explains. "You can only go to court with clean hands." At an Earth First! gathering at Rogue River in southern Oregon, Atiyeh pointed at a cameraman and warned that if he photographed a group leader and him together, he would break the camera. "Earth First!ers are great shock troops, but you gotta know when to send them back into the barracks," he says. "All they do now is damage the cause. You got the press out here already interested in the issue." Atiyeh works the Three C's—the courts, Congress, and the state capital—to achieve his ends.

The present phase of Atiyeh's strategy obligates him to reach beyond his one-man army. Andy Kerr, an indispensable ally, surely ranks as the shrewdest tactician on Atiyeh's side. The model of a professional environmentalist, he is the Ralph Nader of the old-growth-preservation movement. In 1981 the young activist filed the first administrative appeal in the Northwest against a Forest Service timber sale. By 1988, as the conservation director of the Oregon Natural Resources Council, a grass-roots coalition, he was masterminding 220 separate appeals in a single month, creating a legal logjam.

The tactic proved so costly to industry that a House committee summoned Kerr to Washington, D.C., for a special hearing, at which he was attacked by Oregon representative Bob Smith, among others. Yet by raising his profile and drawing national attention to the issue, the politicians unwittingly played into Kerr's hands. Northwestern officials saw environmental-minded colleagues from other regions suddenly move into their domain. "Asking the Oregon congressional delegation today to deal rationally with the end of ancient forest cutting is like asking the Mississippi delegation in 1960 to deal rationally with the end of segregation," he says. "These national forests belong just as much to the waiter in New York as they do to the logger in Oregon. There's almost more credibility not being so close to something because you're not biased. You can't see the larger picture. It's like segregationists saying you don't know those Negroes like we do. We're close to them, we have to deal with them, not like you white liberals in New York." As would be expected, most of the Oregon delegation's offices on the Hill have banned him from their offices.

Kerr recently helped lead a move to file protection for the threatened Pacific fisher, a fur-bearing mammal of the weasel family inhabiting old growth alongside the spotted owl. "How appropriate to send these guys up the creek," laughs Chuck Bennett, a lobbyist working for Atiyeh in Salem. "They'll never have a decent night's sleep with Andy. He'll go through to the food chain's bottom and end up with loggers."

Hirons, viewing the ploy from the other end, heaps enmity on Kerr he would not hazard to direct at Atiyeh. "I heard they may list weasels. They ought to start with Kerr," Hirons rages. "He's not even human enough to be in any captive breeding program." (The U.S. Fish and Wildlife Service subsequently refused to list the Pacific fisher as a threatened species on the grounds that it lacked sufficient information to determine its preference for ancient forests.) Industry contends that Kerr's notoriety has thwarted attempts to find a compromise solution to the logging controversy. "He's the most polarizing force out there," Hirons adds. "I don't really see him differently than an Earth First!er. He practices mental terrorism." Hirons and fellow loggers refuse even to sit down at the same table with Kerr.

Atiyeh and Kerr complement each other's strengths. "Andy grasped the issue from the very beginning," says Atiyeh. "He's a political genius, like a brilliant chess player five moves ahead of his opponents." The virtues Atiyeh lauds in his collaborator belong in equal measure to himself. The last ancient trees still standing owe their lives to Atiyeh, Kerr, and the rest of the grass-roots activists. These men and women came to the forest's rescue well in advance of their allies alongside the Potomac. They brought the first lawsuits to protect the spotted owl, launched the first lobbying campaigns, and participated in the first futile summits staged by politicians in the hope of reaching a settlement.

"This is where the story is happening. Washington [, D.C.] is not in touch with us because those people's judgment is completely clouded. They see the world through the eyes of those who are trying to influence them," Atiyeh says. "I have tremendous respect for the Audubon and Wilderness societies. But I gotta admit some of these folks are the biggest bunch of snobs I know. The national groups kept telling us the issue wasn't ripe yet. Left to their own devices, they would have waited ten years and it would have been over."

It bears noting, though, that once the nation's mainstream conservation groups jumped into the fray, they were a force to be reckoned with. In particular, the Audubon Society's documentary *Rage over Trees* introduced the issue to a national television audience. The Wilderness Society's meticulous surveys of the dwindling inventories of old growth shamed the U.S. Forest Service into fessing up to its total ignorance of how much was left and, at long last, confirm the alarming statistics. The Wilderness Society's superb package of educational materials has enlightened children and adults alike about the importance of safeguarding ancient forests.

Atiyeh's triumphs complement the spiraling awareness of citizens about their role in protecting the environment. The phenomenal success of *50 Simple Things You Can Do to Save the Earth* attests to a growing desire among Americans to make a difference. This modest, ninety-three-page how-to guide has sold more than 3 million copies. Readers follow practical steps to promote energy and water conservation, forest preservation, and recycling of everything from paper to metal to old tires. Its section on reusing old newspapers, for example, points out that it takes an entire forest, more than 500,000 trees, to supply Americans with their Sunday newspapers every week. The simple things to do include sorting and bundling newspapers and magazines for easy recycling at local centers. If U.S. citizens, each of whom goes through 580 pounds of paper per year, recycled 10 percent of their newspapers, the nation could save about 25 million trees a year.

Every page of this national paper parade comes at a price. Ten thousand copies, a typical first printing, of the very book your eyes are scanning at this moment, dear reader, require the equivalent, if converted to board feet, of 200 trees now threatened in the tropical rain forest. That fact comes from a report in *The New York Times* on perhaps the only publishing "tree clause." When Mickey Hart, the drummer for the Grateful Dead rock band, signed a contract for a book on ancient and rare musical and rhythmic traditions, he asked how many trees in Costa Rica would be cut to print it. His publisher offered to match Hart's contributions for planting trees, roughly $500 per 2,000 copies, to replace those that went into his books. The clever provision echoes Hirons's call to arms for Americans to cease taking natural resources for granted.

To bring the issue home, it is worth tracing the timber I have watched Hirons log at Pamelia Creek to see where it exactly goes once it leaves Young and Morgan's mills. Lumberyards throughout New England and the Northeast sell it for the finest homes. Wood chips from just inside the bark of a Douglas fir log go into corrugated paper for cardboard boxes holding television sets and brown bags at supermarket chains up and down the West Coast. The *Los Angeles Times*, *The Denver Post*, and the *Oregonian* derive up to half the "virgin fiber" in their newsprint from white and silver fir, hemlock, and spruce. The balance of the blend consists of recycled paper.

The preservation of the last old-growth forests forces the nation to pick up the slack in timber from outside the Northwest. About a third of U.S. plywood and 15 percent of lumber come from the region, figures that may be sliced in half if 11.6 million acres are set aside to protect the spotted owl. Seth Zukerman, author of *Saving Our Ancient Forests*, outlines a set of policies for maintaining our standard of living without wiping out second growth in the South and Northwest. A family of four in North America uses 1,000 board feet of lumber per year, the highest amount in the world. On this continent the cost of lumber, the lowest anywhere, manifests itself in the dump-bound piles of sound boards outside homes undergoing renovation. Fortunately, "Salvage Merchandisers" listed in the yellow pages are reaping profits from reselling used wood from wreckage sites at the cheapest prices imaginable. Seattle, the city boasting the most comprehensive recycling program in the United States, has set up convenient transfer stations for reusing scrap lumber and wood.

Wise buyers and homebuilders can play a key role in saving forests. Americans can afford to be profligate, because lumber has traditionally accounted for just 7 percent of the price of an entire house. (By some estimates, even a 100 percent increase in lumber costs would add only another 7 percent to a house's price.) In the United States, the walls hold up the roof and upper floors in most wooden homes, a method called "stick framing" commonly used in cheap, easy-to-build tract houses. Europeans prefer timber-frame construction known as "truss framing," whereby posts and beams buttress a building. Truss framing evenly distributes stress points throughout a house through sound engineering principles with a third less wood than a conventional structure. A lot fewer trees give their lives. "[It] requires less material and more labor," Zuckerman maintains, "which could also be an advantage in these times when resources and jobs both become scarce."

A boycott of old-growth redwood at the lumberyard or hardware store requires customers to look for its extra-tight, clear grain before making their purchases. If consumer pressure can force Star Kist and other tuna canners to stop buying tuna caught in nets that function as death traps for dolphins, it can force lumber companies to stick to cutting and selling only second growth.

The United States must rethink its love affair with green gold in the same light it did black gold. In 1970, 111 years after the birth of the American oil industry, domestic production peaked and then began to drop. Two energy crises later, conservation emerged as the battle cry. While the United States will maintain its self-sufficiency in wood, it may no longer be able to afford the environmental costs of putting more than 60 percent of its lumber and 75 percent of its plywood into residential and commercial construction. No other large society has so many homes built of wood. Ever since the conquest of the frontier, Americans have demonstrated an enduring affinity for lumber as the nation's primary building material. In the mid-1800s, the first American settlers in San Diego shuddered at the sight of a town built of adobe, an indigenous and abundant material of sun-dried clay and straw. "They said, 'Hell, no, we're not living in mud huts,' " notes Zuckerman, "and began to bring in lumber." Pioneers who longed to live in wood homes across the treeless Great Plains and southwestern deserts had to order their timber from hundreds of miles away.

Today the United States would be well served going against its cultural grain by matching building materials to local resources. Many of the stateliest homes in the Northeast and Midwest are made of brick, which is merely moist clay hardened by heat. The Southwest leans toward adobe. Sand and gravel for concrete blocks is everywhere. At the turn of the century, Thomas Edison led a crusade to save trees and, for three hundred dollars, enable the "poorest man among us" to afford a lasting home. He invented a process to pump concrete in house-size molds. After a few days of setting, the molds came apart to reveal a quasi-complete dwelling. Before the idea caught on, Edison turned his attention to the phonograph and motion picture camera. In the long term, the American consumer's gain was the forest's loss.

Wood will still remain in use as decoration for paneling and doors even when it ceases to serve structural purposes. The Japanese show a higher appreciation for wood's aesthetic appeal in their meticulously crafted homes largely because they have learned to live with less of it.

In addition to lumber, in their processed form trees enter American's daily lives as paper. Contrary to popular belief, the paper industry was founded on recycling. In 1690, the first paper mill, outside of Philadelphia, manufactured its product from cotton and linen rags. Almost two centuries later, shortages during the Civil War led to new technology and the manufacture of paper from wood. By 1904, recycled rags and waste paper accounted for only 40 percent of American paper. Except for World War II's recycling drives, virtually all paper soon came from pulpwood.

Today a return to the basics appears certain. High-grade paper varying in rag content (including cotton, linen, flax, and hemp) from 25 to 100 percent is doing a brisk business in security papers, legal documents for permanent records, and premium stationery and letterheads. A researcher at Oregon State University, in concert with the Weyerhaeuser paper company, has developed an efficient process for turning straw into paper. Only fifty years ago, all corrugated medium paper was made of wheat straw. In the 1940s, a new hardwood milling process and cheaper fiber sources killed off the product. In commercial manufacturing, today's hybrid would combine 30 percent straw and 70 percent pulpwood. The cost would be at least ten dollars a ton less than using conventional materials, which mostly explains why China manufactures a lot of straw pulp. Researchers have also found straw to form a stronger fiber than wood-based paper, an obvious plus. Besides saving trees, the innovation would help clean up the air in the Northwest, since the eighty-million-dollar grass seed industry in Oregon's Willamette Valley grooms its crops by burning fields in late summer.

Until the new products become widely available, individuals can do their part by recycling. The slim pines and poplars on plantations in the southern United States are grown precisely for paper. Yet trees, in any form, are a fungible commodity, like grain, so that a new supply from one region can replenish the stock depleted elsewhere. Four months before the listing of the spotted owl as a threatened species, the U.S. paper industry announced a national goal of 40 percent paper recovery from recycling by the end of 1995, a leap from 26 million to 40 million tons, based on the growing demand for paper at home and abroad. If industry meets its goal, it could save more than 520 million second-growth trees.

A team of Forest Service researchers has estimated that such recycling would result in a 15 percent overall reduction in the projected quantity of pulpwood that would otherwise be required by the paper industry in the year 2000. Lower demand for pulpwood will ease the drain on timber inventories in the South, allowing this timber to take the place of old growth for two-by-fours or plywood—a third of which comes from the Pacific Northwest.

The proliferation of state laws cracking down on environmental claims like "recyclable" will inevitably lead to federal standards. Mobil Corporation removed the word "degradable" from boxes of its Hefty plastic trash bags, bowing to demands from environmental groups and the threat of legal action by the attorneys general of eight states. The sunlight the bags need to decompose is noticeably absent beneath several layers of dirt and trash in the average landfill.

As the truth-in-advertising controversy shows, *50 Simple Things* fosters the illusion of home remedies as an alternative to serious public policy. In the telling section on recycling, the authors bemoan manufacturers' reluctance to use recycled paper because it costs more than virgin stock. In fact, in the Northwest the costs of new and of recycled newsprint are roughly the same. "I'd like to use more, but it's not available," says Sara Bentley, the publisher of the *Statesman-Journal* in Salem, Oregon. Fault for the disparity between the high demand and low supplies lies with government's failure to spur the fledgling industry by passing com-prehensive recycling laws. Almost half of the families in the United States already separate their garbage, whether mandated by law or not, and even more are willing to fork over extra money for products putting their effort to good use.

Government bears the responsibility for ensuring that slow-footed companies get on board. Connecticut has enacted a law requiring newspapers to be made from 40 percent recyclable paper—a lesson for New York City. Each day New York collects twenty-seven thousand tons of garbage at its main landfill, the world's largest, soon to reach the height of the Egyptian pyramids. Rather than scaling back on the recycling program it recently launched, New York should be expanding it. The city recycles less than 10 percent of its total garbage, mostly bottles, compared to Seattle's 50 percent.

In Washington, D.C., Congress would do well to pass the na-tional recycling bill wending its way through the system. Bill Clinton favors creating and expanding markets for recycled prod-ucts by providing tax incentives that promote the use of recycled materials "whenever possible." Fifteen years ago, standards set in Washington, stimulated by the appeal of Japanese imports, spurred Detroit to meet the demand for cars with higher mileage per gallon. The standard doubled, from 14 mpg in 1974 to 27.5 mpg today. Clinton has also pledged his support for measures raising that standard to 45 mpg. While he and the lawmakers are at it, they can tack on recycling standards as well, combining carrots and sticks.

However much do-it-yourself conservation succeeds in stimulat-ing public awareness, it ultimately weakens people's clout. "No point in letting the news reports and magazine coverage drive you to despair," chirps 50 Simple Thing's Introduction, "even the most 'intractable' environmental problems march toward a solution when everyday people get involved." This sort of guilt-free, arm-chair activism lulls citizens into a false complacency about the gravity of crises beyond the scope of installing a brick in a toilet tank to save water.

Each person can affect the environment when working collec-tively rather than individually. The basic problem, argues Paul Ehrlich, a biologist at Stanford University and author of The Pop-ulation Bomb, is "the scale of human activities relative to what can be supported by the natural systems of the planet." It pays to treat the fundamental disease rather than the symptoms. In the end, a booming recycling business nationwide relieves the pressure on Opal Creek.

On the political front, Atiyeh serves as a model for the average citizen wishing to influence the logging controversy's outcome. He has spread the word through a barrage of well-placed letters to local newspapers, helping to further coverage of the subject. On television, the producers of ABC's *Prime Time Live* and the Audubon Society's documentary focused on Opal Creek because Atiyeh led them there. The formidable powers of persuasion he displays in a hectic schedule of public appearances win him legions of converts. From the regional Forest Service director on down to the local district ranger, all sense his watchful eye on their notices to sell tracts to timber at Opal Creek. Atiyeh's firm grasp of the process has thwarted them time and again. His reputation precedes him on Capitol Hill, where U.S. senators and representatives drawing up wilderness maps remember Opal Creek by dint of Atiyeh's hard labor.

Claudine Schneider can vouch for the method to Atiyeh's madness. Thanks to lobbying from delegations of youths, the U.S. representative from Rhode Island has decided to fly cross-country to see Opal Creek for herself. "You often find people who are very committed and consumed by a desire to change the way people want to think things," she says. "Rarely do you find the basic knowledge and insight as to how to find a solution. George is the activist-pragmatist."

Atiyeh sounds a clarion call to arms to jolt people out of their complacency. "If the Russians became a threat again, we'd immediately build up our defense. No study, bingo, we're going for it. Yet we find it repugnant to fight for the life support systems that sustain us all. Forget studying global warming, just stop it. Why can we react so strongly against a political power and so wimpily to a true threat to our very existence?" he demands. "The environmental movement is not perceived as being macho. Defense is men, defense is soldiers, defense is kicking ass. Defense is John Wayne. Environment is a bunch of liberal East Coast hippies, peace, and love. We need an underlying macho ethic, like Rednecks for Wilderness or Earth Warriors."

The much-vaunted new world order becons him and fellow Earth Warriors to lead the charge. The end of the Cold War and the outbreak of democracy presages a new age based on cooperation among nations in mounting a defense against the "common enemies": ignorance, poverty, disease, and environmental deterioration. In the global village of instant communication and computer networks, the nuclear disaster at Chernobyl and the burning oil wells set off by the Iraqis during the Persian Gulf War broke down international borders. Deforestation's hazards know none, either.

America works best on a mission. In the early 1950s, people banded together on the home front to defeat polio. Today the nation can devote part of the resources and know-how it once applied to military preparedness to improving the health of mother earth. The preservation of the world's last remaining temperate rain forests can rout the common enemies of dirty air, polluted water, and the extinction of species. In his best-selling book *Earth in the Balance*, Vice President Al Gore calls "the effort to save the global environment the central organizing principle of our civilization."

The conservation ethic sweeping the nation will prove short-lived without citizens doing the necessary spadework in politics. Earth First! misses the mark. Trade-offs and temporary defeat are the prices of democracy, the worst system except for all the rest. The United States is blessed with the most easily influenceable government in the world, offering well-organized environmentalists plenty of options for making an impact. In 1909, *The Promise of American Life*, a book of political philosophy authored by Herbert Croly, emerged as the progressive movement's bible thanks to its forceful argument for a national revival. Croly envisioned this revival being spearheaded by the concerned everyman he saluted as "something of a saint, something of a hero." Atiyeh and Hirons, on the opposite ends of the spectrum, are both—two average citizens willing to sacrifice their private lives for their public convictions. The nation needs more of their kind of populism than politically correct shoppers.

Opal Creek's survival will ultimately depend on the contributions of millions of saints and heroes, even on a modest scale. Surgical strikes of letters and faxes to congressional representatives, Forest Service *apparatchiks* in Washington, D.C., and the Northwest, and the president will force them to think twice before wiping out the last ancient forests. A chorus of indignant voices in local newspapers and on local call-in radio shows will keep them honest. Atiyeh is fond of quoting the Sierra Club's maxim "endless pressure, endlessly applied." Power comes in numbers. The expanding membership rolls of grass-roots and national environmental groups enhance their clout. Donations, however small, help finance their vital research and campaigns to stave off the elimination of ancient forests.

Above all, true conservationists exercise their birthright at the voting booth. The polls offer the best means of holding officials accountable to the public will. The League of Conservation Voters and other groups track the records of members of Congress for easy reference. After election day, those still serving in Washington, D.C., will hear the steps of constituents voting with their feet. According to the register in the information kiosk at the entrance of Jawbone Flats, the foot traffic through Opal Creek has doubled each year for the past five, to ten thousand annually, as word of its wonder spreads. At that rate, politicians ignore this jewel of ancient forest at their own peril.

On Friday evening of Earth Day weekend a banged-up pickup pulls in front of the gate at Opal Creek. In the cab and open air bed, the arrivals squint at the darkening mountains in the dimming daylight. On the ride up to the mining camp, they listened intently for the spirits in the woods. "God is nature and nature is God," says Calvin Hecocta of the Paiute Indian Tribe in southern Oregon. "I've seen for myself since 1950 [at age six] that constant cutting means destruction of the land. The hurting part of that destruction is what my father said: 'The taking of these things without prayer or blessing is one of the greatest wrongs against God and nature.' "

Hecocta is joined by Wilmer Stampede-Mesteth. The Sioux medicine man has journeyed a long way, eleven hundred miles, from South Dakota's Black Hills. He and Hecocta are setting foot in Opal Creek for the first time to sanctify the land. The heretical act of logging would then amount to defiling a church.

After a century of struggle, Native Americans are retrieving their heritage to preserve from extinction a culture as ancient as these woods. In the Northwest, their burgeoning alliance with environmentalists puts them at the forefront of the movement to protect critical spawning habitat for the Pacific salmon, a staple of the Indian economy. To Native Americans, the forests also represent an irreplaceable religious resource for spirit questing, cleansing, gathering medicines, and placement of traditional regalia.

Hecocta burns inside from the eradication of the life-style he enjoyed growing up with in the Klamath Mountains in southern Oregon. Land speculators, many of them from California, turned the Indians' grazing space into farms and posted "No Hunting," "No Fishing," and "No Trespassing" signs, stripping the original inhabitants of a birthright they enjoyed long before the white man showed up. "A certain freedom our elders held sacred was taken away from us," laments the forty-seven-year-old Hecocta. Every day he prays for the return of Crazy Horse, the great war chief who deflected the U.S. Cavalry's bullets point-blank in battles. "Crazy Horse would fight this environmental destruction to death."

Centuries ago here at Opal Creek, young Santiam braves embarked on vision quests atop Whetsone Mountain, overlooking Jawbone Flats. Right below the five-thousand-foot summit, a peculiar two-tier outcropping of smoothly rounded rock juts out of the dark waves of fir and cedar like a lighthouse in the ocean. Two pillar-shaped formations flank the two-hundred-foot-high escarpment. On its flattened twenty-foot-wide top rest the remains of a stone wall large enough to seat a man. Atiyeh and others who have used rappelling equipment to scale the great rock and lower themselves down from the summit have often wondered how on earth their ancient predecessors accomplished the feat.

Their superhumanness surely sprang from extraordinary purpose. A tribe's elders decided it was time for a boy, by the time he was twelve or thirteen, to come to terms with his Creator at the mountaintop. On the appointed day, usually in the summer, the youth followed an elder up the strenuous-mile trail to Whetstone. Left alone, the budding warrior sat down inside the ring of stones. For the next three days, while fasting, he was seized by visions of plants, animals, or waterfalls distilling life's essence. By the time an elder returned a sunrise later to pick him up, the brave was ready to make his way back to Opal Creek and into manhood.

Aside from practical considerations, Native American's harmonious relationship with nature underpins their faith; contrary, in large measure, to the Judeo-Christian worldview of subjugation. "In our traditional way of life, we lived off the land and took only what was needed," Hecocta says. "Our people were the first environmentalists, hundreds of years before the word was even mentioned. Responsibility and respect for God's land and God's creatures has been handed down for generations. I'm doing my part to pass down these beliefs to anyone who wants to lend an ear or heart to them." Had his people invented the chainsaw, might this continent have looked different long ago? In light of this weekend's events, it's highly doubtful.

Hecocta's lofty sentiments and practices account for the growing number of Caucasians concerned about ecology who are embracing Indian customs as an antidote to their own civilization's insensitivities. "As far as inspiring people," says Atiyeh, "our native American brothers have the strongest claim to the spiritual arguments for protecting nature."

Atiyeh drags himself to the small common in camp to deliver his first address ever at Opal Creek, to a crowd of Earth Day celebrants. With great fanfare, the public-relations apparatus of Save the Opal Creek Council, a group led by him and allies, has promoted the event in the weekend calendars of papers across the state. In the past, Atiyeh always sought refuge from his daily travails down in the valley in the solitude of his paradise up in the mountains. Ironically, the more attention he drew to the cause through his speaking and media campaigns, the less he could escape.

Here in the eager faces of more than one hundred old and young backpackers picnicking on the grass is living proof that he must surrender his special place to save it. Twenty years before, on the first Earth Day, Atiyeh and his small band of individualists lived in seclusion at Opal Creek, going for months on end without seeing another soul. "We just had a ceremony up in the house sharing our feelings with our Native American brothers who were here long before us. We are so fortunate that my special place still stands. For a long time in my life, we were very private about this land and didn't want to share it," he singsongs. "Now we recognize that the land belongs to all of us."

"On the other side of Stony Ridge is a clear-cut," he says, pointing behind his listeners. "On Whetstone Mountain, look off to the other side, there's a clear-cut. Top of Mount Beachy, look to the other clear-cut. We are literally in an oasis in a sea of clear-cuts."

Free of the television lights and adoring coeds who latch on to him on college campuses, Atiyeh appears at one with himself on his hallowed ground. "This is the Oregon we've lost, the Oregon that used to be. Not this valley, but every valley, including the Willamette," he says. "Saving Opal Creek will take all of the people of Oregon, working, caring, and loving the land together. I see the pain in my friends and I see the pain in Mill City. They are going to lose their jobs and they don't understand why. This is more important than anyone's job. We have to save it and we have to change. If we trade our life support system for money, we're all doomed." The only sound is the wind whistling through the mountains.

Hecocta steps forward to give a soul talk from his unique perspective, but rooted in a universal theme. Nature's elements have weathered his skin as smooth as the contours of the smooth-barked trees surrounding us. "Indian people are taught at an early age to respect the things around them. It's important if you pick something up, you put it back where you found it," he says, his jet-black hair waving in the light breeze. Hecocta scoops up a small stone, holds it aloft, and drops it softly to the ground: "You do that because you respect God and God's land. It's your purpose and mine to take care of the place. We come here today to learn about earth. To feel the warmth of brother sun on your back. Listen to the voice of the wind in the trees. Take time to drink the water you're allowing to cleanse you on the inside. You get a chance to be reborn as people as part of nature and God. When we touch the earth, the things we feel are him. We need to give these things to our children and our children's children. We need to teach the children to leave these things alone."

Hecocta wears a heavy wool shirt streaked with rainbows around his elbows and across his chest to convey personal power. A blue and white sash hanging from the waist ornaments his ceremonial dress. Tied tightly around the head, a bandanna of the same color helps him concentrate on the positive. "It makes me angry to think of how the country I come from was ripped apart with chainsaws by people who had no caring about the things living here. Many of us are still haunted by the grief. When I moved into the Willamette Valley I could see the amount of destruction around here. I feel sad inside it's going to continue."

The picnickers stop eating and hikers fidgeting to hang on Hecocta's every word. "Remember while you're here, you have entered this land that belongs to the wildlife. People live in these little houses," he says, pointing to the cabins in the camp. "Animals live in the ground, trees, and in the water. We can visit, but we have no right to come and tear their home apart and destroy their lives. It's their natural right. My relatives and I are going to be a voice for the people, forests, and animals. The animals and birds cannot be here to talk with you and tell you about fears of losing their homes; the pain on the other side of the mountain when their land is taken away from them like mine was. All they can do is run away and seek sanctuary in a place like this while the rest of the land is bare. Don't let anybody deceive you that everything is okay. The wildlife is hurting out there. It's time to take that message home with you. Teach it to your children. Teach them about love for God's earth and each other."

IX

People and a Place

Chuck Bennett wishes that he and his wife, Cherie, could escape Salem to their weekend home above Mill City. In his mind's eye he pictures himself walking down the path from his backyard to the cliff overlooking the North Santiam River's cool, rolling waters 125 feet below. Ever since volunteering as the point man in Atiyeh's campaign to pass legislation safeguarding Opal Creek, Bennett has enjoyed few good nights of sleep.

Oregon state legislators, once eager to sign on fast as they could to Senate Bill 500, now light into Atiyeh and Bennett in the Capitol rotunda beneath the murals of the 1805 Lewis and Clark expedition and the 1843 covered wagon train. They encircle them in the basement cafeteria and in the parking area. They demand to know what went wrong. If anyone can sense the lay of the political landscape, it's Bennett, a popular, seasoned lobbyist and former state representative. "Don't worry, I have this sucker wired," he kept assuring SB 500's backers. "It'll go through like greased lightning." Bennett had lined up Senate president John Kitzhaber, the body's power broker, as chief sponsor. Atiyeh helped stack the witnesses in the testimony against the timber types. Behind the scenes, they timed the hearings to begin as soon as the bill left the hopper—a smooth parliamentary maneuver designed to minimize attention and speed its passage. For good measure, Kitzhaber frosted the bill with the number 500, a memorable, round number.

Atiyeh presumed right would make might. "Let's stuff that bill and do some horse-trading," Bennett said. "Wait a minute, Chuck," Atiyeh admonished him. "You're going to have to do whatever it takes to keep the package together." With great fanfare, they promised to preserve the largest remaining stand of old growth in the Oregon Cascades. In its original version, the thirty-one-thousand-acre Opal Creek Ancient Forest State Park would have ranked as Oregon's biggest state park, boasting four miles of walking and horseback trails and over fifty waterfalls. In the hearing room, Atiyeh presented a dazzling slide show highlighting the park's older half. Some fifteen thousand of the acres would have encompassed trees ranging in age from five hundred to a thousand years old. Half the state's population live within sixty miles. Bennett appeared to stand on firm ground insisting on SB 500's "mom and apple pie" popularity.

Then all hell broke loose. The mill owners whipped their rank and file into a frenzy. A parade of one hundred log trucks rumbled past the Capitol, honking their horns in a deafening din. Five hundred demonstrators waved signs and chanted slogans. Groups of them splintered off to stalk lawmakers one on one in hallways and offices. Secretaries, unaccustomed to seeing mountainous lumberjacks out of the woods and in town, recoiled from the personal contact. Legislators wondered how so many could afford to take time off in the middle of the day to be there. Freres, one of Mill City's Big Three timber companies, simply shut down its four mills and paid most of its 250 employees to attend. It provided buses for the convenience of 175. "They were there because they kind of were told to go," snapped state representative Dave McTeague. "It makes a mockery of the process to employ that kind of tactic." Four other mills in the canyon turned the lights out for the day.

On the surface, the commotion in Salem appeared wholly disproportionate to SB 500's significance. The log trucks came from as far as Roseburg, 134 miles south of Salem, although nary a tree from Opal Creek would have ended up in the town's mills. Moreover, Opal Creek's location on federal lands gave the U.S. government rather than the state the final say on its disposition, so the bill was mostly symbolic. "During the hearings, I would watch the log trucks and think you're going around the wrong Capital Beltway," said state senator Jim Hill (currently state treasurer), whose district includes Mill City. "Opal Creek shows what can happen with a misplaced symbol. Regardless of what happens, it wasn't going to change federal policy." The proposed legislation would have merely required Oregon to apply for a special long-term lease from the U.S. Forest Service.

Nor, at first glance, did the figures justify the thousands of dollars Rob Freres admitted he lost in productivity in subsidizing his workers' politicking. In one of its worst-case scenarios, industry predicted the park would have removed about 2.7 million board feet, barely enough to build 270 houses. Bill Bradbury, the Senate majority leader and cosponsor, wisely advised the demonstrators to look at boosting the value added to wood products. By his estimate, the timber in the Opal Creek area represented about 3.5 days' worth of log exports from Oregon. Other park supporters added that it would reduce Willamette National Forest production by less than 0.5 percent.

Atiyeh and Bennett discovered their miscalculation during a visit they paid a lawmaker. For both loggers and conservationists, Opal Creek transcended its actuality as a small nest of ancient forest east of Salem. With the spotted owl controversy hitting at precisely the same time, industry homed in on the only bill out there resembling an attempt to define the issue. Opal Creek was the place to draw the line in the sand. "We're in a fight for our lives," declared Kevin Long, hired as a lobbyist for Mill City's timber interests. "It's not the environmentalists versus the timber industry. It's the environmentalists versus rural Oregon. It's a way of life."

Up in Mill City, Long's stoic father, George, broke completely out of character to turn his column in the *Enterprise*, "It Ain't All Roses," into a manifesto. The heartfelt sentiments rise above the unpolished grammar:

> The preservationists and obstructionists will stop at nothing. Their goal is to prohibit timber harvesting on ALL National Forest lands. The spotted owl is but a legal surrogate to preclude timber harvest. The Opal Creek State Park is only a political surrogate to create additional wilderness acreage in the upper North Fork.
>
> We must pray it is not too late. We absolutely have to wake up. Paul Bunyan has been sleeping for a century. While we napped on our majestic pillows crafty preservationists have carved away at our livelihood. The sleeping giant is awakening. We will be heard.
>
> The people must continue to fight Opal Creek in Salem. You, with your yellow arm band and timber industry attire are the most effective Opal Creek lobbyists. You have entered into a game of political hardball. Hearing times will be changed,

delay tactics will be instituted and politicians will do everything they can not to look you in the eye when they cast a vote against Opal Creek. Look the Legislators in the eye and smile when you ask them to oppose Senate Bill 500.

Canyon residents have risen to the challenge. Let us not be discouraged by the process. We will prevail. Opal Creek is the battle that will turn the political tide.

Long supplied the phone number and address of Tom Hirons's Communities for a Great Oregon office in Mill City. In the ensuing days, Hirons needed extra staff to handle the deluge of inquiries.

His client, Jim Morgan, had long since shunted aside his dependence on Atiyeh, to navigate Hirons through Salem's political shoals. In the early 1980s, Atiyeh, the governor's nephew, lobbied for Morgan in Salem to allow drug testing in the mills. Ironically, Young and Morgan took his advice to become politically active by contributing lavishly to the campaigns of local politicians, some of whom became proponents of logging Opal Creek. "It's only when we get shoved against the wall that we come out fighting," he thundered. "We've been shoved and shoved and shoved. That's why we can't compromise on Opal Creek." As though to back up his fighting words, Morgan announced his intention to be first on line to cut the timber there. "I want," he declared to reporters, eyes ablaze, "to build the road into Opal Creek."

Morgan still seethes over the brazen duplicity he believes Atiyeh displayed trying to secure the Opal Creek state park bill's passage. "George played those political games about being [ex-Governor] Vic Atiyeh's nephew and the big name for all they were worth," Morgan says. "Frankly, he lost that round, and George wasn't used to losing. I leveled with him."

In the midst of the tumult at the Capitol, state representative Phil Keisling sought to find common ground. Loggers scampered about tying yellow ribbons, their campaign's trademark, to office phones. Their opposite numbers countered with green ribbons. Keisling, a young Portlander, thirty-five, and a native Oregonian, did them both better by tying yellow and green ribbons to colleagues' phones. "I was showing this isn't a simple issue. A lot of people's lives are affected. We have to work together and try to decide the issue here rather than in the courthouses," he said. "In this state, where politics is fairly civil, I've never seen this anger or demogoguery. The Opal Creek bill crystallized a lot of anxiety and resentment."

For his own part, Keisling came away mesmerized from an excursion into the woods for lawmakers led by Atiyeh. "The point is whether we have saved enough old growth. That's the Opal Creek challenge. Show me," he says. "My gut tells me it's fairly extraordinary." At the time of SB 500, Keisling could afford to stray partway from this goal of objectivity. His urban constituency, polls demonstrate, favored keeping the Northwest's Opal Creeks as an outlet for weekends and vacations. Since then, Keisling's rise to secretary of state (lieutenant governor) obligates him to fuse his emblematic yellow and green ribbons for real.

Atiyeh and Bennett's legislation crumbled before their eyes. Despite lopping off about a quarter of their original proposal, to 22,680 acres, the timber industry threw its weight around. A bevy of their full-time lobbyists, far outnumbering conservationists, from such groups as the Oregon Forest Industries Council, employ strong-arm tactics. As long as King Timber reigns in the Northwest, it can reward friends and punish enemies at the ballot box. In 1986, its chief political action committee laid out $35,000, an astounding sum when the average Oregon race costs about $100,000, to bump off Bradbury's immediate predecessor as majority leader for failing to hew to the party line. In the first election following SB 500, in 1990, according to the Portland-based nonpartisan Western States Center, this single interest group would spend almost a half million dollars on state races, the largest total contribution by far from any Oregon industry.

Senator Wayne Fawbush, an original cosponsor of the Opal Creek bill, justified his vote against it in committee on the odd reasoning that there were not enough votes on the Senate floor to pass it. "Wayne's a wonderful human being and an environmentalist in his own right. The other side just broke arms and legs," Bennett explains. "During the last election, it gave him tens of thousands of dollars. This was the chit they called in." Tabled in committee, SB 500 dies a slow, painful death.

Meanwhile, the enmity between the two former close companions rages. Hirons feels totally betrayed because he had received no advance notice of the bill from Atiyeh. "Here George is going around telling me I'm his absolutely very best friend," Hirons says, "and he doesn't even tell me about this." Hirons testified against SB 500 on technical grounds. A state park, to him, conjured up images of friendly campgrounds and picnic areas. Opal Creek, he argued from the personal experience he drew on from living there for two years, constituted de facto wilderness for all but the experienced hiker. "I've never really had any argument with George over Opal Creek. I've had visions of that gate coming down and people having access. Let's poke a road down the middle so everybody can drive into it and see it," he tells me one year later. "What do you think of when you hear Opal Creek Ancient Forest Park? It ain't all big trees. You're talking about some nasty ground. What about some guy from Kansas City who hears about the park and visits with his wife and three little kids? All they can do is walk into Jawbone Flats and walk out."

Measured against the strident rhetoric of Jim Morgan and his gung ho allies, Hirons appears to be pressing a debater's point. After all, the timber barons care not one iota about the ultimate shape of an Opal Creek park. The act of logging the area to smithereens renders the matter moot. Hirons's nuanced position affords him the moral luxury of opposing SB 500 while keeping a safe distance from the cut-and-pillage crowd. It also reflects his sincerely held view that the best wilderness serves the most people, even if it means cleaving a road through Opal Creek's soul for recreation vehicles.

In the year since SB 500's defeat, Atiyeh grows livid watching Hirons abandon the quasi-neutrality he has steadfastly maintained over the years. Ever since departing from the mines, Hirons refused to become involved in the political imbroglios whenever the U.S. Forest Service spoke of its designs on Opal Creek's timbers. One night during the hearings, they squared off in a heated phone fight. Atiyeh reminded him of an earlier agreement to testify for protection of Opal Creek. "George, what the hell are you asking me to do?" Hirons asked. "You gotta be kidding. I log for these guys. I don't necessarily want to log Opal Creek, but they want some timber out of it. Friendship can go a long way, but not so far that you shoot yourself in the foot." He interrupted his tirade to demand that Atiyeh come clean on his hidden agenda.

"We ain't just going for Opal Creek," Atiyeh shoots backs. "It's the flagship. We're going for all of it."

Atiyeh later shakes his head struggling to figure out his ex-partner's rationale. "He went down there as the principal organizer trying to kill the bill. It's the military domino theory. Opal Creek falls, then goes the rest of the forest," he says. "To tell you the truth, some of the national groups have nightmares about unilaterally saving Opal Creek. The flagship is gone. I've no intention of saving it to sink the fleet."

Salem serves as the fitting battleground for framing the debate between lumberjacks and environmentalists. In this sleepy capital of a hundred thousand tucked away in the nation's far corner, twenty-seven hundred miles from Washington, D.C., each side vies for claim to the largest contiguous stand of ancient forest left in the western Cascades. The bare-knuckle politics on the local level tests Atiyeh and Hirons's mettle as well as the relative merits of their causes. Neither one ever set out to throw himself in the political fray. They were well aware that their aggressive drives would overturn their happy, fulfilling lives. Till this day, Hirons yearns to continue logging full time as dearly as Atiyeh longs to resume running the small mine at Jawbone Flats and ferrying commuters about in his bush plane. They simply had too much at stake and were too good at fighting for it to remain on the sidelines.

As grass-roots activists, Atiyeh and Hirons have proved adept at winning the hearts and minds of politicians, the media, and citizens. Their clash ultimately boils down to a sign held aloft at a timber rally: "PEOPLE, NOT PARKS." The most dramatic words and pictures can never do Opal Creek justice, Atiyeh realizes. Time and again he has swayed the hardest skeptics by bringing them to the mountaintop to experience it for themselves. His challenge, in turn, is to convey Opal Creek's magnificence to the millions far from the towering trees and crystal streams. He is selling the world on absolute wilderness. Hirons seeks to convert it to economic use, airbrushing away the chainsaw as part of his reclamation project to present the logger as the forest's guardian. The other half of his campaign highlights the downside of conservation in the thousands of tragedies befalling families on the verge of losing their heritage.

At a coffee shop two blocks from the Capitol, Atiyeh and Bennett, like a pair of seasoned veterans, are still recovering from the shock of SB 500. "It's a war," Atiyeh says. "They needed something to rally the troops around." Bennett blames the timber barons for perverting the political process. "A bunch of short-sighted local idiots did in the state park. Rob Freres makes a lot of money off the subsidies of the American taxpayer," Bennett erupts. "They have that entire community buffaloed. The average Joe is scared shitless. There is confusion as to who's right. These guys still love hunting and fishing. And a lot of them don't trust the mill owners because they've been ripped off."

A registered Republican and two-time voter for Ronald Reagan in the general election, Atiyeh clings to Oregon's progressive tradition. "I'm a Teddy Roosevelt Republican, socially responsible and fiscally conservative. I was born into a Republican family which didn't say 'Democrat' without the word 'damned.' I'm now a Republican in name only. Gotta bring those other fools around," he chortles halfheartedly. "How can you be a conservative and not want to conserve habitat and go fishing? The root of conservative is to conserve." Critics brand him an opportunist. The long, bumpy ride from TR, the standard-bearer of the modern environmental movement, to RR, his antithesis as a steward of the earth, lends credence to Atiyeh's view that the party abandoned him rather than he it.

George's activities have caused his uncle, Oregon's chief executive from 1979 to 1987, no small consternation. An oriental-rug merchant and twenty-year veteran of the state legislature, Vic Atiyeh became the first governor of Arab descent in the nation. In 1982 he joined the select company of three governors in his state ever to serve two terms, after trouncing his opponent by a two-to-one margin, the highest in thirty-two years. Most voters appeared to respect his low-key decency and integrity in the conservative-housekeeper role he played. Through soothing eyes bearing an uncanny resemblance to his nephew's, the governor, fifty-eight, coveys the reliability of a Boy Scout—befitting his four decades of active volunteerism in that organization and the trinkets decorating his Portland office. He speaks excitedly of a Scout jamboree he recently attended. A cleft chin abuts his lopsided mouth. Square-shaped aviator glasses complement his right-angled head.

His gradual swing from the business corner to the political center on environmental and labor issues generally preserved the status quo. A protracted recession tested his economic credo. In 1979 Governor Atiyeh argued that a principal obstacle to his state's economic well-being was "the miserable image Oregon has with the national business community." "We were too heavily dependent on wood products and agriculture," he says today. "We had to diversify." Yet throughout his reign he staunchly defended the Northwest's economic mainstay, timber. "I just think we have about as much wilderness as we need," he maintained in 1979, before a stream of federal wilderness legislation passed. "The super environmentalists would really like to go back to the days of Lewis and Clark. I worry about people who lose their jobs and who won't be able to retrain," the ex-governor says today. "The super environmentalists only care about natural resources."

The governor was lukewarm to the wilderness bills he feared

would stall Oregon's economic recovery. "Our state is the park for all the millions of people. If that's what you are going to do, you're going to take away our ability to make a living. You can understand the fear if somebody is going to take away your job and you lose your house and family," he says. "All you folks out there who want to enjoy the beauty of Oregon and the Northwest want to lock it up as your playground. So pay us something for it. Do something to allow us to live out there." The angry pitch for just compensation begs the question of wiping out the last 10 percent of ancient forests. "So? I don't want to sound like a cut-and-slash kind of guy," he insists, sounding a lot like one. "There ought to be old growth. But these trees are no longer growing. They will die. We can grow trees again and they will be beautiful." Contrary to his claims of centrism, the governor strikes a hard line against his nephew's arguments for preservation.

His views come as something of a surprise, considering that Governor Atiyeh's affinity for Opal Creek stretches back to 1944, the year he married Dolores Hewitt, Jim "Grandpa" Hewitt's daughter. The couple spent their Christmases, Thanksgivings, and vacations up there. "I wanted to go all the time," Atiyeh recalls, "as often as I could." He enjoyed helping Grandpa prepare the flume line for piping fresh drinking water into camp. The son-in-law fished for rainbow trout and took advantage of the solitude to shoot the black powder muzzlers from his extensive antique firearms collection.

Ostensibly, SB 500 and earlier legislative measures to stop loggers from putting Opal Creek's dying trees out of their misery have posed as wrenching a quandary to the governor as they have to Hirons. The consequences can cut short the careers of politicians and loggers alike, particularly those intimately linked to the issue, such as these two men. "I keep wondering why if this is such a treasure," says the governor, "it isn't part of wilderness."

Opal Creek, as a senior statesman of his caliber ought to know, was excluded from the federal wilderness system and nine other local and national conservation plans his nephew championed precisely because the timber industry has coveted the rare, big trees that make it so special. "My reluctance is I never want any appearance of conflict of interest," the governor adds, betraying his extreme caution. Governor Atiyeh sold his interest in the mines to Thurston Twigg-Smith in 1972 and hasn't visited Opal Creek in six years. Perhaps the gun-shyness dates back to the public sting of fetching his nephew out of jail after he was arrested with Larry McDonald in 1970. The episode honed the damage control skills of the rising star in the state legislature. "I don't really want to spend time talking about that," he says. "It's not a pleasant focus." At the eleventh hour of a wilderness bill in 1984, his nephew pleaded with him to support Opal Creek. Finally Governor Atiyeh sent a telex from Syria, where he was traveling on business and pleasure, to Oregon senator Mark Hatfield in Washington, D.C., asking him please to include Opal Creek. At the same time, the governer discreetly informed the senator he would understand if he didn't help. That cooked it for the legislation.

The uncle and nephew, as two accomplished politicians, strain to dispel suspicions of a rift in the family. "I don't think he'd listen to me any more than he'd listen to his dad," the older Atiyeh says. "You know young people and children." The forty-one-year-old graciously gives his uncle the benefit of the doubt: "He said George doesn't speak for me and I don't speak for him, but we do speak to each other."

They do so across a great divide. "There has to be a distinction between environmentalists and super environmentalists. If George goes beyond Opal Creek, he's a super environmentalist," Governor Atiyeh says. "I have a hard time saving it all." In petulant phone calls to Hirons and in public pronouncements, his nephew has done just that, raising the flag in his special spot at the movement's summit to preserve all old growth. "Opal Creek is the gem, the biggest and best piece we've got. It should carry the other pieces," the younger Atiyeh explains. "There are other gorgeous places, too. I've been given an offer through the back door to exchange Opal Creek for the rest of it. That's not right. It's like saving one elephant and killing the last herd. There must be some place between." So long as he and the governor search in vain to find it, the two will remain philosophically estranged.

Based on appearance, an outsider could easily overlook the silver-haired forty-one-year-old Chuck Bennett in his current capacity as a lobbyist. He's not one to rely on his creed's textbook Three B's—beefsteak, broads, and booze—to do his job. Bennett lately wears Dexters, Birkenstock sandals, and a motorcycle helmet to accompany his preferred mode of transportation. Oregon trial lawyers, chiropractors, and psychologists have all retained his services. Atiyeh takes up about 15 percent of his time. "I don't charge George one dime. I told him I needed something to get to heaven because what I was doing was not paving the way," Bennett says. "There are a very limited number of lobbyists who make it there. You don't walk to heaven in Guccis."

When buttonholing lawmakers, Bennett sticks to the pragmatic reasons for safeguarding Opal Creek. "I reject the spiritual argument. The average person is not going to define the issue in spiritual terms. George has done a real good job expressing it in his personal, high-charged, emotional way," he says. "Almost every bill has an economic value. I'll tell you, honest to God, I look for the economic assets versus the liabilities. I'll tell you, here, there's no comparison." For starters, Bennett cites the potential for tourism and the importance of water quality. "They want to hassle about the owl," he explains. "I think they're going to find that other creatures, including humans, depend on that forest's little hotel." Steam from the coffee he sips slightly fogs the aviator glasses Bennett wears. "The water we're drinking in this coffee came right out of that forest," he says. "It's so sweet because it doesn't require the chlorination and filtration that other water resources do." A regular coffee drinker myself, I can vouch for this brew's tastiness.

A Salem resident, Bennett, turns a cold shoulder to Atiyeh's neighbors in Mill City. "You have to come away from Opal Creek and realize there are no more places like it. I really believe in it. It's the last contiguous stand of its size in the Cascades and one of the last historic mining camps in the Cascades. The thought of cutting Opal Creek just breaks my heart," Bennett says. "They can talk about jobs, but I'll tell you what. I hope Freres shuts down. I'm not going to give up that place to help some son-of-a-bitch buy a Bronco (the all-terrain vehicle of choice for most loggers). It's not just a fair trade."

His scorn extends beyond abstract notions of the adversary to a flesh-and-blood friend of the past decade. Until moving permanently to Salem from a weekend retreat on the outskirts of Mill City down the road from Hirons, Bennett and Hirons regularly enjoyed each other's company. Both share a wry sense of humor and a passion for history. In the early 1980s they banded together to block construction of a local dam threatening their property. On the advice of Hirons, Mill City's timber barons later retained Bennett to try to end log exports.

When a verbal scuffle broke out between Atiyeh and a young logger in the Capitol, Hirons summoned Bennett for help to remove Atiyeh from harm's way, in spite of the opposing politics. The lobbyist took the measure of the man then and there. "I know Tom and like him," Bennett says. "Personally, he's a sensitive and caring person." But professionally he and Hirons have grown far apart. "He acts like a guy from Southern California," fumes Bennett, a native of Washington State, resorting to the ultimate put-down in Oregon, where one's stock is gauged by a family's generations and an aversion to that sinful state to the south flooding Oregon with its refugees. "I'm appalled by his destructive attitude toward the environment. I suspect Tom can't sleep at night. I couldn't."

Since SB 500's demise, Atiyeh and Bennett have no plans to resurrect it in any form. At least they can take solace from the $3 million they estimate their efforts cost the timber industry in 1989. After SB 500 went down, they apprised hostile legislators of their devilish strategy to protect old growth through a flurry of new bills. By their estimates, if industry took one Friday each year to allow employees to attend rallies, it could save the equivalent of all the timber in Opal Creek. By Young and Morgan's own calculations, an eight-hour shutdown cost the Oregon economy almost $1 million a day in lost wages, worker compensation, and taxes.

The black humor helps deaden the pain of Atiyeh's rude awakening in Salem. "I went in there an absolute idealist and figured the righteousness of my cause would shine through," he says. "I got hammered so hard, I couldn't believe it. These guys can still slam-dunk us politically in the state because of the Oregon tradition and who they are as loggers." Atiyeh has shifted his attention to Washington, D.C., to advance his cause. "I think some of my opponents are incredulous that I get the shit kicked out of me," he says, "and keep coming back."

Atiyeh probably never stood a chance in Salem. King Timber still holds sway not only in the political and economic realms but also in the culture's popular mythology. Oregon's Capitol is a handsome building styled in modern Greek architecture and constructed of white Danby Vermont marble. On the front, high-relief carvings in bronze depict the sea otter, beaver, and eagle as created by the sculptor Ulric Ellerhusen. His centerpiece, an original pioneer, is 168 feet above the ground. Rising 24 feet from the cylindrical structure that tops the building in place of a conventional dome, it stands, in the gushing account of a local reporter long ago, as "Oregon's tallest and most looked-up-to native son." Four hundred ounces of 23-carat gold leaf were used to plate the muscled bronze body, accentuating the glittering, 8½-ton heft. The "Oregon Pioneer," or the "Gold Man," as he is also known, symbolizes the spirit of the Northwest's early trailblazing.

In today's supercharged atmosphere, loggers embrace the Gold

Man as the monument to the frontier values they applaude themselves as embodying. They are fond of pointing out that an ax
rather than an owl in his hand beats the birds in the preservationists' bush. "Nobody comments on the tree stump," says a
surprised Cecil Edwards, Oregon's legislative historian, when I do,
upon noticing it at the Gold Man's feet. My tour guide on the
rotunda roof 25 feet below the pioneer quickly corrects himself
after calling him a logger, a four-letter word in some circles. "No,
he's never referred to as that," he hastens to add. From here, the
Gold Man can see and be seen for miles. Visitors to his perch
share the sweeping view of Mount Jefferson, Mount Hood, and
the lush Willamette Valley.

The panaroma appears to bolster the cases of Atiyeh and Hirons, both of whom once spent a fair amount of time enjoying it.
As a Senate page in his youth, Atiyeh brought dates to Salem's
apex. In his college days, Hirons's job as a Capitol janitor en-
dowed him with the key to the roof. He spent many a relaxing
evening smoking cigarettes and doing his homework in the lap of
the vista. From this vantage point, it is possible to look out over
Salem's graceful homes and tree-lined streets, fashioned at the
turn of the century from the prosperity afforded by the state's
abundant natural resources. Toward the east and Mill City, the
eye catches an ugly clear-cut Atiyeh despises for its brazenness.
It leaves the impression of a thumbtack hole in the center of a
pretty postcard.

Today western land users are serving notice that environmental
victories in recent years are unleashing a severe backlash. Scores
of "grass roots" groups are rolling across the political landscape
like tumbleweed, bound together in a common effort to promote
the "wise use" of natural resources for mining, logging, and ranching. Their names sound as wholesome and patriotic as the Min-
utemen—Communities for a Great Oregon ("Communities together
means timber forever"), People for the West, and Oregon Lands
Coalition ("Putting people back into the environmental equation"). OLC unites forty-four community groups representing
more than sixty-two thousand members. Its vast network introduces Hirons and other grass-roots standouts to movers and shak-
ers in the media and in Washington, D.C. The gospel of
"multiple use" the movement preaches rests on the premise of
everyday folk arrayed against environmental elitists.

Hirons runs the Mill City chapter of Communities for Great
Oregon, the state wide group he founded to counter environmentalists, out of a compact two-room office on Highway 22, bank-

rolled largely by the timber barons, and Jim Morgan in particular. At the office, CGO keeps a full line of paraphernalia bearing the trademark yellow that the timber forces have embraced since 1988. (When Oregon's grass-seed industry unwittingly adopted the preservationists' counteremblem, green ribbons, they found themselves being greeted in timber towns by the finger and being run off the road by log trucks.) By early 1991 the Gulf War would mute the yellow symbolism altogether.

Twelve dollars buys membership in CGO and, in Mill City, a subscription to a six-page yellow newsletter. It ranks as good a grass-roots read as any in the Northwest, serving as a billboard for petition drives, letter-writing campaigns, and public protests. The logging companies post notices for community forums to which they donate coffee, doughnuts, and child care. The rank and file will think twice before staying home once they read the wake-up calls—"STOP! LOOK! AND LISTEN! YOUR WAY OF LIFE IS BEING TAKEN AWAY!" Woodworkers and their wives take advantage of the forum to let off steam against the preservationists.

The newsletter's star is its editor. Hirons has developed a crusty style approximating H. L. Mencken at the helm of the *Farmer's Almanac*. He peppers his work with quotes from historical figures, among them Machiavelli: "When neither their property nor their honor is touched, the majority of men live content." The addresses of politicians appear at election time. "The lesson to be taught will be that economy and ecology both stem from the same Greek word and both must be sustainable," Hirons writes on the eve of the Gulf War. "If we fail, the alternative will be the Four Horsemen: famine, pestilence, death, and war." As a media watchdog, Hirons keeps tabs on the spread of untruths as he sees them, from the mundane, *Time-Life*, to the exotic, "NINJA TURTLES MISINFORMED" (about the loggers' much-maligned comrades, cattlemen, and their impact on the land). Mill City's residents are urged to flood Phil Donahue's Rockefeller Center office with letters after an unflattering portrayal of the "timber story." The addresses of the competition, Oprah and Heraldo (sic), are furnished to keep them honest, too, in the future. Hirons's endeavor would be incomplete without a few darts flung in the direction of Mill City's own celebrity who flies "prominent people around and shows them the 'acres upon acres of clear-cuts.' " Atiyeh has heard that the CGO newsletter is such a good read that he has sent in his dues to join.

Perhaps all the energy Hirons pours into his creative outlet numbs the anguish of wanderlust for the woods. His support staff of woodworkers' wives at CGO have occupied his days, lately, seconding each other's ideological notions, creating the effect of an echo chamber in the claustrophobic quarters. He rolls his eyes listening to them read the latest intelligence reports from right-wingers in Montana and Wyoming about assorted conspiracy theories, among them legions of armed Earth First!ers known as "Eco-Kamikazes" plotting to overthrow timber towns from within. "I wouldn't want to give them a sharp stick to hurt themselves," he jokes to a staffer intent on taking it quite seriously. Atiyeh is less funny. From the CGO office, Hirons dispatches his surrogates, whom he calls his "spies," to monitor his ex-partner's public appearances.

In his spare time, Hirons amuses himself playing with the computer Atiyeh, who sells and services them, recommended he buy. Showing off the graphics program to me, Hirons uses a mouse to draw a mountain and in the foreground a stump, the object defined by Aldo Leopold as "our symbol of progress." Hirons rounds it off with an ax stuck in its center. He looks at once tired and wistful admiring his vision of paradise calling to him on the back-lit screen. "I don't want to make my career out of working for CGO," he says. "I'd like to work my butt out of a job here."

Three blocks from the Capitol, Hirons and Jim Morgan work the fourth estate at the *Salem Statesman-Journal.* Dan Postrel, an affable and acerbic thirty-five-year-old reporter, has agreed to have coffee with them in the paper's cozy cafeteria downstairs from the newsroom. "This is our paper," growls Hirons, laying today's edition on a table. It features a story on the thirty thousand jobs the owl will cost, and advertisements paid for with dollars from the timber industry and related products. "We don't make all the right decisions," Morgan chimes in. "We've had trouble getting decent, fair coverage." "Well, you're in the right place," Postrel assures them. Morgan and Hirons spew out their familiar litany of grievances against conservationists, particularly Atiyeh. "You need to be asking some real hard questions about Opal Creek," Hirons says, tugging at his Mad Creek cap and muddy jeans.

Hirons and Morgan's folksy, if crude, stab at political action results from the pervasive sentiment in logging country that media bias has victimized the timber trade. A couple of hit-and-run numbers by East Coast television producers might lend such an impression on the national level. But journalists in the Northwest, with much more at stake, are by and large laboring to strike a balance between the plights of the spotted owl and thousands of workers. The *Statesman-Journal* has run a well-written ten-page supplement on Mill City in its Sunday edition, and the *Oregonian* an encyclopedic three-part series. Michael Donnelly likens the *Oregonian's* devastating, if belated, three-part series on the abuse of forests to the *Detroit Free Press* taking on the auto industry. The statewide paper, a beneficiary of timber companies' advertising and pulp for newsprint, brings home the radical shift in attitudes taking place in much of the Northwest. Perhaps Hirons's camp heaps almost as much enmity on the *Statesman-Journal* and the *Oregonian* as Atiyeh because they're in their own backyard, where they don't take kindly to the treason they perceive.

Atiyeh regards slanted journalism as a product of the truth. "It reflects the outrage of the people of the United States. The media has gone out of its way to give the other side a fair shot," he says. "They've still deluded themselves to believe that if they got their story out to the American public, people would care more about jobs than an entire ecosystem of the ancient forests." Outside the Northwest, the majority of mail in response to a *Time* magazine cover story on the spotted owl goes against the logger.

Ever since SB 500's defeat, Hirons and his allies have mapped out strategies to widen the scope of their public-relations campaign. The log truck wagons from Roseburg, a town of sixteen-thousand in southern Oregon, and elsewhere in the Northwest continue to stimulate the consciousness of urban flatlanders unaccustomed to seeing the big men and bigger machines from the back country downtown. Each event emboldens Hirons's party to top the next. What if they could consolidate all the local protests, such as the rally against Opal Creek in Salem, into a single demonstration so historic that third-growth loggers would tell their children about it well into the next century?

All of a sudden, federal scientists unveil a report calling for the preservation of 8.4 million acres of forest to save the northern spotted owl from extinction. An endless series of dire reports from economists stokes the fears of doom. The word goes out from Brookings, across the California border, to Pendleton to La Grande, near Idaho. A full-page advertisement appears in the *Oregonian*, a state wide paper: "SPOTTED OWL ISSUE. JOBS—NOT HANDOUTS—A DEMONSTRATION FOR OREGON JOBS AND THE SURVIVAL OF OUR COMMUNITIES. NOW IS THE TIME TO STOP LISTENING AND START ACTING."

Friday the thirteenth turns out to be a good Friday for the organizers praying for a solid turnout. Life in Mill City and its sister towns comes to a standstill from the mass exodus to Portland. The Stewarts let their staff go and run their general store by themselves. At their supermarket, the Girods maintain a skeleton crew. The schools grant students excused absences so they can join their families. They would have offered their buses free, as a show of solidarity, but CGO had already charted its own fleet. (Upon discovering that his son Aziz Atiyeh skipped class, his irate father asks his girlfriend Michelle, a millworker's daughter, where on earth he spent the day.) The mills shut down and pay their employees to go to the rally. In Douglas County, where 70 percent of the revenues come from timber cutting, fifty government employees take advantage of an offer for paid time off. Most taxpayers do not object. Other counties pack half a dozen buses and hundreds of other vehicles. Farther north, "The Welcome to Sweet Home" sign receives a face-lift. Today it reads "Closed— Gone Job-Hunting in Portland." Ninety-nine percent of the businesses are shut down. High-schoolers who have yet to get haircuts or buy flowers for tonight's senior prom are out of luck.

Rolling up Interstate 5's northbound lanes in his Ford, Hirons checks in with Jim Morgan on his CB. They rejoice in the phalanx of vehicles souped up in official yellow bumper stickers and ribbons. Sympathetic motorists honk their horns in support. By midmorning, more than a hundred log trucks and buses invade Portland, Oregon's hub of commerce and most populous city. Hundreds of cars carrying the troops for timber further clog Portland's incoming and outgoing traffic.

Hirons arrives early to help set up at Pioneer Courthouse Square, the plaza unofficially known as Portland's living room. He clips yellow ribbons from spools to knot bow ties on the arms of Marlene and friends. Jim Morgan rushes down to a table to fill out a card switching his registration to Republican, the preferred party these days for its prologging stance. Timber families line up to sign a long, yellow oak-tag scroll. Written with a Magic Marker, the letter on it implores the president to take their side. At the front of the stage, someone has placed a totem. The details of a miniature replica of a log truck—painted yellow, of course— are accurate down to the tiny chain binders for fastening a load. A teddy bear atop wears yellow ribbons and the same plugs timber fallers use to protect their ears from chainsaws.

Everyone who is anyone in Oregon's timber industry is here on April 13, 1990. Hirons introduces me to the legendary logging company owner who, years ago, took it upon himself to give a long-haired employee a trim. With a chainsaw. It yanked huge clumps of hair out of his head. They settled out of court for twenty-five-thousand dollars. "Yeah, but it was worth," he recalls fondly, "every penny of it."

As the program opens at noon, Hirons relishes scanning a throng six times the population of Mill City. Ten thousand loggers, millworkers, small-business operators, and their families jam Pioneer Courthouse Square on a sun-drenched day. The crowd comprises the largest political gathering ever in the square. A sea of yellow shirts, signs, ribbons, and decorations engulfs the red-brick grounds, spilling out onto sidewalks and streets. There are grandmothers, grandfathers, and tykes cradled in their mothers' arms. Virtually all the men are dressed in the loggers' uniform of suspenders, and hickory shirts over slogan-emblazoned T-shirts. In a high-rise building opposite the square office workers spell out in yellow copy paper "SAVE OUR JOBS!"

On the ground, crops of hand-lettered placards sprout up in the crowd. Even if the mills supplied the materials, the slogans' pure emotion suggests a sincere, personal touch. "IF MY DADDY DOESN'T WORK, WE DON'T EAT"; "PRESERVATIONISTS WANT TO DESTROY FAMILIES"; "PEOPLE COUNT, TOO"; "WHO'S REALLY ENDANGERED?"; "OREGON HAS OWL'S-HEIMERS"; "SAVE MY DAD'S JOB."

The hour-long rally captures the sultry fervor of an evangelical revival in the Deep South. On the densely populated stage, Republican officeholders in the state join Hirons and other allies in loud renditions of patriotic anthems bookending the event. In three neat rows, they clasp one another's hands above their heads and sway back and forth in unison as Iris Butler from Roseburg leads a tearful rendition of her own composition about pulling together "like one big family." The folksy earnestness leaves the crowd unfazed, confining the rapture mostly to the stage.

More signs: "OUR CHILDREN NEED HABITAT"; "I PAY RENT WITH TIMBER"; "MY LIFE—MY JOB ARE IN JEOPARDY"; "SAVE MY GRANDPA'S JOB. TRY PAYING YOUR BILLS WITH OWLS"; "DOES WASHINGTON, D.C., GIVE A HOOT?"

Environmentalists may be routing the timber forces on every public-relations front but music. Bill Randolph and Dub Debre, a pair of honky-tonkers in midnight shades, pick their acoustic guitars ferociously while reading the ditty they've penned for the occasion. The lyrics' social realism pays offhanded homage to folk balladeer Woody Guthrie:"

> You know it's time to go
> 'Cause the mill's closed down
> And I can't work here no more
> There's a church where I married
> my sweet bride
> There was a sawmill and
> a small-town corner store
> There's a chain on the gate
> Its yard is overgrown
> It's been so long since I
> seen a working day
> But a lock on the door can't keep
> my heart away
>
> People worry about birds and the status quo,
> but they don't remember the forests grow
> People in the city gotta understand
> The timber life folks are the
> heart of the land
>
> So climb in the car kids
> I guess it's time to go
> 'Cause this town's broken down
> We can't stay here no more
> No more

Since 1985, Willie Nelson, John Mellencamp, and Neil Young—three of popular music's top entertainers—have romanticized the hardships of the American yeoman through Farm Aid, a gala benefit concert. The more than $10 million they have raised for American family farmers have funded programs from crisis hot lines to job training. Hollywood glommed onto the cause in the feature films *The River* and *Country*, starring Mel Gibson and Jessica Lange. On the big screen, the farmer emerged as a vanishing cultural icon, an object of both sympathy and worship. His valiant struggle against the corporate fiends foreclosing on his hearth and homestead represented an abject moral in an era of unrepentant greed. *Roger and Me*, a popular documentary about the plight of thousands of laid-off autoworkers, skewered General Motors, their heartless employer. The "timber life folks," in the words of Randolph and Debre, find themselves forsaken as long as ecology remains such a hot issue and loggers receive bad press.

So far, the collection of celebrities Hirons's side has rounded up leaves a lot to be desired. In Washington, D.C., the industry features ex-Baltimore Colts quarterback Bert Jones on drive-time radio spots asking listeners to consider the human costs of protecting the spotted owl. Jones happens to own a lumber mill in Louisiana. Retired Air Force general Chuck Yeager, the first person to break the sound barrier and a member of Louisiana-Pacific Corporation's board of directors for the past eight years, pushes the envelope. On a visit to Eugene, Oregon, the prominent figure in the book and movie *The Right Stuff* puckishly invites reporters to ask him how he celebrated Earth Day. They fall for his bait. "I cut down old-growth redwoods," he quips. Of environmental radicals, Yeager declares: "People like that should really be hung up." Friends like Yeager obviat the need for enemies.

The loggers have plenty of them among the celebrity set. Hirons cannot even escape the ideological static tooling around listening to his favorite country music station. The country group Alabama has penned a mawkish ditty beseeching fans to "feel guilty" about the shape of mother earth passed on to the children. "What the hell should I feel guilty about?" Hirons erupts. He doesn't watch MTV, or he might have imploded seeing Arin Atiyeh's handsome face in a musical montage by the Grateful Dead. Narrated by Paul Newman, the show, *Ancient Forests: Rage over Trees*, focuses on Opal Creek.

Loggers are easy prey for caricature in popular culture in the context of environmentalism's sacrosanct *cause célèbre*. "The outdoors just calls to me," says one fat logger to another in a Gary Larson Far Side cartoon. They sit, surrounded by stumps, atop a freshly felled log. An episode of the television program *MacGyver* revolves around a smarmy mill owner in bed with Japanese mafia stealing logs from the U.S. national forest. The Simpsons cartoon show derides a bumbling logger for bribing a congressman to lumber a local forest.

The timber industry, save a few bruises, can still hold its own on the airwaves, thanks to the immense financial clout it wields. Industry succeeds in intimidating a group of the largest corporations in the United States to reject the Audubon documentary none had ever seen. Stroh Brewing Company withdraws $600,000 for the entire nature series after northwestern loggers, in an industry wide protest, threaten to boycott the Stroh brand. Environmentalists charge Stroh with suggesting changes in the program to ensure that the loggers are depicted favorably. Audubon refuses. Stroh concedes that loggers have pressured the brewer. The nine companies—including Exxon, Dean Witter Reynolds, and Ford Motor Company—slated to sponsor the ancient-forest program on Turner Broadcasting System yank their advertising, forcing Turner to take a bath of $250,000 when he runs the program. Ford dealers in the Northwest express concern that their involvement might have cost them business. The corporations' thin respect for First Amendment principles comes on the U.S. Constitution's two-hundredth anniversary. To its credit, General Electric subsequently agrees to provide a three-year, $3 million grant, but Big Timber has shown how readily Big Business will knuckle under. GE soon decides the controversy is not worth the public service and announces it will bow out once its commitment expires.

Since most people are unlikely ever to avail themselves of Atiyeh's hospitality at Opal Creek, their only window to its wonders may be confined to television shows and movies. The mass audience for programs, including *Rage over Trees*, has fired the public's awareness. The ricochet effect in the media has generated multiple stories about the spotted owl in newspapers and magazines. By no coincidence, Congress immediately gets down to business addressing the northwestern crisis.

When not starring in programs such as *Rage over Trees*, Atiyeh makes whirlwind rounds to enlist the aid of show biz sympathizers. "You talked to him like he's a real person," squeals Arin after his father conversed on the phone with Michael Stipe of the rock group REM. Stipe appears on television wearing an Opal Creek T-shirt, and jokes to his partners about raiding the piggy bank to send him there. Atiyeh glides his Cessna down the Pacific Coast to San Francisco in the hope of staging a benefit concert for Opal Creek. To his dismay, however, he learns he will have to raise $50,000 just to cover the costs of a concert. "It's very hard to take Opal Creek to Hollywood, New York, or Washington, D.C. Gotta take people to Opal Creek. Then it's its own best spokesman," he says. "The forest can take care of itself. My job is just to get people to go there. I've never failed to bring anybody who wasn't moved to our side." Among the celebrities he has recently brought to Opal Creek are rock singers Carol King and Kenny Loggins.

The saddest sounds at Pioneer Courthouse Square this afternoon once the music ends are the grunts of one politician after another whoring after votes. The exclusively Republican cast leading the cheers stakes out a position too extreme to leave

Democrats, who maintain their own ties to timber industry anyway, room at the bargaining table. A union official had been
heralded in an official press release for attending. When he declared his intention to discuss the issue of log exports, the rally
organizers ban him from speaking for pushing an argument popular
among preservationists.

U.S. representative Denny Smith, a square-headed conservative who smiles out of one side of his mouth through thin lips,
sports a yellow ribbon in his dark suit's breast pocket. A Vietnam
veteran and hawk, he has spent his eight-year Capitol career
getting more bang for the Pentagon's bucks. In 1985 he almost
singlehandedly killed the Army's ineffective Sergeant York anti-
aircraft gun. The next year, his campaign to improve the efficiency of weapons manufactured in the United States landed him
on the front pages again. A retired Air Force colonel serving as
a weapons analyst on Smith's staff demonstrated a homemade
seven-foot-long antitank cannon at a gas station in suburban
Washington, D.C., in the hope of selling his invention to the
Defense Department. The weapon fell accidentally, firing shells
through his flatbed truck and into a gasoline pump. In the fiery
explosion that ensued three people sustained serious shrapnel
wounds. Smith's aide jumped in his charred truck and fled the
scene before being arrested.

Smith emerged from the incident unscathed, but voters' anxieties about his attention to matters back home tightened his race.
On environmental issues affecting his state, Smith is apt to sacrifice influence for ideology. After months of waffling during his
first year in office ten years ago, he ruled out any compromise
over Opal Creek to become a diehard enthusiast for logging it.
He tried killing the 1984 Oregon Wilderness and 1986 Columbia
River Gorge bills, which passed in spite of his intransigence. Two
years later, Smith withheld his support for the Wild and Scenic
Rivers Act so he could water it down. He has earned a reputation
for being nobody's man but industry's. Atiyeh will never forgive
him for threatening to torpedo a wilderness bill before congress if
Opal Creek received protection. He bristled on hearing Smith
dismiss Opal Creek's friends, including, presumably, Governor
Vic Atiyeh, as "A bunch of tree huggers." Last election, 1988
the congressman's margin of victory was so narrow, 707 votes,
that a lobbyist called Atiyeh to sing prematurely "The Wicked
Witch Is Dead."

"I've voted against more wilderness," Smith boasts. "The
[radical environmentalists] don't want these trees harvested.

They don't want to treat them as a crop. I need your vote." Judging from his voice's timbre, it is all he can do from dropping down on his knees to plead for support. A week later, Smith lashes back at Democrats critical of his Portland performance. "We're already starting to hurt, even before the potential listing of this dumb bird," he tells the *Salem Statesman-Journal*. In 1990 when the return rate for House incumbents would be 96 percent, Smith suffers the ignominy of going down in a landslide. Clumsy acts of political desperation on the timber issue and hawkish attacks against his opponent for being soft on Saddam Hussein compound nagging doubts about Smith's ties to the S&L debacle.

The most powerful individual on the stage is the least formally dressed of the politicians. All are attired in Wall Street-conservative business suits, except U.S. senator Bob Packwood. In blue jeans and a red sweater with blue stripes, he fancies himself one of the guys. The exaggerated gestures in his performance are those of an outsider straining to conform. His feet tap furiously out of sync to Randolph and Debre's number. His clenched fists give him trouble doing the "Hands Across America" routine. During the program, he projects a demeanor perpetually on the edge of a temper tantrum.

Packwood speaks his people's language. At the height of the fervor for tax reform in 1986, the then chairman of the Senate Finance Committee and a happy beneficiary at election time of the largess of his state's biggest employer earned the nickname "Hackwood" and "Plywood" for larding the main bill with preferences for the timber industry. He had put his parochial interests above the nation's. His colleagues thus felt entitled to help themselves to tax breaks for mining, oil, and gas in violation of the bill's spirit. In a matter of weeks, Packwood did an abrupt about-face and cobbled together new legislation free of all the goodies, apparently mindful of the horrendous press he had received in Washington, D.C., and a close reelection campaign back in Oregon. That he would risk obstructing the most sweeping overhaul of the American tax code in nearly half a century demonstrated the timber industry's stranglehold on him.

At home members of Congress reveal a side of themselves Washington, D.C., seldom sees. Inside the Beltway, moderates admire Packwood for supporting abortion rights, family leave, and other women's causes. (In late 1992 ten women charged him with making unwelcome sexual advances over a twenty-year period. Packwood, refusing to deny the allegations, enrolled himself in an alcoholics' recovery clinic.) In Pioneer Courthouse Square the crowd's sheer magnitude would inflame any demagogue's baser impulses. Packwood shamelessly sinks to the occasion. "I went to the Senate when Vietnam was the hot issue and if you gave any support to Richard Nixon and the thought that perhaps you with-draw gradually from Vietnam you were a pariah, because the cry was no war," he roars in a nonsensical stream of consciousness. "A few years later the issue became, 'Should we take your guns away?' ['NO! NO!' the horde shouts back.] The cry became, 'No guns!' Now the same group is saying, 'No jobs!' I understand their mentality." He must not know Atiyeh, a gun enthusiast and longtime member of the National Rifle Association. Moreover, Packwood scores cheap points impugning his enemies' patriotism, "the last refuge of a scoundrel," in Samuel Johnson's oft-quoted phrase. By Packwood's logic, environmentalists have not been content to aid and abet the Viet Cong or ravage the Second Amendment. Now these anticapitalists aim to drive Oregon out of business. Packwood's exercise in the paranoid style of American politics borders on the bizarre.

The senator dredges up the stereotype of the one-issue voter in his mind. His secretary, he announces, took a phone message from a constituent claiming that "trees are more precious than people." It hardly matters whether the poor soul fits an outlandish caricature on the order of, say, a logger on a killing rampage against the spotted owl. The caller dared to oppose his reelection. "I've reached the end of my patience on this," Packwood steams, politely divulging the man's name and hometown in case anyone wishes to form a mob and set him straight.

The protest's featured speaker violates Hirons's two cardinal rules. "No owl-bashing," cautions the leaflet for loggers attending the rally. "The media snaps it right up," Hirons says. And no press-baiting. Both tactics only backfire. Packwood drops a cryptic reference to Kathie Durbin. As the messenger of bad news lately, the gifted journalist covering environment for the *Oregonian* has incurred the wrath of loggers. The mere mention of her name by Packwood induces a cascade of boos. Durbin, standing near the stage incognito, in sunglasses, hides her embarrassment. "Now, wait a minute, she's a good reporter," Packwood says disingenu-ously, without bothering to explain why her name came up in the first place. He then brings up the spotted owl. "Shoot 'em," shouts a heavyset man behind me on Packwood's cue. "Folks, the owl is not the issue," the senator says. "If the natural predator of the owl swooped in tonight and ate all of the little devils, the issue would not be over."

Unfortunately, a half-baked plan he has hatched may spell doom for the "little devils." His staff has ferreted out a little-used provision of the Endangered Species Act unknown at the time even to the interior secretary. It allows a political committee to weigh economic considerations over scientific evidence. The group would consist of the secretary of agriculture, the secretary of the army, the secretary of the interior, the chairman of the President's Council of Economic Advisers, the administrators of the Environmental Protection Agency and the National Oceanic and Atmospheric Administration, and a representative of each affected state—a lengthy Who's Who in the Bush administration, with one or two exceptions, of industry backers. In effect, the God Squad, as it is informally known, can play God in the cosmos and permit a species to become extinct.

Of the five cases the God Squad has considered in its history, only one, before the Bush Administration registered its symbolic opposition to protecting the spotted owl in 1992, resulted in a ruling against a species. In 1979, the whooping crane—the tallest North American wading bird—was exempted after a compromise between the developer and conservationists to allow a dam to be built. The Endangered Species Committee turned down the Tellico Dam on the Little Tennessee River in favor of the rare snail darter, an infamous and tiny fish. After Congress overturned the ruling, the dam went up and the fish were moved to another part of the river. For the God Squad to override the Endangered Species Act's protection, the benefits of the move must absolutely offset those of saving the species. The spotted owl doesn't appear to meet such criteria at all. The nation's leading biologists have established the spotted owl's niche as an "indicator species," a telltale sign of an entire ecosystem's condition.

The Endangered Species Act, one of the nation's toughest environmental laws since it came into being in 1973 with President Richard Nixon's strong support, is regularly reauthorized with overwhelming bipartisan support. Since coming into existence, it has enshrined the nation's commitment to preventing any species of plant or animal from disappearing. The bald eagle, for one, owes its survival to the law. The last time Congress reauthorized the act, in 1988, the House voted in favor of renewing the bill by 399 to 16; the Senate, 93 to 2. During Senate debate on the spotted owl, Senator Al Gore accuses Packwood of trying to skirt the act to keep on logging as usual in ancient forests. "The God

God Squad is a stacked deck. The views of these people are known. There is no doubt what the outcome would be," said the Democrat from Tennessee and current vice president. "If these forests are destroyed, what happens to these jobs then? The real question is, Do they move to other jobs before or after the remaining ancient forests are destroyed?" The bid failed, 62 to 34. Packwood vowed: "We'll fight another day."

All the consternation about the northern spotted owl creates the impression that laws designed to protect it have done to the American economy what Soviet central planning did for free enterprise. As Timothy Egan reports in The New York Times, from 1987 to 1991 the government planned 34,202 projects in areas affecting endangered species. Virtually every one of the developers had to consult with the Fish and Wildlife Service, and in some cases revise their projects. The government expressed concern in about only 367 of them. And merely 18 of these were scrapped for violating the act. To any rational observer, that seems a small price to pay for averting the bald eagle's extinction.

In Pioneer Courthouse Square today, Packwood winds down. "Count me in this fight," Packwood bellows. "Frankly, I kind of like you people, and I hope to see you around for the next two hundred or three hundred years." He receives courteous, if subdued, applause.

Up close, the gravity of carrying the weight of logging's future on his shoulders appears to have pulled down his earlobes and bags beside his nose, revealing the white at the bottom of his eyes. All the curves in his face create a rising tension, climaxing in his mouth's epicenter. He stares off in space at no one in particular, as if in an angry trance.

With the last notes of "God Bless America" still ringing in our ears, Hirons introduces me to the senator behind the stage. Perhaps he will display his contemplative side away from the microphone. I ask him whether he voted for the Byrd proposal in the Senate to provide unemployment and retraining benefits to coal miners displaced by the Clean Air Act. Packwood, myopic to the parallel problems faced by many of his colleagues in the plight of the miners and woodworkers, voted against it. "We're not asking for welfare for loggers. We're asking to keep the forests on a sustained yield basis and keep the loggers at work," he smolders, the anger still raging in his eyes from his speech. "We're not asking for handouts, we want jobs. Cutting trees doesn't ruin the environment. We plant them again. They get cut again. They grow again."

I ignore the air of condescension and apparent coolness toward ancient forests' uniqueness to probe his concern about woodworkers likelier to lose employment from technological change and overcutting than from conservation. While twenty-five-thousand woodworkers were losing their jobs over the past fifteen years as a result of automation, Packwood kept his voice noticeably silent. "That's happened for years. The loggers are not asking for welfare," he says, at the risk of belaboring a point he's already made. "It's not unlike agriculture. We've become more productive and we have fewer employees. We're not asking for handouts." The repetitious rhetoric sounds like it was lifted from signs at the rally.

Packwood's face turns redder than a forest fire at the mere mention of retraining. "That presumes we're going to shut down the forests," he fumes. "We'll do all right if we keep logging the forests and replanting the forests." But if the owl is going to be listed, at a considerable economic cost, why not cushion the blow not through a political gesture such as the God Squad, which his own Senate colleague Mark Hatfield regards as futile, but with serious programs? "I'm not going to cross that bridge till we get there," Packwood replies. "I'm hoping we don't say, like this fellow who called me on the phone, that trees are more important than people. We will not adopt that attitude."

A few minor scuffles between timber supporters and environmentalists break out. A pigtailed heckler near the stage howls a running commentary on log exports. "We need some security," intones a timber activist on the stage, grabbing a microphone. A small posse routs the demonstrator from the square. At the edge of the crowd three timbermen locked in brawls, and raring for more, are taken into custody for disorderly conduct and intoxication. "No more violence, you fucking Nazi," an Earth Firster! screams at a hostile adversary. An obnoxious nineteen-year-old from Portland State, sporting a peach-fuzz mustache and a T-shirt declaring "THERE ARE NO JOBS ON A DEAD PLANET," insists on delivering sermons to his elders. His band of Earth First!ers hurls a bag of paper towels soaked in chemicals into the square. The stench fouls the air for a block. "I don't know why they need stink bombs," Hirons sniffs. "The Earth First!ers already smell."

As if by a miracle, the politicians' rabble-rousing and the hordes of people don't disturb the peace. The ten thousand on hand to defend their livelihoods look like a riot waiting to happen. Yet there are more arrests at an average Sunday football game. The nonviolence may stem from the soothing midday sunshine following a long wet spell. Ken Kesey has diagnosed this state as that "drowsy fascination that Oregonians label 'tranquillitis' or more graphically 'standin' an' starin'." Maybe a brawl or two would act as aggression therapy, allowing the crowd to vent its collective spleen and experience the momentary sensation of regaining control of its destiny. Clinical reasons exist for the timber workers' lethargy. Psychologists tend to ascribe such behavior to the depression and grief they may feel from the impending death of their profession.

Packwood's performance leaves a residue of cynicism among the voters he expects to pull the voting booth levers for him on election day. "He didn't impress me, but he said something that we all want to hear," Harvey Spears tells me in Mill City a week after the rally. "Well, he's really not offering us nothing." The sixth-grade education Spears is ashamed of obviously has not impaired his ability to see through Packwood's charade.

Far removed from the commotion at Pioneer Courthouse Square in the late afternoon that day, Hirons quietly skips stones from the river's gravel bar running near his home. "I don't trust any fucking politicians. There ain't one of them that has the guts to stand up and tell the truth," he grouses. "To these dirty sons-of-bitches, we, the people of the timber community, are a political liability. None of them really want to get into this issue."

The senator, however, is playing the issue to the hilt. "I've watched Packwood before. I believe that when he stands up in front of a live crowd feeding off its energy that excitement is genuine," Hirons says. "I also know he's had enough experience in the U.S. Senate to be a cold, calculating politician. I think the only reason he's doing this is for his election. The rest of those guys are running for cover. We're not a liability for Packwood because he's not running right now." He would in 1992, against Representative Les AuCoin, and eke out a slim victory after AuCoin exploits his environmental vulnerabilities.

Although Hirons considers programs to retrain woodworkers tantamount to surrender, in keeping with the party line, Packwood's opposition to Byrd's proposal to assist displaced coal miners rouses suspicions about the depth of Packwood's convictions. "I was really interested in your question to him about that," Hirons says—so interested that Hirons calls Washington, D.C., to find out the voting record of the rest of Oregon's delegation: What he discovers doesn't thrill him: "I'm so goddamned pissed off with those assholes."

This afternoon, Packwood manages to come off as antienvironmentalist without being prologger. In January 1963, George Wallace stood on the steps of the state Capital in Montgomery, Alabama, where Jefferson Davis took the oath of office as president of the Confederacy, and proclaimed: "In the name of the greatest people that have ever trod this earth, I draw the line in the dust and toss the gauntlet before the feet of tyranny! Segregation now! Segregation tomorrow! Segregation forever!" Substitute "old growth" for "segregation," and there arises an eerie resemblance to Packwood's harangue. The way of life rooted in old growth, like the Old South, is over, and many of the lumberjacks themselves know it.

A few days later, one of Packwood's constituents, George Schneider from Milwaukie, OR, fires off a letter to the *Oregonian*:

> To the Editor: U.S. Sen. Packwood's speech might have been more effective if it had been delivered from a tree stump, symbolic of a dead issue. Most of our old growth is gone. As a senator, he represents all the people of Oregon. He should be bringing all factions together in a diplomatic way for a solution rather than acting like an agitator for a lynch mob.

Viewing the spectacle on television in Mill City at dinnertime, Atiyeh loses his appetite. "Packwood sounds completely nuts. The last thing we need is a demagogue. By inciting those emotions, violence could break out. It's our fault because we put these people in office," he laments. "We are too easily seduced by sound bites." Atiyeh cannot fathom the senator's motives. "If he keeps it up, he's going to kill the entire timber industry. The worst possible strategy is to fight endangered species," Atiyeh argues. "Nobody in Washington, D.C., is going to care about Mill City. The governor and legislature had the opportunity to solve it. Now every national politician is looking at us. Someone in downtown Manhattan is deciding our fate."

Pioneer Courthouse Square marks the zenith of the loggers' grass-roots campaign. For one shining hour, the esprit de corps has lifted hopes higher than a spar tree. Many of the sturdy, stoic loggers who have prided themselves on their fierce independence have rubbed elbows and souls together for the first time in a common effort.

Then the goodwill soon dissipates like a sun shower in summer. The natural letdown leaves the protest leaders scurrying for devices to translate the energy into tangible results. Just as the demonstrators for a nuclear freeze in the early 1980s proved poor on the conceptual follow-through of their fuzzy notions, so the timber supporters strike a dead end in ideas. The "wise use" movement's exaltation of private property in the domain of natural resources, a hallowed plank in the 1992 Republican national platform, may cost a farmer or homeowner wishing to fill in a wetland. By contrast, most of the loggers here in Pioneer Courthouse Square lose any such ideological claims since they reap their profits from public property on federal lands. Nor can the Northwesterners present this afternoon tap into their urban neighbors' sympathies, according to recent polls. The urbanites' agenda places a premium on the clean drinking water and the natural refuges ancient forests provide.

Over the next few months, the flurry of rallies draws shrinking crowds until the tactic finally becomes extinct. The loggers see little rhyme or reason for showing up. A massive five-state demonstration is planned in Kelso, Washington, to catch President Bush on the fly, en route to commemorating the tenth anniversary of Mount St. Helens's eruption. It fizzles. Loggers apparently have better ways to spend a Saturday than waving at a dot in the sky.

Back in Mill City, Jim Morgan's effusive pride reaches to the sky he tries to take back from Atiyeh. In our casual contacts, he repeatedly vows to shatter the impression Atiyeh left from the plane rides I took with him by taking me up in his own plane— a match of dueling Cessnas. Morgan parks his Cessna 206 on Atiyeh's private airfield. The conservationist magnanimously keeps it open to all pilots, irrespective of their political persuasion. "You try to remain civil," observes Morgan. He first soloed under Atiyeh during his intensive flight instruction.

He and Bert Wright apologize for the heavy clouds cloaking most of Oregon's horizon. Nonetheless, on the forty-five-minute ride retracing Atiyeh's route, they take advantage of ample opportunities to press their case. Down below, the vast moonscape Weyerhaeuser has created on its own land glares at us. "I'm not disgraced by the way Weyerhaeuser would take everything. All the professionals believe it's a mistake that should never have been done," Morgan avers. "This country was born on learning from mistakes, not preserving them and going back to medieval times. I'm absolutely not ashamed of anything. There comes a point when you can't compromise anymore."

The plane angles at forty-five degrees past a ridge toward a green island surrounded by clear-cuts. "That's Cheek Creek, every bit as big and purty as Opal Creek," exclaims Morgan. In fact, at about thirty-five hundred acres, Cheek Creek is less than half the size, according to Forest Service figures. Gliding over truncated stretches of timberland, it becomes fairly self-evident that there are as few "purty" places remaining as there are spotted owls living on Christmas tree farms, as Wright insists. Morgan balks at falling for the numbers game. "I don't think how many are left should be an issue," he says. "Do we need to preserve that much? How many redwoods do we need to look at in the future? How much beauty do we need to enjoy?" The plane suddenly bumps through a pocket of turbulence.

A millionaire mill owner, Morgan preaches an unvarnished utilitarianism at complete odds with conservationists' reverence for the forest primeval. "There is no doubt about it. Clear-cuts are ugly," he acknowledges, gazing through the windshield. "But I see the bad spots as new houses. It's a sign of progress. I see second growth growing up, like kids, a new generation for the future. Trees coming back are like a five- or six-year-old turning into a fifteen-year-old. Then there's a nice stand of timber."

Wright hovers over Marion Forks, a beautiful 160-acre patch of private woods at the confluence of the North Santiam River and Marion Creek and homesteaded and still owned by the Morgan family. Adolescents have sprouted up in the place of the old woods. "There's a private man-made hike. Cutting has not hurt the property value," he adds. The matching crowns of evergreens beneath Morgan's wings form the even shag of AstroTurf, in sharp contrast to the ancient forests' jagged edges.

Morgan views an ancient forest's distinct features through the lenses of a farmer in the Dust Bowl. The site of spike tops on dead and dying trees in a climax forest in rocky wilderness areas prompts the familiar refrain about their worthless decadence. "Is it fair for the rest of the country to let it go to waste? There's the economy," Morgan says. "There are ways of improving nature with management techniques. If we can't do good forestry, we can't provide the American Dream." Within Morgan's narrow definition of the multiple-use concept, nature exists primarily to serve man's material needs. He traces in the air with his index finger a three-hundred-mile hike from North Santiam River to Mount Hood, off on the horizon. But for hikers to enjoy the outdoors experience, they must accept a vista of clear-cuts across the valley as reminders of the homes and other products Morgan furnishes them. Morgan and Wright land, mission accomplished.

As far as Atiyeh is concerned, Morgan is welcome to use his airfield anytime he wants. "The loggers look at the forests differently. Clear-cuts are coming back. They have to make the distinction between old growth and second growth. Nobody has argued you can't replant trees. It's not a forest," he says. "Even if you have trees there, you wonder, 'My God, what used to be in that valley?' That must have been a magnificent forest. I want a legacy of the original forest. I don't want my kids walking through giant stumps ten to twelve feet in diameter in second-growth forests after the ancient forest has been cut down, trying to imagine what the trees looked like and realize they've all been cut down."

At the edge of Salem's fast-food row, Atiyeh dons his finest threads, a brown Levi's Action Wear suit and cowboy boots, to check Hirons's latest moves. Atiyeh and Michael Donnelly, an uncompromising Salem-based conservationist formerly of the Breitenbush community, are leaning on Mike Kopetski, a candidate locked in a bitter grudge match with Congressman Denny Smith. Kopetski favors logging scraps of old growth while protecting large tracts such as Opal Creek. Donnelly argues that any old-growth tree still standing is worth saving.

Kopetski implores him to heed the needs of timber towns he must carry to win. "I come from a poor family. My father was forty years old with five kids. I know what it's like to come home and see your mother crying," he says. "A child doesn't go on vacation because a father's lost a job. I've a strong feeling for the average working person." Even so, his navy pinstripe suit, horn-rimmed glasses, paisley tie, and wing-tipped shoes constitute the uniform of a professional politician, whom Donnelly suspects of waffling.

Atiyeh takes exception to the indifference Donnelly, a Salem native, displays toward timber town residents. "I live in one of those communities. My kids are taking it particularly hard watching their good friends moving away because their fathers are losing jobs. Michael doesn't think we should cut another stick, but there's going to be a minimum of trees we're going to have to give up," Atiyeh patiently explains. "We have a little time, but not much. We're pretty much out of options. It's going to be hard for the timber industry. I want, too, to see us leave something in Mill City other than a legacy of stumps. I know you're in a minefield."

Hirons, for one, is waging his own underground campaign against his archnemesis and the candidate he endorses. Hirons takes out a quarter page in the *Statesman-Journal* denigrating Kopetski. "ARE YOU ANGRY? YOU SHOULD BE" blares the heading beside a crude photo of Kopetski, obviously photocopied from official campaign literature. His left-wing, green credentials—"Mike Kopetski has been in New York raising money to campaign in Oregon"—argue for a vote for Smith. Covering his tracks, Hirons runs a notice at the bottom disassociating connections to any political office. "Paid for and authorized by Howard Hall," says the advertisement. Hirons's front man is none other than the amiable watchman he employs up in the woods to look after his equipment.

The highly partisan debate has sent moderates like Kopetski scrambling to recapture the center. On the last day of a recent convention considering the Oregon Democratic party platform, Leo Rund, the Earth First! member who buried himself up to his head in rocks, took advantage of the sparse attendance on a late Sunday to lead extremists in pushing through platform planks calling for a complete ban on the logging of old growth and an end to clear-cutting on state and federal lands. Republicans are having a field day painting Democrats as zealots. Kopetski tries impressing on Donnelly the wisdom of distancing himself from the convention, historically a haven for the lunatic fringe, by recounting its history in the 1970s. The platform came out for legalization of marijuana, the installation of locks on the inside of jail doors, and the abolition of private property rights.

Kopetski fears the mavericks' infiltration of the party may hasten a shift already under way in the state's political alignment. The timber rally in Portland has already allowed Republicans to pose as the saviors of the working man in the woods. And the Oregon AFL-CIO, a longtime electoral ally of the Democrats, is making noises about abandoning them, thus exposing the labor movement's traditional blind spot toward the environment. Local labor unions, led by the AFL-CIO, opposed creating the Opal Creek park. "There are more members of the Sierra Club than the unionized timber industry," Donnelly reminds him, noting woodworkers' age-old resistance to being organized. "We're going to support you. The question is the degree. Are you going to inspire conservationists?" Kopetski asks him to keep in touch.

In the parking lot, Donnelly and Atiyeh wring their hands in mutual frustration. "Kopetski gives new meaning to the word 'hapless,'" Donnelly says with a grunt. "I felt like saying, 'If you're this wishy-washy, it's scary.'" Atiyeh's pragmatic impulse gives Kopetski the benefit of the doubt. "Democrats like Mike are caught in the vice between jobs and the environment. The impact timber has on small communities isn't lost on him," he notes. "But Opal Creek is a winning issue." On election day, he will go on to win primarily because of Smith's links to the S&L scandal.

Had the election turned solely on timber, it would have been a cliff-hanger. The disagreement between Donnelly in the city and Hirons in the country over the place of wilderness in our world has created a yawning chasm few politicians straddle successfully.

Washington, D.C., power brokers may be aware of the disappearance of old growth secondhand from reading reports or watching television. But the actual experience of going to the scenes turns them into hard-liners. "I don't think anybody can go to Opal Creek and not fall in love with it," Atiyeh says. "Every time I take congressional aides there it seems I have them on my side. But until we get the congressmen there, it's going to be very hard." Fact-finding missions by members of Congress have inspired the most sweeping legislation.

On a crisp Saturday morning, a black-and-white five-seat helicopter touches down, sounding a cacophonous blast in the heart of Opal Creek's upper camp. A pair of environmentalists from Oregon and Washington, D.C.—Atiyeh and Claudine Schneider—scamper out, heads ducked, under the spinning blades. Schneider, a five-term Republican U.S. representative from Rhode Island and committed conservationist, is on congressional recess. While locked in a tight race for the Senate (she would lose in 1990), Schneider puts her campaign on hold back home to find hard answers in the Northwest.

The sight of the Jawbone Flats mining camp transforms Schneider from a cerebral lawmaker into a gleeful tourist. She dips her hand in the water shooting out of the impulse waterwheel. The shed full of old mining equipment—Atiyeh someday intends to convert the shed into a museum—enthralls her. Down the road, he answers all her questions about the camp's history. "This is like something you'd see in the movies," Schneider exclaims. "It doesn't remind you of your day-to-day existence."

Atiyeh leads the way to a natural waterslide he glides down in the summer. "I used to own land in Montana and climbed the Tetons. I know mountain terrains," Schneider tells him above the water's roar. "The trees, the waterfalls—this is really exquisite. I would say in terms of natural areas, it would be in the top 1 percentile of places I have ever been."

Her immersion in Opal Creek has merely stiffened Schneider's resistance toward brooking any compromise over legislation pending in Congress that would safeguard old-growth forests. "Seeing is believing. We have to move this issue to the front burner," she says, before boarding the helicopter. "What I find most shocking, besides the comparability between what's going on here and the Amazon, is the whole breadth of the area affected. To see the vast clear-cuts and that growth has not returned. You hear it grows back. Clearly it does not. The key is to get the whole big picture." As soon as she returns to Capitol Hill, Schneider intends to bring members of the appropriate committees and a group of bipartisan activists from Congress to Opal Creek. All summer long, Atiyeh serves as a full-time host to Washington, D.C., elite.

Both sides, of course, present only one-dimensional views of the situation on the ground. Absent from Schneider's "whole big picture" this weekend is any personal contact with loggers whose livelihoods come from national forests. On their circuit, timbermen purposely skip ancient stands outshining the finest second-growth forests. Atiyeh and Hirons share in common the political liability of crying in the wilderness. The conservationist places a premium on the spiritualism of Opal Creek's cathedral over the clean air and water it yields. His approach lifts the ethereal issue beyond the average voter's reach. Bread and butter, as Hirons knows, come first at election time. Except Hirons, too, tugs at the social conscience of a public beseeched to grasp an abstraction beyond its immediate concerns. The logger's way of life to Americans outside the Northwest, and some there as well, may just not be worth the cost of sustaining it. A slogan at the Portland rally— "JOBS, NOT HANDOUTS"—smacks almost of an entitlement program, or, worse yet, the sort of socialism woodworkers denounce environmentalists for advocating. Years of overcutting ensure a fair share of casualties. The pandering of Packwood and other politicians offers scant hope to many of the loggers doomed to fall though the same cracks as farmers and coal miners.

The discord between Atiyeh and Hirons crystallizes the differences between contrasting value systems. Hirons defines conservation strictly by and for people. Old trees seem superfluous in the context of feeding a family. The striking element of the logger's objection to Atiyeh's case for Opal Creek rests on his aesthetic comprehension of wilderness as an extension of civilization. It brings to mind the "access philosophy" of a pundit in the early 1970s, whereby tramways would whisk Los Angelnos into the Sierras in minutes and a cable car take "ordinary people" down the Grand Canyon's rims. "SHOULD WE ALSO FLOOD THE SISTINE CHAPEL SO TOURISTS CAN GET NEARER THE CEILING?" asked a newspaper headline in response to a proposed damming in the 1960s. James Watt, Ronald Reagan's embattled interior secretary, later carried the access philosophy to an extreme well past Hirons's, on a motor trip down the Colorado River through the Grand Canyon: "I don't like to paddle and I don't like to walk." It bears mentioning that if, by contrast, a logger adopted the same aversion to hiking through the woods, he wouldn't last long in the business.

The lack of picnic areas and campgrounds Hirons bemoaned in his testimony against SB 500 argued for its passage. The Opal Creek Challenge Phil Keisling has issued demands the nonbeliever to "show me" the land "untrammeled by man," as outlined in the 1964 Wilderness Act. "How much beauty do we need?" Morgan asks, hovering over the scattered fragments. A lot more than currently exists in the eye of the beholder. Ninety percent of the ancient forest has already been cut, and much of the rest may follow. The areas already protected are largely confined to the high elevations. The timber industry grudgingly wrote them off due to the expense of reaching the scrawnier trees. The forest higher up provides habitat for fewer species than Opal Creek and other low-elevation stands.

Hirons mistakes natural scenery and beauty for wilderness. The majority of people can already enjoy itself on roads instead of trails. The use of art galleries and libraries by the few scarcely justifies turning them into McDonald's and video arcades for the many. Until Atiyeh can broaden the political constituency for Opal Creek, he must count on the privileged visitors there to carry word of its majestic groves home to the majority. Only then will they see the need for enduring beauty.

X

Little Big Bird

For all his time hiking and working in Opal Creek's ancient forests, Atiyeh has seldom encountered the nation's most controversial bird, the northern spotted owl, though biologists have confirmed their presence. On his way down the trail from Whetsone Mountain in the early 1970s he was puzzled by a strange owl with the bark of a dog like none he had ever heard or seen. Years later, while toiling outside the mines, Atiyeh and his employees thought nothing of being serenaded by loud, distinctive, barklike hoots. At the height of the timber conflict, Atiyeh finally sees one up close. On the mining road leading into Jawbone Flats, an employee happens upon a shredded owl carcass and a shotgun shell casing a hundred feet away. Atiyeh subsequently receives a phone call: "You'll end up the same way if you don't watch it."

Atiyeh immediately hands over the feathered corpse to the Detroit District's chief wildlife biologist. He, in turn, decides that this is a job for the brand-new wildlife crime lab operated by the U.S. Fish & Wildlife Service in Ashland, Oregon, 300 miles away. The first and only facility of its kind in the world, the "Scotland Yard" of wildlife crime identification features state-of-the-art equipment that would be the envy of the most sophisticated police labs. It protects hundreds of species—including elephants, sea turtles, leopards, and numerous kinds of parrots—killed or taken from the wild each year to supply a $1.5 billion business in illegal wildlife products.

One of the ten forensics scientists on staff goes to work on the evidence from Opal Creek. In an effort to match possible suspects and victim at the crime scene, he examines the shredded mass of feathers and flesh along with the shell through stereo and scanning electron microscopes. There remains no doubt about the species' identity. Yet the spotted owl's remains have reached a stage of decomposition too far gone for the sleuths to determine the precise cause of death. "Nobody jokes about killing animals," Ken Goddard, criminologist and head of the forensics lab, is fond of noting. "For some reason people are more outraged about animal crimes than people crimes." With society's heightened sensitivity toward the treatment of animals, few people countenance the abuse of any species, let alone an endangered one. Every dead owl linked to loggers, however loosely, probably results in the saving of dozens more in the wake of public outcry and pressure to save the bird's habitat.

One less spotted owl today counts a lot. The species' population in its native range from British Columbia to northern California is only a few hundred more than Mill City's human population; and, like the lumberjacks in timber towns, on a downward slide. Just thirty-five hundred pairs survive in old-growth forests, half the number of a century ago. In some heavily logged areas, the spotted owl population has declined that much in the past five years. Even if all logging came to a screeching halt, a significant reduction in the existing population would still occur. Its habitat is simply deteriorating too rapidly. Under the best available conservation plan, it would still take the slow-breeding bird a hundred years to increase its total number a mere 10 percent.

In the battle for old growth, this ancient symbol of wisdom has acquired the mythical status of Sasquatch, the hulk of the northwestern woods that children grew up fearing and revering. Both environmentalists and loggers exploit the spotted owl for their own purposes. Environmentalists use it as a stalking horse to thwart the timber industry much in the same way they used the tiny snail darter to obstruct dam builders in the 1970s. Unlike the homely fish, though, the owl provides a telegenic rallying point on television and in magazines. National environmental organizations cannot resist adorning their mailings and publications with pictures of the cute, cuddly creatures. The timber interests, by contrast, rally their troops by reminding them that sacrificing their way of life for the sake of this diminutive denizen of forests is for the birds. "GET AN OWL, SAVE A LOGGER" is but one in a series of bumper sticker slogans crowing man's undisputed reign over the wild kingdom.

Hirons's only rendezvous with a spotted owl, years ago in the brush, barely registered. On the way to a job, he looked up and saw it fly right in front of his pickup. Since then, Hirons cannot put the bird out of his mind. Congress, under pressure from environmentalists, has assigned a team of federal scientists, headed by Jack Ward Thomas, to draft a plan to protect the spotted owl and avert its extinction.

The team is composed of six biologists thoroughly versed in the research and management of the northern spotted owl. For six months the blue-ribbon panel studies the bird with the intellectual intensity of the Manhattan Project. To the utter dismay of loggers and the partial satisfaction of environmentalists, the resulting 427-page report, written in plain English, recommends setting aside more than 8 million acres across Oregon, Washington State, and California as reserves for the birds. The U.S. Forest Service insists the plan would stop logging on 50 percent of national forestland west of the Cacades and claim twenty-eight thousand jobs. The scientific manifesto sounds a clarion call of peril to ancient forests and provides a ready-made recovery plan for the northern spotted owl when the U.S. Fish & Wildlife Service declares it a threatened species in the summer of 1990.

For two weeks the Detroit Ranger District has widely advertised in local papers the Timber Sale Planning Workshop at the Chummery Comfortel in downtown Salem. The stated objective is to thrash out specific problems so that high cut levels mandated by the 1990 congressional logging compromise could be met. According to the official press notice, "General issues such as the harvesting of old-growth timber or the protection of the northern spotted owl are not on the agenda." If only it were so simple for the Forest Service to conduct business as usual.

The Thomas Report has showcased the owl at center stage. "They're all here," says Atiyeh, scanning the Mill City four-wheel-drives in the parking lot. "Anyone who has anything to do with logging. This is their whole world crashing down." Inside, loggers, mill owners, and millworkers spill over from rows of seats into standing room at the side. At the front, district ranger Dave Alexander holds forth in a corduroy jacket and Levi's. The rest of the crowd comes as it is, in suspenders and hickory shirts. Hirons introduces me to Ray Weber, the timber cruiser for Young and Morgan, who eyes me warily in my navy Brooks Brothers blazer and gray flannels from a day of meeting Salem pols. "You buying or selling?" he inquires.

While he was cuing up a video presentation of the Thomas Report, I noticed that Alexander's tall physique adds authority to a brute fact. "It's a whole new ball game, people," he announces. The lights dim, and Thomas, onscreen, seeks to put the best face on the bad news to loggers by way of a friendly fireside chat. "Obviously the best thing we would do for the northern spotted owl would be to cease and desist all timber operations in the Pacific Northwest," explains Thomas, one of the nation's leading big-game biologists, in a sonorous voice. "Obviously that is not within the realm of life, and any conservation strategy that ignores the needs of people is doomed to failure." Listening with the rapt attention of graduate students as Thomas drones on about scientific methodology, none of the loggers so much as fidgets in his seat. "They're scared and depressed," Atiyeh whispers. Long after the lights come back on, the audience sits in stunned silence. Hirons, who stood throughout the show for a better view, mumbles some standard industry rhetoric with the verve of rigor mortis.

Heading toward the second part of the workshop at the other end of the motel, Atiyeh bumps into Randy Moberg of Fred Moore Logging in Mill City, a friend and hunting buddy until the timber conflict drove them apart. The two appear to exchange social pleasantries in the corner, but Moberg then storms over to Hirons. "Just saw your partner," he says with a growl, a subtle dig at Hirons's history with Atiyeh. "Says, 'Gotcha.' " Hirons stares awkwardly down at the floor to avert Moberg's angry gaze. "I just gotta try to thumb my nose at the digs," Hirons says afterward. "It's baggage I drive around with."

Atiyeh emphatically denies ever uttering Moberg's gibe. He still fails to stop another story about his callousness from blowing through Mill City like an ill wind. "Randy came up to me and said, 'Looks look we're going to be flipping hamburgers [in the tourism trade]," Atiyeh insists. "All I said was, 'I'll buy one from you.' "

Out in the dark parking lot, Atiyeh and Hirons proceed to their cars with predictable fanfare. While a coterie of environmentalists dotes on Atiyeh, a Mill City woodworker approaches Hirons to shake his hand for all the work he has done. "You giving him a raft of shit?" Atiyeh jokes to Hirons as I converse with him. In their first face-to-face meeting since the ABC *Prime Time Live* show two months ago, they size up each other as suspiciously as a pair of alley cats. The two share innocuous town gossip and their families' latest doings. In a burst of enthusiasm for the upcoming timber rally in Portland he is helping lead, Hirons stops just short of inviting Atiyeh, as though the old times they once enjoyed together had never really ended.

Many of the loggers and environmentalists who spend most of their waking hours in the woods have never even laid eyes on the spotted owl. Most people in timber towns only know the elusive creature by reputation, from the tall tales they've heard from loggers of it nesting in barns or in young tree farms—anywhere but old-growth forests, where impartial biologists have documented beyond a doubt it primarily resides. My eager hosts at Breitenbush, the alternative community presiding over the hot springs resort, had promised to introduce me to their winged soul-mates during a three-hour hike. Perhaps owing to a slow start, on a drowsy Sunday morning (in daytime, when the nocturnal owls are mostly dormant) repeated calls to the owl went unanswered.

To fullfill my wish, I would have to pay the experts a visit. Jim Farrell, the Detroit District chief biologist, puts in sixteen-hour days and six-day weeks keeping tabs on the spotted owl. He took the job in 1989 expecting primarily to maintain deer and elk for the enjoyment of outdoorsmen—standard fare for Forest Service biologists. "The owl issue exploded a month after I got here," he recalls. When an irate resident of a nearby timber town lit into one of his female biologists at a bakery in the town of Detroit for costing him his livelihood, Farrell ordered his whole crew to lay low. At local coffee shops and general stores, unless pinned down, Farrell speaks in only vague terms about his actual duties for the Forest Service.

The controversy has created a new breed of scientist across the Northwest known as the "combat biologist." Caught in the cross-fire of politics and science, both bird and biologist find themselves under siege. "Folks whose lives depend on timber harvests don't look too kindly on us protecting the owl," Farrell says. "We're on the hot seat for everything we do."

No matter who the antagonist, Farrell has the combat biologist's bearing to stand his ground. "The first time I saw him I thought he was a log truck driver," says Mark Penninger, a specialist on his staff. Farrell's silver-speckled red beard reinforces his steely gaze. Whether in blue jeans or official Forest Service uniform, which he disdains, Farrell never parts with a cowboy hat. The cigarettes he chain-smokes, another idiosyncrasy for someone in his line of work, round out the image of a cross between Smoky the Bear and log truck driver.

A seasoned veteran of wildlife wars, Farrell arrived in Oregon after having squared off with menacing ranchers while researching the threatened desert tortoise in the East Mojave and with angry miners while on the trail of the ferruginous hawk in Wyoming. "I've been around for fifteen years in a lot of places. In California, I knew people who killed desert tortoises just out of revenge and anger. In Wyoming, they shot ferruginous hawks all the time and burned their nests," he says. "This is the toughest job so far trying to get the job done for natural resources and meeting other objectives." Rumors run rampant through Mill City of Farrell usurping the power of timber sales planners to build his own fiefdom. In private, loggers mutter imprecations against him. At public meetings, he must parry their verbal blows. "They're constantly doing something to prove me wrong," Farrell says. "That means you gotta stick to the facts."

His antagonists in timber towns cut him little slack. "Money drives the whole thing," Farrell insists. "And it and politics often thwart good science. I think most loggers you talk to would admit they've cut too much too fast." The uneasy coexistence between humans and endangered species stands to worsen. "The spotted owl and the old-growth logger are endangered for the same reason," Atiyeh says. "They're both running out of habitat."

In an ironic twist, Farrell's strict adherence to the letter of the law can shield the owls from environmentalist threats as well. Members of the Breitenbush community have tangled with him over his decision to close hiking trails near owl nests, including the ones they showed off on our hike marking the anniversary of the Easter Massacre. He has put the kibosh on a summertime folk music concert after the discovery of a pair of owls and two fledglings on a ridge a thousand feet away. "The Forest Service finds the 'sound of music' more detrimental to spotted owls than the roar of chainsaws and crash of ancient trees," reads a news release Michael Donnelly, the environmentalist and ex-Breitenbush resident, faxes far and wide. "Whatever disturbs the owl is not cool right now," Farrell responds icily. He fears the large crowd of concert goers, expected to exceed seven hundred, may scare the owls away from their homes. Since the show must always go on, the Detroit District finally chooses an alternate site one mile west of the original. With recreation eclipsing logging as the principal activity in national forests, the burden will fall on environmentalists to practice what they preach.

Farrell derives his authority from the stroke of a pen on a map. So far he has halted about twenty-five timber sales by finding an equal number of owls. At his office, on a grid of a hundred thousand acres (a third of the district) slated for logging, he has sketched "calling stations" from where owls are summoned. "Owl protocol," a rigid set of guidelines betraying faint Pentagon over-tones, requires his dozen pairs of biologists in the field to inven-tory at night from March through September. They have up to six visits to confirm a pair in a Habitat Conservation Area, the minimal twenty-one-hundred-acre space owls are believed to need to survive.

Mark Penninger, twenty-four, and Monica Cape Lindelin, twenty-five, comprise Farrell's crack strike team. Cape Lindelin came from California and Penninger from North Carolina through a nationwide recruitment of biologists. "A lot of biologists wouldn't touch this because of the social controversy," says Pen-ninger, whose gold earring sets him apart from Forest Service colleagues. "But that's what attracted me. Whatever job I do after this will be gravy."

On a cold, misty morning, Farrell and the two hooters head into the woods in a new pickup, which—in strict accordance with "owl protocol"—has its headlights on in broad daylight. Along the graveled logging roads, they point out black-and-yellow-striped tape designating owl habitat. There is an eerie symbolism to the yellow ribbons—the unmistakable marker for clear-cuts—swirled in a black armband. Detroit is one of the most heavily logged districts in the Willamette National Forest. "You can see driving around here there's not a lot of old growth," says Farrell of the chewed-up terrain. "Over the last twenty years this district is basically the one the Forest Service came to when they came up short on timber volume."

Our very first stop proves an instant success. At the timber conference Dave Alexander had assured me owls will come on cue, as long as you known when, where, and how to look. No sooner have Cape Lindelin and Penninger stepped out of the pickup to begin calling, than one glides down and alights on a branch. Curiously unafraid of humans, spotted owls have been known to respond to slamming car doors and honking horns. Reports have even circulated of them investigating the ding, ding of a logging yarder backing up and the growl of a chainsaw—noises of their mechanical predators.

We owe today's encounter to more than good luck and this bird's trusting nature. Two years earlier the construction of a logging road a few yards away wiped out its nest. It took another couple of years for the evictees to erect a new home, in an island encircled by the road and clear-cuts. (The Forest Service has already sold this "unit," or designated timber patch, but the deal is still pending Farrell's approval.) One unintended consequence of squeezing the owls into smaller areas is to simplify the hooters' task. "It's like what my dad said about a small farm pond home back home in Carolina," Penninger drawls. "If you lower the water, the fish are easier to find."

As the owls' precious living space shrinks from excessive logging, so do their chances for survival. In the fragmented forest high winds may blow down trees at the woods' edge, further erasing the habitat. Packed together in their cramped new quarters, they compete among themselves and with other species for the same food, like poor peasants vying for bread. Defenseless fledglings then face greater risks of predation from great horned owls, northern goshawks, and other raptors—birds of prey. Meanwhile, the displaced spotted owls may lose their territories altogether. Scientists write these victims off as the "floater population."

On maps of the last remaining old-growth corridor between Canada and California, the Detroit and Sweet Home districts form C-shaped swatches. These wide fractures in the Cascade Range create barriers to the spotted owls' northerly and southerly movements. "Connectivity" measures the extent to which linking blocks of habitat allows individuals—typically juveniles—to disperse. The owls need such stopover places for suitable cover and opportunities to forage.

For those owls stranded in isolated stands, the likely inbreeding may well dilute the gene pool. As a result, over the next century there may evolve a northern and southern Oregon spotted owl less fertile and more prone to disease. "The genetic flow has gone on since the last ice age, eleven thousand years ago. Things are in harmony out there," Farrell says. "If you disrupt that harmony, you don't know the consequences. Common sense will tell you that." In 1990 scientists in Oregon and Washington State confirmed the first "sparred owl." In two separate cases six hundred miles apart the new hybrid emerged from the crossbreeding of the northern spotted owl with the barred owl. Biologists were unable to determine whether the hybrid was an isolated mistake of nature or the alarming sign of the spotted owl's end as a distinct species. Regardless of the mystery, they warn, the belligerent barred owl's capacity to thrive in heavily logged areas throughout its widening northwestern range will cut into the spotted owl's space. Sharing the same food supply, the endangered bird's conciliatory nature leaves it the runt's portion.

Perched on a low branch, the owl Farrell has found today swivels its head back and forth 180 degrees to inspect its intruders. The one-pound, fourteen-inch bird has chocolate-colored plumage flecked by white spots on the head and neck. Chestnut brown and white streaks run through the tail feathers. Its dark eyes twinkle like the night sky. A large white molting vest covers its breast. The ear on one side of its head is higher than the other, enabling the bird to hone in on a sound both vertically and horizontally. Even in pitch-black dark, a small mammal scurrying across the forest floor remains starkly exposed to the owl's pinpoint hearing.

The owl posing for our benefit is a male, which is smaller than the female. Among predatory birds that obtain food by killing and consuming other animals—including eagles, hawks, and falcons—the fair sex is usually larger. At this time of the year, the spring, the female spotted owl usually stays put, devoting the day to roosting, or resting, and sitting on her eggs. The male takes care of most of the hunting while the female serves the prey to the young.

The pair, like virtually all spotted owls, makes its home high in the multilayered canopy dominated by towering trees with spacious branches for nests. In the broken-topped dead trees, or "snags," spotted owls make use of natural cavities resulting from snapped-off limbs and rotting trunks. They tend to roost in low perches in the dense understory during warm weather and high in the overstory of large trees when it's cold and wet. A snag's thick walls provide additional thermal cover. By contrast, an even-aged second-growth stand only offers the owl shallow canopies and poorer trees for roosting. Their finicky real-estate requirements aren't meant to accommodate loggers. "Spotted owls, after all," notes the Jack Ward Thomas Report, "are oblivious to our political and institutional boundaries."

Spotted owls depend on old-growth forests to eat and not be eaten. The northern flying squirrels, red tree voles, and dusky-footed woodrats on which they subsist abound here. The pickings are so slim in uniform second growth stands that, as one zoologist has noted, "a blue jay would have to pack a lunch to get across." In the meantime, spotted owls can live in relative comfort because they will not end up as someone else's morsel. Under the closed canopy, the birds have places to hide from great horned owls, one of their biggest predators.

Perhaps wildlife's most distinctive sound in an old-growth forest belongs to the spotted owl. Expert hooters can sound a melody of tongues like masters of a foreign language. Cape Lindelin starts with a four-note location call—hoo-hoo-hoo-hoo—the owls commonly employ to fend off territorial challenges. Females give the contact or begging call—coo-weep! coo-weep!—to solicit food from males. The distinctive bark series—ow! ow! ow! ow!—goes off during territorial disputes and long-distance conversations between birds. To my untrained ear, Penninger and Cape Lindelin's voices are barely distinguishable from the owls'.

The mere confirmation of individual owls presents an incomplete picture of their condition. Biologists must "mouse" to determine whether there are reproductive pairs being sustained, the clearest sign of the species and forest's condition. An owl with no young will kill the mouse—by biting its head off—and eat it immediately or stash the rodent away for future consumption. An owl with a family to feed delivers the meal to the nest while biologists, in hot pursuit, tail the owl through the woods.

From a small plastic box Cape Lindelin deposits a white lab mouse on a young fir tree's bouncy branch. An owl swoops down to a limb's platform twenty feet overhead, cocking its head in recognition of the mousy squeak Penninger simulates by puckering his lips. The bird's sleepy round face, accustomed to nights, when the nocturnal bird is most active, appears to spring to life. "Come on, come on. Take it," purrs Cape Lindelin. "I just heard the female's coo-weep! calling for the mouse." In a sudden flash, the owl dives and grabs a late breakfast a few feet away with razor-sharp talons. On aerial pursuits its primary, fringed feathers muzzle sound, enabling it to sneak up on prey. Hungry owls hop from limb to limb to nab squirrels and other animals trying to flee through the trees. The biologists peer through binoculars to observe the bread winner, and its bloodied beak, serving its mate and two downy fledglings. "Yes! We got a nest here," Penninger exclaims. "Let's give him all four mice."

Furrier than cotton balls, the young offspring arouse keen interest from Penninger and Cape Lindelin. The season is late spring, a perilous juncture in an owl's life. Thirty-five days after hatching, the owlets use their talons and beaks to crawl tentatively across elevated perches. During their frequent free-falls, they overcome their inadequate aerial abilities by fluttering softly onto trees below the nest. The hapless owlets who crash-land scramble toward the nearest tree trunk to climb back up. Their talons grasp the rough bark, steadying them as they amble skyward while flapping their wings. They are as clumsy as they are determined. A rest requires them to hold still and drape their outspread wings against the trunk for a sure grip. The ascent may be steep and grueling, but there's no turning back. Grounded owlets become easy prey for predatory birds, raccoons, and bears. More than one third of the fledglings never live to see autumn.

Potentially graver dangers than nature's high mortality rate imperil the owl. "It's a very real conflict when you start talking about people's lives," Farrell says. "Here we treat nest sites as confidential information. There have been owls shot and there have been threats." At about the same time Farrell arrived in Detroit, sixty-five miles south, in Oakridge, Oregon, the Forest Service discovered a spotted owl that, from all indications, had been hunted down. Its mutilated carcass hung in a noose over a forest fire information kiosk. At least another victim, shot a few months earlier in the Siskiyou National Forest, was spared the posthumous lynching. Maximum fines for killing an endangered species can reach two hundred thousand dollars and one year in prison. But because the crimes were committed before the listing, the punishment would carry a six-month prison sentence and a ten-thousand-dollar fine.

He's willing to endure the extraordinary professional pressure to help avert a species' extinction. "The owl wasn't useless before man came two hundred years ago, except from a money and production point of view," he says. "I'm not a religious person, but I know man didn't put the pieces of an intricate web of connections here, so he shouldn't be the one to take them out. We're not smart enough to know what we're doing."

In timber towns, the federal government's initial steps to list the species provoke the sort of hysteria seldom seen in the United States except in wartime. These small, isolated communities whose way of life has carried on uninterruptedly for most of the century unleash propaganda against the foreign forces of environmentalists befriending that cursed bird. The bumper-sticker brigades display unseemly slogans—"I LOVE SPOTTED OWLS FRIED" and "SHOOT AN OWL, SAVE A LOGGER." (Atiyeh customizes his own baseball cap—"SAVE AN OWL, EDUCATE A LOGGER." He has also boasted to the local paper of snapping up the one "SAVE AN OWL, EAT A LOGGER" the Gates General Store sold, though I've yet to see him wear it.) Tailgaters cruising through Mill City editorialize on pickup trucks: "NO TOILET PAPER, WIPE YOUR ASS WITH A SPOTTED OWL." Rubber chickens representing the spotted owls distant cousins dangle from rearview mirrors. Papa Al's, Mill City's fast-food joint, features such daily specials as "Endangered Logger" (a cheeseburger) and "Spotted Owl Soup" (homemade chicken and dumplings) on its menu board alongside the daily fare of fries, corn dogs, and milk shakes. A mock Campbell's soup can bearing the off-color brand "Cream of Spotted Owl" sits atop a file cabinet in mill owner Jim Morgan's office. An employee of Verl Moberg of Fred Moore Logging gives him a jar of "pickled owl," a rubber chicken floating in liquid.

Swept away in the frenzy, Siuslaw National Forest officials terminate one of their own marquee owls. Woodsy Owl is grounded at elementary schools in the forest area. For two decades he has enjoyed a star run as Smoky the Bear's pal and as the symbol of the refrain "Give a Hoot, Don't Pollute." Children singing the "The Ballad of Woodsy Owl" are now left wondering whether their feathered friend "knows what is best" after all. "We certainly don't want to get Woodsy and the spotted owl confused in the kids' minds," a public-relations officer explains. "Sometimes you have to be prudent and withdraw rather than inflame the situation." The press has a field day reporting the owl that gives a hoot gets a boot. In an informal survey, the Forest Service contacts six local teachers, five of whom demand Woodsy's return. One week after his ouster, Woodsy stages a dramatic comeback.

In due course, the vilification of a Bambi with feathers offends the sensibilities of visiting tourists and the national media. After all, environmentalists don't drive around with bumper stickers proclaiming "I LIKE MY LOGGERS FRIED." To counter the severe backlash, industry and Hirons have cautioned rank and file at meeting and in leaflets announcing timber rallies to cease all "owl-bashing." They've had less control over the enterprising owner of the general store, next door in Mehama, where I purchased a T-shirt with the inscription "INVITE A SPOTTED OWL TO DINNER." The message encircles the image of a Neanderthalish logger holding a knife and fork as he prepares to dig into a turkey-size bird. "Damn him, damn him," Hirons says of the proprietor. "The tourists just eat that stuff up." They also bring them home as tasteless souvenirs for friends.

Much of the rhetorical fury belies the ambivalence workers in the woods feel toward a creature few of them have ever seen. You won't find any "I LIKE MY SPOTTED OWLS FRIED" slogans on Harvey Spears's pickup. "Everybody keeps pissing, moaning, and groaning about it," he says. "It's not the owl, 'cause everybody is using this poor little bird as leverage. The damn birds are totally innocent. It's the people."

Up the road a short piece, Jack Stevenson articulates the passions of legions of loggers unable to fathom all the commotion. "I can't see where that owl is gonna make a difference in the goddamn world. Can you? A little-bitty *owl?*" says the senior member of Hirons's crew. "I don't see where that owl contributes anything. If it kills rodents, I'll buy some mousetraps. They work pretty good catching a lot of mice. We don't need owls. Let's cut down the trees." Stevenson heaps most of his contempt on environmentalists' never-ending land grab. "You think anybody gives a fuck about that owl? There's going to be no more old growth, but there's no more dinosaurs or cavemen. They used to call it progress. Now it's bad."

Spears and Stevenson are both right. The spotted owl is in fact being used as an effective vehicle in the fight to save ancient forests. Since there exists only an Endangered Species Act but no Endangered Ecosystem Act, ecologists have sought to protect one species after another for their own sake and as vehicles for protecting their threatened habitat, including ancient forests. One Mill City logger happened upon a baby owl while driving around. He immediately brought the owlet to the local Forest Service and tried trading it for a thousand acres of timber. In a moment of political mischief, Hirons hatches a devious plot calling for an ally to sue to protect the western snowy plover, a white and gray wading bird inhabiting some of the West's toniest coastal communities and numbering fewer than fifteen hundred. His gimlet eyes betray Hirons's glee envisioning disrupting the Malibu set's way of life as conservationists have his. Might he consider bumper stickers to popularize the cause? "Yeah," Hirons exclaims, not missing a beat, "and they'll say 'FUCK THE SNOWY PLOVER.'" The U.S. Fish & Wildlife Service recently listed the plover as a threatened species.

Since 1976, the federal government has been required to manage wildlife habitat by choosing and keeping track of "indicator" species. Two other species besides the spotted owl belong to this select group of natural barometers in ancient forests west of the Cascade Range. There lives no bigger woodpecker in North America than the pileated woodpecker, measuring up to twenty inches. Earlier this century, ornithologists feared for the red-crested giant's future. But in the East the bird has staged a remarkable recovery thanks to conservation initiatives and its ability to adapt to its altered habitat. In the Northwest, where it has declined sharply, the pileated excavates its home out of large snags and feeds on the ants living in decaying logs and trees. The Forest Service predicts that by the year 2030, national forests will sustain fewer than half the number of pileated woodpecker pairs they did in 1984. The population in the Willamette National Forest is expected to drop from about eighteen hundred in 1984 to about three hundred in 2030.

On an evening hike along the mining road into Opal Creek, I meet a pine marten emerging from a log—an amazing stroke of luck, considering that the animal has proved so elusive that even biologists tracking them can go for months without spotting the speed demons, except in traps they set to study them. The lean, kitten-size, short-legged animal appears as startled as I am. Its thick coat of rich, brown fur blends into the scenery. While, in some areas, they have been trapped to extinction largely for their valuable fur, the logging of forests in the Great Lakes extirpated the population in that region. A member of the weasel family, the marten dwells inside an ancient forest's large, old, decomposing logs and stumps, where it can hunt for food, hide from predators, and keep warm.

They play the role of the dying canaries that once alerted coal miners to perilously low oxygen levels. Indicator species reflect the health of the planet at large. "Aldo Leopold wrote that 'to keep every cog and wheel is the first precaution of intelligent tinkering.' " Farrell says. "If species at the top of the food chain take a nosedive, then there is something seriously wrong with our environment." The spotted owl's decline represents not just an isolated tragedy, but also the breakdown of the earth's life support systems. The fates of the logger and the bird are intertwined.

The public may presume biologists can simply propagate spotted owls under artificial conditions and release them in the wild. "I've had a vision in my mind's eye," Hirons says. "I thought Opal Creek could be set aside with some timber harvesting and as a study area for all the spotted owls in the vicinity. You could do captive breeding like they've done with the condors." Atiyeh shares an interest in breeding the endangered species. "If loggers kill the owls, they're going to be endangered," Atiyeh says. "If I was a logger, I would be breeding them."

Although a captive breeding program could be launched for spotted owls, as was done for the California condors and peregrine falcons, the Endangered Species Act's objective was never to reproduce zoo specimens. The removal of all California condors from the wild may defeat the law's purpose. "When the vultures watching your civilization begin dropping dead," wrote the nature writer Ken Brower of the condor, "it is time to pause and wonder." The success of captive breeding programs for endangered animals remains in further doubt if, once a zoo reintroduces them to nature, they have nowhere to go. The zoologist Gerald Durrell has termed the continuing loss of habitat the "There Syndrome." As Gertrude Stein once noted, "There is no there there." Captive breeding is at best an expensive, stopgap response. The spotted owl's case underscores the importance of conserving entire ecosystems.

Once upon a time, the passenger pigeon, a blue-backed and pink-breasted migratory bird, filled North America's skies. The naturalist John James Audubon calculated that flocks flew over him at a rate of over 300 million birds an hour, according to Paul and Anne Ehrlich in their book *Extinction.* The roar of wings from a flock sounded their impending arrival from five miles away. The population is estimated to have been 2 billion birds, an abundance that early settlers enjoyed in their diet. They merely scooped the birds up from the ground where they dropped from overpopulated nesting spots. Then hunters began shipping passenger pigeons to markets in New York, and the dense oak and beech forests, where they dwelled, continued to be cleared. Throngs of pigeons suffocated from burning grass or sulfur deliberately set beneath their roosts. Others were fed grain soaked in alcohol and carted off. People swatted the pigeons down with long sticks or simply shot them to death. Hunters shipped them live by the millions, at a wholesale price of fifteen to twenty-five cents a dozen, from the Midwest to New York for target practice in shooting galleries. (The term stool pigeon—an informer, especially a spy for the police—is derived from the decoy pigeon attached to a perch or stool.) The survivors plunged from nesting mishaps and inbreeding. By the turn of the century, the passenger pigeon had perished in the wild. The last captive bird, Martha, breathed a final gasp in the Cincinnati Zoo in 1914.

The same railroads that had transported millions of dead passenger pigeons shipped East the tongues, hides, robes, and bones of the bison. The rest of the immense, dark beasts' carcasses was left to rot. Almost 4 million bison once blanketed the Great Plains. Professional meat hunters like Buffalo Bill Cody boasted of slaughtering 4,280 in a single year. "A ranchman who had made a journey of a thousand miles across northern Montana, along the Milk River, told me," wrote a young Theodore Roosevelt of this era, "during the whole distance he was never out of sight of a dead buffalo, and never in sight of a live one." By 1883, hunters had wiped out the last significant herd, numbering 10,000. At the turn of the century, 500 stray animals still roamed the Great Plains. About 25,000 today reside in parks and private herds.

The mass die-off of species we are witnessing is unprecedented in the annals of humankind. The biologist E. O. Wilson estimates that we have recently begun to extinguish other creatures at a pace ten thousand times faster than natural processes. Three species of plants and animals become extinct each day.

The northern spotted owl receives federal protection as the 578th addition to the federal list of endangered species. It thus joins the great grizzly bear—a massive, hump-shouldered carnivore reaching 8 feet in height and 800 pounds in weight—which numbered 100,000 in the lower 48 states at its historic high. Shooting, trapping, and poisoning have slashed the population to fewer than one thousand. The whooping crane is the most statuesque American bird, standing more than 5 feet tall. It can cover a yard with each stride, but not fast enough to escape the gun or the plow. About 270 still exist. Merely 500 American crocodiles—bit-toothed reptiles attaining lengths of 23 feet—ply the Florida Keys and tidal marshes.

Since its passage in 1973, the Endangered Species Act has lived up to its billing, keeping at least 700 plant and animal species from going under. Among them is our national symbol. The once-common bald eagle sank to 400 nesting pairs in the early 1960s from shooting, habitat loss, and such pesticides as DDT, which weakened eggshells. A ban on DDT and the preservation of nesting areas have brought the number of pairs back to 2,700 in the Continental U.S. The U.S. Fish & Wildlife Service believes the bald eagle no longer teeters on the brink of extinction, giving it grounds for "down listing" its status from endangered to threatened. Comparable comebacks—from the Columbian white-tailed deer to the Aleutian Canada goose—may become a memory should President Clinton and Congress fail to reauthorize the Endangered Species Act as legally required, a responsibility lost on the Bush administration.

"If we screw up over the long term, new life forms will evolve on the planet. We're babies. The last mass extinction occurred when dinosaurs roamed the earth 10 million years ago. This is a big mass extinction we have going on now, but nothing compared to what we had going on before. We could extinguish ourselves and all our fellow beings at this point and evolution will continue in another 2 million years when new life forms will evolve," Atiyeh says at Opal Creek. "We can't destroy the planet, but we can destroy ourselves and almost everything on it. We're being very selfish. If we care anything about our children and children's children, we have to pay the price for saving our species. The price for not doing so is nothing compared to what they'll pay."

Humans derive a multitude of benefits from the thousands of species belonging to natural ecosystems. They comprise a veritable storehouse of foods and drugs of untold value to health and medicine. Research has spurred the development of anticancer and heart drugs from exotic plants such as the Pacific yew that George Atiyeh points out on his hike. Paul and Anne Ehrlich, *Extinction*'s authors, enumerate additional examples found in nature. Plants have been used to treat cancer at least since the time of Hippocrates, four centuries before Christ. Today a derivative of a plant related to the periwinkle plant helps control high blood pressure. An extract from the leaves of a periwinkle species yields an effective chemical for treating Hodgkin's disease. In 1928, Alexander Fleming discovered a mold that spawned the first antibiotic, penicillin. The animal world's drug potential awaits to be tapped as well. The venom of vipers serves as an anticoagulant, preventing the formation of blood clots leading to heart attacks. Bee venom relieves arthritis. Over half the world's population depends on three species of grass—rice, wheat, and corn—for food. Humans foreclose the possibility of widening their range of agriculture by eliminating potential crop plants that have long been staples of indigenous peoples in the tropics. And the world would be a lot poorer without the dyes, fabrics, insecticides, perfumes, and lotions created from nature.

With every species lost, we impoverish some of the earth's finest resources. The biological progeny of dinosaurs, gigantic reptiles, live on in the form of crocodiles and alligators. Tourists flock to the remaining swatches of the Florida Everglades preserved in parks to enjoy the beings closest to small dinosaurs. "What a thrill it would be in national parks if people could see great lumbering brontosauruses weighing forty or fifty tons grazing across the landscape," wonder Paul and Anne Ehrlich, "or herds of ceratopsian dinosaurs roaming like rhinoceri with three gigantic horns." While dinosaurs ultimately fell victim to natural forces, humans bear responsibility for the latest extinctions.

The nation has the choice to avoid turning the spotted owl into one of this age's dinosaurs. The owl represents—as David

Ehrenfeld, author of *The Arrogance of Humanism*, defined all endangered species—an "expression of a continuing historical process of immense antiquity and majesty." The ineffable beauty of a spotted owl's "coo-weep!" for food or its glide toward its prey transcends the prosaic concerns of economics and politics.

In the vast historical continuum, simple compassion grants other creatures the right to exist. Our solemn obligation as the earth's stewards calls for us to ponder the moral repercussions of extinction. The affectionate pats Harvey Spears gives his dog while expressing sorrow for the owls under attack convey the sensitivity of humanity's higher calling toward the whole community of living things. Humans can sympathize with helpless creatures less able to adapt to their environments.

Many past environmental mistakes are reversible. For example, pollution control has brought the Hudson River and Lake Erie back from the dead since the 1960s. But extinction is forever. Once an ancient forest disappears, all that can reappear is a collection of trees. When the spotted owl blinks a final time, there are no more where it came from. We ought to ensure the species' longevity for its profit and our own.

XI

Logrolls and Logjams

Tensions between the U.S. Forest Service and members of Atiyeh's Shiny Rock crew continue to smolder like lit kindling. The agency claims it's merely carrying out its duty to keep a close watch on public forestlands at Opal Creek. Atiyeh and company regard the constant surveillance as an intrusion and an underhanded attempt to proceed with plans to sell off the area's stately trees for logs. They are willing to go to extraordinary lengths to outcraft their antagonists, just as Jim "Grandpa" Hewitt kept the Forest Service at bay generations before.

On occasion, the clash between Shiny Rock and the federal government degenerates into zany antics reminiscent of Spy vs. Spy, *Mad* magazine's send-up of Cold War espionage featuring a pair of agents, one cloaked and hatted in black and the other in white, each plotting to annihilate the other. From his clean wood-paneled office above Detroit Lake, Dave Alexander serves as the ranger at the Detroit District encompassing Opal Creek. In both size and stature, the six-foot-nine forester towers as chief arbiter, auctioneer, and law-enforcement officer.

Bent on exposing the mining operation as a sham to run Atiyeh off the land, he dispatches men to monitor his every move. They slink around testing waters and taking hundreds of pictures. "My people are telling me this is a facade and we're being bluffed out," Alexander says. "I'm thinking, 'Holy cow, this is kind of absurd.' "

Atiyeh posts "NO TRESPASSING" signs and threatens to

have the foresters arrested. Alexander warns him to desist from interfering with his men performing official duties on a national forest. Atiyeh upbraids a forester for removing the first Opal Creek sign he posted and tossing it in the woods. After Atiyeh lashes out at Alexander by phone, the district ranger orders his forester to take down license plates of all vehicles entering and leaving Jawbone Flats—on the pretense, he insists, of establishing the Forest Service's innocence in any vandalism occurring at Jawbone Flats. Atiyeh accuses him of harassment.

For the better part of this century, Opal Creek has existed as a pin that refused to go away on the Forest Service's map. Above the friction of egos, the dispute has raged first and foremost over ideology. The moment Jim "Grandpa" Hewitt swung his first pick into Jawbone Flat's ore, the agency began fighting to regain its perogative to determine Opal Creek's disposition. Atiyeh won the acid test in the courts by proving that his claims hold economically significant mineral deposits, thus allowing him to maintain private ownership of ninety-five acres at Jawbone Flats smack in the middle of government timber sales.

The showdown at Opal Creek has intensified ever since the U.S. government began wholesale logging of national forestlands in the 1950s to help meet postwar construction needs. By overcutting on private lands, lumber companies had already left a legacy of log shortages and mill closures throughout the Northwest. In the heart of the Willamette National Forest, which sells more timber than any other national forest in the United States, Opal Creek's dense stands of valuable old growth beckoned to Forest Service officials like wheatfields to a farmer. Lumber companies have liquidated, by conservative estimates, thirteen thousand acres of old growth in the Willamette annually since 1985.

Since the 1960s the conservation ethic's firmer hold on Americans' consciousness has put politicians, federal forest agencies, and the timber industry on the spot to satisfy both economic and environmental demands. For fifteen years the Northwest's elected officials, in particular, have ignored the incessant pleas of objective scientists and dispensed cheap old-growth timber as so much pork barrel to buy votes back home.

The sorry statecraft practiced in Washington, D.C., leaves both owl and logger in the lurch. When the last ancient tree pounds the earth, timber workers will still prove big losers in the end. Washington has misled them for decades about the amount of trees still available to maintain their industry. Even without conserving the Northwest's Opal Creeks, they would still run out of

woods to cut within ten years. As a result, the government fore-
closed the possibility of a gradual transition to a second-growth
supply of logs.

The week Dave Alexander arrived from his Forest Service job
in California in 1981, a fresh document authorizing the logging
of Opal Creek sat on his desk, awaiting his signature. The seven
alternatives on his desk ranged from leaving Opal Creek alone to
exploiting its timber potential fully. After touring the site and
poring over the environmental data, he whipped out a pen to
notify Willamette National Forest headquarters in Eugene of his
decision. The ranger ruled out a helicopter logging plan that
would not require any roads be built or another proposal, for
dispersing the cuts over the area because of the subtantial cost
and low payoff, $272,000. Instead, he called for the construction
of 7.3 miles of logging roads and the production of 12.4 million
board feet of timber then worth $689,000, enough to build 1,200
houses. Alexander would end up fighting environmentalists over
Opal Creek throughout his stormy reign from 1981 to 1990.

Atiyeh and his allies remain poised to spring into action at a
moment's notice the day the Forest Service elects to confirm their
worst fears. "All we have to do now is announce a sale and we'll
have an appeal," Alexander says. "I've managed to meet my targets and leave that area alone this long. I have agreements with
George and others that we're not going to sneak up on them. No
surprises." His agency's latest management plan would allow logging on more than 4,000 acres in Opal Creek's 6,800-acre basin
at a rate of 5 percent every decade. Except for a couple of modest
wilderness patches surrounding Opal Lake and Opal Pool and a
500-yard "scenic corridor" along the creek, the basin would be
open to a network of new logging roads and intensive timber
cutting. Atiyeh fears not only losing the heart of Opal Pool but
also the adjoining stream basins. The Forest Service's plans call
for logging in 14,480 acres of the 37,725-acre Opal Creek area
known as the Little North Fork Basin.

Alexander has only been doing his job. Opal Creek's misfortune
centers on its location in the Detroit District in the Willamette
National Forest—1.68 million acres, more land area than the
state of Delaware, and stretching along the western slope of the
Cascade Range for 110 miles in western Oregon. As the top
timber producer among 156 national forests and perhaps the
world, it accounts for almost 10 percent of all timber cut in the
national forests. "The public has been saying, 'Don't cut Opal
Creek. The Forest Service has said, 'That's good, but you gotta

make the volume up somewhere else.' We are being held account-able for that production. I'm having to cut at a faster rate else-where than I wanted to," Alexander says. "As manager of this land, I don't have a problem not harvesting Opal Creek, as long as my target reflects it not being in the timber base. If that's considered part of the land for timber management, I'm going to do it. I'll go straight to court if I have to. But we've decided not to advertise any sales there right now because I know that in no time flat they would be held up by new litigation. How many court cases do you need in a day? At the moment we just keep heading straight to the courthouse, where no one wins. The merry-go-round continues."

The district ranger pays mores than lip service to the domino theory making the rounds in Mill City. "The environmentalists want us to stop cutting old-growth timber at Opal Creek. I know I'm sounding like I'm arguing for the timber industry, but I'd be willing to make you a bet," Alexander says. "They get that thirty-two thousand acres and do you think that would be the last we'll hear of appeals and opposition to timber sales? All we need to do is satisfy George. And what about the Breitenbush community? And, and, and?" And Alexander would have to shift his district's emphasis from timber to the recreational, spiritual, and ecological values of the forest.

Events have already forced him to adjust his thinking about Opal Creek. He remains fairly unclear about Atiyeh's possible motives for investing so much time and expense to gain patents and ownership of the land near Opal Creek. "We think, in the long-term management, it would be better to have land in public rather than private ownership," Alexander says. "Who's to say someone won't build condos and an exclusive resort in there? What if they decide they are going to build a ten-foot-high chain link around each of those parcels? What if you, the public, wants to hike Opal Creek and doesn't have access through those par-cels?" Given that Shiny Rock's crew rather than the Forest Ser-vice maintains the trails throughout the area the lumbering of 12 million board feet of timber will mar the hiking experience, Alexander's argument doesn't seem to wash. Moreover, the thou-sands upon thousands of man-hours and almost $1 million racked up in legal fees for nine years appear disproportionate to the ninety-five measly acres at stake.

The power play pits Alexander's wish to log Opal Creek against Atiyeh's to preserve it, contrary to the district ranger's claims. "No, no, I've told you timber is not our only business. We are

benignly not doing anything about harvesting in there right now,"
Alexander snaps. "Opal Creek is not linked to the patent of the
land. They are in fact separate issues."

The enormous costs to Atiyeh and Persis, Shiny Rock's parent
company, and his own personal history for the past thirty years—
not to mention the court's ruling—tend to argue in the conservationist's favor. "The Forest Service is not neutral," Atiyeh says.
"They want to get rid of us because they want to exploit the area
and we're standing in their way."

The animus between Alexander and Atiyeh has spilled over
into an ongoing spat. "Alexander said he would bulldoze the camp
and sell the mining camp for scrap metal," says Joe Weber, an
ex-Shiny Rock employee, who adopts a skeptical attitude toward
Atiyeh's wilder claims. "He was one of the founding members of
the Get George Committee and called him a sawed-off little
runt." While Alexander denies any personal grudge, he's anything
but shy about attempting to discredit Atiyeh whenever the opportunity arises. "Let me tell you, what he doesn't know about forestry could fill whole volumes," the ranger exclaims on an official
forestry tour he leads with Hirons's Communities for a Great Oregon group, after I mention flying with Atiyeh. Alexander likes
the line so much he repeats it a few minutes later for the benefit
of loggers on the tour who may have missed it.

Atiyeh returns the favor. "The Forest Service has been a truly
evil agency. They would have done just about anything to cut
that thing," he says. "Alexander can play real hardball. There
have been times when I've wanted to throw rocks at him."

Physically, Atiyeh would have been hard pressed to find a more
imposing adversary than Alexander. A big, bearded bear of a
man, at six-foot-nine he ducks to go through doorways at his
wood-paneled Forest Service station above Detroit Lake. The absence of wrinkles from stress or age on his large baby face accentu-
ates a man at ease with himself.

Some people looking so far up at him to reach eye level miss
the quiet smile that flickers when he's talking about interests
unrelated to work, such as the Portland Trail Blazers basketball
team. "Dave's an old-growth kind of guy," Atiyeh jokes, in deference to height better suited for an NBA center than a bureaucrat.
The soft-spoken Alexander's cordial demeanor, leavened further
by a sweet Texas twang from growing up in Grand Prairie, under-
cuts the bully label some conservationists try pinning on him. "I
treat them with courtesy. I can't help being the size I am. You
could be no more six-feet-nine than I could not be," Alexander

explains. "We've had some intense discussions; normally I'm sitting down then. I seldom become more agitated when I'm
standing."

Alexander even displays a sensitive side, wiling away his off-
hours whittling world-class carvings of birds in a studio at home.
His intricate, beautiful figures project a singular attention to detail. The screech owl he shows me looks so lifelike, it appears
ready to take flight. He recently sold one of his creations to Allen
Funt, creator and host of television's *Candid Camera*, for $4,500.

The ranger personifies an agency in the throes of upheaval. On
hunting trips as a boy in Texas, he dreamed about becoming a
wildlife biologist, but the wider array of career choices led him
to forestry school in the South. He received training in the "harvesting" and growth of timber. "I was basically educated to be an
intensive manager of forest crops," he says. "I have evolved into
something else." He has spent more than half his forty-five years
in old-growth stands, starting in 1966 in the Klamath National
Forest in southern Oregon, where he entered large basins of old
growth to design the first roads and timber sales. "Our whole
management scheme was that we needed to be cutting enough so
that as we cut old growth we would have young growth to take
its place. That's purely a business-biological approach. We always
figured that was okay because we always had another ridge or
basin we hadn't gotten to yet," Alexander says. "But it hasn't left
room for the spiritual side. We're just being sent a message that
it ain't enough for a lot of people."

Even if he belongs to the old school of old growth, Alexander
defies any conservationist to paint him as antiforest. "You cannot
have a viable timber industry and not cut trees. We're not talking
here as many in the press would have it, about the rape, pillaging,
and plundering of our land," Alexanders fulminates. "Most of the
people east of the Mississippi don't know diddley about what's
going on here. I don't want to belittle the old-growth issue, but
when you're reading about this back in New York, you don't quite
catch on to the fact we're not cutting it all down. It will not be
back as old growth, but it will be back. We'll go out the back
door and I'll show you a clear-cut from not so long ago."

I follow him later, right outside his ranger station, through a
patch of woods a local railroad logged sixty years ago. The "even-
aged stand," as Alexander describes it, consists of healthy, if ordinary, Douglas firs planted a few decades ago. Many loggers in
Mill City have also extended invitations for me to visit their
favorite tracts of second growth—on a par with many of those

I've seen in the Northeast. They miss the point. What attracted me here in the first place is the majestic one-of-a-kind giants that, by Alexander's own admission, are irreplaceable.

His employer remained in the dark until it was too late. "I don't know if it is 10 or 9 or 12 (percent), but it is around that," Forest Service chief Dale Robertson says of the remaining "old trees" under questioning from lawmakers the month following the northern spotted owl's listing in 1990. The chief had no other choice but to validate the dire warnings conservationists issued all along. Actually, less than one tenth of the ancient forest remains.

For years the agency's unsubstantiated forest inventories based on timber values, not ecological criteria, grossly overestimated the amount of old growth actually left—as anyone can see looking out a plane window at the Northwest's patchwork quilt. The federal government's field workers do "laborious and time-consuming manual methods," the Forest Service's specialists note in an internal agency report criticizing the agency's shoddy work. The Wilderness Society has completed the first comprehensive analysis documenting forest fragmentation ever done, using sophisticated tools including high-resolution digital satellite imagery and computerized mapping.

Alexander's heightened consciousness in recent years of ancient forests' uniqueness stops at Opal Creek's borders. "I don't mean to imply that because we can grow trees fast and well that there's not a value to old growth. You gotta have awe standing in one of those places. One of the things I get out of being in this business is being in places like that," he says. "It's a distinctly different ecosystem than you're going to get in a young growth stand. Each has a place. The only question is how much is enough." Despite visiting Opal Creek several times in a professional capacity, Alexander laments the full day he feels it requires and the challenges it poses to hunting big game. Instead, he and his son prefer spending weekend afternoons bow-hunting in second-growth forests.

"Opal Creek is not in and of itself a more special piece of ground than other places," he says. "It's a beautiful stream, but I could show you many others on this forest." He begs the question of Opal Creek's ecological significance as one of the last continuous stands of old growth, dwelling on the dispute's political dimensions. "Every issue has a flagship, and Opal Creek has become the focal point here," he says. The dormant plans to log the 6,800-acre basin call for the preservation of two patches, containing, Alexander notes, "some of the most spectacular visuals" along the waterway and Opal Lake. Yet since much of this ground is too unstable to accept future planting, it remains off-limits to chainsaws anyway. "We would only be cutting 62 percent, through small clear-cuts of 30 acres," Alexander says, flipping through plastic, transparent overlay maps in the timber-sale department. "In eighty years, what we cut would grow back bigger than what you just saw outside."

Since 1950, the volume of timber sold in the Detroit District in the Willamette National Forest doubled, then tripled. The 298,000-acre tract became the most productive ranger district of the 650 in the United States. District rangers—functioning as "line officers"—perform all the on-the-ground work in their territories, from preparing and administering timber sales to maintaining recreational facilities. On orders from Washington, D.C., the Detroit District emerged as a timber powerhouse, averaging more than 119 million board feet in gross annual sales before wilderness additions in 1984 and 105 million board feet through the rest of the go-go 1980s—enough to build 110,600 houses. "It's one of our major districts," says Dave Hessel, chief of the Forest Service's timber-sale department in Washington, D.C.

Mill City's local logging companies and mills, which purchase 84 percent of the timber cut in the Detroit District, wax nostalgic about these cut levels the federal government will never again achieve. They've milked the cash cow dry. "Industry looks at us as their supplier of raw material. They're not particularly interested in other things besides that," Alexander says. "We've been pretty commodity-oriented in the Forest Service for many decades."

So long as district rangers' performances are evaluated for "getting the cut out," as Washington, D.C., terms the process, Alexander will receive stellar marks. Since the 1970s, national forest employees have scrambled to meet sky-high congressional sales quotas. To ensure that the timber is sold, the Forest Service assigns sales targets to the nine forest regions, based on their capacity. Each regional forester must come within 5 percent of his target or feel the heat from Washington.

Once the Forest Service began selling off its trees in mass quantity during the early 1950s, young foresters have ridden the tidal wave of new revenues. To get ahead, they've had to go along, enhancing the agency's influence in bureaucratic circles by expanding budget and number of staffers under their supervision. By contrast, the forester disposed toward wilderness ends up on the slow track or, worse yet, searching for a new job. Modern forest management under these conditions gives recreation, wildlife, and natural beauty short shrift.

As a result, Alexander and other land managers have walked a tightrope between failing to meet timber targets or incurring lawsuits from breaking environmental laws. In either case, they suffer professional setbacks. The political impetus from Washington, D.C., however, has compelled the Forest Service to continue selling timber along scenic rivers and in municipal watersheds. Seventy-eight percent of Salem's water comes from the Detroit District. "Our customer is the user who turns on his tap and expects a high quality of water," Alexander says. "That's no less a product than timber." He introduces me to a hydrologist from Salem, who happens to be on the premises running a test on the purity of the district's streams. Mounting concern about drinking water motivates the installation of new water filtration systems throughout the region.

Alexander is held accountable for the forests' multiple uses, particularly the wilderness experience. He has come under scathing criticism lately for authorizing a series of clear-cuts near popular trails and campgrounds. "It's a different value system. Congress says, 'We want you to cut timber off the national forest. But don't do it here, here, and here,' " the ranger says with a shrug. "Well, how do you cut this much and not cut here, here, and here? You can't have it all and save it all. It's a no-win deal." With new marching orders from the courts and Congress to ease up on commodity output, Alexander foresees the balance shifting back to conservation. "There's no question old growth hasn't been a priority," Alexander says. "We're going through a big transition."

As his legacy, Alexander is striving to restore peace to the district. "When I joined the Forest Service twenty-two years ago, after I got out of college, I had no idea what I was going to get into," he says, scratching his thick beard. "I don't think anyone then could have predicted the intensity of this conflict." In his waning days at Detroit, he is exploring the possibility of brokering a compromise at Opal Creek through a neutral third party, such as the governor and the Nature Conservancy, a land trust. "We have to get the personalities George [Atiyeh], Dave [Alexander], and Tom [Hirons], and Jim [Morgan] out to find some common ground." Toward that end, he entertains visions of an education center at Jawbone Flats containing both an environmental center and a timber exhibit, funded by industry. "I'm trying to sell a

concept," he says. "If I pull it off, no one will ever know I did
it." Like a negotiator on the scene in the Middle East, he is
painfully aware of the dangers. "It's kind of like walking in land
mines," he adds. "As long as you're still walking, you're probably
doing okay."

The roots of the current ancient-forest crisis date back to the
conquest of a young nation's frontiers. Last century, boundless
optimism about the country's endless forests prompted the federal
government to sell off public lands at bargain basement prices or
give them away free. Heeding Manifest Destiny's call, homesteaders grabbed their acreage and laid the nation's economic foundations. Railroads and timber companies abused the privilege, to
reap massive windfalls. Public outcry about watersheds and future
wood supply spurred Congress in 1891 to grant the president authority to establish "forest reserves," lands set aside "to preserve
the forests therein from destruction." President Benjamin Har-
rison designated the first timberland reserve, next to Yellowstone
National Park. He and his immediate successor, Grover Cleveland, withdrew almost 40 million acres. Six years later, the first
law for managing federally protected forests proclaimed its purpose
to be securing "favorable conditions of water flows, and to furnish
a continuous supply of timber."

Such unvarnished utilitarianism motivated Gifford Pinchot, the
father and first chief of the Forest Service. Upon graduating from
Yale, the aristocratic Easterner chose to pursue forestry as a career.
Since the United States lacked a single forestry school, he had
to go to Europe for graduate training. The Old World, stripped
nearly bare of its virgin forests, taught him the principles of maximum "sustained yield," the prudent philosophy ostensibly guiding
national forest management until this day. It obligates the Forest
Service not to sell more timber than it grows each year. Pinchot
returned home to launch the first comprehensive education programs in forestry and determined to implement his principles in
the nation's timberlands someday. He found an attentive ear in
Theodore Roosevelt, an avid outdoorsman and nature lover. The
president had issued a comprehensive report documenting how
the nineteenth century's cut-and-run practices had caused massive
erosion, transforming fertile land into desert.

Pinchot had impressed on TR and Congress the gravity of a
"timber famine" looming on the horizon and the dire need for
wise stewardship. A conservative at heart and a progressive in
practice, Roosevelt embarked on a mission to rescue the timber

beasts from their own recklessness. In his first message to Congress in 1901 he declared:

> The fundamental idea of forestry is the perpetuation of forests. Forest protection is not an end in itself; it is the means to increase and sustain the resources of our country and the industries dependent upon them. The preservation of our forests is an imperative business necessity. We have come to see clearly that whatever destroys the forest, except to make way for agriculture, threatens our well-being.

In 1905, the U.S. Forest Service was born, and Pinchot, an esteemed member of Roosevelt's kitchen cabinet and a confidant on all matters of conservation, became its first chief. Pinchot wanted the federal government to oversee all of the country's forests. He and Roosevelt had to settle for designating millions of acres out of loggers' reach. In 1907, the timber industry, in keeping with its unrepentant indulgence of the past century, bullied Congress into stripping the president of the power to do so anymore. Pinchot and Roosevelt acted swiftly to protect an additional 16 million acres days before creating the national forest system, igniting a fire storm of anger from members of Congress and private lumber companies. All told, they managed to safeguard the first 148 million acres.

Irate timber barons did protest too much. They had already helped themselves to the richest timberlands, largely forsaking less valuable leftovers on remote, thin-soiled, snowy uplands. Moreover, Pinchot adhered strictly to the pragmatism ingrained in him in Europe. Today, contrary to the popular view, national forests fall outside the domain of the national park system under the Interior Department's authority. Instead, the 191 million acres of national forest (24 million acres of which are in the eastern and southern states), comprising one of every 12 acres in the United States, belong to the Agriculture Department. Its administrators treat much of the lands as they do oats and livestock. "Wood is a crop, forestry is tree farming," Pinchot proclaimed. The "multiple use" concept he advanced for the Forest Service now accommodates 14 percent of the nation's commercial timber output, cheap grazing land for thousands of cattle, and multimillion-dollar mining operations.

Pinchot believed the nation could enjoy its forests and log them, too, setting him against John Muir, the literary naturalist and putative standard-bearer of the modern conservation movement. Ironically, these close friends' affinity for the woods united them on excursions through the western wilds of Montana and the Grand Canyon. Their falling out—paralleling that of Atiyeh and Hirons generations later—occurred once his hiking partner's paramount loyalty to commerce dawned on Muir. The preservationist always supported the sound management of resources to satisfy the material needs of a nation on the move. But by the turn of the century, the naturalist was denouncing Pinchot for sacrificing "thousands of God's blessings" in the nation's "virgin forests." Muir and his allies inveighed against Pinchot as a "deconservationist." The chief forester, in turn, dismissed his foe's defense of nature for its own sake as the impractical, ethereal notions of prairie fairies, posy sniffers, or wind kissers

During the first half of the twentieth century there remained sufficient forests for the followers of Muir and Pinchot to coexist. The proverbial ranger in a fire tower played the benign role of caretaker. Following the Forest Service's creation, about one piece of significant legislation affected its operation per decade. In the 1950s, the decade before an avalanche of new laws began turning the agency on its head, the only law affecting the agency was the Smoky the Bear Act, passed to "protect Smoky's name and character from misuse." Industry paid lobbyists a king's ransom in Washington, D.C., to block logging on federal lands because they feared the timber would drive down the price of their own private holdings. Had the companies cut only as much as they grew, they would have been prepared to meet the surging demand of the post-World War II housing boom. But having liquidated their own timberlands, they executed a perfect about-face and lobbied Washington to open the virgin national forests for business.

The federal government was happy to oblige, as Hirons is fond of noting, to do its part in fulfilling the American Dream for GIs. As a result of the shortage of timber on private lands, alternative materials for home construction—including concrete slabs with asphalt tile flooring, cement blocks, and composition roofing— were enjoying a wider market share. In response, lumbermen teamed up with the National Association of Home Builders to convince architects to use more plywood, shake roofs, wood flooring, and wood siding. The annual cut on national forests, which had started during World War II to fill the military's urgent needs, climbed in peacetime—from 3.5 billion board feet in 1950 to 9.4 billion board feet a decade later, up to its peak of 12.7 billion board feet in 1987.

Industry had to cut more trees per acre on national forests, situated primarily on poorer sites, than it had cut on its own private holdings to maintain volume. Meanwhile, the Forest Service spawned a new element of the industry, wholly dependent on publicly owned supplies of old growth. Politics have weighed heavily against conservation. In their budgets, Congress and administrations since Harry Truman's have promoted timber at the expense of fish and wildlife, recreation, soil, and water.

Over the past thirty years, new constituencies have emerged to check industry's influence in Washington, D.C. The ranks of the Sierra Club and other conservation groups continue to swell from baby-boomer backpackers appalled at the despoliation of their favorite hiking trails and campgrounds. The number of visitors to America's 341 national parks has doubled, to 300 million, over the past two decades, and could jump to 500 million by the year 2010. Meanwhile, a chorus of scientists is advancing arguments to concentrate attention on the importance of safeguarding drinking water sources, wildlife, and genetic diversity.

In 1964 the ideas of John Muir finally bested Gifford Pinchot's, on the day President Lyndon B. Johnson signed into the law the Wilderness Act. This radical measure, marking the culmination of more than a quarter century of dogged lobbying by conservationists, established wilderness areas "where the earth and its community of life are untrammeled by man, where man himself is a visitor who does not remain." The new designation prohibits not just logging and grazing but also vehicles, tramways, hotels, and the bear feedings commonly scheduled in national parks. The 91-million-acre wilderness system—extending from the Great Bear in Idaho to Virginia's Shenandoah—remains perpetually free of human intrusion.

Wilderness is a uniquely American idea. While other nations have set up national parks, virtually none has preserved expanses of land in a primitive state. "Clinton Anderson [a senator from New Mexico and chairman of the Committee on Interior and Insular Affairs at the time of the Wilderness Act's passage] viewed wilderness as a sign that we're a nation rich enough to save some of our resources. When we reach the stage where we have to cut the last tree, mine the last piece of ore, drill for the last barrel of oil, cut the last blade of grass, we are through as a civilization," says Robert Wolf, a retired congressional staffer who helped draft the law. "Anderson firmly believed that a wilderness bill had a profound meaning to society." The national wilderness preservation system includes national parks, national forests, national wildlife refuges and land overseen by the Interior Department's

Bureau of Land Management. "The timber companies were the leading opponents of the original wilderness base in the late 1950s," Wolf recalls. "Whenever there was any move to take out land, as crummy as it was, from the cut base, industry fought it tooth and nail every damn time." Over the past decade, the Reagan and Bush administrations tended to resist additions to wilderness areas, foiling congressional plans to preserve Opal Creek and other natural lands from logging.

In 1976, public alarm about the rise in lumbering on federal lands drove Congress to pass the National Management Act, requiring the Forest Service to balance the goals of conservation and resource development. On paper, the redefinition of multiple use would reconcile water, wood, wildlife, minerals, and recreation. In practice, the flawed legislation fueled controversies by promising all things to all users. In effect, Congress told the Forest Service to keep getting the cut out while protecting the environment at the same time, creating a void for the courts to step into as the final arbiters. In the past two years, since 1991, the Northwest's timber cut has dropped by more than half, chiefly because of injunctions. Judges, most of whom nobody elected, have assumed responsibilities for tackling problems that politicians responsible for land management created but are too afraid to solve themselves.

The Forest Service keeps fumbling, unsure of its mandate on the ground. Atiyeh encounters frustrations large and small in dealing with it. The Detroit District leaves it to him and his crew to maintain the trails through Opal Creek to avoid appearing more partial toward recreation than timber. Atiyeh once asked a forest officer why he approved razing a historic, spectacular lookout tower atop Whetstone Mountain. The official explanation he received was to prevent vandalism.

Hirons himself has had numerous occasions to lambaste Alexander and the timber-sale planners at the ranger station. At the time of the hotly contested logging of old growth at North Roaring Devil's Ridge, otherwise known as the Easter Massacre, he becomes sucked into the controversy. Hirons heeds the request of producers on assignment from the national breakfast show *Today*, to take a camera crew up to the scenic gorge where the Breitenbush community had built a trail. At the end of a road into the woods, they are greeted by a clear-cut in full view. A series of other clear-cuts on a hill at the turn of the bend further assaults their senses. Once again, millions of Americans see adorable spotted owls and flattened forests on their television screens. Hirons seethes over taking the rap for this public-relations debacle.

"Damn it, Dave, the first thing you face crossing the South Breitenbush River is the butt end of a clear-cut," Hirons lights into Alexander. "Couldn't you put the clear-cut back five hundred feet so those folks hiking through don't have to see it and you don't ruin everybody's experience driving up the highway?"

Perhaps Hirons vents his anger at the wrong culprit. "The Detroit District is probably the most heavily fragmented in the Willamette," he concedes. Unrealistic timber targets set in Washington, D.C., have shrunk the land base beyond the point of affording Alexander and other rangers the wiggle room to weigh aesthetic considerations. In the Northwest, the frantic rate of logging has caused egregious mistakes in areas preserved strictly as wilderness. Not long after Hirons's outburst, for example, Willamette National Forest officials found themselves deflecting charges about the accidental logging of 3 million board feet of standing timber on 41 acres within Three Sisters wilderness area south of Opal Creek.

A thicket of euphemisms has sprung up to obscure the Forest Service's actions, rivaling another unpopular agency, the Internal Revenue Service, sugar coating taxes as "revenue enhancement" or the Defense Department "delivering ordnance"—that is, dropping bombs. The Forest Service has exorcised the word "log" from its vocabulary, preferring to talk about "harvesting old growth," as the yoeman farmer would plow a crop. Atiyeh views the loaded term within the larger scheme of the Forest Service's systematic deceit. "How do you harvest what you've never sowed? I don't have any problem cutting down second growth," he says. "If they got 92 percent of the land base industrialized and can't have sustained yield, then sustained yield is a myth. Multiple use has become abuse."

The chief of timber sales in Washington, D.C., refers, in Orwellian tones, to trees as "standing inventory." His agency has been known to sanitize clear-cuts as "grove enhancement." By contrast, biologists on the ground are partial to calling the mounds of dirt and charred stumps a "nuked" forest. "Thinning," according to a reverential Weyerhaeuser publication, translates into a selective cut "in immature stands which increases the rate of growth and improves the quality of trees that remain." The removal of a dead timber, standing or on the ground, meets the definition of "salvaging," a truly patronizing notion. Ancient forests survived for ten thousand years on their without needing human assistance.

Dawn breaks over Mill City early on Friday, enveloping the town in a clean yellow-white light. Inside the Dutch Inn, the pungent smell of coffee intermingles with the heavy haze of cigarette smoke. The mills' managers frequent the Dutch Inn almost every day at breakfast. Shop talk about timber contracts and similar matters fills the room. Hirons sits down at a table with Jim Harris, a timber cruiser from Young and Morgan. Harris, dressed in a flannel shirt and polishing off a plate of biscuits and gravy, insists Jim Morgan is so desperate for wood that he has purchased three trees in a woman's backyard. It almost sounds like a tall tale to Hirons. He prefers talking about his big day ahead helping stage a forestry tour. Harris wishes him well and reminds him of the Indians visiting Opal Creek over the weekend. "I hear Atiyeh is leading a hike up there. Maybe we ought to have someone bury themselves up to their neck and fell a tree in front of Opal Creek. Second growth, of course," Harris jokes, borrowing a page from Earth First!'s protest strategy at North Roaring Devil's Ridge. Hirons sets down his cup of coffee to guffaw.

Billed as an "Earth Day Celebration" by its cosponsors, the Communities for a Great Oregon and the U.S. Forest Service's Detroit District, the forestry tour presents forty years of timber management from the ground up through a series of photo opportunities and upbeat talks worthy of Madison Avenue. Dan Postrel, the acerbic reporter for the *Salem Statesman-Journal* covering timber issues, likens the experience to *Our Friend the Atom*, the films trumpeting nuclear power many American school children were subjected to in the 1950s and 1960s. Today two hundred local high-school students and their teachers show up. Staffers at the office of CGO, the grass-roots group Hirons founded, have spent weeks druming up interest in the Willamette Valley and coordinating the itinerary with a timber-sale planner at the ranger district.

At 7:30 A.M. a small contingent of public officials, reporters, photographers, and sympathetic foresters fill about one third of the upholstered tour bus, a disappointing turnout in view of all the publicity. Perhaps people are just too timbered out these days to pay much heed. The head of Dave Alexander, today's featured speaker, grazes the bus's ceiling. We roll past the Whitewater clear-cuts, logged eight years ago. A viewshed, or scenic corridor, hides the damage. These are curtains of trees the Forest Service designs to—as the tour's organizers sweetly put it in the fact sheet they hand out—"have a low impact on the traveler. This is a place that elks are often seen grazing and when the bear grass is in bloom it is a beautiful sight."

The fringes of trees environmentalists deride as "fool 'em strips" for concealing the Forest Service's true mission actually provoke controversy within the agency and among loggers themselves. In certain instances—except, perhaps, the *Today* show fiasco at North Roaring Devil's Ridge—Hirons believes they obstruct motorists' open vistas and waste valuable timber. Yet in these trying times Dick Posekany, the timber and land manager for Frank Lumber in Mill City, reiterates the importance of good public relations: "You know those windshield foresters say, 'Damn loggers, they clear-cut the whole thing."

Moreover, as Alexander and his superiors in Washington, D.C., explain to me repeatedly, recreation constitutes a major part of national forests' business and automobile driving a major part of recreation. According to a comprehensive Forest Service study, driving ranks as the second most popular outdoor activity on its land, as measured by number of trips away from home in millions (421), second only to swimming (461), and twice as much as walking (267). Begging the question of whether the popularity of steering wheels over hiking boots points to a nation gone soft, the Forest Service includes scenic corridors in virtually all of its long-range plans as a marketing strategy to cater to its clientele. "When people drive over the top of the McKenzie River Forest they don't want to see a clear-cut," says George Leonard, deputy chief of the Forest Service. "They want the natural experience." Besides, as conservationists have maintained all along, the less people know what really goes on in the nation's woods behind the green smoke screens, the safer it is politically for the Forest Service. In 1791, the Russian statesman, Grigori Potemkin, constructed glorious fake villages along a route Catherine the Great was to travel, to hide the peasants' true misery from her. Ever since the media and conservationists began knocking down the U.S. Forest Service's own false fronts a few years ago, many of the "windshield foresters" Posekany curses are asking the government hard questions for the first time.

Our first stop on the field trip is at the Hoover Campground, near the headwaters of Detroit Lake in a stand of second growth that took root after the area was logged in the 1920s. This plush spot in the woods is one of 386 campsites around the lake within easy access of two thirds of Oregon's population. "We've been bursting at the seams for years," Alexander says. "In wilderness areas man is supposed to be a visitor. We're going to have to restrain the public through a permit system and ticket books. We don't have a choice but to preserve wilderness at a certain level." The Detroit District plans to emulate a toll-free 800 number the Mckenzie District farther south has established. Campers nation-wide call ahead to reserve a spot and date of their choice.

This week, on the eve of the opening of the trout fishing season, the Detroit District is busy getting the campgrounds into shape. Last year the district enjoyed almost 1 million visitor days, a unit of measure representing an individual's twelve-hour stay, in the lake area and surrounding trails, a recreation paradise for picnickers, boaters, and backpackers. Across from the Hoover Campground, their pleasure from the natural experience may be adulterated by the jarring site of a clear-cut on private land. The forest is littered with others just like it.

The government's inattention to recreation reflects its out-moded priorities. The overwhelming lion's share of the forest ser-vice's billion dollar-plus budget goes toward making timber available for logging—as opposed to managing water and air or maintaining trails. In the Willamette Forest there are 6,360 miles of roads (enough to reach from New York to Los Angeles and back, and then take a round trip to San Francisco) primarily for logging, and 1,298 miles of trails. Timber accounts for 85 percent of the Willamette's $56 million annual budget. Since the profu-sion of public works projects throughout the national forests dur-ing the Great Depression, Keith Ervin shows in *Fragile Majesty*, the government has let its trails go to seed. Back then there was one mile of road for every two of trails. Since then the proportion has switched in favor of roads by three to one nationwide, af-fording loggers ready access to timber.

The future lies in reversing the equation. In its new manage-ment plans the agency finally appears ready to build more trails than roads. The Forest Service's own research indicates that recre-ation yields four times the benefits of timber and sixteen jobs for every one derived from cutting trees. But the agency's planners spend four times more on timber than on recreation. According to a study conducted by Oregon State University and funded in part by the Forest Service, the expected boom in tourism and recreation in Mount Hood National Forest will create twenty-five hundred jobs and more than $100 million in sales over the next decade. On much of this forest, the government could earn more money selling recreation permits than timber.

Clearly, a strong conservation ethic toward the national forests will pay off for old growth and the Treasury in the long run. Randal O'Toole, a forest economist and author of the trenchant *Reforming the Forest Service*, advocates giving the agency incentives to manage for wildlife and other nontimber activities by charging user fees for recreation. If bureaucrats had a stake in protecting ancient forests, they could then take the money generated from hiking and fishing to expand wilderness areas and campgrounds. A Forest Service planning paper estimates that such fees could bring in more than $5 billion annually, three times more than what the agency makes in gross receipts from an unprofitable timber program propped up by $8.5 billion in federal tax dollars over the last 14 years. People surveyed are willing to fork over from a few dollars for picnicking to about $30 a day for big-game hunting.

The Forest Service has announced plans to boost recreation fees on national forests by 70 percent, charging visitors for the first time to use such sites as picnic areas and boat ramps. The agency believes the change will almost double its revenues from recreation fees to $24 million. Visitors to national parks are used to paying entrance fees and additional charges for camping privileges. Yet, incredibly, the Forest Service has charged only for the use of campgrounds with full water, toilet, cooking, and garbage facilities. Of the thirteen campgrounds highlighted during the forestry tour, almost a third are free. The Clinton administration is considering raising user fees on public lands for recreation, hiking, hunting and camping.

The government has barely scratched the surface of reaping the profits it deserves as the caretaker of America's national treasures. Under an old sweetheart contract at Yosemite, the largest and most significant concession in the park system, a private company running the park's lodging facilities, restaurants, shops, and services passed on less than a penny for every dollar of the $90 million spent in the park by visitors each year! The deal brought to light the national parks' outdated concession system, established decades before soaring attendance at parks turned them into profit centers. Under a new agreement that goes into effect in late 1993, the National Park Service will take in 25 cents for every dollar.

The contract at Yosemite could become a model for future concession contracts, ensuring that the government receives a fair share of the income. Two Interior Department investigations have revealed that concessionaires at national parks had generated millions of dollars in earnings while in certain instances paying less than 1 percent of their gross revenue in government franchise fees. According to the department, concessionaires earned $500 million in gross revenues in 1988 but returned only $12.5 million in franchise fees, an average of 2.5 percent of receipts. The Interior Department is seeking to raise all fees to at least 22 percent and to open the contracting process to competitive bidding.

Much of the public already pays recreation fees in places besides national parks. Hunters and anglers have had to buy licenses for years. In eastern national forests, hunters pay a surcharge to the state wildlife department. Campers and swimmers are accustomed to dipping into their wallets on public and private land. Ski resorts turn handsome profits charging skiers for lift tickets. Outfitters and guides command up to $100 a day for hunting, fishing, boating, and horseback riding. The premier river guide accompanying Hirons, Randy Moberg, and me in fishing for steelhead in Oregon charges $500 a day and can hardly keep up with the demand.

Some of the fiercest opponents of setting aside old growth stand to gain the most from such reforms. The windfall would exceed the money Mill City and other timber towns currently receive from logging sales. Programs could be funded to speed business diversification and assist displaced workers. Private woodlot owners would watch the value of their holdings rise, since federal timber would cease to compete with private. They could also charge for camping, hiking, and picnicking on their lands just as the government would on its own.

Environmentalists who accuse O'Toole of discriminating against the poor end up shortchanging everyone. Perhaps they remain too fixated on shedding their image as elitists. As he demonstrates, user fees are more equitable than the present system of taxation to support recreation since only those who use the forest must pay for it. Recreation fees pale in comparison to the cost of vehicle or a pair of new hiking boots. Because most recreationists tend not to be poor, it probably defies fairness and budgetary realities to start another entitlement program subsidized by the rest of the public. "If fees are truly a deterrent to low-income people, some form of 'recreation' stamps could be provided by the Department of Health and Human Services," O'Toole argues. His unassailable faith in "marketization" leads him to libertarian extremes about the wisdom of providing any subsidies at all for outdoor recreation on public lands. "Why should Disneyland, baseball games, movies, or concerts cost money if outdoor recreation is free?" O'Toole asks. "Taking this argument to its logical conclusion, the government should subsidize video games, dirt bikes, and bowling." In effect, unlike a Dodger or Mickey Mouse fan, the permitholder affixing a sticker on a car window to enter a national forest would be performing a public service.

The Forest Service's distorted budget harms both ancient forests and taxpayer's pocketbooks. In the future, self-sustaining wilderness areas would be inured to the special-interest legislation that has long promoted logging ancient forests. The public had better become accustomed to helping defray the costs of preserving ancient forests through user fees or else risk losing them altogether and being the poorer for it.

At the Pamelia Trailhead, a log's roll away from Hirons's current job, a timber-sale planner introduces the high-school students and dignitaries to a classic patch of old growth. He directs our gaze to two of the ecosystem's basic characteristics, a multilayered canopy above a four-hundred-year-old thumper, and a winter storm blow-down biologists now require Hirons and other loggers to partially leave behind as a means of replenishing the soil. The forester asks the youth what they see on the ground. "Down, woody debris," Hirons interjects, invoking the technical term to the laughter of colleagues standing beside him.

Back on the bus, timber executive Dick Posekany tries preempting positive discussion of Opal Creek among the guests by harping on its drawbacks. "You hear a lot about Opal Creek and opportunities for tourism," he avers. "The hills are steep. The place needs to be made a lot more accessible for a lot more people. Tom knows it better than I." Hirons appears somewhat taken aback at being trotted out by his peer as a character witness against his old stomping grounds, but is willing to oblige: "In my twenty-five years of logging I've gone up and down a lot of hills. Opal Creek has as nasty ground as I've seen." Challenged later in the day to present the case for logging it, Posekany himself hems and haws.

During the 1970s and 1980s the Forest Service hired ecologists and wildlife biologists to supplement traditional road engineers and timber managers. While the agency's policy remained the same, the new recruits stimulated consciousness about resources besides timber. At the Willis Timber Sale we meet a pair of archaeologists responsible for surveying sites for cultural artifacts prior to a timber sale's release.

Atiyeh has touched the flesh and blood of ghosts from vanished tribes through prehistoric artifacts discovered at Opal Creek. As a boy, Atiyeh and friends were hiking far up in the cliffs one day when they stumbled into a cave painted with pictographs of animals and hunting scenes. He has been unable to find the spot since.

His miners at Jawbone Flats unearthed a trove of arrowheads and shards of stone. Native Americans hunted, fished, and picked berries throughout the Northwest. These activities, plus the baskets and canoes they constructed from cedar, demanded sharp tools. A Forest Service biologist examined the obsidian pieces—black volcanic glass Indians shaped into tools—and estimated them to be two thousand years old. Atiyeh proudly displays a few of the arrowheads at home and at the camp. His collection also contains yellowed, dog-eared maps detail Indian trails along the ridges surrounding Jawbone Flats, leading to aboriginal summer camps. (The Indians, much like people today, enjoyed the valleys' warmth in winter and escaped its summer heat in the mountains.) Retracing the primeval steps while holding the lustrous weapons, it excites a hiker's imagination to picture an intrepid hunter stalking his prey—perhaps an elk or bear twice his size—before the birth of Christ.

On the tour, the two young women archaeologists in hiking boots and jeans look fit and trim from all the scurrying they do up and down slopes in advance of the onrush of chainsaws. In this area they have excavated evidence of civilizations dating back five thousand years. The discovery of flakes or chips of obsidian here indicates the presence of ancient peoples. Though fewer than 5 percent of these historic sites are on federal lands, lengthy bureaucratic procedures can create a roadblock for loggers. "Gravesites are a cultural resource. You cannot willy-nilly disturb them. If you find an area, we ask you to circle it on the map," pleads one of the archaeologists. "Call and let us know. Call us. Call the Bureau of Land Management. Call the library. Let us know where it's at." Hirons and Posekany exchange glances and stare at the ground, tabulating on their mental calculators the number of board feet the woman can cost them.

The archaeologists holds aloft an ordinary-looking round stone with a groove cut down the middle. "We realize from electron microscopes that this was used for straightening arrows and sharpening tools," she exclaims. "This is a rare, unique find." Hirons looks nonplussed. "A couple of archaeological asses come along to find obsidian chips and say, 'Let's go have a dig here,' " he later fumes. "The cable from a yarder probably ran across their rock."

A few miles down the road running through the freshly logged Willis Timber Sale, today's tour culminates in the Forest Service's proudest symbol of progress, tree planting. It puts decades of logging on public forests in the most favorable light possible, laying to rest any suspicions of the old cut-and-run practices ever returning. Who could protest cutting down woods if they are eventually going to be replaced? "We're right on top of our reforestation," Alexander insists. "We're planting a million and a half trees per year. This year we have already planted 500 acres of young trees and are going to plant 1,700 acres more." Forest Service chief F. Dale Robertson boasts of replanting 492,000 acres, the most since the forest system's creation in 1905.

A silviculturist, trained in the care and cultivation of trees, demonstrates the proper technique for planting trees to give students hands-on experience with the agency's extensive "reforestation" program. Each student then receives a tiny eight-inch seedling of Douglas fir, red cedar, or western hemlock and a hoedad, a hybrid between a pick and a shovel, to dig their holes. "Go do your part for Earth Day," says a state politician on the tour. Fanned out across the slope, the students pierce the soft, moist earth deep enough to cover the roots. On the advice of foresters giving instructions, the students delicately pat down the soil with their hands instead of stomping it with their feet. These youths, proclaims a CGO press release, are sowing the seeds of "tomorrow's forest."

The idyllic scene looks a little too good to be true. What we are watching today represents one stage of what the Forest Service terms "intensive management," the industrial tree-farming techniques of clear-cutting, burning, applying chemical fertilizers, planting, spraying herbicides to prevent the growth of unwanted species, controlling pests (i.e., bear and elk), and reentering in forty-five to sixty-five years to log again. The new man-made landscape foresters and loggers refer to as "reprod," short for reproduction, bears only a distant relationship to a natural ecosystem. In fact, the Forest Service has not reforested a single piece of land as nature does, any more than a geneticist has cloned a human being. It cuts down the forest, then restocks its cash crop with trees of the same species, the same size, and the same height. The mysterious, complex old growth at Opal Creek embodies big and small trees, moss-draped boughs, carpets of decomposing logs, and nutritious mushrooms for a diversity of wildlife not found in man-made forests.

The government has largely failed to do even a particularly good job in producing tree farms. The law requires the land to be replanted within five years of logging and prohibits logging outright on sites unfit for intensive management. Yet plenty of timber activity has gone on on sandy, rocky soils and steep slopes at high elevations where seedlings cannot possibly take hold. A congressional study shows that the Forest Service is regrowing less than two thirds of the volume of timber being cut. Robert Rogers, forest silviculturist at the Sequoia National Forest, concluded in 1988 that "less than 10 percent of the reforestation records were complete in all respects, and in most cases there were no measure of the reliability of the data."

The Forest Service's incomplete and downright deceptive records on restocking have measured the number of trees planted instead of those that actually live, a method worthy of the National Wildlife Federation's derisive term "voodoo forestry." The agency can thus claim 99 percent success rates in certain northwestern forests where trees have not grown back at all, despite half a dozen attempts. Since the late 1960s, the agency's own soil scientists have warned about the dangers of irrevocable damage. In his public-relations battle, Atiyeh keeps the Forest Service on the defensive concerning a mountain logged around Opal Creek in 1970 and still bare.

Alexander's office would have steered clear of those poor soils, he admits, had he the chance to plan that timber sale again. Yet even the original environmental assessment for the first Opal Creek timber sale on his watch uses such phrases as "the land is not well suited for regeneration" and "shallow, excessively drained . . . on steep side slopes and ridges." Trees on some soils, it says, should not be cut, particularly where replanting poses a problem.

The ranger regards criticism of the worst mistakes as 20/20 hindsight. "Look at dietary things. We're really into oat bran and exercise. Where were we in 1960? Our value systems are changing in a whole different bunch of areas and we're trying to go on. If you've got a heart problem today, you take it to Portland, where they'll cut you open and replace a couple of veins and arteries and in two months you'll be back out," he explains. "In 1960 you would have died. The point is we don't look back and say it's criminal that my grandmother died because the medical profession couldn't deal with that. Does it appear any more reasonable to chastise the Forest Service for what happened back then? In 1960 we didn't care a hell of a lot about spotted owls, just like we couldn't fix your arteries back then."

At least Alexander avoids bureaucratic obfuscation. But his analogy is strained at best. The medical field's main mission down through the ages, health maintenance, has stayed constant, irrespective of evolving value systems—in the best interests of Alexander's grandmother and all others. Heightened sensitivity toward the disappearance of wilderness does not excuse the Forest Service's violation of the basic precept of sustainable yield Gifford Pinchot enshrined at the turn of the century, a precept the public had every right to believe the Forest Service still upheld. The government's insistence on cutting down more trees than it grows will continue to plague the forests.

The Forest Service has embarked on the correct course by experimenting with "stewardship contracts" to foster symbiotic partnerships between land managers and foresters. These contracts are awarded for upgrading the ecosystems' health and productivity, as opposed merely to turning them into wood factories. Tree planters receive financial bonuses for high survival rates rather than for the number of seedlings sunk into the ground.

The government can go one step farther and elevate the position of "reforestation worker" to its rightful position. These men and women are the unsung heroes of the second growth our children will depend on. On the job, they take up residence in trailers, campers, and tents, leading an itinerant existence that may mean four or five moves over three months. Like loggers, planters frequently toil in the wretched weather of blistering heat and drenching downpours. On top of that, they sweep across the slopes while carrying 40-pound bags, of 150 seedlings each, strapped to their backs and stopping every 10 feet to stick their hoedads in the ground and launch the lives of embryonic trees.

Brain drain at Forest Service dims the prospects of it developing innovative programs to confront today's or tomorrow's challenges. In a major report, the normally conservative Society of American Foresters, the largest collection of government and university leaders in its field, has condemned current forest research in America as underfunded and uninspired. The Forest Service's budget for research, it notes, has dropped by about 14 percent over the past decade. The number of agency scientists has fallen from 1,000 to 740 since 1980. Their equipment and facilities are dilapidated. And the number of graduates in forestry each year—100—lags woefully behind the demand. "Forestry research must change radically if it is to help meet national and global needs," the report concludes. It proposes boosting the Forest Service's research budget, restoring competitive research grants that the agency eliminated, and strengthening the teaching of forestry to attract more and better students. Agency officials applaud the recommendations, perhaps ushering in a new era for America's woodlands.

The "radical approach" in the vein of the Society of American Foresters' proposals really amounts to a return to the basics. In its opposition to continuing research, the Reagan administration went through the motions by recycling old scientific studies. For example, it slashed federal programs providing small woodlot owners with technical advice. Yet the 4 million acres of the so-called Third Forest in the lowlands of western Washington State and western Oregon comprise some of the richest second growth anywhere and the grist to keeps sawmills operating. Jeff DeBonis, a former timber sale planner in the Willamette, calls on his ex-employer to shift 180 degrees back to its original mission of stewardship, and assist private landowners in taking proper care of their forests in such areas as rehabilitating logged land. Interior Secretary Bruce Babbitt favors raising user fees on all public lands to "give incentives for good management of the land."

With the sun sliding behind the mountains in the early afternoon at the ranger station, the Forest Service treats the tour group to a seedling as a going-away present to take home and plant. Hirons watches the students file into the office in a long line. The accompanying information card—on recycled paper, of course—hedges its bets, observing that by the year 2020 one seedling can either contribute to reducing the greenhouse effect or yield sufficient wood to produce 4,700 newspapers. "I don't need a tree," Hirons mumbles, as if to distance himself from the sappy surfeit of Earth Day symbolism. He returns a few moments later, sheepishly holding five seedlings. "What the hell."

On the ride home, Hirons sits on the armrest and reaches for a microphone to amplify his stump speech. Seizing the moment thirty-three hours before the real Earth Day, he rues the science and politics conspiring against him. "I've had a real hard time over the past few years figuring out if ecology is a science or a cult," he says. "Man is not a cancer. There's a whole line of thinking that after getting done creating all the fish in the ocean, God said, "Stop, that is enough." His voice trails off in the bus's hollow silence.

A summer steam bath soaks Washington, D.C., in wet heat. The father of our country, who selected this site for his new nation's capital, was not around to suffer the consequences of the swampland bubbling underneath the pavement till this day. The bright sun reflects off the imposing bronze doors housing the Interior Department, the government's largest collection of land management agencies. In Room 7000A, a continent away from Mill City, blue curtains and an American flag embroider the ceremony's pomp and circumstance. The podium bears the Interior Department's seal, a bison pointed left. James Watt failed to move it permanently rightward in the name of ideological purity. On June 22, 1990 at 11:00 A.M. sixty print reporters and sixteen television cameras, including those of the networks, pack every square inch to record today's history. A simulcast will break into the morning breakfast shows from San Francisco to Seattle.

A decade of scientific studies and lawsuits has finally reached a climax. John F. Turner adjusts his reading glasses to declare formally that the little big bird is a threatened species. "The biological evidence says that the northern spotted owl is in trouble," says the director of the Fish & Wildlife Service, a division of the Interior Department. "We will not, and by law cannot, ignore that evidence." The decision triggers the broadest application ever of the Endangered Species Act, one of the toughest environmental laws on the books. It also caps perhaps the fiercest conservation fight in decades, setting the stage for the protection of the ancient forests. Compounding the economic troubles of timber towns, it could slash logging in half on seventeen national forests in Washington State, Oregon, and northern California.

Turner wholeheartedly endorses the Jack Ward Thomas report recommending that 8.4 acres be preserved for northern spotted owl habitat, the minimum needed to maintain a viable population. "This is without a doubt," Thomas recently said of his strategy, 'the largest conservation strategy for a single species that's ever been considered anywhere."

Today's event borders on the theater of the absurd. Specially printed placards in the hallway outside billed today's event as the "Spotted Owl Press Conference." But Interior Department spokesman Steve Goldstein immediately tries to dampen expectations. "This is a press availability," he solemnly announces to gales of laughter. "It has been downgraded from a press conference." (Chuckling at his agency's exclusion from the event, a Forest Service official I meet later in the day jokes about the downgrade, a term weathermen invoke during hurricanes and other high-grade storms.) In a comic effort at spin control, the press conference's organizers have shoehorned the media into a small room turned unbearably hot by the camera lights. A six-hundred-seat auditorium was available in the same building. In a separate document Turner has mysteriously urged the Forest Service and the Bureau of Land Management to rely on the Thomas

Report, which most observers have assumed all along would serve as a ready-made recovery plan. Still, Turner's announcement lacks specific steps either to protect the owl or to cushion the blow to timber towns.

Political operatives at the White House intervened in the hours leading up to the declaration to stifle the professional scientists backing the epochal Thomas Report. Orders have come from high up to scrap the Thomas Report and continue logging as much as possible of the last 10 percent of ancient forests. In doing so, they ignore a three-and-a-half year process in which the Fish & Wildlife Service conducted four major public hearings and evaluated more than twenty-three thousand public comments on the proposed listing. "[The decision] is based on the most comprehensive scientific inquiry ever made by the Fish & Wildlife Service in preparation for a listing decision," Turner says. "[The Thomas Report] contains some of the best biology I've seen." (Even the timber industry's own scientist on the panel refrained from writing a dissenting opinion.) Yet senior officials in the Agriculture and Interior departments and Forest Service chief F. Dale Robertson find themselves relegated to the sidelines for standing behind the scientists' biological findings. A senior official in Washington, D.C., has called regional agency chiefs to advise them not to sign a letter endorsing the report's credibility.

Secretary of the Interior Manuel Lujan and Cy Jamison, director of the Bureau of Land Management, two of the holdouts who ultimately prevailed with the White House's blessing, have clued in no one on how they intend to improve on the plethora of solid science. On his travels through the West, Lujan, who had compiled a dismal record on environmental issues over his twenty years in Congress as a New Mexico Republican, has assured loggers of his plans to cut the area for owl habitat and expressed befuddlement about the purpose of the Endangered Species Act. "Nobody's told me the difference between a red squirrel, a black one, or a brown one," he says in Denver, weighing in in the debate over whether to permit construction of an observatory in Arizona that may cause the extinction of the Mount Graham red squirrel. "Do we have to save every subspecies?" During a field trip, he later claims he saw an owl whose species was unimportant since they all pretty much look the same.

The Bush administration's fiercest opponent of the Endangered Species Act refuses to let hard science cloud his judgment. Literally interpreting the Bible, he informs *Time* that he rejects Darwin's theory of evolution regarding the rise and extinction of species. "I just look at an armadillo or a skunk or a squirrel or an owl or a chicken, whatever it is, and I consider the human being on a higher scale. Maybe that's because a chicken doesn't talk," Lujan says. "Here's what I believe. God created Adam and Eve, and from there, all of us came. God created us pretty much as we look today."

Lujan's alliance with the Bureau of Land Management (BLM) raises serious doubts about the extent of his concern for the spotted owl. By an act of Congress in 1937, the Bureau of Land Management manages its 2.4 million acres of land in western Oregon, including about 15 percent of the old growth left, predominantly for timber production, with minimal regard for environmental protection. Thus it came as scant surprise when BLM director Jamison, in testimony before Congress, voiced his objections to the Endangered Species Act.

Bill Clinton would do well to avoid his immediate predecessor's repeated missteps in the northwestern logging issue. It remains to be seen whether the new president will fulfill the promise in his campaign to preserve our ancient forests for their "scientific and ecological importance" and leave the Endangered Species Act intact. "Planning and good long-term management can help us protect jobs and the unique, old-growth forests that are as much a part of our national heritage as the Grand Canyon or Yosemite," the president said this past spring before a historic forest conference he and his conservation-minded Vice President Al Gore held in Portland to find a solution. Bruce Babbitt, Clinton's Interior Secretary, describes the current process for protecting endangered species as a "train wreck" waiting to happen. He proposes to focus less on saving one species at a time, adopting instead a multispecies approach to protect entire ecosystems for all the animals and plants within an area.

Bush, like Bob Packwood and a legion of other politicians, managed to be antiowl without being prologger. Bush's insistence on playing politics with both their fates exacerbated the mutual suffering. Timber towns fear that the decay in devising a long-term management plan for forests will further cloud their futures. Environmentalists have vowed to return to the courts to halt logging. And members of Congress outside the Northwest are feverishly pushing their own programs to preserve large reserves of ancient forests.

In his 1988 campaign for the White House, Bush cynically coopted symbols in a pledge to become the "environmental president." But as a conservative Republican president closely allied with big business, he consistently tempered his promises of support for environmental causes on the gamut of issues from protecting wetlands to controlling global warming by insisting that economic considerations must also be taken into account.

Watching his political fortunes slip away in 1992, Bush lurched from the "environmental president" to the "reelection president." To win votes in the West, he weakened laws and regulations so that industry could exploit the nation's natural resources. Coal companies were given the go-ahead to strip-mine millions of acres of public parks and forests. With the aid of Vice President Dan Quayle, who headed a federal panel aimed at relaxing governmental regulations, more than fifty rules for clean air were gutted. (Bush thus undid the Clean Air Act, which he had touted as a major accomplishment of his administration.) New rules at the Interior and Agriculture departments infringed on the public's right to appeal and stop logging, mining, oil drilling, and grazing.

The Bush administration blatantly subverted the lawful mission of professional land managers to practice sound stewardship. In 1991, two senior officials overseeing millions of public acres disclosed that they had been ousted from their jobs for resisting political pressure to increase logging because it threatened fish and wildlife, from large trout to grizzly bears. A tearful John Mumma, a regional forest manager based in Missoula, Montana, and a twenty-eight-year veteran of the agency, disclosed to a House subcommittee that he had been transferred from his position to a desk job in Washington, D.C., for failing to meet his annual timber goals. He accused industry executives and western senators and congressmen, through Chief Robertson, of demanding his head. "I have failed to reach quotas only because to do so would have required me to violate federal law," Mumma, fifty-one, said. He decided to retire rather than compromise his ethics. Under a congressional subpoena, Lorraine Mintzmyer, a thirty-two-year veteran of the National Park Service who worked her way up from secretary to become the agency's only female regional director, said the White House leaned heavily on her to water down ecological protection for Yellowstone National Park. She was then ordered transferred to Philadelphia.

Bush left that "little furry-feathery guy," as he referred to the northern spotted owl, on a more precarious perch than ever. The seldom-used cabinet-level committee known as the God Squad voted to override the Endangered Species Act and allow timber sales on seventeen hundred acres. In early 1993, a federal appeals court ordered an investigation to determine whether the administration improperly pressured members of the squad to permit the sales.

The meaningless symbolism underscored Bush's abdication of responsibility and the urgency for Clinton to take decisive action now. "Hey, old George Bush, you're saying, 'The hell with it.' The administration can blame it on the law, the courts, or on Congress. They're punting again. Bush is saying, 'I want this to last until my presidency is over and it's somebody else's problem,' " U.S. representative Bruce Vento, a Democrat and leader on conservation issues, told me the week of the owl's listing. "This is the mentality of the robber barons from the 1890s in the 1990s. If Bush, the president, representing the entire nation, can't face up to the facts, who the hell can?"

In 1991 the administration received a stunning rebuke, its ironic source amplifying the message. Seattle-based U.S. District Court judge William Dwyer, a Reagan appointee, ordered sales in sixty-six thousand acres of prime old growth in national forests suspended until federal agencies produced an effective protection plan for the spotted owl. In addition to that tract on the cutting line, he noted that four hundred thousand acres of owl habitat had already been logged since 1984, risked pushing the "species past a population threshold from which it could not recover."

Judge Dwyer stated:

A great conifer forest originally covered the western parts of Washington, Oregon, and northern California, from the Cascade and Coast mountains to the sea. Perhaps 10 percent of it remains. The spaces protected as parks or wilderness areas are not enough for the survival of the spotted owl.

The loss of old growth is permanent. To bypass environmental laws, either briefly or permanently, would not fend off the changes transforming the timber industry. The argument that the mightiest economy on earth cannot afford to preserve old-growth forests for a short time, while it reaches an overdue decision on how to manage them, is not convincing today. It would be even less so a year or century from now.

More is involved here than a simple failure by an agency to comply with its governing statue. The most recent violation of the National Forest Management Act exemplifies a deliberate and systematic refusal by the Forest Service and Fish & Wildlife Service to comply with the laws protecting wildlife. This is not the doing of the scientists, foresters, rangers, and others at the working level of these agencies. It reflects decisions made by higher authorities in the executive branch of the government.

The Bush administration's procrastination after the owl's listing offered timber workers not much more than a summer's worth of work. Logging returned to a standstill as a result of a series of court decisions that stopped logging because the administration continued to violate environmental laws.

Bush's stall tactics only prolonged the misery. He threatened to veto any legislation providing special help to woodworkers displaced by the spotted owl's protection. Moreover, his administration persisted in ignoring proposals to retrain them or assist their distressed communities at a time when certain northwestern legislators and organized labor made such aid a precondition of support of any bill saving the last remnants of old growth.

Some form of worker benefits presents the surest course for breaking the political logjam. The amelioration of economic maladies would negate the industry's principal argument against protecting the northern spotted owl. How can timber barons block anything so useful to their aggrieved workers and still retain their credibility? Environmentalists have belatedly recognized the wisdom of defraying the immediate human costs of preserving ancient forests. Above all, a comprehensive strategy gives more than a stick in the wind to loggers such as Harvey Spears preparing their families and themselves for the tough times ahead.

The Northwest serves as an ideal testing ground for laying out a cornerstone of Clintonomics, worker retraining. A first step in the "green conversion" from environmentally insensitive industries to productive ones is clearly outlined in a study the Bush administration suppressed and withheld from a congressional committee. The fifty-two-page report, prepared by the Forest Service and the Bureau of Land Management, details government initiatives to soften the impact from implementing a conservation strategy for the spotted owl. It focuses on improvements in trade policy to ban the export of raw logs; bold efforts in community outreach to give dislocated workers new skills; family support; packages of loans and grants to the hardest-hit towns; revenue sharing to offset the drop in timber sales; and "land stewardship" through public works to build trails and enhance fisheries. Best of all, taxpayers should like the plan because it could save more than twenty-one-thousand jobs, as many as might lose their jobs from saving the spotted owl, merely by shuffling funds already earmarked for existing programs.

Tom Hirons, a familiar figure in Washington, D.C., from his grass-roots lobbying trips, felt such disgust with political gridlock following the owl's listing that he virtually gave up hope of working within the system. Joining a delegation from the northwestern timber industry, including Mill City's Jim Morgan, he was treated to the classic capital run-around. At the Forest Service, the chief was genially noncommittal. The interior secretary reiterated his exasperation with the economic problems of endangered species. He and the agriculture secretary, in another meeting, shifted the blame to Congress.

During a half-hour meeting in the White House's West Wing with the President's top aides, from which conservationists were excluded, Hirons and his delegation received a particularly heavy dose of cynicism, opening with even more whining over the Endangered Species Act's futility. In an uplifting pep talk aimed at raising their flagging spirits, the then chief of staff, John Sununu, warned them to augment their ten-thousand-strong ranks considerably or they would never be taken seriously as a special interest.

Sununu's bloodless political calculation reduced the real lives of panic-stricken people in the nation's far corner to the abstraction of so many votes on election day. President Bush's right-hand man held out a slender reed for Hirons to lean on. At the eleventh hour of the beginning of the end of logging in ancient forests, loggers looked in vain for government to rationalize their world's chaos. That afternoon the group called on Mark Hatfield, Oregon's senior senator. "Senator," Hirons said, looking him straight in the eye, "I feel like a milk pail under a bull."

Over the years, Atiyeh and Hirons realized they had to criss-cross the continent if they were to master a scintilla of their destinies. While running North Forking Logging in the mid-1970s, the pair lobbied together in Washington, D.C., for programs benefiting small timber companies. They both found the high-pressured environment overwhelming. At hearings on Capitol Hill, Hatfield snapped three times at him that he, Hatfield, could read Atiyeh's testimony faster than he could.

At that time, they left empty-handed and, country boys at heart, bewildered by the big city's exotica. Atiyeh hoped to seize the chance to indulge in the ethnic cuisine matching his heritage. "George, we ain't going to no more eigh-rab restaurants," Hirons snapped. "What the hell am I going to eat? Those chickens must have been starved to death."

By the time the ancient-forest issue explodes in Washington, D.C., fifteen years later, the two men are stars and staying in separate hotels. National timber and conservation groups pick up their travel expenses. "George is so effective because the best witnesses are the grass-roots people who have power in their backyards," says Rindy O'Brien of the Wilderness Society. Gushes Fran Hunt of the National Wildlife Federation, "His logging and mining background don't make him a stereotypical environmentalist. He's handsome, articulate, colorful, and bright. He flies in his plane. He's hands-on-oriented and from Oregon. For all these reasons, George commands authority and respect." At the National Forest Products Association, Dave Ford, the very model of a Washington, D.C. lobbyist in a white shirt and gray flannel suit, depends on Hirons to project the bona fide attributes he lacks. "I'm just a hired gun. Tom has a lot more credibility," Ford says. "He comes from timberland and is a real person."

In 1989, Atiyeh and Hirons take their seats at the back of the hearing room in the Longworth House Office Building, eyeing each other warily and waiting their turns. The logger feels decidedly uncomfortable in the Sunday best he calls his "zoot suit." The conservationist wears his inseparable-from-him cowboy boots. "This is the hottest day I've ever spent," Hirons mutters, mopping Washington's humidity from his eyebrow. "God almighty, this place is a griddle." He could just as easily have been referring to the political atmosphere surrounding the first hearings ever on old growth, held by a joint House subcommittee in the dim hopes of forcing a legislative solution. "I can think of few conflicts so severe," announces cochairman Howard Volkmer, a Missouri Democrat.

Three months earlier, at Atiyeh and Hirons's last appearance at a capital, in Salem, they quarreled face to face over the Opal Creek Park bill. Today they confine their differences to oratory they've spent the past few weeks crafting. Perched on an elongated, semicircular wood lectern, Hirons introduces himself to the U.S. representatives as the owner and operator of Mad Creek Logging Company. (Upon hearing the name, the sober mien of cochairman Bruce Vento, a Minnesota Democrat, dissolves into laughter.) "Preservationists have duped a large number of Americans into believing that there are only two choices: either total preservation or total destruction. This is not true! These absolute choices deny man's basic need to be creative and utilize technology," Hirons proclaims. "We are an essential part of the earth's ecology. Working together, we can plan a reasonable and certain future for the people and the forest of the Detroit Ranger District, and throughout the forestlands of this great country."

Atiyeh rises to the occasion as well: "The love of one place, Opal Creek, has pulled me into a battle that I never thought I would ever have to face. It has turned many of my friends against me and earned me more threats than I care to count. When the death threats failed to dissuade me from speaking out with the truth about our national forests, my children were harassed along with anyone who did business with me. Most disturbing of all, I learned that Opal Creek was but a small part in a drama that was being played out across the Pacific Northwest. Most of the special places with the big trees that have made Oregon famous have not been protected, they were just the places that the saws hadn't reached yet."

Ron Marlenee, a pugnacious ultraconservative Republican from Montana (who lost in his bid for reelection against a conservation-minded candidate in 1992), appears unmoved. Among his provocations today, between witnesses he jokes into an open microphone that "spotted owl tastes like chicken." The only laughter in the room comes from him. (Spotted owl probably tastes like bald eagle, too.)

All week long, Atiyeh and Hirons race about town against the clock and their own disillusionment. Each morning the logger leaves from the Holiday Inn across the street from the National Rifle Association's headquarters, where he's staying with fellow industry representatives, to call on members of the House and Senate. "Yeah, yeah, my mind is already made up," growls one of the few members of Congress he talks to in person. Atiyeh fares hardly better in his rounds on Capitol Hill with Aniese, his daughter, in tow.

The pair of Mr. Smiths arrive home from their travels to Washington needing long showers to cleanse themselves of the muck. "It's scary that the aides, a bunch of smartasses, are telling congressmen how to vote," Hirons says. "And, as I've told you, I don't trust any damn politicians." Atiyeh concurs about the federal government's divorce from reality. "You can actually feel the power floating and know this is where the decisions affecting America are. The more times I go there, the more I realize how perverse it is," he says. "Men don't go to Washington, D.C., and change it. It changes men who go to Washington. I haven't seen anybody it hasn't happened to."

The government recognized its mismanagement of the public's forests decades ago. In a study the Forest Service commissioned in 1969 to increase supplies of timber from Douglas fir, the agency first acknowledged it was pumping the well dry. Once these trees were cut, the annual cut in the subsequent rotation would drop almost in half. Nonetheless, the report justified nearly doubling the allowable cut in the 1970s at enormous expense to future timber yields and—it admitted outright—water, fish, and recreation. Few in Washington, D.C., seemed to lodge much protest.

In 1970, however, a group of esteemed foresters released a study highly critical of the Forest Service for abusing resources besides timber on national forests. Although biologists such as Eric Forsman of the Forest Service had researched the spotted owl extensively since 1968, federal agencies neglected his work. By studying it to death, they bought time to continue logging. In 1976 Bureau of Land Management biologist Mayo Call alerted his superiors to the dire need to save the spotted owl or else face drastic cutbacks in timber logged on federal lands once the spotted owl landed on the federal list:

> With the present allowable cuts and rate of cutting old growth timber, it is estimated that ALL old growth forest habitat will have been cut inside the next twenty years [1996]. This includes BLM, private, state, and Forest Service lands. It is, therefore, imperative that action be taken to assure that spotted owl populations be maintained in suitable areas throughout western Oregon. It is not enough to provide last-minute habitat protection to species teetering on the brink of extinction. We have equal responsibility to manage wildlife habitat so that no species gradually slips into a state of irreversible oblivion.

In the late 1970s, the Forest Service sold 5.2 billion board feet of timber—enough to put up 52,000 houses—each year from Oregon and Washington State.

Ronald Reagan, a devout believer in development, appointed John Crowell, a former attorney and lobbyist for Louisiana Pacific—the largest single buyer of federal timber—as assistant secretary of agriculture overseeing the Forest Service. From day one, Crowell resolved—no matter how many federal court orders and national environmental laws tried to stop him—to double or even triple the amount of timber cut on national forests. Throughout the 1980s lumber companies put the arm on Washington, D.C., to replace the supply of old-growth timber long since exhausted on private lands. In response, Crowell actually boasted of violating the principle of sustainable yield to boost the forests' productivity. Meanwhile, the administration slashed money available for recreation, wildlife management, and replanting. It eliminated vital inventories of ancient forest and a five-year study of the requirements of animals residing in them. Planners in several national forests protested the environmental degradation, to no avail.

Crowell's extremism virtually mirrored James Watt's, another fox in the Reagan administration entrusted to guard a chicken coop. The notorious interior secretary declared a moratorium on new listings of endangered species in the early 1980s. Crowell, his ideological soulmate, was "sure" environmental groups had been "infiltrated by people who had very strong ideas about socialism and even communism." The ancient forests' uniqueness fell far outside his intellectual purview. Crowell insisted that the spotted owl was not endangered, contrary to the mountain of scientific proof. "How many owls can we afford to protect?" he snapped. From day one in office, Crowell embarked on a mission to liquidate ancient forests and replace them with fast-growing young trees. "From an economic standpoint those trees are doing nothing but standing there rotting," Crowell declared. "We could get more value by cutting them down and growing a new crop." Crowell, an unabashed apologist for the industrialization of the last old growth, harbors few regrets about sowing the seeds of today's crisis.

Under the 1976 forestry law, Congress required the agency to draft new management plans reflecting realistic outputs of timber on each forest and the protection of other values, including water quality, wildlife, and recreation. The law prohibited the Forest Service from cutting on lands where trees could not grow back. Forest Service planners intended to drop the cut by 20 percent in the Northwest. Industry lobbyists crawling through Washington, D.C., had other ideas. So had Crowell. He consulted his deputy, Douglas MacCleery, formerly a timber analyst from the proindustry National Forest Products Association.

On the heels of objections to the proposed cutbacks from their ex-colleagues among lumber companies, Crowell and MacCleery ordered the Forest Service to revise the plans. The land managers went back to the drawing boards, only to arrive at about the same numbers. The Reagan administration threatened to supplant the agency's top officials with political appointees unless the plans met their wishes. Forest supervisors in the Northwest met with the Forest Service chief to argue for measured reductions. Former northwestern regional forester James Torrence—who, upon his retirement in 1989, criticized politicians for demanding higher cuts than science justified—claims the inaction "strung out the planning process."

Conservation delayed was conservation denied. With the planning process creeping forward at the speed of a tortoise in spite of objections raised inside the Forest Service, logging went on as usual, thanks to officials in the Reagan administration pressuring the Forest Service to maintain high volumes of timber at record levels in the mid-1980s—though less than Crowell had sought. "The Pacific Northwest plans are late, because of several attempts by the timber industry and the administration to raise the allowable cut," wrote a key congressional analyst in a confidential memo to his boss prior to the first hearings on old growth in 1989. "The industry has had four extra years of timber sales, at a volume which the Forest Service's data shows is unsustainable."

Upon Crowell's departure in 1985, George Dunlop carried on where his predecessor had left off. All national forest plans in the Pacific Northwest had to increase logging or he would veto them. "The administration intervened once again, this time through Assistant Secretary Dunlop with McCleery still as deputy," notes the congressional memo. "Dunlop ordered the Forest Service to develop a 'no change' policy that would keep 5 billion board feet. The Dunlop-MacCleery intervention cost the agency $500,000 and delayed the plans six months to a year." Between 1986 and 1989, the last year before environmentalists went to the courts en masse to halt timber sales, 20 billion board feet came off the national forests in the Northwest.

Meanwhile, the Fish & Wildlife Service steadfastly shirked its responsibility to protect the northern spotted owl. In 1985 it received a detailed math analysis forecasting the bird's inexorable path toward extinction. The agency and the Forest Service agreed to ignore it. In 1988 U.S. District Court judge Thomas Zilly found Fish & Wildlife's decision not to list the owl "arbitrary and capricious and contrary to the law" and directed the agency to explain its decision. Later the General Accounting Office, an investigative arm of Congress, revealed that Fish & Wildlife officials had doctored substantial parts of a major study to play down the northern spotted owl's desperate condition. Researchers admitted they felt pressured to "sanitize the report" by substituting data from the timber industry. By 1990 the agency had run out of excuses and declared the northern spotted owl threatened.

Economics and politics, not biology, drive Congress. Ever since the creation of the Forest Service, the federal government has become socially responsible for the livelihood of loggers. The hallowed doctrine of "community stability" it promotes shields timber towns from the markets' boom-and-bust vicissitudes. Counties are entitled to 25 percent of gross timber receipts in lieu of lost prop-

erty taxes because these lands are federally owned. The government earmarks the revenues ($306 million in 1992) for local roads
and schools. In a vicious cycle to retain their portion of the purse,
county commissioners and state politicians lobby Congress and
agency officials to maintain astromically high cuts, regardless of
the biological expense.

Members of the northwestern delegation have set unreasonably
high timber targets for the Forest Service through the appropriations bills. From 1980 to 1985, the cut on all national forests
exceeded the actual growth of sawtimber by 61 percent. During
the decade 40 percent overcutting was common in the Northwest's richest timber-producing forests and even reached 70 percent. According to the Forest Service's own conservative data,
for the past few years every national forest has been selling timber
at least 23 percent above the level of sustained yield. Some forest
planners have argued that those figures should be tripled.

A parade of Forest Service officials up to the chief has fessed
up to overcutting on national forests. But, in a macabre dance
among the branches of government, the agency nods and winks
at being mandated to log more than it desires. The Forest Service's officials care most about bloating its budget, keeping their
jobs, and bolstering the status quo. Senators and representatives,
backed by successive presidents, bring home pork to stay in office.
The Forest Service has served as a convenient whipping boy because the agency sells the timber and deals most intimately with
the lumber companies. But once it began retreating from its excessive cuts in the mid-1980s, only for Capital Hill to jack them up,
the true culprit emerged. "We propose and they [Congress] dispose," says Jack Ward Thomas of his agency's role.

Egged on by the timber industry, Congress has practiced the
time-honored art of logrolling, otherwise known as regionalism.
Senators and representatives from the affected areas serve on sub-
committees where they can budget the funds for such pork-barrel
projects as dams, highways, bridges, and—in the nation's far corner—timber to promote community stability. Members of the
Northwestern delegation have been traditionally appointed to appropriations committees controlling federal purse strings. Mark
Hatfield, the ranking Republican on the Senate Appropriations
Committee and an influential five-term lawmaker, has almost singlehandedly dominated federal timber policy for two decades from
this committee.

Hatfield, a progressive Republican from Oregon with a moderate record on environmental issues outside of forest policy, evokes

visceral reactions from loggers and environmentalists. "I genuinely like the guy," says Tom Hirons, contrary to his dim view of politicians in general, "and I have a great deal of respect and admiration for him." Atiyeh has revised his grass-roots speeches to train the spotlight of culpability almost entirely on the Oregon delegation. "It's not the fault of loggers, the Forest Service, or environmentalists for letting this go on as long as it has, but the people in Congress, for making promises they couldn't keep. They managed the forest as though it could go on forever. We have to beat up on Hatfield. He's the primary villain and he's not doing a damn thing to save a public resource. In these communities the rubber band is pulled so tight, it's going to snap," Atiyeh says. "Look, I don't say any of this lightly. I've known him since I was a kid in a political family. He and my Uncle Vic went into the legislature together. They were great buddies and still are. Hatfield used to come over and I'd look at him as a second uncle. I've only started going after him over the past year."

During his first term, Hatfield played a prominent role in persuading President Richard Nixon to drop an executive order restricting clear-cutting on federal forests. While cosponsoring the National Forest Management Act in 1976, he jockeyed to weaken environmental provisions. The senator won language in the law authorizing the Forest Service to depart from the principle of sustained yield, against the wishes of other sponsors in the Senate, effectively giving lumber companies carte blanche to overcut public lands as they had on private.

Hatfield rests his environmental laurels on his sponsorship of the 1984 Oregon Wilderness Act. The legislation preserved 850,000 acres of federal land and removed more than 300,000 acres from logging. Industry allies excoriated him for his infidelity, overlooking the preponderance of wilderness consisting of rocks and ice at high elevations. Conservationists attacked Hatfield for protecting only 200,000 acres of old growth. He vowed never to allow another wilderness bill in his state again. As if to make good on his pledge, in 1987 Hatfield and James McClure—an Idaho Republican and powerful colleague in the Senate in his own right from a timber state—larded appropriations for roads with $50 million more for timber roads than the $229 million requested by the pavement-happy Reagan administration.

Frenzied speculation in the late 1970s inflated the bids on public timber. The housing market's collapse in the recession a few years later enslaved timber companies to high-priced, long-term contracts on which they had to default. Billions of board feet of timber gained a reprieve as living trees. Mark Hatfield came to the rescue, passing a buyback law in 1984 to bail out his pet industry. The government tore up $2.3 billion worth of contracts and allowed the mills to repurchase the same timber for $113 million! "We would have lost 60 to 70 percent of small to medium mills," the senator now tells me. "I introduced contract relief to get them out of the great recession." His unmitigated boondoggle also wasted an incredible amount of government funds through political favoritism.

Hatfield's legislation, by all accounts, had drastic repercussions for the Northwest's economy and forests. "Whenever the Oregon economy has gotten into trouble, the politicians have thrown out timber as pork barrel without looking at the long-term effects. All of a sudden we had this big flood of timber on the market. The volume coming into the mills exceeded production capacity. It didn't end until five years later. Why do anything else but waste the resource as long as you're making money because the raw material is so low?" Atiyeh says. "Politicians are notoriously shortsighted. Instead of scaling back, they propped up mills with junk equipment that should have gone out of business ten years ago. Had Young and Morgan and Freres been forced to retool their mills, they would have become more efficient. Hatfield prevented the survival of the fittest by not letting the mills be weeded out like an elk herd."

Until losing his Senate race against Packwood, Les AuCoin teamed up with Hatfield from his position on the Appropriations Committee in the House to pump up the cut far higher than the Forest Service wanted. The Oregonian Democrat, in the top tier of unreconstructed liberals in Congress for his leadership on measures to slash defense spending and for public funding of abortions, also boasted credentials so green that he routinely earned nearly perfect ratings from Washington environmental groups. His wife, Sue used to work for the Wilderness Society, one of the harshest critics of her husband's policies. AuCoin belonged to a select group of five schizophrenic legislators in Washington who received at least $10,000 in campaign contributions from each side in the fight over ancient forests in the eight years preceding the spotted owl's listing. He ranked first in Congress in political action money from the greens, $31,896, and tenth in the House in donations from the forest and paper products industry, $41,164. According to records kept by the Federal Election Commission, in his last election to the House, AuCoin received $4,464 from the Forest

Industries Political Action Committee, the largest amount by far from that PAC in Congress.

His strange bedfellowship with Oregon's senior senator shows the grip of the Northwest's peculiar institution on its politics. AuCoin's merciless grilling of former Forest Service chief Max Peterson in 1986 for failing to meet the allowable cut went down in history as a defining moment. "The Forest Service has recommended one cut for the last twelve years, but two heavy players have raised the ante: Hatfield and AuCoin. As the flow came faster and faster, the forest had to be raped," Atiyeh says. "Rather than metering out the resource, they've tried dumping cheap old-growth timber. The days of unlimited resources are over."

Atiyeh holds Oregon's hydra in Congress personally responsible for imperiling Opal Creek and infecting Hirons with the disease that ultimately quarantined them from one another. "The ultimate big lie is the promise Congress made which it couldn't keep. The members have consciously hooked Tom and other loggers on cheap old growth. Now the pushers are out of supply for the timber junkies," says Atiyeh, falling back on his favorite analogy. "Whether it's Tom, Senator Hatfield, or AuCoin, not one of them will deal with reality. These people are all in absolute denial. By continuing to flood the market each year with federal timber, we make the problem worse and the ultimate day of reckoning that much harder to take."

Hatfield and AuCoin appeared willing to do just about anything to shore up their falling house of timber. As a last resort, since the mid-1980s conservationists have bypassed unsympathetic politicians to win federal court injunctions halting timber sales. In retaliation, Hatfield and AuCoin tacked on to appropriations bills a series of riders barring judicial review to allow logging to proceed regardless of the environmental implications. This antidemocratic restriction on citizens' ability to appeal to the courts flying entirely in the face of their strong support of civil liberties in the past, caused such an uproar that it's unlikely even to pass again.

AuCoin has insisted that he was only guarding the Northwest against competition from southern and Canadian timber. When pressed further, the congressman disengenuously blames top Forest Service officials for not warning him. The historical revisionism smacks of damage control. "I will not accept criticism from any quarter that I force-fed this agency with more timber sales than the agency could accept," the congressman snapped at the *Oregonian* for an incriminating account of his performance.

Les AuCoin can lash out at his hometown paper or the demonstrators at rallies waving "LESS AUCOIN" placards, but not hide from his own peers. "Congress has compounded the Forest Service's crisis-oriented policy by expanding the allowable cut. They've both been trying to live in a fantasyland based on assumptions of an endless supply of timber," says Bruce Vento, the chairman of the Interior Subcommittee on National Parks and Public Lands, where one in seven laws originates. "I don't think we can keep prostituting the laws." Vento has introduced legislation to stop AuCoin and his allies from doing just that.

All American taxpayers foot the hefty bill for Hatfield and AuCoin's raid on the Treasury. Robert Wolf, as if by pure serendipity, happens to be hiking on the old mining road into Opal Creek in the rain when Atiyeh and I give him a lift to a cabin at Jawbone Flats. On a visit to see his family in Portland, he is checking out for himself the block of ancient forest as he has heard so much about back in Washington, D.C. At Congress's behest, the avuncular Wolf—a forester, author of the National Forest Management Act, and emeritus economist with the Congressional Research Service—has pored over the Forest Service's books to disprove its claims that it earned $255 million in 1992. "These mythical profits are achieved by accounting alchemy," Wolf argues. By Wolf's estimates, despite a $793 million congressional appropriation, the Forest Service showed a negative cash flow of $536 million in fiscal year 1992, and $8.5 billion over the past 14 years. Evidently the Reagan-Bush administrations' aversion to government waste excluded moneylosing timber sales in national forests.

Among the creative bookkeeping Wolf has discovered was the omission of $306 million, the usual 25 percent cut of the gross sale receipts to county governments, though a conventional business subtracts taxes from profits. In addition, the Forest Service spread the costs of building logging roads over hundreds of years. One dirt and gravel logging road, built to last 25 years, in Alaska, is amortized over 1,800 years, a gimmick one congressional staffer likens to the Italian government still paying for the Appian Way. The Forest Service has admitted it has lost money on about half its 155 national forests. Congressional critics put the number at 100.

Homesteaders and railroads in the nineteenth century took the richest tracts of fertile lowlands because it wasn't worth their bother logging the arid, mountainous regions for which the Forest Service later assumed responsibility. But who can pass up a fantastic bargain when the seller, the government, picks up the tab for building the expensive roads (providing easy access for workers and machinery), insect control, and other costs, and sells off the trees for prices often far below market value.

The cozy deal has gone on for so long that industry views it as an entitlement. "Years ago, at hearings on federal timber sales in Medford [Oregon], I remember a mill owner saying," Wolf recalls at Jawbone Flats, sipping coffee by a hot wood stove, " 'I'm against socialism and I'm against communism, but I'm for a planned society.' " The losers are private tree-farmers struggling to compete with the artificially low prices the federal government creates, thus exerting further pressure on ancient forests.

The Forest Service has quit trying to defend its profligacy, diverting attention instead to missions unrelated to timber. "Our charge from Congress is to manage for net public benefit," says George Leonard, associate chief. "That's a concept that was developed to recognize that there are values to the national forestlands that are unquantifiable." Timber revenues fund programs for erosion control and saving the red-cockaded woodpecker in the Southeast. Of course, neither would require much help in the first place, absent logging. The Forest Service's perverse logic is tantamount to burning down a house to collect on the insurance for home improvement.

Waving the flag of deficit reduction, the Clinton administration is seeking to phase out subsidized sales and charge market rates for timber on national forests. Western lawmakers, long accustomed to repelling such reforms, may face a tougher challenge in this era of budgetary constraints. The mills and politicians beholden to them have only themselves to blame for the economic blows they are probably about to receive.

On the eve of the spotted owl's listing, the timber twins Hatfield and AuCoin take a final turn at bat for their special interest. They introduce a bill so extreme that even a neutral official from the Forest Service responsible for studying it describes it as "pro-timber." The legislation environmentalists deride as the "Timber Tantrum Act" would enable the Forest Service to open up areas presently off-limits to logging, such as protected wilderness, in exchange for others to protect the spotted owl—an unprecedented move. The legislation also gives the agency forty years to ratchet down the cut, by which time it would be too late. Hatfield and AuCoin deconstruct the concept of multiple use, turning the forests over to the mills for a single purpose.

In a move reeking slightly of an election-year conversion, the Oregon representative cosponsors daring—for him—bipartisan islation. It would override parts of the Endangered Species Act but establish significant old-growth reserves and protect Opal Creek. Displaced workers would receive assistance for retraining and expenses to relocate their families. "The truth is that Pacific Northwest timber harvests are coming down and will never be the same again," he tells the Portland Chamber of Commerce. "The truth is that the American people have spoken on the Endangered Species Act. They're not going to gut it."

The senator has agreed to talk at his office in the Hart Senate Office Building the day he introduces the bill. To his credit, he is not evading the hard questions while the congressman generally lays low during these eventful days, citing vital appropriations business. Hatfield's rugged good looks, a strong profile, and short-cropped, neatly combed silver hair command instant attention. His elegant, conservative suit fortifies his senatorial bearing.

Hatfield emphatically denies ever violating the principle of sustainable yield. "It's not true the Congress has forced an unrealistic cut," he says, pitching his latest legislation. "I've chosen to stand in the middle with a plan to preserve the owl with the least impact on seventy threatened communities," the senator adds in a broad indictment of the heartless obstructionists.

Throughout his discourse Hatfield drops the expression "lock up," a loaded term only used by the timber industry. Everybody else speaks of "protection" or "set aside" of wilderness. "You're talking about managed forests, watersheds, fisheries, and timber production—multiple use," he explains. " 'Lock-up' means no mining, no forestry, or agriculture." His affability surrenders to a cold gaze concentrated through stern blue eyes; as if to say, "Are you questioning me?" Oregon's voters and reporters are taken aback by Hatfield's chronic petulance. Cocking his chiseled chin and arching one eyebrow to press a point, the senator exudes the imperious aura of a man carved in stone in his own lifetime. And Hatfield is. A majestic marble bust of him has graced the Oregon Governor's office for almost a decade.

Oregon's senior senator, born in 1922, is far too intelligent and complex a public official to dismiss simply as a timber hack. The ponderosa pine of state politics has led a charmed life, compiling a perfect election record in his races since his first race to the state legislature. Whether or not Oregonians agreed with him on every issue, respect for his high-mindedness cut across party lines. His deep religious convictions motivate his opposition to abortion and the death penalty. A militant dove, he broke ranks with his party and the president in a courageous vote against the Persian

Gulf War. In its ratings, the *National Journal* has ranked him as the most liberal Republican senator.

In recent years, the brown hair has turned grayer and the jowls have sagged farther. A growing number of admirers speculate that his extraordinary length of incumbency, four decades, has compromised his renowned integrity. The latest in a long series of startling ethical lapses involve him accepting and failing to disclose thousands of dollars' worth of gifts, including artworks and travel expenses from a former university president who lobbied him for a government grant. Listing thirteen gifts, including ten—from a $400 compact disc player to $17,000 in home improvements—valued at $43,000, the Senate Ethics Committee rebuked Hatfield for "improper misconduct." Oregonians counted yet another chip falling out of their statesman's bust.

Hatfield's Beltwayitis on natural resource issues locks him in the bygone era before he left Oregon to begin his professional life in Washington, D.C. In 1966 he could still picture the endless stretches of the Northwest's frontier he enjoyed in his youth. The proximity of ancient forests to his front door back then appears to have anesthetized him permanently to its fragile splendor almost half a century later. Clutching to the timber industry's fading glory in Oregon, he refuses to face up to its diminution as a factor in the state's economy.

Of course, his own political fortunes turn on perpetuating the past. Hatfield's financial disclosure reports could suggest, as environmentalists charge, that the timber industry has "bought and paid" for him. In the first quarter of 1990, covering his most recent reelection and leading up to the "Timber Tantrum Act," he collected $45,000 in timber contributions—about a third of his receipts over that period. In the period spanning his last two elections the same industry showered him with $68,980, the second-highest total from that industry in the Senate.

The money seems well spent, given the senator's proclivity toward hewing the company line. "I'm very reluctant to get into job retraining and relocation in a public way because there's so much fear and frustration out there in those mill towns," he says in his office. "Why should I add to the anxiety by saying I've already caved in by already throwing in the sponge?" In principle, Hatfield actually supports assistance to workers. He has eagerly backed Senator Robert Byrd's amendment to compensate miners displaced by clean-air laws and approved a line item in appropriations providing comparable assistance to the Northwest's woodworkers. "I would prefer not to be linked to that," he admits. In practice, he is pandering to the timber lobbyist gallery, dead set against any concessions. In unofficial Washington, D.C., they refer to such behavior as "skirt-lifting to special interests." Oregon loggers looking to their senator for a helping hand receive the back of his.

Hatfield could see the worries in their eyes for himself were he to take the six-hour flight back home more often. Lately he has maintained a surprisingly low profile at home. "I've never been to one of those public [timber] rallies. That's deliberate," he says. "I don't think you resolve any issue out there when it's all political theater and drama. I've never engaged in that. It's not my style." The thinly veiled swipe at Packwood, Oregon's junior senator and rally enthusiast with whom Hatfield maintains a frosty relationship, shows commendable restraint for refraining from grandstanding. Yet in his grass-roots newsletter Hirons lumps Hatfield in a group of figures under suspicion for failing to show up at the timber rallies. The moment Hatfield sees it in his in box, he drafts an irate, three-page letter to Hirons and shouts at him on the phone. "I was almost stunned, it was not my intention to piss off a U.S. senator," the logger says. "But I didn't apologize. At least he remembers who I was."

With November fast approaching in 1990, an election year, the possibility of looking for new work begins to cure Hatfield of his Olympian aloofness. For most of the summer and fall he campaigns at the same methodical pace as he does in-off election years, hunkered down in Washington, D.C. In the meantime, Harry Lonsdale, a little-known Bend businessman and political neophyte, mounts a spirited challenge, putting him within striking distance in a late September poll and giving Hatfield the scare of his public life. Suddenly the senator's urgent business in Washington can wait. He hustles home to glad-hand Hirons and his neighbors at a breakfast in Mill City in one stop on a barnstorming tour through countless timber towns. His margin of victory—54 percent to 46 percent—is his lowest in almost two decades, and this against an inexperienced candidate, and months before the major ethics scandals surfaced. For all his earnestness, Lonsdale—at least in my estimation, based on personal interaction with him—appeared out of his depth on certain issues, except the two he was running on, abortion and logging. Lonsdale hammered away at Hatfield as a "timber beast" and a "timber pawn."

Alternatives to Hatfield's solution abound on Capitol Hill. Bruce Vento, the chairman of the House Interior Subcommittee on National Parks and Public Lands and presiding over the hear-

ings Atiyeh and Hirons attended, would create the Pacific Northwest Ancient Forest Reserve, spread over 6.3 million acres in
western Oregon, Washington State, and California and based on
the Thomas Report. His bill provides for number of measures
designed to alleviate economic distress in timber country, including technical assistance to boost productivity in mills and woodlands. He supports programs to construct recreational facilities
and enhance new wildlife habitat and watersheds, creating 10,000
new jobs—as many as the low-end estimates for the loggers' job
losses. Over the next five years, the amount of national forest
receipts returned to affected counties in the three states would
double, from 25 percent to 50 percent, speeding their diversification. Workers on the verge of falling through the safety net would
be entitled to $150 million in job retraining, counseling, and
placement.

That a congressman from the Midwest should present himself
as a savior of the old growth is no coincidence. He is striving to
recapture a piece of the paradise lost in his own backyard. "In
northern Minnesota, Michigan, and Wisconsin the virgin forests
were all gone 125 years ago and they won't come back," Vento,
fifty, says just before the office buzzer summons him to a floor
vote. "I remember growing up seeing those big, beautiful white
pines in the rafters of old homes. Now they're few and far between. These great forests of the Northwest are truly a national
treasure."

On Capitol Hill the so-called outsiders incur the wrath of the
northwestern delegation for meddling in their affairs. AuCoin and
Hatfield condemn other lawmakers for poaching on territory once
considered exclusively their own. "It's a bill dead on introduction," AuCoin asserts, reacting to Vento's legislation. "This does
unneeded economic damage to our region." "What about the
economy?" Hatfield asks non-Northwesterners. His aide overseeing timber issues amplifies the senator's sentiments. "The final
decision will still be made by our delegations," says Mike Sals-
giver. "Anyone who misreads that is not aware of how Congress
works."

His assumptions about the primacy of regionalism, or logrolling,
are about a decade out of date. The burgeoning environmental
movement, spearheaded by a network of members and potent
lobbyists, weakens Northwesterners' vice grip on natural resource
policy. Had the delegation exercised a modicum of restraint over
the past three decades, only a few biologists might ever have

heard of the spotted owl. Today much of the American public knows and, judging from polls, cares about the imperiled species.

The Northwesterners' supreme asset, a Speaker of the House from Washington State, so far takes a backseat. Tom Foley, far removed from any action in Congress setting the Democrats' agenda, appears indifferent to the conflict engulfing his home state. In response to reporters, inquiries about legislation assisting dislocated workers, Foley once referred vaguely to a bill aimed at communities in northern California that he recalls passing in the late 1960s. A five-minute phone call from an aide would have set him straight about its actual passage a decade later. Once he finally spoke out, all Foley could think of is emasculating the Endangered Species Act.

In his failed bid to retain the White House, George Bush perpetuated his woeful performance on the logging issue. North of Mill City, at the foothills of the Cascades in Washington State, he railed against the Endangered Species Act in the strongest terms ever by a president, likening it to a "sword aimed at the jobs, families, and communities of entire regions like the Northwest." He promised to use the full force of his office to topple every legal roadblock in the way of logging the last ancient forests. "Its time to put people ahead of owls. This will not stand," the president declared, borrowing his tired phrase from the Gulf War while pumping his fist in the air and grimacing. "I mean it." The president couldn't resist his "red meat" rhetoric, jabbing at Clinton in a debate for pandering to the "the spotted owl crowd." A Clinton presidency, he later asserted, would mean "no timber workers, only a bunch of owls."

Hirons scoffed at the president's desperate ploy to keep his job. "I don't trust him," he says. "Why'd he wait so long?"

The 1992 presidential election's outcome may have helped lay to rest the false choice between environmental protection and job growth, from which Bush and Dan Quayle struggled to make political hay against their opponents. Clinton acknowledged that he learned such trade-offs are counterproductive. They boost environmental clean-up costs without creating any new jobs. As Arkansas governor he improved his mix record on conservation by preserving thousands of acres of wildlands in his state and promoting the safeguarding of endangered species. As further proof of the false choice, Al Gore argued more strenuously than any other member of Congress that in the Northwest loggers would lose their jobs when the last, irreplaceable trees fall anyway. Exit polls on election day revealed that Bush's general environmental views cost him a lot, particularly among suburban voters, for whom these issues cut deeply. The Clinton-Gore team even swept the Northwest with plenty of room to spare.

A growing number of economists and environmentalists advocate shutting down all national forests to logging. After all, the timber famine the Forest Service has warned the nation about since the agency's founding has never materialized. Timber use in this nation peaked in 1908, before oil and gas heat supplanted wood-burning fireplaces and stoves. Per capital wood consumption has declined ever since. Modern agricultural techniques have accelerated the growth and cultivation of trees, accounting, in part, for their greater quantity today than in 1920. More than 70 percent of the nation's forestlands now belong to private ownership in less environmentally sensitive areas. The elimination of taxpayers' subsidies for timber in a free market would give small tree-growers the incentive and edge to pick up the slack from the loss of federal lands. Timber towns would reap the ancillary benefits of a new source of dollars from recreation on intact ancient forests.

However valid, these approaches, largely espoused by the northeastern intelligentsia, develop policy as though in a vacuum. An immediate halt to logging would wreak social havoc on timber towns such as Mill City already beset by uncertainty. By contrast, a steep, graduated reduction over the next five years and infusion of aid from timber receipts would ease the transition to new economies in concert with their environmental surroundings. The government owes these good people that much, having weaned them on cheap old growth. Atiyeh, living and breathing the discord in Mill City, favors prescribing to loggers scraps of biologically insignificant scraps of old growth as their "methadone program" rather than forcing them to go "cold turkey." Despite the burgeoning popularity of ancient forests as a cause in Washington, D.C., the lumber companies' omnipotence precludes an ideal solution. Atiyeh realizes how hard it is to achieve any ban on logging, let alone a total one. He and his moderate associates will settle for saving Opal Creek and the remaining blocks of ancient forest of a comparable magnitude.

This crisis would never have reached such monumental proportions had public officials husbanded a precious resource instead of selling it for a song. Big industry and politicians are guilty of colluding to bend the rules in their favor. The grim facts about the consequences of their actions stared them in the face for twenty-five years. They orphaned the spotted owls, last vestiges of old growth, and, ultimately, the loggers themselves for their own short-term expedience.

The problem transcends any single issue to the breakdown of American government. Strangled by special interests and collective shortsightedness, the government seems unable to meet the country's growing challenger. Washington, D.C., has obscured the federal deficit through legislative tricks and dithers about enacting sorely needed education reform. The last decade's government by symbolism has rested on a montage of photo opportunities in which a president can pose in a national park in L. L. Bean clothes to certify his environmental credentials. The missed opportunities in Washington, D.C., reinforce the rampant cynicism among Americans about government's ability to improve their lives. Small wonder Americans turned out a sitting president in 1992.

In the end, however, Americans bear the burden for leaving loggers and spotted owls out on a limb. Though we live in a system far from Athenian democracy or a New England town hall meeting, the republicanism envisioned by the founding fathers affords considerable opportunity to translate private decency into public interest. The deterioration of government—unlike other troubled institutions, from the church to the family—is nothing that cannot be addressed on election day. In 1992, Americans expressed the strongest desire in a generation to become involved again and to back an activist government. Now the responsibility falls on Clinton and Gore to fulfill their promise and balance the spiritual and practical urgency of saving Opal Creek against the fundamental fairness of granting Hirons the new lease on life he has earned.

XII

Buzzsaws and Olive Branches

The fragmented old growth Hirons and other loggers need to feed the mills cuts into the conservationists' plans to set aside at least a few pieces for posterity. Two ill-starred efforts to forge a compromise succumb to bitter political sniping. In the ugly aftermath of SB 500, the bill establishing a state park at Opal Creek, Atiyeh calls Jim Morgan and Hirons in a conciliatory mood to help release some timber that environmentalists have ensnared in legal injunctions. They whip out maps of the Detroit Ranger District and the list of sales stuck in the pipeline. Atiyeh flies them over the forest in his plane.

"George, we're not getting anyplace," Hirons says. "You can't sign off for all the crazies on this shit."

"I know what they're interested in and not interested in," Atiyeh replies. "No one cares a lot about the biologically insignificant fragments." His generosity stops at Opal Creek's edge, of course.

After a month of hypothetical horse-swapping, an exasperated Hirons turns to other matters and delegates his responsibilities to Ray Weber, a timber cruiser who estimates standing timber for Young and Morgan. Atiyeh gives him a table and free rein of his own Save the Opal Creek Council office at the airfield. They work with environmental groups and Senator Mark Hatfield's office. Nothing comes of it.

A few months later, during the midsummer, Detroit District ranger Dave Alexander makes a last-ditch effort to forge a compromise. Officially his creation is known as a local advisory group.

Atiyeh would soon end up dubbing it the Fruitless Discussion Group. Alexander boldly seeks to take the thorniest issue on his watch, Opal Creek, out of the hands of politicians, who had flubbed the park bill, SB 500, and uphold the principle of self-determination for the citizens directly involved. He and a pair of his staffers appoint a dozen of the pivotal players from both sides of the conflict to mediate. They tap Atiyeh, Hirons, and Jim Morgan. The participants agree to focus on Opal Creek, a hot spot close to home and ideally suited to serve as a microcosm for issues about the forest at large. Alexander budgets twenty-thousand dollars, and hires a Seattle-based mediator with a forestry degree and skilled in western natural resources disputes.

Three evening sessions at the Chummery in Salem, site of the spotted owl conference, leave everyone where they started. Hirons and industry demand a constant, guaranteed flow of timber over a certain land base encompassing Opal Creek. Atiyeh and the other environmentalists counter that Opal Creek is nonnegotiable and must receive federal protection as pristine wilderness. On the sidelines, Atiyeh privately plans to barter land for logs, lopping off six thousand acres of thirty-one thousand acres from the original state park proposal and agreeing to drop most of the appeals they have filed against sales in the Detroit District covering spotted owl habitat. His plan never even has a chance to hit the bargaining table.

Politics and personalities dash all hopes for the compromise from the start. Since inflaming passions in state capitals through log truck demonstrations against the northern spotted owl and counterprotests on the owl's behalf, industry and the environmentalists have galvanized national attention. Both sides have thus deemed it in their interest to export the issue to Washington, D.C., where they've been accumulating plenty of frequent-flier miles rushing off to lobby U.S. representatives. "They're saying, 'If I can get my situation settled in Congress, I don't need to fool around with these local people,' " Alexander says. "They may have the force of laws behind them in Washington [,D.C.], but in truth the best solution is with the locals." On the heels of the verbal confrontations in the hearing rooms, the rancor still runs deep leading up to the opening bargaining session. "It was a very uncomfortable situation," Alexander says afterward. "People came to meet after they had been at each others' throats."

The line Hirons's group had drawn in concrete denied it any room to maneuver. In their view, all restrictions on logging in the Opal Creek area imperil logging's future. "Every damn thing we've worked for in the last twenty-five years was on the line and those motherfuckers sat there with their arms folded across their chests. A waste of fucking time. The only thing we're being asked to negotiate is our extinction," Hirons roars. "I'd sure like to know the true motivation behind their agendas. The National Wildlife Federation, Audubon—all those high-paid jerks in Washington, D.C. The timber industry guys are a bunch of hacks, just as much as the other side. Just by their nature, the more there's controversy, the more need there is for them."

Atiyeh and his cohorts have boxed themselves in by putting Opal Creek totally off-limits to their adversaries' chainsaws. "They're dumb," he explains. "What they have to do is give me Opal Creek. We're not talking morals, just straight political strategy. They can have all the fragmented stuff, which is most of what's left. If they'd save the last four big blocks of it, they'd cut the knees out from the environmentalists. Their constituency would have to start completely over from scratch trying to build name recognition for places. By that time the issue would be over. It's like someone poisoning the Tylenol capsule. The manufacturer pulls every bottle. So does Perrier [whose bottled mineral water became tainted]. It defused the issue. You're always better off doing the right thing and controlling it yourself at the same time. The loggers are losing the battle themselves. I've told them they were the best fund-raisers for the environmental groups that have ever come down the pike. Politically, they're idiots."

Hirons doubts Atiyeh can hold up his end of the bargain in any pact. "Jim and I would be glad to give him Opal Creek. But he wouldn't shut up and go away," Hirons says. "He's told me it's the flagship. You'd have to give him and the others everything else. The preservation movement's standard line is to save all the old growth." Industry's domino theory—whereby the fall of Opal Creek to the conservationists will bring the entire forest with it—forestalls any concession.

"Everyone was feeding off each other and looking for me and Tom to have a confrontation with George. He was looking for some sort of compromise to save his own soul," Jim Morgan says. "I told him, 'We're going to the wall, win or lose.' The time to compromise isn't when you're sitting there shooting each other. It was a secret mission. Most people in the community don't know about it. I don't know even if I want them to know about it. They'd think we're talking to the enemy. We couldn't do that publicly. Even if we wanted to have coffee, we wouldn't dare."

By a bizarre quirk of fate, Atiyeh and Hirons are scheduled as the two speakers at an Earth Day seminar at Linn-Benton Community College in Albany, Oregon. Hirons briefly considers backing out when he learns with whom he has to share the stage, but thinks better of it. He is going only because he once attended the school and the son of an old logging friend has extended the invitation.

The most recent row over Opal Creek and logging of ancient forest has kept Atiyeh and Hirons apart for two months, the longest stretch for them since they first met twenty years ago. The awkward and brief interlude at the owl conference in Salem augurs poorly for any sort of détente in the near future. Still, out of personal concern and professional curiosity, I discreetly broach the idea to each of them, in private, of the three of us meeting over a cup of coffee after their speaking engagement. The suggestion doesn't go down particularly well at first.

Hirons shoots one of his legendary glowers, as if I had just tipped the yarder over on his job, and throws the "rigging fit," a logger's temper tantrum he specialized in while running North Fork. "I've told you George and I can't talk for five minutes without pissing each other off. Look, I haven't had a paycheck in three months. Besides that, I've always been the one to break the ice for over twenty years. So let George break it this time."

Atiyeh suffers conflicting emotions. "I think Tom's scared. He's quit coming over. I feel the animosity isn't on my side. It's Tom's responsibility and I'm disappointed in him. His fucking job compared to Opal Creek is worth shit as far as I'm concerned," he fires back to me in his half of the Atiyeh-Hirons monologue. "I'll walk into a buzzsaw ten times and be kicked down, but Tom is going to have to accept it. It's pretty hard to offer an olive branch when they won't take it."

The conservationist still clings to the dream, perhaps an illusion, that in the end Hirons will come around. "I would do anything but give him Opal Creek. I cannot shut up. I know what I'm doing is right. They don't really understand. I would love to settle this more than they would. I want to see Opal Creek saved and I don't want to see the loggers hurt more than is necessary. If Tom asked me to do anything, if he needed help, I'd do it. Even though we're still on the outs, that relationship is still very important to me."

Hirons tosses the compliment back in Atiyeh's face. "He's so slick, he can afford to speak highly of me. He has my fucking back against the wall."

"I hope Tom can sort out the politics. I know, deep down, he doesn't believe," Atiyeh replies to me. "It's been a real strain on both of us lately."

Bouncing back between the two adversaries like a harried Middle East envoy, I reiterate my offer to broker the meeting. "I'll meet him on one condition: We don't talk issues," Hirons erupts. "And I DON'T want no touchy-feely shit."

George laughs at the precondition and agrees. "I'll do it. I don't know if Tom really wants to," he says. "The only way this thing is going to be settled is if Tom has a way of saving face."

Another day older and deeper in debt since the Fruitless Discussion Group, Hirons believes his only choice is to stay the course. Aside from hard economic facts, he would no sooner scrap the career ingrained in his identity than Atiyeh would allow Opal Creek to be violated. "I'm a logger, a damn good logger," he avers. "If I wanted to quit what I'm doing, I would." Hirons has made it clear he regards retraining as a "cruel hoax."

"In a lot of ways, it's impossible for Tom and me to be seen in public," Atiyeh says. "I tell people he's my friend, but he can't. I think that's kind of weird." The anger swells inside Atiyeh in anticipation of his hopeful rapprochement. "These guys have created a strange reality among themselves. They are driven by the people around them. You know what I'm going to tell him?" Atiyeh fumes. "His hero was Hank Stamper in that book [Ken Kesey's *Sometimes a Great Notion*, a northwestern epic set in timber country and that Hirons has read twice], and Tom's just the opposite. He had this tremendous respect for Hank Stamper, who would say 'Fuck you!' I'm the one who's ended up to have to do that. Stamper didn't interfere with what he felt was right. He lost his wife, his brother. Everything. Tom's never been a coward before. Maybe he's more concerned about his social standing than I've ever been."

Hirons admits industry's long arm keeps him a safe distance from Atiyeh. "If Jim and I tried anything," he says of the mediation sessions, "we would have been isolated from the rest of the industry." Had Atiyeh taken leave of his senses when he approached him? "If I had testified, I would never have another logging job in this state again, they would have put so much pressure on Young and Morgan to get rid of me. Jim would have sold me down the river," Hirons says. "There are lots of players I can't afford not to get along with. I gotta walk a soft path out there."

The verbal pyrotechnics appear to preclude them from repairing their friendship and, perhaps, cutting their own separate deal as a lesson to the other disputants. "If Tom and I came up with a solution by ourselves we would self-destruct pretty fast. The community feels it has lost already, so the climate isn't ripe for that yet. And as the issue became nationalized, we lost control," Atiyeh says. "Stamper said, 'Never give an inch.' The frustration is why we have to go to such extremes to settle. The state park bill started this process, and then industry raised its head and went crazy. I'm very sad it has become so vicious. I've stuck my hand out and had it slapped, so I figure it's stupid to do it anymore."

Personalities aside, Atiyeh laments the narrow window of compromise years of overcutting have closed. "The big problem Tom and I have in trying to work this thing out is there ain't hardly enough for either side to give on," he says. "The less each side has to give, the less chance it has of bringing the others along."

Hirons harbors identical doubts. "I've asked George, 'When you're going on about those fragments of forest, what the hell are you talking about, 50 million board feet, 30 million board feet?' He doesn't know. It's really hard for us to talk about Opal Creek or even the Detroit District as though this goddamn thing existed in a vacuum," Hirons says of the issue's elevation to the national arena. "George and I are both packing a helluva lot more baggage than a few years ago. George has this whole community against him. I have this whole community lined up behind me. Maybe Jim and I could talk about it. But you can't approach a lot of the other guys [mill owners]."

They both admit to being burdened by the baggage Hirons dwells on. "I can't speak for everybody on my side." Hirons says, "just like George can't speak for everybody on his side." Adds Atiyeh: "I'm willing to call it quits anytime they are. But I can't do it unilaterally. And it would take a lot of courage on Tom's part."

At Linn-Benton Community College, a modern complex 90 miles from Mill City, Atiyeh delivers his fifteen-minute speech while dressed in a leather jacket bearing the insignia of Project LightHawk, the green air force for which he flies to publicize the loss of ancient forest. He highlights his lifelong affinity for Opal Creek and his concerns about neighbors in trouble. The audience claps enthusiastically.

During a short intermission, Hirons takes the last drag on a cigarette in the hallway. Atiyeh walks offstage and out the door and straight into him. Their dance in the dark is about to end. "Hey, George," Hirons says. "How's Aziz? I heard he rolled the rig."

"He's fine, Tom. You see my speech?"

"Nah. I don't want to come up there and refute everything you said."

Atiyeh laughs loudly. "You mind if I watch you?" Atiyeh climbs up stairs to a distant corner of the amphitheater by himself.

Hirons is the first speaker from the timber industry these students have ever heard. Atiyeh has learned through the environmental grapevine of plans for a band of Earth First!ers to harass Hirons. On the drive over, he vows to come to his defense. Hirons's address goes on without a hitch. His former friend sits in rapt attention, chin in hand far up in back in the auditorium's elevated rows, sublimating his urge to fire questions at his nemesis. With the framed Opal Creek poster Atiyeh left behind still standing against the podium, Hirons recounts his descent from a proud American yeoman, providing essential material for success, to a probable bankruptcy victim. He muses on a road to Opal Creek and the valuable timber. Pregnant pauses between his points of emphasis heighten the dramatic impact. A middle-aged woman keeps shaking her head. In the question-and-answer period she challenges Hirons to come clean about his true intentions regarding the elimination of ancient forests. "I assume you've already made up your mind," Hirons shoots back, as though upbraiding one of his crew, before giving her a quick biology lesson on old growth.

He receives less applause than Atiyeh. His old logging friend's son mounts the stage to express his gratitude. "I really want to thank you for coming," the student says. "I really believe that for you to face a stacked deck took a lot of courage." He touches on the very quality that Atiyeh believes Hirons must display to risk coming to terms with him.

Off the stage, Atiyeh asks me, then Tom, if we'd like to grab some coffee. Hirons agrees. He glances around to double-check whether a woman from his Communities for Great Oregon office, who spoke of attending his speech today, showed up. He won't even hazard a guess about the repercussions if the town finds out about his clandestine rendezvous.

At the T&R Restaurant, a classic truck stop, the three of us wedge ourselves into a booth, Atiyeh and Hirons on opposite sides. A huge truck driver at another table devours a gargantuan steak and two glassfuls of milk. Atiyeh and Hirons break the ice chatting about family.

"How about going back to what you were doing?" Atiyeh asks.

"Going in and buying and selling farmers' patches? Leverage the hell out of them. I know it's hard, but you're smarter."

"I'm not so sure about that," Hirons replies. "I guess I'm not as smart as I thought I was. I'm afraid we're in the process of biting the dust and picking up the pieces. I'm beginning to wonder if the goddamn hassle is worth it." Hirons bemoans his cash-flow problems and the creditors hounding him ever since he purchased the costly yarder.

Atiyeh shakes his head over the piece of equipment he begged Hirons not to buy. "I'm not saying nothing," he interjects before cutting himself off.

"What's got me down is there's nothing out there. The only thing that gives me a glimmer of hope is the windfall [blown-down trees]. When push comes to shove I can do what I did in the late '70s and early '80s. There's enough to pay the bills, put some beans on the table, and keep me alive. I've been told if I want it, to get my ass up there fast. Damn, it ain't much. But I could use that right now. Just for morale's sake."

Hirons broaches the prickly subject of the *Prime Time Live* show, the source of so much bad blood between them. He assures Atiyeh his anger is directed not at him, for his embellished résumé as a former logger, but at the reporter Chris Wallace for sucker-punching him about cutting down ancient trees. Atiyeh is sympathetic. "The thing that pissed me off about that show," he says, "is that I keep saying the politicians are the villains. They're the ones who created the crisis. They're the ones with the solution."

"Those bastards!"

"We have common ground there," Atiyeh says, swallowing a mouthful of apple pie smothered in cheddar cheese. "How much sympathy do you think you'll gain on the national agenda?"

"I don't think we'll gain any. The public mind-set is that we can let so many millions starve every year in developing countries if we have to. It doesn't seem to bother anyone too much. You know forty thousand laid-off autoworkers in Detroit don't get half a sound bite on the national news. If nobody feels it, it ain't there. All the guy in Cleveland sees on television is an ugly clear-cut or a cute spotted owl up a tree. He hears about ancient forests. 'Goddamn, yeah!' We'll never overcome the visuals. Never, even if I make the world's best speech. But the pendulum is going to swing back. Everybody is willing to pay the price of a better environment till they have to."

"We'll see."

"In our rush to protect the environment," Hirons says, "we can't sacrifice all our physical and economic values."

"Our life-style is going to change, no matter what. I gotta disagree with you when you say poverty is the root of the problem. Look at the rate of consumption. The full model of success is not the United States. We're not the example, and that's what we're trying to sell. The more wealth, the more you are consuming. Donald Trump ought to be killed."

"The American Dream of a house is not achievable for the average American," Hirons replies.

"As long as the Japanese are competing with us for lumber supply that argument isn't going to hold water. You can't say we're cutting forest to provide housing to Americans when a great portion of it goes to the Japanese market. That's the one thing that really bothers me. We ought to be producing more dollars from our lumber. You can never lose the market share for quality."

Hirons returns to the troubles lying ahead for timber towns. "What the hell are we going to do for these communities that take the biggest hit? Retraining and economic diversity have a hollow ring."

"We need tax credits and other assistance for timber-dependent communities so you're all not going to be tour guides. Congress created the crisis. Congress has an obligation to stop it. It's even worse than a national disaster because they did it. They're the problem."

"You have to be very careful about how you provide assistance. You know the nature of the industry. Jesus Christ, we're independent contractors and we're not taking nothing for nothing. Everything I've gotten in my life I've worked for. I ain't taking no fucking handout. When push comes to shove, if the government wants to buy that 208 [yarder], they can have it for exactly what I owe on the damn thing."

"It isn't a handout, Tom. The polarizing rhetoric has to change. You guys are hurting yourselves by blaming, quote, 'the radical preservationists' because it isn't true."

Each man gazes intently at the other. Hirons drums his fingers softly on the brown Formica table while talking and rests his chin in his cupped right hand while listening. A napkin and an empty Marlboro pack lie twisted and crumpled next to his coffee cup. Atiyeh draws lines on the table with a fork and a spoon. He then puts his utensils down to stroke his mustache with his fingers. Since checking their egos at T&R's door, the two are stripping away public personas down to fundamental disagreements over principles.

Both men look weary in the artificial light. "I'm too out of shape to get up the mountains," Atiyeh grumbles.

"I can't hike up the sides on my logging jobs either." Hirons removes his aviator glasses to rub his eyes.

"I want to go back to the life before. I really want it over with."

"I'm going to go out of my rabbit-ass mind pretty quick if I don't get back in the brush. I'm on the verge of being a basket case now. I'm trying to stay mellow around the house. I've lashed out at Marlene. It lasts only a few seconds. There was a time when that would have been a great excuse to go out drinking. However unjust it might be, what do you expect? You just get into an uncontrollable rage."

"It's tough on my kids growing up. Arins can't take it anymore. When he comes home and tells me his friend is moving because of the owl, I tell him he knows that isn't what it's all about, but he thinks he's gotta carry the whole burden on his shoulders. Do you like all this political shit? I don't."

"Fuck, no. I hate it with a passion. You running around with an 'ENVIRONMENTALIST FROM HELL' bumper sticker and me running around with yellow ribbons. That is polarization. What I'm trying to do is work myself out of a job at the CGO office, if at all possible." Once again, Hirons blames the conservation and timber groups in Washington, D.C., for perpetuating the conflict. Atiyeh concurs.

"Probably together, we could do it," Atiyeh says. "But I don't know how."

"I think that's a pipe dream," Hirons responds. "What are you and I gonna do? Call a national press conference, sit down, and hug each other?"

"Fuck that shit, Tom. What I'm saying is you and I can come up with a solution. We have so much invested in all of this. I've found I can still influence what goes on in Washington. If you orchestrate your end with a coalition so it's not just two guys sitting up there saying, 'We've known each other and been friends.' If you could bring people in and I could, there's a possibility."

"I don't know how we're going to do this." Hirons clears his throat.

Atiyeh starts to laugh. "How about doing it as our parting shot? Let's order a one-way ticket out of Mill City."

"Damn right. Better make that two tickets. You're astute enough to know there are people out there capable of doing that, too."

"I've had threats," Atiyeh says. He updates Hirons about the spotted owl carcass recently found at Opal Creek and subsequent threats he received on the phone.

"I've had threats, too," Hirons reminds him. The two of them commiserate further between slurps of coffee.

Far from the crush of cameras and notebooks, the two men are engaged in the painful process of restoring a friendship battered by months of relentless abuse. I sit back in silence to watch the natural thaw of this cold war. Mutual affection unites them in the high-minded gambit they are conceiving hand-in-hand. "Hunger is the handmaid of genius," Mark Twain wrote. Atiyeh and Hirons hunger peace and sanity. From today's intellectual interaction emerges the embryonic stages of the Albany Accord.

They pick up where they left off at the Fruitless Discussion Group, bandying about swatches of forest in their budding peace plan. "Give me a place to start with," Hirons says. "We can talk about the Detroit District. You and I can agree on that real quick." Opal Creek. Elkhorn. Devil's Ridge. Cedar Creek, Box Canyon. Hirons inquires about federally protected wilderness areas.

"No, no, Tom," Atiyeh admonishes him. "Politically, that issue would blow up. There's a real emotional attachment to those places in this country." Atiyeh directs his attention to the small, unconnected blocks of forest: "Nobody's going to get emotionally attached to isolated hundred-acre pieces out there."

"We're talking about a 50 percent reduction in the twenty-year timber supply," Hirons says. "I understand we can live with a one-third reduction. We need to get together a whole package."

Of course, the spotted owl constitutes the wild card looming over any proposal. Atiyeh promises to consult Jim Farrell, the Detroit District's chief biologist, to evaluate its habitat requirements and study his unique collection of maps. "I'll talk to him and do some digging. I don't know if we can go anyplace. You and I'll have to try to identify timber sales together."

"You start talking about drawing lines on a map, we need a neutral third party," Hirons says, "someone to send messages back and forth."

"Yeah, to settle the thing."

Hirons swigs his umpteenth cup of black coffee. Neither of the traditional rituals of conciliation—smoking a peace pipe or breaking bread—could possibly induce the caffeine high he and Atiyeh share in upholding their lofty ideals at this moment. My own fingers tremble from the overdose. Over the three hours we end up spending at T&R, I must excuse myself three times. Atiyeh does once. Hirons remains fixed in his seat. His intestinal fortitude or iron constitution, reinforced by his penchant for swallowing snuff juice, never cease to amaze. This afternoon, his Olympian powers of concentration block out the distractions of mere mortals.

"I think you and I could pull it off," Hirons says. "But I don't know if we could ever get the others to agree with us. We tried it before at last year's Opal Creek sessions."

"Tom, let's keep all the lines of communication open."

"That's not going to be nearly as easy as it was even last time [at the Fruitless Discussion Group]. Jim [Morgan, Hirons's client] knows we're talking."

"He's the only one who needs to know," Atiyeh says. "Unless our phones are tapped, we don't need to tell anybody else."

But if nobody knows, Atiyeh and Hirons realize they are only play-acting in the vacuum they've brushed against all along. Any plan requires allies. At the same time, they understand the perilous consequences if they're caught consorting. Atiyeh wants the death threats to remain just that, threats. Hirons is already in dire straits. The mill owners could blackball him right out of Mill City and into financial ruin. "Our idea is a start, but it doesn't mean shit," Atiyeh says, "if we still have all the turmoil around us." He and Hirons are trapped by an intractable dilemma.

"You and I aren't going very far alone, George. I gotta have more players in the camp and I can't do an end run around them."

"You know, Tom, if you and I do it we're both going to get run over. We have to bring in players from both sides. I have no problem with Jim." Atiyeh asks Hirons about Rob Freres, a mill owner and his implacable foe from Mill City since the hostilities broke out. "Robby looked so bad on *Rage over Trees* [the Audubon special], there's no way for him to save face," Atiyeh says. "That's a real stumbling block."

"You can't count him out." Puffs of a Marlboro mask the worry lines on Hirons's face. "Anyway, within two or three weeks, we could be back to our rhetoric."

"Oh, no, Tom. My speech has changed. I don't go after industry or after the Forest Service. Only after the Oregon delegation [in Congress]. I'm going to be shutting up pretty quick. I'm pretty much burned out. This is the last chapter, no matter what happens. I would like to see a solution. We have to do serious homework. I don't know if it's a pipe dream, but let's exchange information."

"It would sure screw up the whole debate," Hirons says. "We ought to do it just for kicks."

"I think I ought to get out of town, you get out of Mad Creek, and we'll blow everybody's mind," Atiyeh chimes in. "Fuck 'em all. That will be the happy ending."

Bright daylight has turned to grayish dusk and then black dark in the restaurant's windows. The trucks' headlights knife through the dark parking lot. Hirons peeks at his watch. "We've been drinking coffee for three hours," he says with a gasp, as though snapped out of a hypnotic state. Time has stood still for the moment.

On the trip back to Mill City, an overwound Atiyeh analyzes Hirons, the man, and his predicament. "He's gotta get out of this, I can't do it. 'I'm too old to start over again. Woe's me.' That's the saddest part in this whole damn thing, and I wanted to jump over him for it. He's been pushed to the edge, hanging on to something that's gone," Atiyeh says. "I'm not any smarter than Tom. I don't have any more self-confidence. I have to accept that I'm going to have to adapt. My life is going to change. This is a guy who has spent his whole life fighting. He's just fighting for the wrong cause. He's still Tom. He's going to have to climb back out of this SOB and kick some ass."

The lingering mental image of Hirons's haggardness eats at him. "I worry about him. Goddamn it, he won't quit smoking. He's hunched over. I don't know if his back is bothering him. You know the guy's been through the ringer. He ran his truck off the side of the mountain."

Despite his friend's travails, the meeting of the minds has lifted Atiyeh's spirits about their unique opportunity. "I have tremendous empathy for Tom and don't want to see him get hurt. I think he cares enough about Opal Creek, the thing I'm in love with, to bring us together."

I see Hirons the next day back in Mill City. Emotionally drained, he prefers letting the experience soak in to fumbling for the right words. "That was a gut-wrenching experience yesterday. I'm still sweating."

In weeks to come he mulls over the Albany Accord. "I'm ready to cave in on Opal Creek. If George and I could figure out a way to do an end run around Andy Kerr [of the Oregon Natural

Resources Council], I'd have to figure out a way to do an end run around the big boys down the road [the mill owners]," Hirons ventures. "I'm thinking strategy out loud with you. It would be easy to get the rug pulled out from under us. Right now and for the immediate future we gotta be damn careful who we talk to."

Atiyeh envisages his own breakthrough. "If Tom and I came up with some solution, we probably could force the debate. We have to ratchet logging down on a basis sustainable for the environment while ensuring timber is going to be cut in perpetuity. I want to work something out with them as a moderating influence because they need help. The whole issue has to be what is good for the land and the people."

XIII

Epilogue

One year since my last visit, Hirons plies the familiar but treacherous Forest Service road up to Opal Creek in his Ford XL, admiring the spectacular scenery only as a logger can. A jarring clear-cut, still left from last summer, stares from the opposite slope. Atiyeh, who has never lost a legal appeal protecting Opal Creek, did not try to block it since he thought the logging site was over the next ridge. He continues to scourge himself for allowing the blemish—where trees may never grow again on the fragile terrain—to assault the senses in the gateway to Opal Creek. Hirons expounds on the benefits of producing additional lumber here: "It would be good forestry to take out a third of the trees to get rid of these clumps. Instead of competing for space and sun, it would release the dominant ones to grow bigger and you'd never be able to tell there had been a logging job. George always said that when I drove through this I start salivating."

In fact, Hirons comes not to bury Opal Creek, but to hike it with Atiyeh and me through the ancient forests and down memory road. He and Atiyeh have spent the past year since their secret mission in Albany reassembling the pieces of their broken friendship. Today they are closer than ever. Besides daring to have coffee with him in public and in Mill City, Hirons is back to fraternizing with him on a regular basis during daily visits to Atiyeh's home at the airfield. They have serious work to do together. Their mutual fears, frustrations, and hopes have emboldened them to craft a bold political compromise to resolve the ancient-forest crisis. It promises to ensure Opal Creek and the logging industry's survival at the same time. In preparation for a landmark bargaining session at the Detroit District office, Atiyeh and Hirons agree to joint tours of a historic logging camp and Opal Creek to understand each other's viewpoint better.

Although my modest proposal for Atiyeh and Hirons to meet in Albany proved auspiciously timed in sowing the seeds of their relationship's renewal, the initial overtures would doubtless have occurred anyway. Perhaps the development was an inevitable by-product of my quiet intervention. Atiyeh, a science enthusiast, cites Heisenberg's uncertainty principle of quantum mechanics on a subatomic-particle level. The observer, by his sheer measurement of events, influences their outcome. "You've become a key character in bringing Tom and me together. The rapprochement would have been at a different time and it may have been too late," Atiyeh explains. "Even though we still disagreed after you left, we at least started talking again."

Atiyeh and Hirons's rapport has glued their newest partnership. "Philosophically, we are diametrically opposed, but by talking again we've come to some reasonable conclusions," Atiyeh says at his airfield while waiting for Hirons to arrive. "We are friends, and that friendship transcends all."

Healthy disagreements that once ruptured their relationship now sustain it. "In my speeches I've talked about the hole inside people. Tom defines his arguments in the Bible's Judeo-Christian tradition. They don't necessarily have to be mutually exclusive, but at the same time Opal Creek is still my church," Atiyeh says. "I don't put man above the other beings that live in the forest. Tom believes that human beings are made in God's image. But he cares about and loves the forest. Riding with him through it the other day, I said, 'What the hell are you doing, counting logs?' He said, 'Hell, no. I'm really enjoying it. The forest's really beautiful.' "

Atiyeh's supercharged idealism obscures the gritty pragmatism underlying their compromise plan. He is still racing against the clock to save Opal Creek. No sooner had the court ruled against the U.S. Forest Service and awarded Shiny Rock patents to Jawbone Flats' mines than the Bureau of Land Management dredged up musty documents from Grandpa Hewitt's reign in the early 1950s to dispute Atiyeh's title to other claims he has used so effectively to fend off timber interests. He has scampered across the Northwest to track down a pair of miners in their nineties who worked with Hewitt and could vouch for his enterprise's legitimacy. In Washington, D.C., the political stalemate leaves Opal Creek as vulnerable as ever.

While the tempest in Mill City is largely subsiding, the vital interests at issue mitigate against halcyon days returning again. As Marlene Hirons points out, the anger has mostly shifted from Atiyeh and the state capital to Washington, D.C. "In human terms, I have to live with these people in town. I can't sit back and be calling them a bunch of dirt bags and slimeballs forever," Atiyeh says. "Tom and I are working for the whole good and want to be bringing the whole community back together."

Last year, Hirons railed against anything reeking of "touchy-feely" before agreeing to sit down at the same table with Atiyeh in Albany. Since the reconciliation between Atiyeh and him, he has hardly undergone a radical transformation to a New Age-sensitive man. "I don't pack a grudge," he says, "but we're not exactly going to walk down the streets with our arms around each other." Hirons is the first to concede he's acting as much out of self-interest as altruism. Over the past year, his business woes have only worsened. Spiraling prices for the timber bought by logging companies and a depressed lumber market have put the wood trade on hold. Hirons and Mad Creek Logging stayed inactive for four straight months at one point. The possibility of declaring Chapter 11 bankruptcy looms over him like a constant virus. This past winter he applied for unemployment benefits for the first time in his life. Hirons depends on the $211 a week for which he and his crew are eligible, a far cry from their earnings in the brush. Hirons thinks his entitlement is richly deserved. "I've been paying taxes for more than twenty years," he says. "I might as well collect a little bit."

His plight appears to justify his gambit with Atiyeh. "There's a sense that if something doesn't happen," Hirons says, "a whole bunch of us are going off the edge of a damn cliff in the next six months." As a result, Hirons has assiduously courted Jim Morgan and the rest of the moderate wing of Mill City's timber barons. He has written off the irreconcilables, Atiyeh's sworn enemies. Rob Freres and company are now pillorying one of their own, Hirons, for betraying his community. "So? They see me as a threat. Been shot at and missed, shit at and hit," says Hirons, sounding a lot like Atiyeh. "What the hell have I got to lose? It's all gone anyway."

In midmorning Hirons sits at Atiyeh's Save Opal Creek Council office at the airfield, grousing, as usual, about the "rotgut" coffee. The conservationist salutes the logger's brave move in a context they can both relate to. "To put it in logging terms, you're hung up. You keep going ahead on the line till something snaps rather than slacking it off—maybe draw the line, put a roll on it, doing something a little bit different."

"That's what we've been doing the past year," Hirons says.

"You've been doing it, but you're about the only one. Now they're starting to follow you."

"Well, somebody has to pull rigging on this fucking crew."

Hirons grips the steering wheel of his Bronco while conversing with Atiyeh, sitting in the front passenger seat. I sit in the backseat, leaving them to their own intellectual devices. We cruise along the steep, narrow roads of the Tillamook Burn State Forest, the crowning monument to modern forestry. Atiyeh and Hirons once joined thousands of other schoolchildren replanting what had been a three-hundred-thousand-acre wasteland in northwestern Oregon. Helicopters did the aerial seeding. Seventy-three million trees later, the vibrant second growth put life back in the slopes.

We step out to survey the scene. Hirons eyes some of the stouter timber ripe for cutting. "I'll tell you what, George. It's time to let a little daylight into this swamp."

Atiyeh recoils from the sight of areas already logged in the vicinity. "Why did they do all this shit? Look how little the stumps are."

Back on the road, Hirons surrenders the wheel to his friend. "Really stupid way to move around, if you think about it," the environmentalist muses aloud. "Steel box on rubber doughnuts on smashed rock. There has gotta be a better way."

"You sure got a way with words," Hirons interjects, no slouch himself. Atiyeh invites him to a forest conference later in the week. "Nah, I ain't gonna puke."

The close companions, reunited once again, have their repartee's timing down pat. Indeed, all their movements seem synchronized. The moment Atiyeh adjusts his sunglasses with both hands, Hirons reaches over to handle the steering wheel and prevent us from sailing off the mountainside.

At lunchtime we arrive at Camp 18, an enticing roadside attraction comprised of a logging museum and a log cabin that functions as a restaurant, about forty miles west of Portland. Atiyeh and Hirons have hamburgers; I eat fried fish. The cuisine, however, is incidental to the stunning ambience. All of the timber used in the building has come from these parts. Camp 18's co-owner hauled, hand-peeled, and draw-knifed it with the help of family and friends. He also cut the lumber himself on the property across Humbug Creek. An eighty-five-foot ridge pole—the horizontal beam at the ridge of the roof and to which the rafters are attached—steals the show at Camp 18. The ridgepole, believed to be the largest in the United States, weighs twenty-five tons and contains fifty-six hundred board feet. Nor is there any overlooking the restaurant's main doors, made from genuine old growth, four and a half feet thick and tipping the scales at five hundred pounds.

"They talk about letting a little daylight into the swamp [as Hirons did at the Tillamook Burn Forest]. Can you imagine coming into the Willamette Valley? We're really piss ants compared to a big old-growth tree. Can you imagine having to clear those bastards by hand?" Atiyeh asks no one in particular. "What a challenge. Man, they'd get rid of the trees and burn those stumps for years. You'd have to be willing to bust your ass and fight in order to get them out of the woods. Part of that attitude goes to the heart of the Oregon character. The way you get something done is to put your head down, charge, and fight."

Atiyeh swallows another handful of french fries. "If you're talking about a new economy for Mill City, this is it," he declares to Hirons and me.

"What the hell is there to see in Mill City?" Hirons replies. "It's on the way through."

"What Sisters [a thriving tourist town between Mill City and Bend] got? You went through there twenty years ago and would say, 'What the hell would anyone want to live here for?' You've got a lake [at Detroit, eighteen miles away]. The golf course could be developed. Everybody has to get off their asses and the mentality, 'Oh, no, we can't do anything.' "

Chewing over his food and Atiyeh's ideas, the logger is willing to engage in a brainstorming session. That Hirons would give tourism, a four-letter word last year, any credence at all attests to the long ideological distance he has traveled. They talk animatedly about launching a Camp 18 in Mill City. Visitors might have their pictures taken with a Paul Bunyan mascot. Hirons suggests serving food family style, like they do in Amish country—where he has vacationed on trips to Washington, D.C.—with heaping plates of turkey, mashed potatoes, and stuffing passed around the table. "Well, if I can give tours of Opal Creek and maybe a mining museum up there, Tom," Atiyeh says, "you can give tours of a logging museum down in Mill City. Why doesn't one of the mills start something like this in Mill City?"

"I'm not sure they have enough class or imagination," Hirons concedes.

Atiyeh laughs. "You think we can stick a Camp 18 for Mill City into one of the congressional bills?"

His former business partner isn't smiling. "Timber has provided a quality of life, George."

"Yes, as far as economics. I don't know about livability. We need sustainable growth and a sustainable environment. Look, I don't want to see Oregon turned into a national park. I just want to see it accommodate all the other uses. There are going to be some trade-offs."

Hirons tries shifting the conversation back to Mill City's doldrums. "Go ask the merchants," Atiyeh challenges him. "Are they hurtin'? Go ask the merchants."

"That ain't the whole fucking story, how the merchants are doing," Hirons snaps. "Talk to Cherie [Girod, of the Canyon Crisis Center]."

"She lives in the worst part of it. I'd have that perspective, too, if I ran the center. If you spend your time looking at all the shit, that's what you're going to see. I agree. I don't want to lose Mill City's values. I don't want a situation where I have to lock my door, either."

"Last year Cherie had nine hundred calls. This year she's had seventeen hundred. Worker retraining and relocation. That's thrown out as some great panacea, but it's closing eyes to the real problem. What the hell does it all do for Mill City? It doesn't do anything for the people underpinning the community. There's a lot of resignation."

"Yeah, first there was denial, then there was frustration, now there's resignation. You don't need to retrain the entrepreneurs. I'm not advocating a tourist economy. I'm saying there are a lot of other things we can do. We can attract and build businesses. I don't know if it will all filter down to the most unskilled people in the mills. I don't look at those people as the lifeblood of the community anyway. They have been traditionally transient. So many people paint Mill City as a dying town, but it's growing and robust."

I stop in at Camp 18's gift shop on the way out. In addition to a couple of books on northwestern history, I purchase a key chain consisting of a miniature log truck hauling three logs. It ends up being the only three-log load I see on this particular visit to Oregon in 1991. These days it takes a half dozen undersized second-growth logs to fill a truck's bunk.

The opposite conclusions Atiyeh and Hirons draw from their same hometown reflect the tale of two Mill Cities. In the midst of social upheaval from environmental and economic forces beyond the control of timber towns, two ways of life compete for the society's soul. The old culture, based on wood products, is surrendering to the new, rooted in the exaltation rather than the eradication of natural assets.

Mill City is anything but drying up and blowing away like the Oregon ghost town Valsetz. Businesses begun by footloose entrepreneurs are actually booming. Over the past year, baseball card, T-shirt and an appliance shop have occupied storefronts left vacant since the last recession, in the early 1980s. An environmentally sensitive, Utah-based mining company, Plexus, is developing a modest copper mine in Cedar Creek Valley, on the outskirts of Mill City. Plexus sets up shop in the old building once housing the Hammond company store and bearing the painted inscription "WELCOME TO MILL CITY." The venture will create 90 new jobs. Wilbur Harlan can hardly keep up with orders for his painted saws of logging and nature scenes, proving his cottage industry has legs. In an ironic sign of the times, Cherie Girod's Canyon Crisis Center recently lost its home. The Dutch Inn, the local meeting place, needs the space for expansion to satisfy the growing tourist trade. (She later sets up at the meat market across the street from her husband's grocery store.) The price of real estate in Mill City continues to rise as retirees from California, small-business owners, and bedroom commuters to Salem snap up houses at record rates.

Hirons and other timber activists are having a hard time rallying the troops as they did so effectively last year. Dirty and faded, the only yellow ribbons left hanging from trees flap sullenly in the wind. The timber rally as a political tool is extinct. A badly corroded "WE SUPPORT THE TIMBER INDUSTRY" wood sign mulches in the wet grass on Harvey Spears's front lawn. For all of Spears's bluster about maiming Atiyeh, the unemployed logger and onetime brawler speaks in the hushed tones of a beaten man. "Things have died down. People have given up," he says. "I think they figure they are fighting a losing battle." A few dozen yards away from his home, a small plane mill that shut down for good last year reminds him of his misfortune every time he walks out his front door.

Spears has endured a rougher year than most. In the five months since his last job, the longest dry spell for him ever, he has waited in vain for the phone to ring. While his wife, Ellen, stays afloat doing the hair of the retirees at her salon, the timber wives have cut their visits in half. She has started selling Avon on the side. "Every penny helps," her husband says in the family mobile home's cramped living room. "In a little while these lights and telephone may go off."

Spears rubs his beard and looks down at his haggard hickory shirt while mulling over the personal degradation. "I keep laughing and joking," he says, "but inside I'm crying." The experience has been sobering enough to keep him away from the taverns that once proved his undoing. Still, he cuffs his children and exchanges angry words with his wife, just to let off steam. "The ones leaving Mill City now are the bum loggers. The majority staying are steady," he says. "Hell, the old lady and I can both work the same shifts making eight dollars an hour at the Dairy Queen. This family is going to plumb starve to death before I work at a job like that."

The timber sign rots in his front yard largely because of Spears's own political evolution. Rather than stand his ground clinging to a lost cause, he is preparing to abandon his roots and move his family out of the Northwest if he can find work elsewhere. A year ago, environmentalists espoused retraining and relocation programs for timber workers while loggers inveighed against them as defeatist. Spears will take any help he can get these days, including legislation pending in Congress to defray his moving expenses. "I would like to see some of that and health insurance so I don't have to beg, borrow, or steal," he says. "This country owes me a job. I don't want a handout. Just what's due me for working all my life." Spears has kept his gas credit card empty in case of a sudden move. He has stashed away a cash reserve just large enough to feed his family and him till they reach their destination, wherever it may be.

Following his excursion to the Tillamook Burn State Forest and Camp 18 with Atiyeh, Hirons upholds his end of the peace pact by returning to Opal Creek. He pulls up to the notorious gate Atiyeh's detractors in Mill City charge him with controlling to maintain his power base. The privileged few who know the combination to the lock are limited to the U.S. Forest Service, Shiny Rock employees, and family. Yesterday Atiyeh entrusted Hirons with the combination, perhaps the sincerest expression yet of faith in his old friend.

Even so, Hirons, the consummate handyman able to repair complex logging machinery in a single bound, fumbles with the lock. He asks me, so bereft of mechanical ability I've had to prevail on him to turn off high beams in my rental car, to try. I pop the lock's cylinder right open. There appear to remain a few psychological barriers for Hirons to hurdle.

In Atiyeh's cabin at Jawbone Flats, Hirons laces up his corked boots. The sharp spikes on the soles he relies on to grip logs will come in handy for climbing Opal Creek's steep trails. "You allow corks here?" Hirons asks.

"Hell, it won't be the first set of corked boots," Atiyeh responds, half laughing. On the hike Atiyeh led me on last year he wore a baseball cap bearing the inscription "SAVE AN OWL, EDUCATE A LOGGER." This year he dons, of all headgear, one of Hirons's black Mad Creek caps.

We hug ourselves against the cold, driving rain through woods as dark as night under the low ceiling of clouds. Crossing the Little North Fork, Atiyeh and Hirons point out a chunk of the massive log they had to blow up with dynamite in their logging company's salad days.

The conservationist holds aloft a skein of moss. "Hey, Tom, you know what this is? What are you gonna do if you're in the forest and cut your hand? It acts as a natural Band-Aid. It's called lungwort and it also fixes nitrogen right out of the air from the sides of those trees," Atiyeh says, pointing to the moss-draped spires. "If you have any air pollution, it's the first thing to die."

"Yeah, that stuff is everywhere." Hirons removes his glasses to wipe the fog off the lenses.

Atiyeh points to a Pacific yew, the small, rare tree containing the powerful cancer-fighting chemical Taxol. "See, Tom, we don't know what's here."

Hirons shifts our attention to a heroic ancient tree bulging at the trunk. "That's one righteous cedar," he exclaims.

A smile on Atiyeh's face flickers through the rain dribbling off his cap's bill. "I have to admit I would have once looked," he says, walking up to the cedar, "to see how many bolts [wood bars] are in this."

"Hmm. How many shakes." Hirons refrains from calibrating the number of thick wood shingles.

His friend eggs him on for fun: "I wouldn't blame you for counting logs." Hirons hoofs down the trail.

Back at Atiyeh's cabin at Jawbone Flats, he stokes the wood stove. The damp smell of our coats drying on top suffuses the heavy air. The three of us wash down slabs of whole-grain bread torn from a loaf, and cheddar cheese with ultrastrong black coffee. Atiyeh kicks up his feet on the rustic wood coffee table to expound on his and Hirons's vision. "Tom really cares and feels for the forest, and I really feel for the people. We've both come to the conclusion that we're going to lose some jobs and some trees. Neither of us are very happy about it, but we've come to recognize the solutions are always someplace in the middle. How do we best influence these solutions rather than letting Congress or the northwestern delegation do it? The politicians are so removed they only care about themselves. I didn't throw the first punch and I don't want to fight anymore."

"Our delegation is paralyzed," Hirons interjects, nodding his head. "The ones who are supposed to be part of it and represent us ain't doing a goddamn thing. We've got to do an end run around the national industry and environmental groups, which have their own agendas."

The compromise plan gestating from the Albany Accord is so sensible and well modulated, perhaps it could have emerged only from two headstrong figures as close to the ground as Atiyeh and Hirons. The plan sets out three distinct classifications to manage land in the Detroit District and beyond. The first category, Ancient Forest Reserves, recognizes the largest remaining blocks of old growth as dynamic ecosystems worth preserving as research areas. "The big places like Opal Creek ought to be never cut. Their time has come to be left alone. These are the ones with large constituencies," Atiyeh explains. "Instead of Earth First!, the well-dressed ladies and guys with three-piece suits are going to be out there if anyone tries logging them. In pristine condition, we'll finally see what kind of interest we're getting off the trust account." The primary emphasis on research and recreation, to the exclusion of all logging, will ensure these forests' biological legacy. The beneficiaries include the spotted owl and hikers.

The second category incorporates the latest principles of the much-vaunted New Forestry. Under this approach, loggers would abandon traditional clear-cuts in favor of mimicking natural processes. The techniques call for leaving living trees and woody debris behind to help regenerate the forest for plants and wildlife while still allowing logging to continue. The habitat should prove suitable for a variety of species, from elk to the spotted owl. The U.S. Forest Service is promoting such concepts under the rubic of "New Perspectives in Forestry" and has established a number of experimental stations testing them across tens of thousands of acres.

Atiyeh knows Jerry Franklin, a forest ecologist in the University of Washington and guru of what the scientist himself terms the "kinder and gentler forestry," from his tours of Opal Creek. "These are smaller unroaded tracts with biological significance but without particular constituencies. Using Franklin Forestry, we deal with each piece on a case-by-case basis. The classic example is the road from the gate to Jawbone Flats," Atiyeh says. "Loggers have been taking dead and down for a hundred years. We can pull interest off the trust account by maintaining ecological viability. We'll be managing not only for timber, but water and recreation. This central category of our plan ought to be driven by the quest for knowledge, not just the quest for wood."

The most recent of Hirons's three meetings with Franklin occurred last week, at a conference in Portland. Since new logging roads would be prohibited in these areas, they batted around ideas about helicopter logging and skyline logging with sufficient lift to reach over the forest's canopy. Either technique would cause minimal disturbance to standing trees. "Franklin seemed to think the plan George and I've come up with is biologically defensible," Hirons says. "And isn't that today's catchphrase?"

Hirons's main concerns center on the much smaller volume of timber in the three- and four-acre clear-cuts Franklins envisages replacing the standard forty-acre clear-cut. "He told me, 'Tom, you'll be pleasantly surprised.' The big unknown question is how much. Well, you're going to let the forests themselves decide rather than the politicians," Hirons says. "The other thing we've talked about is what we do to get from here to there. You can't simply stop what you're doing one day and start something else the next." His and Atiyeh's plan addresses that concern by providing a bridge till the second growth comes on line. As far as economics, the relative scarcity of timber will boost its value, particularly for premium products made from old growth instead. Moreover, the sophisticated new logging techniques ought to put the exceptional loggers of Hirons's caliber in higher demand.

The Albany Accord's third and least glamorous class calls for industrial forestry lands. These highly fragmented pieces of lesser biological significance would be treated basically as farmland—with one caveat. The highest sustainable yield possible must occur on an ecologically sound basis. The presence of game and other wildlife promises to afford at least some recreational opportunities. If maximizing timber at negligible cost to the environment smacks of an oxymoron, it probably is. "These industrial fragments are going to provide the transition time for loggers," Atiyeh says. For all intents and purposes, he's willing to write off the scraps to preserve the jewels such as Opal Creek.

A provision separate from the three categories offers industry immediate relief. "The mill owners are going to be a helluva problem," Hirons says. "I mean the guys who made a commitment to their employees and bought timber no matter what the price was." Atiyeh and Hirons support some form of legislation to loosen existing timber contracts with the U.S. Forest Service. On top of that, they advocate earmarking federal and state grants for community crisis centers and economic diversification, starting with new value-added manufacturing for wood products.

"What we're talking about in our overall plans is what I thought multiple use was all about," Atiyeh says, taking another swig of coffee, "whether it's timber, recreation, or wildlife habitat. My only fear is human nature, that we won't do anything unless there's a crisis. If we buy three more years of breathing time, will that time be used effectively, or will it mean politicians lying and forestalling the day of reckoning?"

"We have everybody's attention, George. Nobody's going to set the cut levels at the historical highs. It's certainly going to alleviate the mess Congress has caused."

"This is the first time that anybody from either side has ever sat down and agreed on anything."

"What I'm hoping is that it will have so much appeal," Hirons says, "it will be accepted. If only the media would latch on to it."

"We have to have it all together before we start lighting fires," Atiyeh cautions him.

"We're not that far away."

"Kopetski told Tom and me we could do whatever we want."

Atiyeh, who supported Mike Kopetski's election to Congress for backing Opal Creek's preservation, advised the freshman representative to mend fences. The timber industry enthusiastically backed Denny Smith, his opponent and staunch anticonservationist. "I told him Tom is one of the more reasonable of the bunch," Atiyeh says. Kopetski agreed to meet Hirons in his district office.

"No, I didn't support you in the campaign," Hirons remembers telling him. "Now it doesn't make a difference; you're my congressman." The congressman has promised to champion wholeheartedly in Congress whatever plan his two activist constituents hatch. Tomorrow a legislative aide will attend a negotiating session of all the key players.

Hirons reaches for another hunk of bread. "Politics is getting in the way of good forestry. The question is, can man extract what he needs without ruining it?"

"Where's the line between a little and too much?" Atiyeh asks him. "We know how to grow trees, but do we know how to grow forests?"

"I'm so fucking tired of this fucking debate," Hirons snaps. He stands up and walks outside. The three of us burst into laughter.

We follow him. The skies have finally broken, bathing Jawbone Flats in a supernal light. "This sure is a great place to visit," Hirons muses in the context of the two years he and his family lived here two decades ago. "It will always be a special place." He points to Whetstone Mountain, whose craggy peak he scaled twenty years ago. "I remember flashing mirrors to Marlene who stood there at such-and-such a time to let her know I got there. She'd flash back." Hirons abruptly cuts off the nostalgia, lest he appear overly sentimental.

I ask him to elaborate on his reaction toward the cedar he hailed as "righteous" earlier today. "I've seen a lot bigger trees than that," he erupts, perhaps with some justification, for asking him so leading a question. "A big tree turns me on for a lot of different reasons. It's neat that it's been there for so long. When I look at a big tree, I can't help but see logs. It's just second nature, 'cause I've been doing it for so damn long. But I also recognize it ain't never gonna be again, so there ain't no use to worry about it. Do I get a religious feeling from a big tree, something mystical? No, leave it to whoever [i.e., George and company]. It don't do it for me. Never has done it. But those people who do have a religious experience need a place for it." Amid last year's acrimony, Hirons steeled himself against Atiyeh moralizing about Opal Creek. It took a return to friendship and Opal Creek to bring him back to his moderate senses, the grist of compromise.

The secret meeting convenes at nine-thirty at the Detroit Ranger's office, an austere wood-paneled room with industrial orange carpet. At the long rectangular table sit Hirons; Mike Miller, a fellow logger; Denny Frank, representing the mill owners; Raul Gagne, from the Detroit timber sales department; and Ted Corvine from Kopetski's office. The conservationist Michael Donnelly had to bow out for personal reasons, leaving Atiyeh alone once again at the bargaining table, though he has come to admire Kopetski's boldness. "You need more people on your side," Hirons quips, turning to Atiyeh amid mutual chuckles.

Corvine urges Atiyeh and Hirons to tread carefully on their

upcoming trip to Washington, D.C., to sell lawmakers on their plan. "You're both dynamic and motivated," he says. "I don't want you rocking the boat. Wait till we have legislation."

"We're not going to torpedo anything we have spent so much time and effort on," Hirons assures him.

Atiyeh seconds the notion. "We've been putting our heart and souls in this for a long time. This is all about Tom's livelihood and a place very special to me."

Hirons reminds him of his duties to develop alliances. "My peers cannot see me suing for a separate peace."

"There is a heady allure and seduction that goes on when you think you're on the fast track's bullet train," Corvine says. "I recognize how pivotal you are as players in this process."

Throughout the session, one stumbling block surfaces over and over again. Corvine repeatedly strains to pin down a precise cut level in the Detroit District acceptable to both sides. "What is it you need to sign off on?" he pleads. "This is a pig-in-the-poke process. Do we have any idea what the logging is going to be? I don't want you guys leaving here agreeing on 25 million board feet and later saying, 'Screw this.' "

Neither party appears willing to commit to a hard number, preferring to leave the matter to so-called experts. As Atiyeh has warned all along, industry and conservationists alike must swallow some sacrifices. "My goal is to mitigate the impact as much as possible," Atiyeh says. "I do care about my community and I do care about my friends. I want to find a way to make the transition without the human costs."

Sensing an opportunity slipping through their fingers, Hirons throws out figures. After considerable back and forth, he, Atiyeh, and the others decide the wisest course would be to ratchet down gradually from the historic averages in the Detroit District of 115 million board feet during the 1980s to 40 million board feet in the mid-1990s. Denny Frank, with 150 workers, the third-largest employer in Mill City, behind Young and Morgan and Freres, looks skeptical. "George, it sounds like you want us to die slow or die quick," he says. Atiyeh accepts a bridge—or "glide path," as the Forest Service terms it—of roughly 5 million board feet per year, from 65 million board feet to about 40 million board feet in fifteen years. By then the second growth will kick in.

Frank still shakes his head. "Sixty-five million board feet is going to be a bloodbath. Forty million board feet is going to be a disaster."

"No matter how good we try to make it," Hirons counsels him, "it's going to be bad. My sole objective is to help the community."

"You're the most efficient of the mills," Atiyeh says, turning to Frank. His company is, in fact, the industry's future, and it works. Young and Morgan and Freres, of Mill City's Big Three, depend heavily on old growth for plywood and lumber. Frank's mills are to a greater extent tooled to process a steady supply of second growth from the 16,000 acres of privately held land it owns.

"Two of the three mills will survive and they'll be cutting back from two shifts to one," the mill owner says. Frank, a slender, taut man, draws a deep breath and glances in Atiyeh's direction. "We've been fighting for too many years. Frankly, I'm getting tired of it."

Frank reserves his deepest scorn not for conservationists, but rather his own brethren, the mill owners. The presence of the spotted owl on the endangered species list has touched off panic buying, grossly inflating timber prices. The auction winners, including Young and Morgan, regret overbidding. The losers, such as Frank, who finished sixth at the latest auction, evince scant sympathy for competitors they regard as foolhardy. "We're against standing contract relief. It's the same people at the timber sales who produced too much before," Frank says. "The mills are playing chicken with each other." The internecine conflicts among the timber barons risk undermining a key part of the accord designed to bring them all aboard.

By midafternoon, the session has already lumbered on for five and a half hours. Atiyeh and Hirons's single-mindedness has snuffed out any attention to lunch. The rest of us are famished. Denny Frank's stomach growls the loudest, like a little chainsaw. Mike Miller hustles outside to grab a package of mini Oreos from the candy machine. He graciously spills them across the table for us to share.

Dusting off cookie crumbs, Hirons scores a telling point at the center of all loggers' anxieties. "In twenty years we can always go back and clear-cut the whole thing," he says. Humans always reserve the right to alter whatever protection they devise. Nature, it's worth noting, does not enjoy the same privilege.

"In the shakeout, we need retraining and health insurance for workers," Frank says. "They are the ones who are going to be hit the hardest. They're gonna take a helluva lot of help." Harvey Spears would be pleased to hear that.

Hirons issues a plea on his own behalf for entrepreneurial, low-

SHOWDOWN AT OPAL CREEK

interest loans to spur new business opportunities. A $200,000 yarder of the variety Hirons owns commands $15,000 on the auction block today. "We've got to remove the stigma of backruptcy," he says.

Frank excuses himself to return to his mill. "This meeting is in confidence," he says. "Right?" Atiyeh and Hirons affirm it is. They need to cross a few t's and dot a few i's before unveiling their plan publicly.

"There's a spirit of real agreement here today," Corvine says in summation. "A real sense of compromise and progress. Who else will come along?" He aims his gaze at Hirons.

"As they said in *L'il Abner*," says the glint-eyed Hirons, "what's good for General Bull Moose is good for the U.S.A."

Tomorrow he and Atiyeh embark on a joint mission to Washington, D.C., to sway the mighty there on the wisdom of the Albany Accord. "Just the fact that Tom and I are walking down the halls together," Atiyeh says, "will open some eyes."

The next day I accompany Atiyeh and Hirons to Portland International Airport. The stubborn drizzle clashes with their boundless optimism. Two weeks ago, an assistant agriculture secretary in Washington, D.C., contacted a timber group allied with Hirons's Communities for Great Oregon to determine whether any grass-roots activists were talking at all. "George Atiyeh and I are the only ones with an open line of communication between the two sides," Hirons informed him. Once in Washington, the official acts as a liaison between them and the powers that be outside the Oregon delegation. The two friends work Capitol Hill and the federal bureaucracy as never before on their solo lobbying excursions.

The trip proves a mixed success. "We've snapped a few heads around," Hirons says. Atiyeh is less sanguine about the prospects for breaking the political logjam. On a side trip, they stroll the Gettysburg battlefield, pondering the history lessons taught them in elementary school. "Tom and I have suggested building the world's greatest trash compactor and sticking Washington in it," Atiyeh jokes after rubbing up against the egos and agendas subverting his proposal. His disappointment verges on the shattered idealism of Mr. Smith going to Washington.

Back in Mill City, Atiyeh and Hirons run up against a local roadblock. Rob Freres, an incorrigible hard-liner, follows up a high-decibel harangue against Hirons on the phone with a visit to the CGO office while he is out. Atiyeh and Hirons accuse him of purloining a copy of the compromise plan Hirons left on the desk and proceeds to whip up a frenzy against it. "I opposed another splitting of the baby," Freres says. "It's no secret I don't like George Atiyeh. I've never had any problems with Tom." "That bastard," Hirons fumes. Atiyeh is equally furious: "I'd like to take my AK-47 and put a few holes in Robby's Porsche." The Albany Accord's spirit rises and falls like Camelot eclipsed by reality—for the time being.

But the die had already been cast. Atiyeh and Hirons can take solace in history's long view, having set the standard by which all other measures could be judged. Indeed, elements of the Albany Accord eventually found their way into congressional legislation, thanks to Atiyeh and Hirons's perseverance. Both men have had indirect input in the Clinton administration's effort to resolve the crisis.

As the spring wears on, Aziz Atiyeh graduates from high school but is unsure of his first job. His father puts in a call to Hirons for his mechanically oriented son, landing him work as a rigging slinger in Mad Creek's crew. The ironies abound. In his capacity as the driver, Aziz parks the crummy, the loggers' bus, at the airfield of the environmentalist George.

Later in the year, Aziz leaves Mad Creek to pursue another career, cleaning up hazardous waste sites. To his credit, he only hires ex-loggers. At Marlene's video shop in Mill City, Tom's son Wes strikes him as worry-weary from his mounting bills. His father heaves a deep sigh. "You need some work?" he asks. "Yeah," Wes responds. Wes returns to Mad Creek as a rigging slinger, Aziz's temporary job, thus completing a topsy-turvy year's full circle. Jim Morgan has awarded Hirons, for all his political efforts, a plumb job logging prime second growth at low elevation. The father and son are soon working side by side once again.

Atiyeh still navigates among the political shoals. Senator Mark Hatfield tacks an amendment onto a defense appropriations bill, directing the secretary of the interior to issue a patent to Shiny Rock's claim. The amendment finally gives the company clear title to the land, a linchpin in Opal Creek's long-term protection. Atiyeh is willing to overlook the political calculation of a senator eager to shore up his standing among environmentalists after compiling such a lackluster record on the ancient-forest issue. Hatfield delivers at the right moment. Thurston Twigg-Smith, the owner of Persis, has decided to retire and, in a corporate restructuring, to unload most of his holdings, thus ending his two-decade-long support of Atiyeh's crusade. Twigg-Smith donates his tracts of old growth, valued at $12.6 million, to Atiyeh's public interest group

Friends of Opal Creek—reportedly the largest private gift of conservation property in U.S. history. Unless Atiyeh and his new partner Tim Hermach, executive director of the Native Forest Council, can raise enough funds, the title to the land will revert back to the Forest Service, which still covets the timber. Both men must move fast to keep alive their dream of establishing an ancient forest and education reserve at Opal Creek.

Until Washington, D.C., grants wholesale protection to Opal Creek, Atiyeh must crusade as if he hears chainsaws at the gate. Until then, he works on borrowed time, mailing off a flurry of desperate fund-raising appeals for his nonprofit organization Friends of Opal Creek. Barring the arrival of another financial angel like Twigg-Smith, Atiyeh contemplates selling off assets, including his beloved plane, to raise money. He and Hirons are trying to a launch a business together again, this time in the manufacturing of finished wood products.

When Hirons drops by the airfield for coffee and conversation, the topic invariably turns from family to the fates events have forced them to share. Each buoys the other's spirits, reminding him their situation could be far worse. Neither Opal Creek has been logged nor Mad Creek has gone belly up. Hirons has preserved his proud way of life and Atiyeh has conserved one of the last best places on earth for at least another day.

Bibliography

The following books, articles, and reports provided a wealth of information and insight:

Anderson, H. Michael, and Jeffrey T. Olson. *Federal Forests and the Economic Base of the Northwest: A Study of Regional Transitions.* Portland, Oreg.: Wilderness Society, 1991.

Barnhardt, David and Lisa. *Axidental Murder.* Gates, Oreg.: Niagara Publications, 1989.

Breetveld, Jim. *Treasure of the Timberlands.* New York: Scholastic Magazines in Cooperation with Weyerhaeuser Co., 1967.

Byrnes, Patricia, et al. *Wilderness America.* Layton, Utah: Gibbs Smith, 1980.

Caufield, Catherine. "The Ancient Forest," *The New Yorker* (May 14, 1990),pp. 46–84.

Churchill, Sam. *Big Sam.* Garden City, N.Y.: Doubleday, 1965.

Copeland, Cherie. *Fairview Cemetery/King's Prairie Burying Ground, 1883–1983.* Gates, Oreg.: self-published, 1988.

―――. *Santiam Legend,* Vols. 3–4. Gates, Oreg.: 1990–91.

Daniel, John. "The Long Dance of the Trees," *Wilderness* (Spring 1988), pp. 19–34.

Dawson, William, et al. *The Advisory Panel on the Spotted Owl.* New York: National Audubon Society, 1986.

Durbin, Kathie, and Paul Robertstein. "Northwest Forests: Day of Reckoning," *Oregonian* (September 16, 1990), pp. 1, 26–29 (September 17, 1990), pp. 1, 10–13 (September 18, 1990), pp. 1, 11–15 (September 19, 1990), pp. 1, 14–17 (September 20, 1990), pp. 1, 17–19.

Ehrlich, Paul and Anne. *Extinction.* New York: Random House, 1981.

Ervin, Keith. *Fragile Majesty.* Seattle: The Mountaineers, 1989.

Fleetwood, Evangelyn. *Just a Few of Our Memories.* Mill City, Oreg.: privately published, 1988.

Forsman, Eric. *Distribution and Biology of the Spotted Owl in Ore-*

gon. Corvallis, Oreg.: Cooperative Wildlife Research Unit, Oregon State University, 1987.

Gustafson, Alan. "A Vanishing Way of Life," *Salem Statesman-Journal* (December 30, 1990), pp. 1–8.

Holbrook, Stewart. *The Far Corner.* Sausalito, Calif.: Comstock, 1986.

———. *Holy Old Mackinaw.* Sausalito, Calif.: Comstock, 1980.

Hovee, Eric. *Strengths, Weaknesses, Opportunities, and Threats: Analysis for Mill City, Sweet Home, etc.* Salem, Oreg.: Oregon Economic Development, 1989–90.

Kelly, David, and Braasch, Gary. *Secrets of the Old Growth Forest.* Salt Lake City: Peregrine Smith Books, 1988.

Kesey, Ken. *Sometimes a Great Notion.* New York: Viking Penguin, 1964.

Knize, Perri. "The Mismanagement of the National Forests," *The Atlantic* (October, 1991), pp. 98–112.

Lipske, Michael. "Who Runs America's Forests?" *National Wildlife* (October/November 1990), pp. 24–28.

Lucia, Ellis. *The Big Woods.* Garden City, N.Y.: Doubleday, 1975.

Maclean, Norman. *A River Runs Through It.* Chicago: The University of Chicago Press, 1976.

Maser, Chris. *Forest Primeval.* San Francisco: Sierra Club Books, 1989.

———. *The Redesigned Forest.* San Pedro, California: R&E Miles, 1988.

Matthiessen, Peter. *Wildlife in America.* New York: Viking Press, 1959.

Norse, Eliott. *Ancient Forests of the Northwest.* Washington, D.C.: Island Press, 1990.

O'Toole, Randal. *Reforming the Forest Service.* Washington, D.C.: Island Press, 1988.

Robinson, Gordon. *The Forest and the Trees.* Washington, D.C.: Island Press, 1988.

Smith, Jill. "Can't See the Forest," *Willamette Week* (September 13–19, 1990), pp. 1, 9–13.

Sorden, L. G. and Vallier. *Lumberjack Lingo.* Madison, Wis.: North Word, 1986.

Steber, Rick. *Loggers.* Prineville, Oreg.: Bonanza, 1989.

Thomas, Jack Ward (chairman). *A Conservation Strategy for the Northern Spotted Owl: Report of the Interagency Scientific Committee.* Portland, Oreg.: U.S. Department of Agriculture, 1990.

Tisdale, Sallie. "In the Northwest," *The New Yorker* (August 26, 1991), pp. 37–62.

Tower, Madalyn, *Timber Talk* (a monthly newsletter of the Young and Morgan companies). Mill City, Oreg.: 1989–91.

Weber, Joe. *The Cultural History of the North Santiam Mining District.* Gates, Oreg.: Shiny Rock Mining Co., 1983.

Whitelaw, Ed, and Ernest Niemi. *Looking Beyond the Owls and the Logs.* Eugene, Oreg.: Economic Policy Institute Northwest, 1989.

————. "A More Civil War," *Old Oregon* (Winter 1990), pp. 22–25.

Wilcove, David. "What I Saw When I Went to the Forest," *Wilderness* (Spring 1988), pp. 47–50.

Zuckerman, Seth. *Saving the Ancient Forests.* Venice, Calif.: Living Planet Press, 1991.

To obtain additional information or to make a contribution:

Friends of Opal Creek
P.O. Box 318
Mill City, OR 97360

Oregon Lands Coalition
247 Commercial Street, N.E.
Salem, OR 97301

Index